GROUP
FIRST

WESTMINSTER
KENNEL

D1736810

ASHBEY

*Dedicated to Samantha, our own very special "Miss Poodle,"
who epitomizes all the fun, charm, and great intelligence of this lovely
breed as she shares our daily lives and that of the Beagles.*

Our own Miniature Poodle, Samantha (a granddaughter of the famous Ch. Pixiecroft Sunbeam) belongs officially to Marcia Foy but is loved by everyone in the household for her intelligence and endearing ways.

© **1982 T.F.H. PUBLICATIONS, INC. LTD.**

t.f.h.

ISBN 0-87666-736-1

Distributed in the U.S. by T.F.H. Publications, Inc., 211 West Sylvania Avenue, PO Box 427, Neptune, NJ 07753; in England by T.F.H. (Gt. Britain) Ltd., 13 Nutley Lane, Reigate, Surrey; in Canada to the pet trade by Rolf C. Hagen Ltd., 3225 Sartelon Street, Montreal 382, Quebec; in Canada to the book trade by H & L Pet Supplies, Inc., 27 Kingston Crescent, Kitchener, Ontario N28 2T6; in Southeast Asia by Y.W. Ong, 9 Lorong 36 Geyland, Singapore 14; in Australia and the South Pacific by Pet Imports Pty. Ltd., P.O. Box 149, Brookvale 2100, N.S.W. Australia; in South Africa by Valid Agencies, P.O. Box 51901, Randburg 2125 South Africa. Published by T.F.H. Publications, Inc., Ltd., the British Crown Colony of Hong Kong.

Frontispiece (opposite): Ch. Ivardon Love Song, owned by Margaret Durney.

Front Endpapers:

Mutual admiration society! Bob Walberg and Ch. Lou Gin's Kiss Me Kate after the judging at her final dog show, where she attained her 140th Best in Show, a record not even closely approached before. Terri Meyers and the Jack Phelans own this spectacular Poodle.

Champion Rimskittle Ruffian pictured winning the Non-Sporting Group under Mrs. Thelma Brown at Westminster Kennel Club, 1980. Tim Brazier handling. Ruffian has 25 all-breed Best in Show wins to her credit, 10 Specialty Shows, and has won the Non-Sporting Group on 75 occasions as this book is written. Owned by Mrs. Margaret Durney and Edward Jenner.

THE BOOK OF THE
POODLE

Anna Katherine Nicholas

With special sections by HAYES BLAKE HOYT,
Wendell J. Sammet and Joseph P. Sayres, DVM

Overleaf:
Ch. Holly Berry Tempest with her "doting father" John P. Berridge waiting to go into the Toy Group ring. Owned by Mrs. John P. Berridge, Seaford, Delaware.

WINNERS

OX RIDGE
KENNEL CLUB

SEPTEMBER 1978

ASHBEY

Contents

Overleaf:
The handsome black Standard Poodle, Ch. Alekai Psyche, owned by R. E. Peterson of Greenwich, Connecticut, is shown finishing its championship at Ox Ridge Kennel Club, 1978. Handler, Wendell J. Sammet; judge, Robert A. Hetherington; bred by Alekai Kennels.

Overleaf:
Ch. Bel Tor Simon of Story Tale, a beautifully balanced, handsome Standard, handled by owner, **Mrs. J.
A. Mason**, to a good win under Mrs. Ramona Van Court Jones.

BEST OF
OPPOSITE

GILBERT PHOTO

In Appreciation

Having loved Poodles and having been involved with the breed as a judge for more than several decades, I undertook the project of writing this book with excitement and with keen anticipation, for I was determined it should be an *outstanding* book, one that could be used and referred to by Poodle fanciers, both novice and experienced, over many years to come. The success of such a project is necessarily largely dependent on the cooperation one receives from others who also have been active within a breed: from the breeders and owners of leading kennels, from professional handlers who have shown important dogs, and from judges. To those who have responded so graciously and helpfully with facts about dogs they have owned, bred, or piloted to victory in the show rings, my gratitude is boundless, for you have been great. The almost total response I received was heartwarming.

A very special vote of thanks goes to Wendell J. Sammet for his magnificent chapter on trimming and clipping the Poodle coat. No one will dispute the fact that the knowledge of how to do this *correctly* is second to none in importance where presentation of show Poodles is concerned. Those who are familiar with the appearance of his dogs will surely agree with my opinion that Wendell Sammet is a master of the art. We are very proud of his chapter. Additional thanks are due him, too, for the dozens of pictures from earlier days, of important dogs and important occasions, and the resumes of his clients' breeding programs which have added enormously to the interesting features we've been able to collect for your pleasure.

In the latter area, appreciative acknowledgment goes to Henry Stoecker for having loaned us pictures of Mrs. Erlanger and the great Pillicoc Poodles and to Frank Sabella and Ben Burwell, both highly successful in their former handling days, who like Bill Trainor and the Forsyths, literally "combed their files" finding me exciting photographs of important dogs and never-to-be-forgotten people and occasions. For every photo we have been loaned, for every kennel story, and to every breeder who has contributed information, we are thankful.

Our esteemed friend Joseph P. Sayres, D.V.M., again merits our thanks for what we consider to be an especially outstanding section, *The Veterinarian's Corner.* Dr. Sayres is particularly well-versed in the point of view of dog breeders and owners in addition to being a highly respected and well-accredited veterinarian. He grew up in the world of purebred dogs, the son of famed terrier breeder and professional handler Edwin A. Sayres, Sr. and the brother of Ed Sayres, Jr. and the late Henry J. Sayres, both of whom earned positions of respect in the Fancy. Dr. Sayres himself is an Irish Terrier breeder and an American Kennel Club judge. His knowledge, expertise, and experience in his profession are very clearly evident as one reads the pages he has written.

Marcia Foy has contributed much time and effort here at home in helping gather facts for this book, as have the friends who have loaned me books from their libraries and other valuable sources from which to research and re-check information.

Thank you, each and every one.

Anna Katherine Nicholas

Overleaf:
Ch. Valhallas In Command, an all-breed Best in Show winner, a Specialty winner, and a Top Producer; this magnificent Standard is a son of Ch. Acadia Command Performance from Ch. Puttencove Perdita. Owned by Catherine Kish.

About the Author

Anna Katherine Nicholas from earliest childhood has been associated with dogs. At first her earliest pets were a Boston Terrier, an Airedale, and a German Shepherd. Then in 1925 there arrived her first Pekingese, a gift from a friend who raised the breed "just for the fun of it." Now her home is shared by a Miniature Poodle and a dozen Beagles, included among them her noted Best in Show and National Specialty winner, the Beagle Champion Rockaplenty's Wild Oats, one of the breed's truly great sires along with having been the nation's top show Beagle in 1973; Champion Foyscroft True Blue Lou; Foyscroft Aces Are Wild; and, in co-ownership with Marcia Foy who also lives here, Champion Foyscroft Triple Mitey Migit.

Miss Nicholas is best known to the Dog Fancy as a writer and as a judge. Her first published magazine article was in *Dog News* about 1930, a column featuring Pekingese. This was followed by the widely acclaimed *Peeking at the Pekingese*, which appeared over at least two decades in *Dogdom* and then in *Popular Dogs*. During the 1940's she was Boxer columnist for the *American Kennel Gazette* and for *Boxer Briefs*. More recently, many of her articles of general interest to the Fancy appeared in *Popular Dogs* and the *American Kennel Gazette*. Currently she is a featured writer and monthly columnist for *Kennel Review, Dog World, The Canadian Dog Fancier*, and *The Canine Chronicle*. She also has written for *Poodle Showcase* some years back, for the *World of the Working Dog*, and has occasional articles in *Dogs in Canada*.

It was during the late 1930's that Miss Nicholas' first book appeared, *The Pekingese*, published by the Judy Publishing Company. This book completely sold out and is now a collector's item, as is her *The Skye Terrier Book*, published through the Skye Terrier Club of America during the early 1960's.

In 1970 Miss Nicholas won the Dog Writers Association of America award for the Best Technical Book with her *Nicholas Guide to Dog Judging*. She is proud that in 1979 the revision of this book again won the Dog Writers Association of America Best Technical Book Award, the first time ever that a revision has been so honored.

In the early 1970's Miss Nicholas co-authored with Joan Brearley five breed books for T.F.H. These are *This is the Bichon Frise, The Wonderful World of Beagles and Beagling, The Book of the Pekingese, This is the Skye Terrier*, and *The Book of the Boxer. The Wonderful World of Beagles and Beagling* attained an Honorable Mention award from the Dog Writers Association the year it was published.

Other awards for her writing have been received by Miss Nicholas from Gaines (the "Fido" as Dog Writer of the Year in the late 1970's) and from *Kennel Review* (the "Winkie" as Dog Journalist of the Year on two separate occasions). Also, her *Dog World* column, "Here, There and Everywhere," has just received the Best Series in an All-Breed Magazine Award from the Dog Writers Association for 1980.

Soon to be released are two other books written by Miss Nicholas for T.F.H., *Successful Dog Show Exhibiting* and *The Book of the Rottweiler*, and she is now starting work on *The Book of the Springer Spaniel* and *The Book of the German Shepherd*.

Overleaf:
Ch. Clardon Sno' Foolin', the well-known Best in Show Toy Poodle, belongs to June and Dave Suttie, is handled here by Donald Walker. This homebred was No. 6 Toy Poodle in 1979, and at the time promised to climb still higher in the ratings for 1980.

BEST IN SHOW

ROARING FORK
KENNEL CLUB

Graham

Heathermaid of Fircot and Round Table, the dam of
Champion Round Table Cloche de Neige. Owned by
Round Table Kennels, Middletown, Delaware.

Overleaf:
Bill Trainor with Harmo Kennels' fine apricot Miniature, Ch. Harmo Polaris, January, 1973.

CHAPTER ONE

Origin and Early History of the Poodle

Am., Mex., Int., F.C.I. Ch. Daktari Apogee Macho, apricot Miniature, owned and bred by Daktari Apogee Poodles, A. Monroe McIntyre and Nancy Hafner.

In many people's minds, the Poodle is considered a French breed of dog, which is a natural assumption since his popularity in that country has been such that he has frequently been called the "National Dog of France." That he originated there, however, is not true, historians tell us, and they substantiate their statements with strong evidence that they are correct. The truth is that the Poodle is a German breed that first reached favor during the revolutionary wars when some of these dogs accompanied the troops into France. Later they appeared and were received with enthusiasm in Spain, Great Britain, and the Netherlands, and they also have enjoyed popularity in Russia.

We quote the famed authority Jardine in his reference to "the water dog or Poodle" being "of German origin in its most perfect state," which words appear in his widely respected *Naturalist's Library*. We note too the fact that the breed name, Poodle, is undoubtedly derived from "Pudel," the early German identification for these members of the "Canis familiaris aquaticus" (or "water dog family") which were fond of "pudelin" ("splashing in water").

As long as they have been known, Poodles have excelled as water retrievers, swimmers, and true sporting dogs. Both in conformation and performance this has been evident, and their ability as water dogs has been attested to wherever the breed has appeared. They are marvelous companions, too, the darlings of society (especially the Miniatures and Toys) due

to their amusing personalities, and are talented in many ways. But their background is the water dog—the instinct, particularly in the Standard size, remains through the ages.

In France the early Poodles were admired as duck retrievers, using noteworthy intelligence and skill in collecting wounded birds after dark. The British sportsmen also found them fine retrievers, as have the Americans who have worked them as such. Superior thinking ability combined with a splendid "nose" (i.e., strong sense of smell) and the conformation of a tireless, powerful swimmer all combined to make these Poodles retrievers on which one could depend. The sole natural drawback was the Poodle's tremendously heavy coat. So started the custom of the "lion clip," as the shaving of the hind-quarters from ribs to stern was called, as then the dog was no longer burdened by excessive hair, which was a real encumbrance when soaked with water. Poodles in France became so associated with duck retrieving that they often were referred to in France as the "Chien Canne," which like "Caniche," by which the breed was also known, derives from "canard," which is duck in French.

Poodles were also known and popular in Russia long ago, and that country, like Germany and France, drew up a description of the early dogs as the breed was developed there, a "Standard of Perfection" as we think of them nowadays, which we will quote for you a bit later on. Only three colors were permitted as correct in these

18

This beautiful figurine is one of the most handsome and famous ever done of a Poodle. By Royal Doulton in the 1930's.

countries, Germany preferring the browns, France the white dogs, and Russia the blacks. Later on France became the first country to develop the blue and silver colors.

As one of the earliest canine breeds, Poodles were involved with the foundation and improvement of other breeds and with experimenting in developing them. The Germans created a "Poodle cross" (we are not exactly certain why), and at various times we have seen reference to "Poodle Griffons," "Poodle Pointers," and "Poodle Pomeranians," particularly in some English books of the early part of this century. Poodles of course have been credited with having helped create the Irish Water Spaniel and the Curly Coated Retriever, both of which so strongly resemble the breed in conformation.

"Doing what comes naturally." Wycliffe Amina Electra, the sister of four champions, demonstrates that the retrieving instinct still thrives in Poodles. Owner, Mrs. Donald Lyle, Wycliffe Kennels, Canada.

Everything about the early Poodles was not serious business, however. In olden days circus owners quickly discovered that here were mighty clever dogs, fun dogs which seemed to possess a sense of humor along with intelligence and which had (and still have) a natural agility and talent for walking or "dancing" on their hind legs. Thus Poodles went down in history as "circus dogs," and many a performing troupe brought pleasure and entertainment by dancing to music and performing acrobatic feats and other tricks. A very famous individual who has been written-up in history was one named Domini. He is credited with having been able to tell time by the clock, hold his own in a game of

Ch. Snow Boy of Fircot of Blakeen, "Boysie" to his friends, an English import born in 1945. He won the 1949 Quaker Oats Award for dog winning most Groups in that year. His show record stands at 60 times Best of Variety, 38 Non-Sporting Group Firsts, 17 times Best in Show, and twice Best in the Interstate Poodle Club Specialties. Boysie can be found behind many of the top winning white Miniatures of today.

checkers, and match numbers on cards to produce any requested total. Royalty and the public alike have been entertained for thousands of happy hours by the talents of performing Poodles.

Poodles have been popular subjects for great artwork right from the first century, when they were depicted in bas-reliefs along the Mediterranean shores, until the present day when we have countless gorgeous sculptures and paintings, old and new, of famous members of the breed to collect and enjoy. It is interesting that those first century bas-reliefs depict Poodles unmistakably the same breed as we know it today. Albrecht Dürer helped establish the Poodle in Germany during the fifteenth and sixteenth centuries with his drawings. In this same period Bernadine Pinturicia painted a charming series entitled 'Patient Griselda' which featured a neatly clipped Toy Poodle. The famous painting 'Tobit and his Dog' of the sixteenth century, by Martin de Vaux, featured a clipped Poodle, and the popularity of pet Poodles in Spain's early days was attested to in the work of the Spanish artist Goya. Regarding Poodles in Spain, it has been rumored by some historians that there may possibly at some period have been a link.

The smaller members of the Poodle family earned fame in a field of their own long ago as truffle dogs! Quite likely these were the ancestors of the original Toy Poodle breed that

Eng., Am. Ch. Bonny Brighteyes of Mannerhead of Blakeen, English import born January 1935. Shown four times in the States, Bonny won four Bests of Breed and 2 Non-Sporting Groups, becoming a champion. Bred by Mrs. G. E. Boyd, imported and owned by Blakeen Kennels.

was so widely prized in England, Spain, and Germany (where truffles were a popular industry) for scenting and digging up the edible fungus known as the truffle and considered to be a rare and coveted delicacy. Small, light-footed dogs with an excellent sense of smell were needed for this work, "small and light-footed" so as not to break or tear the truffles in digging them and "an excellent sense of smell" for locating these "goodies" efficiently. It is felt that what became known as the Truffle Poodle was quite possibly a composite dog with a slight infusion of terrier outcross, which latter may or may not have been true. We understand that the Truffle Poodles were especially in demand in England

Ch. Rudolph of Piperscroft (left) winning his first Challenge Certificate at the Richmond, England, Championship Dog Show in 1953. On the right is Ch. Braeval Black Nylons.

from the late nineteenth century until the time of World War I. Photographs depict them as white Poodles with black heads and tails and sometimes with a few black spots on the body. These parti-colored dogs were shown at the Botanical Gardens and other English dog shows at that period, having their own classification and enjoying wide admiration despite their coloring. We understand that brown and white dogs and also lemon and white dogs were seen as well as the black and white. A Mr. Cowan exhibited four of the especially successful winners, and there was another dog named Peter (whose owner is not identified) who was described as having a lovely long, lean head of correct type and a very short back. All of the Truffle Poodles had huge coats of hard texture. One of the big Truffle kennels prior to World War I was at Salisbury, England, and King Edward VII was said to have taken a lively interest in its work.

Ch. Prince Philip of Belle Glen taking Best in Show at the Poodle Club of America Specialty, 1966. Owned by Mr. and Mrs. Frank Smith, Jr., handled by Richard L. Bauer, Mrs. Milton Erlanger, judging.

Mrs. Marjorie A. Tranchin's Ch. Highland Sand Star Baby, a black Miniature dog. Highland Sand Kennels produced many outstanding champions awhile back.

A study in Miniature Poodle excellence. Ch. Beaujeau On The Beam, from the late 1960's, is the sire of three champions and is himself a Best in Show winner. Bred and owned by Mrs. Marjorie A. Tranchin, Dallas, Texas.

Ch. Moensfarm Marcelle of Montfleuri, stunning black Miniature Poodle is winning Best in Show at Mid-Hudson Kennel Club, June 1961.
Owned by Mrs. Nathan Allen and handled by Howard Tyler.

Ch. Carillon Colin of Puttencove winning the Group at Greenwich in 1948 for Mr. and Mrs. George Putnam.

Poodle Development in England

England's first Poodle specialty club was founded in 1886. Others came during later years, among them the Curly Poodle Club, the Miniature Poodle Club, and the International Poodle Club. The latter was founded close to 40 years later, in 1932 to be exact, by which point in time exciting progress had been made in Poodles as a breed and in popularity. When the International Poodle Club held its first specialty show at Ranelagh in 1933, its entry of 202 made up of 82 individual Poodles set a record for a Poodle specialty until that period.

Both abroad and in England, Poodles did well during the early 1900's. Originally the corded variety of coat was the more popular in the show ring, but then the tide began to turn in favor of the curlys, always preferred by the pet owners. For, while the pre-war cordeds were marvelous dogs, this type of coat definitely was not for just everyone to own, as growing the cords and keeping them clean and attractive were quite an art.

The English Poodle breeders applied to the Kennel Club for a distinct separation of the two varieties of Poodle, with a separate stud book kept for the cordeds and the curlys. After due consideration, it was decided that basically the two coats were the same, the difference being in the manner handled, so the application was denied. This probably led to the formation of the Curly Poodle Club to help promote that coat

Nunsoe Madelon, the dam of Phidgity, pictured in the late 1920's in England. Bred by V. Dering, by Nunsoe Chivalrous from a dam of Whippendell breeding. Miss Graham Weall, owner.

type. The cordeds became increasingly less popular and eventually disappeared from the ring.

The English breeders had always favored the French standard for Poodles, but developments toward the 1930's brought about some minor differences of opinion. The French standard's description of "well let down and straight hocks" certainly did not agree with the English conception of correct Poodle hindquarters. Nor did the word "wooly" describe texture of the curly coat, which the English preferred to be "harsh." Then the French standard provision that "Poodles must be born without dew claws on the hind legs or be disqualified" seemed a bit stern, as in England breeders were in the general habit of removing the dew claws on the front legs and always on the hind legs if they appeared, with no penalization for Poodles that had been so treated. Also, the French considered a perpendicularly carried tail to be faulty, preferring it to be carried on a line with the back. For these reasons the Curly Poodle Club set up its own standard, on which the Poodle Club of America eventually based our first one after its foundation early in the 1930's.

Phidgity Jessie, born in 1929, by Joker of Garston ex Nunsoe Madelon. Another winning Standard from Miss Graham Weall's kennel.

22

As must be realized, Miniature Poodles were bred down in size from Standard Poodles by judicious selection of the most suitable specimens for this purpose. French breeders, English breeders, and those in America did a magnificent job perfecting the Miniature editions of their breed, and the excellence and popularity of Miniature Poodles prospered around the world.

It was Miss Brunker, owner of the highly influential Whippendell Poodles, who in 1895 brought out the first blue Miniature shown in England. Pierrette Jackson, as the dog was called, made an immediate impression, as did the color. Other leading early English breeders included Mrs. Jack Taylor, well-known for Champion The Monarch, and Mrs. Hudson, known for the exquisite silvers Champion The Blue Boy and Champion Silver Gnome. Mrs. Arthur Willett's Champion Spriggan Bell played a leading role as a valuable producer, as did the same owner's silver, Champion The Ghost. Spriggan Bell was born in 1927 and became a leading winner along with being a fine producer.

Mrs. Walpole Harvey and Miss Rose Armitage were active in small whites and especially noted for Champion Kasha.

Mrs. Crimmins, who lived in Edenbridge in Kent, owned the Barbet Poodles that are familiar to both English and American breeders.

This is a corded Poodle of about 1900, as the breed was most usually seen at that time.

The Phidgity Kennels, belonging to Miss Graham Weall, were noted for fine Poodles in the 1920's-1930's period. Here are three winning Phidgity Standards from that time period.

Ch. Gondolette, bred by Miss H. C. Thorowgood, born in March 1924, by Cadeau from Champion Ambritte.

Ch. Spriggan Bell, born in 1927, was a great winning Miniature of the late 1920's and 1930's. Sired by Ch. the Monarch. Bred by Mr. A. Willett.

King Leo of Piperscroft, the first Poodle to take part in an obedience trial. He did remarkably well, earning even more credit for Mrs. Boyd.

Champion Barbet Mala Sirius was born in 1930, bred by Miss Kalender by Sepperi von der Vils ex Seigerin Dicta Sirius. She was evidently of German bloodlines and won her first two Challenge Certificates for Mrs. Crimmins in 1931. Champion Barbet Chita was another well-known Miniature owned by Mrs. Crimmins. Two white Miniatures imported by Mrs. Crimmins from Germany were later sold to Mrs. Boyd, owner of the fabulous Piperscroft Poodles and one of the world's most successful and influential Poodle breeders, as you will realize as you progress further into the pages of this book. These two German imports were credited with improving the heads and pigmentation on small white English Poodles. Punchinello of Piperscroft, an early winner, was a son of this German bitch.

It was Mrs. Boyd who promptly stepped in and purchased the available Chieveley Miniatures when that excellent kennel disbanded. She became at that time the owner of England's strongest and largest kennel of black Miniatures, although she continued her interest in silvers and whites. Her purchases from Chieveley included a line-bred dog and bitch, and among the offspring of the dog, Petit Ami of Piperscroft, were at least several champions. The future impact in the United States as well as in England of both Chieveley and Piperscroft dogs and bitches and their descendants could almost fill a book in itself, as you will see. Mrs. Boyd was the first English Poodle breeder to train dogs for police work and also had the first to appear in obedience there. She was also the first English judge to come over to officiate at an

American Poodle specialty, which she did for both the Interstate Poodle Club and for the Poodle Club of America. She was a lady of many accomplishments who did inestimable good for Poodles.

Mrs. Ralph Inglis was another important Miniature breeder of that period in England.

Turning to the Standard Poodles, we find Miss Jane Lane, whose Nunsoe prefix was almost a household word in Poodles over several decades. Undoubtedly this was England's most respected and dominant Poodle kennel of its period for Standards. The foundation here was a bitch named Nunsoe Aunt Chloe, a daughter of Whippendell Drapeau from Trifle, bred by Mrs. Lovett. She became a noted winner and produced several champions, among them Nunsoe Clever, a consistent certificate winner. Another

Ch. Barbet Mala Sirius, Miniature Poodle of the early 1930's, was of German breeding and did a great deal of winning during an exciting English show career. By Sepperl von der Vils ex Siegerin Dicta Sirius. Bred by Miss Kalender and owned by Mrs. E. C. Crimmins.

Ch. Barbet Chita, another of Mrs. Crimmins' well known winners in England around the 1930 period.

Miss Jane Lane, famous owner of the Nunsoe Poodles, with black Ch. Nunsoe Lady Mary, and the white Int. Ch. Nunsoe Duc de la Terrace before he came to America to the Blakeen Kennels of Mr. and Mrs. Sherman R. Hoyt.

of Miss Lane's finest Standards, this one a black, was Champion Nunsoe Lady Mary, considered among the most outstanding black bitches of her day.

There can be little question that Madame Reichenbach's renowned Labory Kennels in Switzerland held a unique position in the world of white Standards and in its influence on the breed. This truly fabulous lady was a breeder of stature. Several Poodles went from Labory to Miss Lane's Nunsoe Kennel, one of which was the immortal of the breed, Tri-International Champion Nunsoe Duc de la Terrace of Blakeen. Miss Lane acquired Duc in 1932, then re-sold him to Blakeen Poodles in America not long thereafter, for what "was reputed to be a record price for a Poodle." He sired five litters in England before coming to his eventual home in

America, four from bitches belonging to Miss Lane and one from a bitch of Mrs. Boyd, the latter Samite of Piperscroft, litter sister to Champion Nunsoe Nikola's Christopher Robin. Mrs. Boyd's Poodle activities encompassed Standards as well as Miniatures, and Knight of Piperscroft was the first Duc son to be shown in England. By the time he was a year old, he had a Challenge Certificate from Crufts, one from the big Kensington Canine Championship Show, had taken Best in Show at Brighton, and had won 34 prizes.

Nymphaea Jasper and Nymphaea Jason represented the results of some excellent breeding done by Mrs. Hutchinson from European whites she had imported. These two were subsequently exported to the United States. You will see them mentioned further along. Also the lovely Standard bred by Miss Brunker, Champion Whippendell Poli, was among the important Poodles to come to the United States from Great Britain.

Ch. Knight of Piperscroft, born in 1933, bred by Mrs. Boyd, by Tri-International Ch. Nunsoe Duc de la Terrace ex Samite of Piperscroft.

Miss Lane's famous Standard Poodle, Ch. Nunsoe Nikola Christopher Robin, a big winner in England during the 1920's.

The magnificent Ch. Alekai Luau, bred by Mrs. Henry J. Kaiser, owned by Ann Seranne and Barbara Wolferman, handled by Wendell J. Sammet.

Earlier Standards of the Ideal Poodle

Breed standards as we know them today are not recent innovations. Their roots go back into history, since for as long as there have been breeds of dogs developed for specific uses there have also been descriptions of those dogs and the features best equipping them for their work or making them most desirable.

As time has passed, in many cases changes have occurred in the occupation of various breeds and changes have taken place accordingly in the standards as modifications and refinements have crept in through the years. Yet the basic dog remains, although in a modern version many times far removed from the working or sporting dog it was in the beginning.

In my research for this book, I have found reference to three early descriptions in the three countries where so far as we know the original Poodles were most popular, Russia, Germany, and France.

Ch. Whippendell Carillon, a black Standard Poodle born in England in 1923. Owned by the noted breeder, Miss Brunker.

A very handsome English-bred Miniature dog, Lochranza Benedict belongs to Mrs. Ball and is handled by Pat Norwood.

An especially handsome picture of the great white Miniature dog, Ch. Round Table Cognac, handled to Best in Show by John Brennan, at the Virginia Kennel Club, 1966. Owned by Mr. and Mrs. Alden V. Keene.

The **Russian** description is as follows:

Rather leggy dogs, the head long and wedge-shaped with very little stop. Eyes in the best specimens are dark red, but many otherwise good dogs have yellowish eyes. Ears are set rather high and lie close to the cheeks. The legs are straight and muscular, the feet rather splayed and webbed halfway down the toes. The usual color is black, but there are also sometimes whites or black and whites. The coat, which shows little inclination to curl and none at all to cord, is long, coarse, and almost wiry.

The **Germans** liked their Poodles as follows:

Compactly built, powerful, with deep narrow brisket somewhat similar to that of a Greyhound, slightly arched strong loin with square back. Hindquarters powerful to propel the dog through the water. Feet round, compact, toes webbed to the nail. Head wedge-shaped but with more stop and more cheek than the Russian, very broad and nearly flat between the ears for great brain capacity. Occiput strongly marked. Eyes placed far apart, rather small, intelligent and lively in expression, a stupid expression most undesirable. Ears low-set, long and pendulous, leather reaching tip of the nose when stretched forward, hanging along the neck when head is erect. Lips close and tight, barely covering the incisors. Nose coal black in black specimens, a dark pinkish brown in whites. Bony, muscular, strong neck set into long sloping shoulders and of sufficient length to permit the dog to carry whatever retrieved well above water. Colors are black, white, black and white, and occasionally liver color, the latter regarded with suspicion as possibly indicative of Spaniel blood. Rich dark red eye in black dogs, dark brown in white. In coat the German Poodle is unique inasmuch as the hairs should felt or cord in long slightly knotty or wavy strings of the thickness of a crow quill. The entire coat, from base of skull to root of tail, divides evenly down the back, making a clearly defined part. Coat cords over the entire body excepting eyebrows and moustache, which should be straight and even with no wave and slightly glossier in texture than remainder of the body. Cords on head should fall away from the center leaving a well-defined crown, with no tendency to stand erect. Tail is usually docked, should be perfectly straight and carried at an angle of about 70 degrees with the back. A dog with a curled tail should not be debarred.

A stunning Miniature Poodle from Highland Sand Kennels, Ch. Highland Sand Magic Star II is an important little dog in Miniature history.

The **French** standard preferred:

A smaller and more slightly built dog than the German Poodle, colors being the same, solid colors absolutely essential in a good specimen. Well-defined stop, very broad top-skull with pronounced dome. Eye larger than the German Poodle, clear dark red in black dogs or dark brown in white, with no inclination to weep. Ears set rather high, leather seldom reaching tip of nose. Moderate length of neck, somewhat upright shoulders, body well-ribbed with strong arched loins. Feet slightly splayed, round, webbed to the toes. Legs long and muscular, hindlegs rather straighter than those of the German Poodle, with rather stilted action. Coat on entire dog should incline to curl, separating into ringlets. Must have no inclination to cord.

And now the **English** standard adopted by the Poodle Club of England in 1886:

General Appearance: A very active, intelligent, and elegant-looking dog, well built and carrying himself very proudly.

Head: Long, straight, and fine, the skull not broad, with a slight peak in the back.

Muzzle: Long (but not snipey) and strong. Not full in cheek. Teeth white, strong and level, gums black, lips black and tight-fitting.

Eyes: Almond-shaped, very dark brown, full of fire and intelligence.

Nose: Black and sharp.

Ears: The leather long and wide, set on low, hanging close to the face.

Neck: Well-proportioned and strong, to admit of the head being carried high and with dignity.

Shoulders: Strong and muscular, sloping well to the back.

Chest: Deep and moderately wide.

Back: Short, strong, and slightly curved, the loins broad and muscular, the ribs well sprung and braced up.

Legs: Set straight from the shoulder with plenty of bone and muscle.

Feet: Rather small and of good shape, the toes well arched, pads thick and hard.

Tail: Set on rather high, well-carried, never curled or carried over the back.

Coat: Very profuse and of good texture; if corded, hanging in tight even cords.

Colors: All white, all black, all red, all blue, etc. The white Poodle should have dark eyes and black or dark liver nose, lips, and toenails. The red Poodle should have dark amber eyes and dark liver nose, lips, and toenails. The blue Poo-

dle should have dark eyes, lips, and toenails and should be of even color without patches of white or black. All the other points of the white, red, and blue Poodles should be of the same as the perfect black Poodle.

The above standard was published in the **United States** in 1905, with the following additions:

Add to *Coat,* if non-corded Poodle: The coat should be very profuse and of hard texture, of even length, and should have no suggestion of cord in it and can be either curly or fluffy.

Add: The Toy Poodle should resemble the Poodle in every respect except Coat, often softer and silkier. Height, under 12 inches. Weight, under 10 pounds.

Scale of Points:

General appearance	10
Head	15
Eyes and expression	10
Neck and shoulders	10
Shape of body, loins, and back	10
Legs and feet	10
Coat	15
Carriage of stern	10
Bone, muscle, and condition	10
Total	100

We think that our readers will find it interesting to study these early standards from which the present ones have evolved to note the differences and the similarities along the way and the gradual merging of ideas into our present official description of the breed.

Ch. Trumbull's Silverblu owned by Ms. Barbara Primus, bred by Rawl Torres, sired by Ch. Ledahof Silverissimo ex Baybrier Calico.

Ch. Jolero Black Sunday, Winners Bitch at the Poodle Club of America National Specialty, June, 1977, finishes her title at the Fayetteville Kennel Club, March 26, 1978, under judge Frank Landgraf. Handled here by Richard Koester, owned by Mr. and Mrs. William Tow.

The Group winning Standard, Ch. Bel Tor Payoff, making an early win, still in puppy clip, at the Greenspring Poodle Club Specialty, April 1958. Owner-handled by Mrs. J. A. Mason.

Winning Best Non-Sporting Brace at Westminster, under judge Mrs. Milton Erlanger, in 1968, the handsome white Standards, Ch. Alekai Luau and Ch. Alekai Bali are owned by Mayfair Poodles, Ann Seranne and Barbara Wolferman. Handled by Wendell J. Sammet.

Ch. Round Table Cognac winning the Non-Sporting Group at Westminster, 1966. Mr. and Mrs. Alden V. Keene, owners. John Brennan, handler. Louis J. Murr, judge.

Round Table Kennels' black Miniature, Ch. Moulin's Belle Fleurette, winning Best in Show at Ft. Lauderdale, 1960. Judge, Robert Mosely. Handler, Anne Rogers Clark. Owner, Mr. and Mrs. Alden V. Keene, Middletown, Delaware.

An exquisite headstudy of Ch. Sherrode Carefree Beau, bred and owned by Emiline Krucker, Tucson, Arizona. Handled by Wendell J. Sammet.

CHAPTER TWO

Early Poodles in the United States

Early 20th Century

A fantastic headstudy of a gorgeous Miniature Poodle taken for **LIFE** magazine back in the 1960's, this is Ch. Tedwin's Top Billing, owned by Colonel Ernest E. Ferguson and later by Frank Sabella. "Billy" was a spectacular Best in Show and Specialty winning dog, one of the real standouts in Miniature Poodle history.

Little did Poodle owners ever anticipate, as this century came into being, that their breed would become one of the world's most popular as the years advanced, that it would earn fame in three separate size varieties, and that its smallest members would eventually be regarded as one of the breeding marvels in all canine history. That is how it all has happened, though. The Standard Poodles and the Toy Poodles as they were seen previous to World War I formed the background and the heritage that have developed into the three Poodles, Standard, Miniature, and Toy, that are prized for so many reasons by people in all walks of life in our present world.

Even previous to World War I, Poodles were raised and shown in the United States, both Poodles and Toy Poodles, to be specific. Show classification was divided by coat type rather than by size, Miniatures and Standards competing together as one breed with classes for curly Poodles or corded Poodles the only division, while Toy Poodles were considered an entirely separate breed. It may surprise some of our modern Poodle fans to realize that Toy Poodles were bred and shown in those days, for now we are more apt to regard them as a man-made creation that came several decades later. In a way the latter is true, for the Toy variety of Poodle, modern style, is really quite a different looking dog from those old original Toy Poodles. Still, they are behind present day Toys, which were created by judicious breeding of

them to small Miniatures for a gradual standardization of type, just as a decade or two earlier than this the breeders had created modern Miniatures by breeding them with the smaller Standards for the same purpose. The overall result has been that Poodles are now a breed in three different sizes all adhering to the same type. The Miniature is a small replica of the Standard, while the Toy is a tiny Miniature in appearance. Only dedicated and knowledgeable breeders could have accomplished all this so well within a comparatively short length of time.

But we are getting ahead of our story, except that an explanation seemed necessary at this point in order to avoid confusing the novice readers who might be puzzled were these facts not clarified.

Both Poodles and Toy Poodles had extremely loyal followers during the teens and pre-teen years. As far back as 1890 we find a single Poodle registration, with two in 1891 and 20 in 1893. By 1915, 245 Poodles were registered, with no separate Toy Poodle registrations. In 1918, as World War I drew to a close, there were 47 Poodles registered and two Toy Poodles.

Who were the early Poodle exhibitors? Before World War I, we find references to the Red Brook Kennels at Great Neck, Long Island, which was owned by two ladies, Miss Lucille Alger and Miss Louise Grace. Among their dogs were two well-known importations, Champions Windward Sauteur and Orchard Sunstorm, while among the homebreds Champion Red

Bob and Jane Forsyth in April 1960 are both handling Poodles from Mrs. J.A. Mason's noted kennel. With Bob is Ch. Bel Tor Stay Better Mousetrap, while Jane has the lead on Ch. Bel Tor Head of the Class.

Baby Doll, Champion Little Tiny, Champion Peaster's Little Beauty, Champion Peaster's Little Doll, Champion Peaster's Little Toy, and then later many others carrying the La Rex Doll prefix which she eventually selected for her Toy

Ch. Wynwood's Favorite Fella completing his title, handled by Bob Forsyth, at the Poodle Club of Massachusetts Specialty, June 1965. Mrs. Nora Andrews judging.

Brook Lightfoot was one of the best. These ladies were obviously serious breeders and active exhibitors for whom it was not unusual to put ten or more of their Poodles on the bench at a single dog show. Nor was it unusual for them to garner all of the principal awards. Miss Alger preferred to do the handling (always taking what she considered to be the best dog), doing so in an entirely business-like and professional manner, right down to being neatly attired in a crisp white smock. These ladies are the ones credited with having been the first exhibitors to initiate the custom of brushing out the Poodle coat, in contrast to the more popular practice of the day, dampening it to bring in a tighter curl. Quite truly they were the forerunners of our modern exhibitors. Sadly, we find little reference to Red Brook Poodles following the close of World War I, which is a pity as these ladies obviously had been knowledgeable, forward-looking Poodle breeders. Very likely they would fully appreciate what has been done to the breed over the years.

Other exhibitors of the teens in the New York area, which is where practically all United States dog show activity centered at that time, were either local or, in at least two prominent cases, from the Philadelphia area. Mrs. J. B. Moulton, H. G. Trevor, Miss Marie Louise Whittlesey, and Theodore Verkitz are some to whom we have found reference. Mr. and Mrs. Hartmann of Pennsylvania were very successful breeders of Toy Poodles over an extended period of time, producing an impressive number of those which completed championship. The other famous breeder from the Philadelphia area, Mrs. Harry S. (Bertha) Peaster (owner of Champion Little

Poodles and Chihuahuas), was one who bred and continued winning from this period right on into the 1940's. Mrs. Peaster's niece, Mrs. Florence Gamburg, is still an active member of the Fancy, being a highly respected multiple breed judge and a breeder of Pugs.

An early Poodle fancier who became an important and influential breeder, exhibitor, and judge was a little girl who grew up to be Mrs. Leonard (Flora) Bonney. Attending a dog show while a child, she saw and fell in love with Poodles and in 1912 purchased a black Standard puppy as a gift for her mother, who showed and did some winning with the dog. Mrs. Bonney gained fame in the Fancy not only through Poodles, of which she later owned some excellent champions, but also through great Chow Chows and Dalmatians at her Tally Ho Kennels at Oyster Bay, Long Island.

The 1920's were somewhat unspectacular so far as Poodles were concerned, though this was the calm before the storm, as one thinks back on it with knowledge of what was to follow. A few people loyal to the breed were raising and showing some Poodles. Registrations, however, ranged more or less in the area of two dozen Poodles yearly, with perhaps half that number of Toy Poodles, and show entries were correspondingly poor. Obviously the breed had not yet caught the admiration of the general public.

I find mention of several breeders as having been active during the 1920's. One was Mrs. Reuben Slote, whose kennel name was Reubette. She was the first person, so far as I can find, to

Winning the Non-Sporting Group under Melbourne Downing in 1967 is Ch. Alekai Marlaine with her handler, Wendell J. Sammet. Bred and owned by Mrs. Henry J. Kaiser.

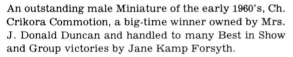

An outstanding male Miniature of the early 1960's, Ch. Crikora Commotion, a big-time winner owned by Mrs. J. Donald Duncan and handled to many Best in Show and Group victories by Jane Kamp Forsyth.

own a black Toy Poodle or for that matter one of *any* color other than white (which almost without exception is the color Toys were in those times). Mrs. Tyler Morse was a Poodle enthusiast but is more likely to be remembered in connection with Old English Sheepdogs. We have already referred to Mr. and Mrs. Thomas Hartmann, who through their Toys were perhaps the most active of any Poodle breeders right then. It was late in the 1920's that Alice Lang (Mrs. Byron) Rogers, of Misty Isles Kennels [not to be confused with Mrs. William (Olga Hone) Rogers, Anne Rogers Clark's mother, of Surrey fame, who came later], started turning her interest from Cairn Terriers to Poodles at her Bedford Hills, New York, establishment. Alice Rogers was definitely one of the "pioneer breeders" of the modern Poodle, providing foundation stock to many of the most successful kennels of the 1930's and also owning and developing some excellent Miniatures.

Also from the Bedford area of New York (which was quite a hotbed of Poodle breeders over at least a couple of decades), Mr. Henry J. Whitehouse and his daughter, Mrs. Whitehouse Walker, were becoming a force in the Poodle world. Mrs. William Jacobs showed a brown dog by the name of Toto during the late 1920's that became a champion in 1930. It is interesting to note that almost a decade later Mrs. Sherman R. Hoyt imported a descendant of this dog that became Champion Cajus v Sadowa of Blakeen. Thus the stage was set and waiting for the influx of the following decades.

Washington Poodle Club Specialty, 1965. Richard L. Bauer handled the Best in Show winner, Ch. Lady Margaret of Belle Glen, owned by Mrs. Helen Cosden.

Poodle Club of America Winner, 1964. Edris Bet-A-Million, black Miniature male bred and owned by Priscilla Richardson; handled by Wendell J. Sammet.

The 1930's

Where does one even begin to describe all the wonders of the 1930's that led to the rapid and spectacular advance of Poodles into the heart of the American Dog Fancy? In chronological order, obviously; thus we will start out by recording that the Poodle Club of America was founded in 1931, applying for membership in the American Kennel Club during July of that year, with a slate of officers that consisted of Mr. Henry J. Whitehouse, President; Mrs. Delancey K. Jay, Vice-President; Mrs. Whitehouse Walker, Secretary-Treasurer; and Mrs. Leo Brady, Mr. H. G. Erwin, Mrs. William Jacobs, Mr. Loring Marshall, and Mr. Byron Rogers as Directors, with Mr. Marshall serving as delegate to the American Kennel Club. The membership list consisted of ten people.

The first serious decision facing the new group was the adoption of the Standard for the Breed, whether it was to be based on the German type or on the Anglo-French type. There were differences between the two (see our section on early Poodle standards), and the majority of people making up the Poodle Club of America at the time favored going with the Anglo-French type as adopted by the Curly Poodle Club of England, although it was the German type that had been dominant in the United States previous to that time. One of the principal areas for difference involved coat and clip. With the German corded style, the "lion type" Continental Clip was used (hindquarters closely shaved), with the Anglo-French calling for curly coats separated into small tight curls with no tendency to cord, and these were clipped in the English Saddle style (hindquarters adorned with pack and bracelets). Since only pink skin was correct according to the European breeders, who thus demanded it, I must admit that some of these early Poodles did look a bit bare and that in those days the English Saddle Clip was more attractive.

The decision having been made, the Poodle Club of America requested permission of the Curly Poodle Club of England to adopt its same rules and standard, which was granted.

Suddenly things started happening in the Poodle world. Numerous dogs were imported from England, undoubtedly a direct result of a rush to breed Poodles which would excel under the new standard. Even so, the German dogs continued to demand respect, and in August, 1931, a handsome one, International Champion Donar v Eisentor, completed his title here for his owner, Mrs. Slote. Imported from Germany and of German breeding, this Poodle has been described as one of the true "greats" of the breed.

The year 1931 was also one in which an imported bitch, Anita v Lutterspring, was bred by her owner, Mrs. Byron Rogers, to the imported dog Nymphaea Pice, whelping her litter on April 23. Included in these puppies were the two which Hayes (Mrs. Sherman R.) Hoyt chose as a gift for her husband, who long had loved the breed. These became the first two champions finished by the Blakeen Kennels, and in the case of the bitch, Blakeen Roulette of Misty Isles, the first champion bred by Alice Lang Rogers. The dog, Blakeen Paul of Misty Isles, finished shortly thereafter. When one considers the aggregate number of Poodle championships completed by "Blakeen" and "Misty Isles" and by the descendants of their dogs since that time, one realizes how definitely this was "the start of something big."

Ch. Blakeen Roulette of Misty Isles (black), with kennelmate, Int. Ch. Nunsoe Duc de la Terrace of Blakeen, both owned by the Blakeen Kennels of Mr. and Mrs. Sherman R. Hoyt.

Blakeen puppies bred and owned by Mr. and Mrs. Sherman R. Hoyt.

The Standard of the Poodle Club of America was officially approved by the American Kennel Club in 1932, during June of which year that organization's first specialty took place in conjunction with the North Westchester Kennel Club, which, if memory serves me correctly, was held on Mrs. Tyler Morse's estate at Mount Kisco, New York. There was an entry of 23 for judge Leon J. Iriberry, an all-rounder from Brooklyn. Nymphaea Jason was Winners Dog for five points, Blakeen Roulette of Misty Isles also gaining five points for Winners Bitch. Best of Breed was Champion Whippendell Poli of Carillon.

The Poodle Club of America took cognizance of the plight of the Miniature during 1932, making a strenuous effort to gain status of a separate variety for these smaller Poodles, which were being somewhat lost in competition against the Standards. They succeeded up to the point of getting separate classification for each variety through the point of the Winners awards (thus two Poodles of each size were enabled to earn championship points rather than both sizes being judged together) and a Best of Variety was judged in each size, but this was followed by a Best of Breed award, which meant that still, for a while longer, only one Poodle was permitted to compete in the Non-Sporting Group. This division of Miniature classification led to a great rush to bring in good Miniature stock for breeding. The first champion Miniature was finished in 1933, a black dog, Chieveley Chopstick, who was more than eight years of age at the time. Soon thereafter the same owner, Mr. Charles Price of Boston, Massachusetts, finished his and the breed's second Miniature champion, also an importation, King Johnny, bred by Mrs. Taylor in England. Whippendell Picot, Johnny's half brother, who had been the first dog of England's famous "Vendas" breeding brought here (Mrs. Tyndall owned the Vendas Kennels) and was seven years old when he completed his title, was the next to follow with titular honors. This all serves as a comment on how badly the separate Miniature classification had been needed, when it had taken these obviously good dogs such a long period of time to gain recognition, undoubtedly due to having been up against the stiff competition provided by the greater early admiration for the Standards!

Some important Swiss Standards, descended from the German bloodlines, were brought to America in 1932, proving themselves valuable in breeding programs here. Most famed of these was Erik Labory, from Mme. Reichenbach's kennel, sent to Mrs. Byron Rogers.

A Poodle, Standard of course in those days, for the first time ever won the Westminster Non-Sporting Group in 1933. He was Champion Whippendell Poli of Carillon, Best of Winners here the previous year. Mrs. Whitehouse Walker owned this impressive black dog who was born in 1929, was bred by A. Brunker, and was sired by Whippendell Carillon from Whippendell Lolita.

Salmagundi Kennels, which became so highly successful for Mr. and Mrs. Justin W. Griess over several following decades, made its first champion also in 1933, a brown Standard bitch, Victoria, who subsequently produced the first of Salmagundi's many homebred champions.

Other 1933 Poodle happenings include the Sherman R. Hoyts' first appearance as Westminster exhibitors, with Blakeen Paul of Misty Isles and Blakeen Roulette of Misty Isles taking Winners Dog and Winners Bitch respectively; Mrs. Whitehouse Walker completed the title of her third champion; and a black bitch was born that later became the foundation for Cartlane Kennels of the Bedford, New York, area. Cartlane was to be operated successfully for many years by Miriam "Midi" Hall, producing outstanding Standards and Miniatures and eventually making its impact felt in Toys through the marvelous tiny Champion Cartlane Once a decade or two later.

But, unquestionably the most important event of all for Poodles that year was that Mrs. T.

Both black and white Poodles were in residence at Pillicoc Kennels. Here Mrs. Milton Erlanger is pictured with two of each. Photo courtesy of Henry Stoecker.

Whitney Blake imported, as a gift for her daughter and son-in-law, Mr. and Mrs. Sherman Reese Hoyt, then of Katonah, New York, a white Standard Poodle bearing the titles and name Tri-International Champion Nunsoe Duc de la Terrace. The Hoyts had seen and tremendously admired this magnificent Poodle while traveling abroad. Upon their return from this trip, Mrs. Blake asked if they had seen a truly *superb* Poodle. Indeed they had—Duc—but he was not for sale. Mrs. Blake took the information in her stride, and next thing the Hoyts knew, Duc was arriving in America, his destination Blakeen.

Duc was first shown at Westminster in 1934, an eye-filling dog that immediately caught everyone's attention, including mine. By going Winners Dog in Standard Poodles, Best of Breed, and on to first in the Non-Sporting Group, Duc became only the second Poodle in history to win the latter award at this show. Later in February he took Best in Show at Buffalo and some other nice honors, too, prior to his return to Westminster in 1935. Another of the Blakeen imported Standards, Knight of Piperscroft of Blakeen, accounted for Best of Winners, and then in came Mrs. Hoyt with Duc. Before she had left that show that year, her handsome big white dog had won the breed, then repeated his Westminster Non-Sporting Group win of the previous year, and rounded out the occasion by becoming the first Poodle in history to win Best Dog in Show at Westminster, at the same time making Hayes Blake Hoyt the first woman to handle any dog to Best in Show there.

The Poodle Club of America's second specialty was held in conjunction with North Westchester, this time drawing 16 dogs for the specialist judge. Miniatures and Standards each had their own classification. In the former, Barbet Stainless Stephen gained three points with Best of Winners, and Blue Jewel of Misty Isles took equal points with Winners Bitch. Reserves were Vendas Arrow of Silver and Gladmore Susette. In Standards, Blakeen Paul of Misty Isles took three points for Winners Dog, going on to Best of Breed. Pierrette Labory of Carillon was the Standard winning bitch; Stillington Xmas of Carillon and Whippendell Cliquette were reserves.

The 1934 Poodle Club of America Specialty, its third, was judged, as had been the first, by Leon Iriberry. Sparkling Jet of Misty Isles was Winners Dog in Miniatures; Misty Isles Algie of Piperscroft took Reserve. No Miniature bitches

A headstudy of Int. Ch. Nunsoe Duc de la Terrace of Blakeen, the first Poodle ever to win Best in Show at Westminster, which he did owner-handled by Mrs. Hoyt in 1935. Bred by Mme. E. Warney, by Prinz Alexander v Rodelheim ex Leonore v d Seestadt. This magnificent dog had a tremendous impact both as a sire and in the show ring. Among his noted progeny are Ch. Blakeen Eiger and Ch. Blakeen Jung Frau.

were present. Best of Winners for Standards was the dog Antoine of Misty Isles. Winners Bitch was Albricias of Blakeen, and the Reserves were Carillon Polisson and Gaillarde of Misty Isles. Best in Show was Tri-International Champion Nunsoe Duc de la Terrace of Blakeen. This year Duc also won Best of Breed at Morris and Essex.

Another event of 1934 was the completion of the championship of the first American-bred Miniature Poodle to gain the title, a black bitch named Marcourt Julie, by Chieveley Chopstick ex a daughter of King Johnny and a Standard bitch.

In 1935, many important Poodle events took place. The first homebred to gain championship for Mrs. Milton Erlanger did so; this dog was Cadeau de Noel, a brown Standard by Stillington Christmas of Carillon from Nunsoe the Mite. Cadeau de Noel goes down in Poodle history as a famed producer, too, having been the sire of the fabulous record-making black dog Champion Pillicoc Rumpelstiltskin. It was in August of 1935 that Pillicoc Toisin D'Or and Pillicoc Vedette completed their titles, these the first two champions bearing the Pillicoc prefix, and Rumpelstiltskin, litter brother to Vedette, finished in September of the same year.

Edelweiss du Labory of Salmagundi, by the same sire as Duc from a bitch named Nelly v d Schneeflocke, added another title to the growing list at Mrs. Griess's kennel. Mrs. Hoyt subsequently imported Nelly to breed to Duc, which later proved to have been an extremely wise decision. In August of this same busy year, Mrs. Hoyt finished Blakeen Mary Mont, the first homebred champion from this kennel. Also Mrs. Hoyt completed titles on the brothers Champion Blakeen Cyrano and Champion Blakeen Durante. "Cy" had a thrilling show career, both before and after being sold to Miss Mary McCreery to head her Lowmont Kennels at Greenwich, Connecticut. I judged this dog on one of my first Poodle assignments and could never forget his glorious brown beauty. Howard Tyler, now a highly successful all-breed judge, handled "Cy" and the other Lowmont dogs for Miss McCreery and managed Lowmont Kennels.

Headstudy of the brown Standard. Ch. Blakeen Cyrano, born 1934, by Ch. Nunsoe Darling David of Blakeen ex Blakeen Vigee le Brun, bred by Mr. and Mrs. Sherman R. Hoyt. Cyrano's show record includes 106 Best of Breed wins, 46 Non-Sporting Group Firsts and eight Bests in Show. Cyrano defeated all the best Standard Poodles of his day with the exception of Eiger and Jung Frau, Mrs. Hoyt notes.

Champion Blakeen Durante also distinguished himself by going to England, an exciting happening as this was the first time that a Poodle bred in the United States had been exported there. Certainly this was a compliment to Mrs. Hoyt and the excellence of the Poodles being produced at Blakeen. Cyrano and Durante were sired by Champion Nunsoe Darling David of Blakeen from Blakeen Vigee Le Brun and were born in 1934.

Spring of 1935 saw silver Poodles coming into their own. The first Standard of this color to finish was Champion Griseley Labory of Piperscroft of Blakeen, owned by Mrs. Hoyt, who was making "firsts" in so many areas. This dog was part of a dominant producing line, as he sired 14 champions himself in the United States. One of his sons was imported by Mrs. Whitehouse Walker and sired four champions, among them Champion Puttencove Impetuous who became the sire of 11 champions. The latter included the impressive black dog Champion Carillon Colin of Puttencove (a great favorite of mine who did much winning under me in the 1940's), Colin in turn siring 21 champions, as did his son, Champion Annsown Sir Gay. This latter dog sired Champion Bel Tor Marceau Choisi and Champion Bel Tor Gigadobs, each of whom were top producing sires as well (see the Bel Tor Kennel story in a later chapter).

On the Miniature side, this same year two silvers became champions, both of them importations. They were Fee D'Argent of Piperscroft and Grayling of Eathorpe-Carillon.

By 1936, Poodle activity had started to spread throughout the United States, with California particularly coming onto the "Poodle map." Ernest E. Ferguson, who later made so many records with his Poodles, purchased Champion Knight of Piperscroft of Blakeen, an English-bred son of Duc, from the Hoyts. Mrs. William Coleman, who had previously purchased two champions from Mrs. Hoyt, gained title on the first California-bred Poodle champion, the black bitch Roulette of Fair Acres (Champion Nunsoe Darling David of Blakeen ex Champion Blakeen Mary Rose). In December of 1936, pioneer Pekingese breeder Miss Lydia Hopkins finished the first Miniature Poodle champion bred in California, who was also the first Poodle champion bearing the Sherwood Hall identification. Miss Hopkins had also bred the first California-bred Pekingese champion—she was a lady who contributed a good deal to both of her favorite breeds.

Ch. Pillicoc Rumpelstiltskin, C.D., winner of the American Kennel Club Award for gaining the greatest number of Variety Groups in the United States during 1937. Best of Breed at the first separate Specialty of the Poodle Club of America, 1938. First in Non-Sporting Group, Westminster 1938, and at Morris and Essex 1937. Owned by the Pillicoc Kennels of Mrs. Milton Erlanger. Handled by Henry Stoecker.

In 1936, Champion Nunsoe Duc de la Terrace of Blakeen won the Non-Sporting Group at Westminster for the third time, breaking still another record.

In 1937 it became apparent why Mrs. Hoyt had been so wise in importing Nelly v d Schneeflocke for breeding to Duc. As the first of the white homebred Standards from Blakeen, Champion Blakeen Schneeflocke appeared in the ring, took Winners Bitch at Westminster, and quickly gained her title. It was another bitch, however, and a dog from this litter that truly made history. These were Champion Blakeen Jung Frau and Champion Blakeen Eiger. Who, once having seen this pair of sensational white Standards, could ever possibly forget them? Type, soundness, balance, style, showmanship—all the requisites of great show dogs were there. Together these two as a brace took Best Brace in Show on at least five occasions, among them Westminster, Morris and Essex, Eastern, Poodle Club of America Specialty, and Interstate Poodle Club Specialty, during their careers in the show ring. Separately, Jung Frau was shown 62 times, won 19 Bests in Show, 40 Non-Sporting Groups, and 42 Bests of Breed; Eiger had 17 Bests in Show, six times was adjudged Best American-bred in Show (an award of that period that was later discontinued by the American Kennel Club), won 57 Non-Sporting Groups, and won Best of Breed 69 times. In those days, such records were nothing short of

fantastic, as we had hundreds fewer shows annually in the United States than now and exhibitors were not in the habit of traveling all around the country as in present times. When there were shows in your area, you attended them, but only for truly prestigious occasions, such as Westminster, Morris and Essex, and specialty events, did exhibitors take their dogs from one part of the country to another.

In June, 1937, Carillon Memoire became the first homebred Carillon champion. Shortly afterward, Carillon Courage, C.D.X., who became the first Poodle to win a Non-Sporting Group and an Obedience Trial at the same show, completed championship, too. Miriam Hall's first champion, a homebred from Misty Isles breeding, Cartlane Bricoleur, gained title during this year. Another important Poodle to finish during 1937 was Champion Rettat's Slick, a black English importation by Marechal of Piperscroft ex Phidgety Swallow. He was a grandson of Tri-International Champion Nunsoe Duc de la Terrace of Blakeen, and he made considerable history as a sire. Among his progeny were Champion Pillicoc Pegasus, sold to Ernest E. Ferguson where he became the West Coast's foundation white stud as well as a successful show dog; Champion Pillicoc Pearl; and Champion Cartlane Caprice. Champion Pillicoc Pearl gained fame as a producing bitch, having been the dam of Champion Ensarr Glace, Peggy Githens' great white Standard; Champion

The fabulous litter brother-sister brace, Ch. Blakeen Jung Frau and Ch. Blakeen Eiger (Int. Ch. Nunsoe Duc de la Terrace of Blakeen ex Nelly v d Schneeflocke) bred and owned by Mr. and Mrs. Sherman R. Hoyt. Born in 1935, these perfectly matched Poodles won Best Brace in Show on at least five occasions at some of the country's most prestigious events: Eastern Dog Club, Westminster, Morris and Essex, the Poodle Club of America Specialty, and the Interstate Poodle Club Specialty.

Salmagundi's White Queen, who became a noted winner for Mrs. Leonard W. Bonney; and Blakeen Surrey Romance, who produced Champion Pillicoc Barrister.

It was during the autumn of 1937 that Mrs. W. French (Peggy) Githens made her first champion when she finished Carillon Corbeau. Selected by Mrs. Githens as a puppy, this dog was by Champion Whippendell Poli of Carillon from Champion Pierrette Labory of Carillon. This dog, with Champion Manon Labory of Blakeen, provided the foundation line from which Ensarr Poodles originated.

Also in 1937, Blakeen Ebony became the first of many champions finished by Miss Mary McCreery at Lowmont Kennels and Champion Bonny Brighteyes of Mannerhead completed title for Blakeen, as did Champion Arnim of Piperscroft of Blakeen, the first white Miniature to win a Non-Sporting Group in the United States.

A year of considerable Poodle progress was 1938. Two outstanding "happenings" were the first specialty show held by the Interstate Poodle Club and the first independent specialty show held by the Poodle Club of America.

First a word about Interstate. With the increasing, virtually skyrocketing interest in Poodles and the number of people now showing and breeding them, it seemed as though the interests of the breed could best be served by the addition of a second specialty club. Mr. and

Mrs. Hoyt, Mr. and Mrs. George Putnam (becoming very much involved as breeder-exhibitors at this period with Puttencove), Mrs. Irene Stowell Morse (whose wonderful Diablotin Miniatures contributed so greatly), Mr. and Mrs. Githens, Mr. and Mrs. Hugh Chisholm, and several other breeders were at the helm of Interstate, and through their efforts this club truly had considerable impact. There were no affiliate clubs with Poodle Club of America so far at that time, and Interstate applied for permission to also become an American Kennel Club member club. The merits of their request were looked upon as valid, so Poodles became the first breed ever to have two specialty clubs both admitted to American Kennel Club membership and sharing equal responsibility for the future of their breed.

Interstate's first specialty show was held on May 27, 1938, and it was a unique occasion as this show was judged by the English breeder Mrs. G.E.L. Boyd. The entry was limited to American-breds. Here there were Best of Variety awards in both Standards and Miniatures, with Champion Blakeen Jung Frau taking the former and then going Best in Show, and Champion Cheri of Misty Isles coming from the classes to take Best Miniature.

The Poodle Club of America's eagerly anticipated first independent specialty was in September at Far Hills, New Jersey. Best of Variety for both Standards and Miniatures was

These two handsome white Standard Poodles with their breeder, Mrs. Milton Erlanger, are Ch. Pillicoc Pearl and Ch. Pillicoc Pegasus, descendants of Tri-Int. Ch. Nunsoe Duc de la Terrace of Blakeen and Ch. Pillicoc Rumpelstiltskin. Pearl became the dam of Ch. Ensarr Glace, Ch. Salmagundi's White Queen and Blakeen Surrey Romance (she the dam of Ch. Pillicoc Barrister). Pegasus went to Ernest E. Ferguson in California, where she served as foundation for white Standards on the Pacific Coast. Photo courtesy of Henry Stoecker.

awarded here, too. Champion Cheri of Misty Isles, now a "Special," won Best Miniature; Champion Pillicoc Rumpelstiltskin was Best Standard and Best in Show. He also won the Non-Sporting Group at Westminster this same year, while Champion Blakeen Jung Frau won the Non-Sporting Group at Morris and Essex.

Champions that finished during 1938 included the famed white producing bitch Princess du Labory of Salmagundi and the Blakeen-owned Cajus v Sadowa, a brown German importation. It was during 1938 also that Mrs. Hoyt imported Lucas du Briole of Blakeen, who was to become an important white sire.

I guess that 1939 really should be referred to as "the year of the Miniatures," for during it the Hoyts, Mrs. Erlanger and Miriam Hall were all among those breeding this variety. It was during this year that Blakeen showed their imported Champion Platinum of Eathorpe, who through his son Champion Platina would be involved in the foundation of Ruelle Kelchner's fabulous silver Miniatures. Mrs. James M. Austin, already a very famous breeder of Pekingese and Brussels Griffons at her Catawba Kennels on Long Island, imported the excellent black Champion Vendas The Black Imp of Catawba. The Imp's eight champions included a dog named Black Magic who in turn sired Champion Magic Fate of Blakeen, bred by Ruth Burnette Sayres, that in his turn became the sire of Dorothy Thompson's Highland Sand Magic Star, foundation stud at this lady's Highland Sand Kennels. Magic Star sired at least 17 champions. Champion Vendas The Black Imp of Catawba was also behind the black and brown strains developed by Ruelle Kelchner at "Hollycourt," a line kept entirely separate from the silvers. Champion Cartlane Valentin, a

Mrs. Milton Erlanger with four of her famed white Standard Poodles, Ch. Pillicoc Polaris, Ch. Pillicoc Pegasus, Ch. Pillicoc Pearl, and Ch. Pillicoc Purity.

silver, was representing Miriam Hall's Miniatures. Mrs. Hoyt finished her imported black, Moutit de Madjige, who was selected to enhance her breeding program in black Miniatures. Mrs. P.H.B. Frelinghuysen was importing and breeding exquisite Miniatures at Smilestone Kennels, and Mrs. Saunders Meade, who owned one of my Standard favorites, Champion Seafren Ange Gardien, was getting intensely interested in Miniatures, too.

Nor were Standards idle. Champion Blakeen Jung Frau won the Non-Sporting Group at Westminster 1939, and her brother Champion Blaken Eiger, won it the following May at Morris and Essex. Champion Chosen Dame of Salmagundi won Best of Breed at the Poodle Club of America Specialty in June (Champion Vendas The Black Imp of Catawba was Best Miniature here), and Champion Blakeen Eiger was Best in Show at Interstate in September, where Miniatures were led by Sparkling Lady of Raybrook.

Ernest E. Ferguson finished his first two homebred Champions, white Standards, in 1939. These were Donna de la Nuit Blanche and Duchess de la Nuit Blanche, litter sisters by Champion Knight of Piperscroft of Blakeen ex Blakeen La Reine (a Duc daughter). Torchlight Kennels in the Midwest was getting under way with an English bitch, the black Champion Nunsoe Little Audrey of Torchlight. Thus the groundwork had been accomplished for still greater Poodle glory to follow in the decade of the 1940's.

The Standard bitch Ch. Blakeen Jung Frau, litter sister to Ch. Blakeen Eiger, by Int. Ch. Nunsoe Duc de la Terrace of Blakeen ex Nelly v d Schneeflocke of Blakeen, born 1935. Shown 62 times, Jung Frau was Best of Breed 42 times, 40 times Non-Sporting Group First, and was 19 times Best in Show including at Morris and Essex, at that time the largest dog show in America.

The 1940's

It was in 1940 that a Toy Poodle, then still considered to be a separate breed, for the first time gained a Group placement at Westminster. This dog, Karitena de Muriclar, bore the kennel name of Muriel Clark from California but was owned by Mrs. James M. Austin, who had become quite intrigued with the tiny Poodles. Karitena was also the first Toy Poodle to win first in a Toy Group at any show in the United States. Mrs. Austin had several splendid Toy Poodles going for her during the period, in addition to her Miniatures. Champion Vendas The Black Imp of Catawba won the latter variety at Westminster this same year.

Probably the biggest excitement of 1940 came in May, when Mrs. Hoyt piloted her homebred white Standard bitch, Champion Blakeen Jung Frau, to Best in Show at Morris and Essex. This was the largest and most prestigious event at which a Poodle had won the highest award since Jung Frau's sire, Duc, had won it at the Garden

some five years earlier, and with the added frosting that this time the winner was American-bred. All the more remarkably, the award was gained in a pouring rain, hardly the most ideal conditions under which to show a white Poodle. But Jung Frau and her owner-handler took all that in their stride, happily coming through with flying colors.

The brother-sister Blakeen duo, Eiger and Jung Frau, was very dominant in the eastern section of our increasingly Poodle-oriented country, which is where the tough competition was centered at this point in time. Eiger won the Poodle Club of America Specialty that first year of the new decade, then in 1941 took the Non-Sporting Group at Westminster.

Now the Miniatures were starting to take over in popularity, quality, and success to the extent of being an amazing tribute to their breeders. They had received little attention in Group and Best in Show competition during the previous decade, but that was quickly changing due to judicious use of splendid importations interbred with both the smaller Standard and Miniature stock already available here. Poodles were beginning to emerge that were truly miniature replicas of the Standards. As we have previously mentioned, careful interbreeding of the two varieties was quite acceptable at this stage, and the results proved to be successful. Stunning little Miniatures were truly causing the judges to "sit up and take notice."

It was at the 1940 Interstate Specialty that a Miniature named Champion Monty of Gilltown became the first of his variety to win the top award at *any* Poodle specialty in the United States. A black dog bred by the Viscountess Furness, he was a son of Sparkle of Mannerhead ex Mattana Sirius of Gilltown; he was an English importation belonging to Mrs. Peter H. B. Frelinghuysen and handled by Walter Morris.

Two years later, in 1942, Champion Ramoneur of Catawba became the first Miniature to win the Westminster Non-Sporting Group. This one was also a black, and it is interesting to note that he was a grandson of the first U.S.A. Champion Miniature, Chieveley Chopstick, and that he went back to the Whippendell strain and to the Early Chieveley dogs.

It was another great descendant of Champion Chieveley Chopstick that in 1943 achieved the greatest victory up to that time for Miniatures. This was a stylish, elegant black bitch, Champion Pitter Patter of Piperscroft, that earned her niche in Poodle immortality when she sailed around the great ring at Madison Square Garden

Mrs. William H. Ball, owner of so many famous winning Poodles, photographed with a dearly loved favorite back in the 1940's.

A historic moment on a rainy day! Mrs. Sherman R. Hoyt has just won Best in Show at the Morris and Essex Kennel Club event May 25, 1940, with her famed white Standard bitch, Ch. Blakeen Jung Frau. Mrs. M. Hartley Dodge presents the trophy.

Looking back into Poodle history we find this photo, taken in 1946, of Mrs. Saunders L. Meade, Seafren Kennels, handling her noted Miniature bitch, Ch. Nelly Bly, to a Non-Sporting Group First at Bucks County Kennel Club.

Ch. Ensarr Navy, black Standard Poodle owned by Mrs. W. French Githens and handled here by Henry Stoecker, taking Best in Show from the author at Susquehanna Kennel Club in 1946.

under the guidance of her handler, Walter Morris, to become the *first Miniature* and only the *second Poodle in history* to win Best in Show at Westminster. Jubilation was high that night among Miniature fans as congratulations were lavished upon Mrs. Frelinghuysen, her owner, and Mr. Morris.

The years of World War II took their toll on the American Dog Fancy, with cancellations of many shows. Those that did continue, with the exception of Westminster, dropped to quite a small size. Armories (the usual site of indoor shows in those days) were needed by the government for "the purposes for which they had been intended," and the difficulty of travel, rationing, and shortages forced fanciers to cut back. Morris and Essex cancelled for 1942, 1943, 1944 and 1945. Interstate held no separate specialty between 1942 and 1945 inclusive, and the Poodle Club of America did likewise. Searching through the records, it appears that both of these specialties supported Westminster in lieu of their own events those years.

The Poodle people were not inactive during the first half of the forties despite limitations imposed on their dog shows. Westminster, as we have noted, did continue, and there were enough other small shows going on to, at least in some way, satisfy the yearning of a dog show exhibitor to have somewhere to take his dogs.

Among the exciting Westminster "happenings" of this period, we note that a Miniature, Champion Black Magic, bred in the United States by Mrs. Delancey K. Jay and sired by Champion Vendas The Black Imp of Catawba, won the Non-Sporting Group there in 1944. Champion Blakeen Luzon, a white Blakeen Standard bitch by Champion Broadrun Cheerio ex the Duc daughter Blakeen Nelly, bred, owned and shown by Mrs. Sherman R. Hoyt, did likewise in 1945. We also note the two future "greats" in the Standard Poodle world that were Winners Dog and Reserve Winners Dog at Westminster during that year, Carillon Colin of Puttencove and Carillon Jester, respectively, owned by Mr. and Mrs. George Putnam and bred by Mrs. Whitehouse Walker. They were both out of Champion Carillon Colline. Carillon Colin became a very popular and widely admired Best in Show and consistent Group winner—a truly magnificent dog. As for Jester, he probably did more to make the general public appreciate Poodles than any dog ever in breed history! Owned by Louise Branch and bred and handled by Blanche Saunders, he was a half brother to Colin, being from the same dam. His

Another of the many famous Best in Show Poodles owned by Mr. and Mrs. Sherman R. Hoyt. Ch. Broadrun Cherry, son of Lucas Du Briois of Blakeen ex Blakeen Nelly won eight Bests in Show, 16 Groups, 18 times was Best of Variety, and with his brother, Ch. Broadrun Cheerio, won Best Brace in Show at Westminster 1943. Bred by Mrs. J. L. Luke; born 1939.

The stunning and very successful white Standard bitch, Ch. Blakeen Luzon, born 1940, bred by Mrs. J. L. Luke, by Ch. Broadrun Cheerio ex Blakeen Nelly. A Group and Best in Show winner owned by Blakeen Poodles.

accomplishments included (in addition to his bench championship, a U.D.T. title in the United States, and an International C.D. title) a very busy career as an obedience demonstrator with Miss Saunders in the movies, on television, and in New York City annually for the National Dog Week observance which was held at that time at Rockefeller Plaza each September. No one who ever saw Jester could forget him. He was a dynamic, beautiful Poodle personality.

Everything started up again in 1946. The war was over and people were in a mood to "make up for lost time," not that the breeders had been inactive during this period, as many fine young dogs began to appear in the show ring.

The Poodle Club of America resumed its separate specialty shows in May of that year, this time locating at the lovely Garden City Hotel in Garden City, Long Island, a "picture spot" which remained its home for a good many years. This was always a big week end for Poodles, as the Ladies Kennel Association of America held forth on the same grounds the following day (this was a club in which many Poodle people were involved, including Mrs. Bonney, Mrs. Austin, and several others) and the Long Island Kennel Club, another big, beautiful show, was nearby on Sunday. As was becoming quite usual, it was a Miniature that was the "star" on this occasion, Champion Paquette, a black bitch by Ack Ack of Misty Isles (note the consistency with which Misty Isles remained in the limelight) from Picaroon. Mrs. Boyd, who had done Interstate on an earlier occasion, came from England to judge here. She was the owner of the Piperscrofts, you recall, that have earned such fame throughout the Poodle world.

Interstate also resumed its specialty in 1946, with Alva Rosenberg, so highly esteemed by all exhibitors, doing the honors. Two handsome brown dogs of Mrs. Hoyt dominated on this occasion, Miniature Champion Blakeen Eldorado (Champion Vendas The Black Imp of Catawba ex Champion Vendas Winter Sunshine of Blakeen) and Standard Champion Blakeen Colorado (Champion Berkham Isaac of Sunstorm ex Broadrun Cinnamon). Each won its variety that day, and I do not have a record on which went Best of Breed. Eldorado was one of the truly great Miniatures in this writer's opinion. He was the first brown Miniature ever to win a Best in Show in the United States, and he was the first Poodle to win Best in Show at the illustrious Eastern Dog Club event in Boston. His record, from 43 times shown, included 35 times Best of Breed, 17 times first in the Non-Sporting

Ch. Pillicoc Pegasus at 13 months. Purchased by Ernest E. Ferguson from Mrs. Milton Erlanger, this handsome white dog was a strong influence on West Coast white Standards during the 1940's. Photo courtesy of Henry Stoecker.

Ch. Pillicoc Reverie, black Standard bitch by Pillicoc Rigolo ex Dream of Piperscroft, was the Top Winning Poodle of 1941. Bred and owned by Pillicoc Kennels.

Ch. Blakeen Enchantress, one of the many great winners belonging to Mr. and Mrs. Sherman R. Hoyt.

Group, seven times Best in Show, and four times Best American-bred in Show. Three times he was Best of Variety at Interstate specialties. Another very famous Miniature took Best of Opposite Sex in that variety that day. She was Champion Platina, a silver bitch owned by M. Ruelle Kelchner who has the distinction of her own listing in the book *Who's Who in American Dogdom.* Platina was bred by Miss Kelchner and sired by Champion Platinum of Eathorpe of Blakeen ex Flora of Piperscroft. It is noted that she became the dam of four male champions, these having been Hollycourt Platinum, sire of seven champions; Hollycourt Light of Star Tavern, sire of 12 champions; Hollycourt Osmium of Paragon, sire of five champions; and Petit Pierre, sire of ten champions. She also had a champion daughter who whelped three champion offspring. At the time this was written in *Who's Who,* 1958, Platina had 125 champion descendants, including most of the silver-grays in the United States, a list that has undoubtedly grown even longer through the ensuing years.

Miss Kelchner contributed tremendously to Poodles throughout her many years as a breeder. Her kennel, Hollycourt Poodles (active since 1937), developed several different color lines over the years. Miniatures were her principal interest, although she did have some champion Toys and Standards, too. I only regret that she died a few years ago and thus cannot give us first hand the complete resume of her records as a Poodle breeder. At least, thanks to the kindness of Wendell Sammet and my own good fortune in

At the Interstate Poodle Club Specialty, September 1948, are two great ladies of the Poodle world who contributed much to the development and progress of this breed in the United States. Left, Olga Hone Rogers, owner of Surrey Kennels; right, M. Ruelle Kelchner, Hollycourt Kennels.

having some of them in my own files, we are able to bring you pictures of a number of her dogs. She was a Director of the Poodle Club of America for many years (of Interstate, too, if I recall correctly) and was a charter member of the Poodle Club of Massachusetts. It was she who received the first Torchbearer's Trophy from the Poodle Club of America for "breed improvement and promotion."

Strathglass Kennels, owned by Mr. and Mrs. Hugh J. Chisholm of Portchester, New York, was also an exhibitor at the first post-war Interstate. Mrs. Chisholm was active with Miniatures, and Mr. Chisholm, always so genial, was more interested in Airedales and Welsh Terriers. The Chisholms were devoted Interstate members, hosted the specialty most graciously upon occasion, and were delightful fanciers. Their son Bill is still "in dogs" as an officer of the Westminster Kennel Club.

Still another Interstate exhibitor this first post-war year was Mrs. Irene Stowell Morse. As you read the kennel stories in this book you will see the impact that Diablotin, even though a small kennel and of short duration due to its owner's untimely death, had on later generations of Miniature Poodles, as her dogs are in the background of some of our most widely admired strains. Noted for black Miniatures, Mrs. Morse had dogs of type and elegance. She was a *good* breeder and an ardent devotee of this breed.

The Morris and Essex came back in 1946 to have its Non-Sporting Group won by a Standard bitch, Champion Lowmont Lady Luck, owned by Miss Mary McCreery. Mrs. Saunders L. Meade took the Miniature variety that day with another favorite of mine, Champion Nelly Bly. Bred by Mrs. A. O. Jimenis (who had some nice Miniatures in those days and was keenly enthused) and Mrs. Byron Rogers, Nelly was by Champion Bibelot of Misty Isles from Moira of Meredick.

The Poodle Club of America in 1947 had quite a number of Ruth Burnette Sayres' Bric A Brac dogs in competition and winning well. As kennel manager for Mrs. Austin at Catawba, she had developed a sound eye and keen knowledge for the breed, which certainly carried on well into her own breeding program. Bric A Brac dogs did some excellent winning in keenest competition, always perfectly presented by their talented owner. This Poodle Club of America Specialty in Miniatures was won by Champion Cartlane Dernier Cri and in Standards by Champion Lucite of Salmagundi.

Showing Miniatures in 1946 were Miss M. Ruelle Kelchner of Hollycourt (closest to judge), Mrs. Olga Hone Rogers of Surrey, and Mrs. Irene Stowell Morse of Diablotin.

Mrs. Ruth Burnette Sayres winning a Group from the author in 1948 with one of her handsome Bric A Brac Miniatures.

At the 1947 Morris and Essex, Mrs. Hoyt won Standards and the Non-Sporting Group with Champion Blakeen Osprey. Bric A Brac Blackbird, who had been Winners Bitch at the Poodle Club of America, came from the classes to go Best Miniature.

Champion Blakeen Osprey won Standards at Interstate that year, while Champion Ensarr Salute, Mrs. Githens' new venture into Miniatures, took that variety while being handsomely handled by Henry Stoecker. This little dog went on to win Best of Breed at the Poodle Club of America the following year and then, a week or so later, first in the Non-Sporting Group at Morris and Essex. He was a black, bred by Ruth and Henry Sayres by Bric A Brac Barker ex Bric A Brac Cinderella, she a daughter of Champion Vendas The Black Imp of Catawba.

In September, 1948, it was my own (A.K.N.) pleasure to judge the Interstate Specialty for the first time. Champion Snow Boy of Fircot was Best of Breed, and Champion Carillon Colin of Puttencove was Best Standard. Olga Rogers took the purple in Miniature dogs with Clairwell Him Especially. I shall always recall the flair with which this lady handled a dog—cool, calm, collected, and with beautiful expertise. Her

daughter Anne has always been admired for her touch, her "good hand on a dog," which was directly inherited from her mother, as anyone who knew and admired Olga Rogers can tell you. Olga Rogers bred and handled Poodles and English Cocker Spaniels at that time under the Surrey prefix. Anne was just on the threshold of her great handling career.

In 1949, the close of another decade, Champion Snow Boy of Fircot and Champion Carillon Colin of Puttencove were the two dominant Poodles. Both won their respective varieties at Westminster, with Colin also adding the Best of Breed award from the Poodle Club of America Specialty. Colin and Snow Boy were winners again at both Morris and Essex and Interstate, on these occasions Snow Boy going on through to first in the Non-Sporting Group at Morris and Essex and at Somerset Hills, with which event Interstate was held in conjunction that year.

With the future in mind, let us note who was entered and with what Poodles at Morris and Essex 1949, of which I have a catalogue. Mrs. Erlanger judged Miniature and Standard Poodles. The Miniature entry was made up by Blakeen Kennels with six, Mrs. Peter Frelinghuysen with six, Seafren Kennels with

Ch. Blakeen Osprey, born in 1944, by Ch. Broadrun Cheerio ex Ch. Blakeen Aigrette, was a Specialty Show, Group and Best in Show winner for the Blakeen Poodles of Mr. and Mrs. Sherman R. Hoyt.

Perfection II, Champion Cartlane Hillandale Cadenza, and Champion Vicki of Lottal. Two white Standards who would accomplish much in the 1950's, Ensarr Glace and Ensarr Cygne, were entered in the classes, Glace in Open Dogs and his son Cygne in Puppy.

Dog people did their share during the war years through supporting Dogs for Defense and other activities. One of them, Mrs. Milton Erlanger, deserves a special tribute for her part in the organization of Dogs for Defense and the great contributions she made to the war effort. She was actively concerned with the War Dog Program. She was a consultant to the United States Government on War Dogs, 1942-1947, and author of the technical manual *Training War Dogs*, 1943-1945. She received the Exceptional Civilian Service Award presented by the Secretary of War in 1945, and the Gaines "Fido" for Dog Woman of the Year in 1946. The Poodle Fancy, and all of us in pure-bred dogs, were very proud of her indeed!

Ch. Carillon Colin of Puttencove belonging to Mr. and Mrs. George Purnam, Manchester, Massachusetts, a very famous winner of the 1940's is being awarded first in Non-Sporting at the Interstate Kennel Association in 1948 by Mrs. Sherman R. Hoyt.

two, Miss Kelchner with three, and Roadcoach Kennels (Mary Barrett, also well-known for her marvelous Dalmatians) with two. Marjorie Siebern, who became a tremendously popular judge, had one, as did Mrs. George Goff, who is perhaps better known through her Puckety Boxers. Also entered were Mrs. Arthur Vogel (later Mildred Imrie), Mrs. Byron Rogers, Olga Hone Rogers, Mrs. Arthur M. Wells, Star Tavern Kennels, Diablotin Kennels, Lucy Magnus with litter sister puppies, Tilo Kennels (Laura Niles—still active), Marion Kafaroff, Mrs. James M. Austin, Mrs. Thomas Smith, Mrs. Githens, Strathglass Kennels, Rodyar Kennels, and Mrs. Clarence D. Allen. The Specials class consisted of Snow Boy, Champion Bric A Brac Blythe Spirit, and Champion Smilestone's Bric A Brac. Champion Blakeen Snow Flurry and Champion Seafren High Falutin were among those in the large class competing for the Dodge Memorial Trophy, a popular and coveted award for Best American-bred Dog or Bitch in each breed. Many of the same exhibitors had Standards entered, plus Carillon, Verdant, Hillandale, Lowmont, and Lottal along with some single entries from names unfamiliar to me. There were five Standard Specials—Colin, Champion White Cockade of Salmagundi, Champion Blakeen

What a lot of nostalgia this picture generates: with the black dog is Bill Trainor; Ruth Burnette Sayres with Ch. Fircot L'Ballerine of Maryland, Bob Forsyth, and Anne Hone Rogers Clark with the Toy, Ch. Wilber White Swan, at the Quinnipiac Poodle Club Specialty, July 1955.

Ch. Marney's Marquis de Lafayette, bred and owned and shown by Mrs. Margaret Durney, was Top Non-Sporting Group winner for 1954 and 1955. "Willy" was from Mrs. Durney's first litter out of her foundation bitch, Ch. Ma Vielle of Blakeen, C.D.X., and won many Best in Show and Group victories prior to retirement.

Ch. Highland Sand Brown Dream at Long Beach, California, handled by Ben Burwell.

The Standard Poodle, Ch. Caledonia Cassandre, winning the Non-Sporting Group at Marion Ohio Kennel Club, 1953. Co-owned by Mr. and Mrs. William Schmick, handled by Mr. Schmick, then of Greenwich, Connecticut. The judge is Miss Iris de la Torre Bueno.

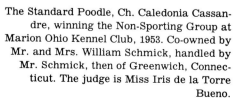

The 1950's

If anything, Poodle popularity and success seemed to gain momentum as the second half of the twentieth century got under way. Poodle interest was spreading throughout the country at a rapidly escalating rate, with new kennels popping up, the older ones holding their own, and increasing outstanding show ring honors for all three varieties of the breed.

The great Standard of the 1950's was unquestionably Champion Puttencove Promise, who took Best in Show at Westminster in 1958 along with a whole string of other exciting awards. A magnificent dog who was to prove a tremendous producing force in Standards as well as a success in the show ring, he was owned by Mr. and Mrs. George Putnam, handled by Bob Gorman, and had legions of friends and admirers.

Another Standard Poodle making its presence strongly felt during this period was a white male, Champion Alfonco v d Goldenen Kette, a class entry from Lottal Kennels at Westminster in 1954. Later, when owned by Clairedale and Pennyworth Kennels and under Bob Forsyth's handling, he became a famed Best in Show and Group winner. Mrs. Claire Knapp Dixon owned Clairedale and her daughter, Mrs. Margaret P. Raynor, owned Pennyworth, the home of so many successful Whippets.

Then there was Champion Blakeen Bali Hai, starting his career under the Sherman R. Hoyts' ownership and later sold to the George Putnams, who continued to campaign him. A beautiful, successful dog and a dominant sire, he was by Champion Pillicoc Barrister from Blakeen Morning Star.

Louise Branch, owner of Carillon Kennels (then located at Pawling, New York), won the Poodle Club of America Specialty in 1952 with her imported blue dog, English and American Champion Frenches Blue Marvel. A son of his, Champion Carillon Blue Boy, made his title in the very short span of exactly two weeks, start-

Mr. and Mrs. George Putnam's glorious white Standard dog, Ch. Puttencove Promise, handled by Bob Gorman to Best of Variety at the Interstate Specialty and a Non-Sporting Group First later that day at Somerset Hills Kennel Club.

ing May 15 at Poodle Club of America by taking Best of Winners and finishing on May 31. Other well-known dogs from this kennel at that period were Champion Carillon Jongleur (by Blakeen Popover ex Carillon Jestina), Santos Labory of Carillon, and Champion Carillon Commando.

Already in the 1950's Edward Jenner, who through the years has gained so many prestigious honors with Poodles bred, owned, or co-owned by him, was active in the breed. We note a Standard dog of his, Forest Flamingo, by Champion Puttencove Midshipman ex Champion Fanfaron Dark Splendor, entered in the Open Class at Westminster in 1954. Frances Angela is another noted Standard breeder entered at this show, with Torchlight Polka Dot (also by Midshipman but from her Champion Torchlight Clementine). Other entries included Dr. Donald Davidson, Fanfaron Kennels, Tally Ho, Bel Tor, and Puttencove. Cynthia and Bill Schmick had their Best in Show Standard bitch, Champion Caledonia Honey Bear, entered as a "Special," as were Katherine Drake's (Larry Downey, handler) Champion Puttencove Soubrette and the Putnams' Champion Blakeen Bali Hai.

Some of the important Poodle events of the 1950's involved the founding of two outstanding successful Miniature kennels—Dunwalke, owned by Clarence Dillon (who was later Secretary of the United States Treasury), and Tydel, owned by Mrs. Marguerite Tyson (who was a famous socialite from Washington, D.C., and sister of Perle Mesta, who had been U.S. Ambassador to Luxembourg and was extremely popular in diplomatic circles).

The well known and splendid white Standard dog, Ch. Ensarr Cygne, winning Best in Show owner-handled by Mrs. W. French Githens, Rockland County Kennel Club, 1953.

Mrs. Leonard W. Bonney, owner of Tally Ho Poodles, here admires the winners she has selected at the Poodle Club of America Specialty, May 1957. The Toy is Ch. Fieldstreams Bojangles, owned by Audrey Watts Kelch, handled by Ben Burwell; the Miniature is Ch. Hollycourt Florazel owned by M. Ruelle Kelchner, handled by Wendell Sammet; the Standard is Ch. Puttencove Promise, owned by Mr. and Mrs. George Putnam, handled by Bob Gorman.

Bob Gorman is handling Puttencove Promise, one of the truly great white Standards, for Mr. and Mrs. George Putnam to First in Non-Sporting at Queensboro Kennel Club, 1957.

The Seafren Kennels of Mr. and Mrs. Saunders L. Meade owned this highly successful imported Best in Show winning Miniature, Ch. Fircot L'Ballerine, handled by Ruth Burnette Sayres, here taking the Non-Sporting Group at Troy Kennel Club, 1955.

Ch. Bouchiene D'Amour photographed in 1957.

The imported silver-brown Miniature, Ch. Spider of Piperscroft owned by Helen R. Thompson, Winelist Kennels, Prospect, Kentucky.

A Group winning Standard of the early 1950's, Ch. Bon Mar Cavalier, owned by Marjorie Fraser of California, handled by Ben Burwell.

The white Miniature is Ch. Icarus Duke Otto, owned by Mrs. Robert Tranchin, handled by Jane Kamp Forsyth. The black Standard, Ch. Bel Tor Suivez Moi, handled by William J. Trainor at the William Penn Poodle Club, May 1957.

Ch. Hillandale C'est Vrai, handsome Standard of the 1950 period, owned by Dr. Donald Davidson and handled by Ben Burwell to Best in Show honors.

A white Standard that was a formidable contender in his day, Ch. Alfonco von der Goldenen Kette was owned by Clairedale and Pennyworth Kennels and handled by Robert S. Forsyth. Pictured here winning Best in Show at Ox Ridge Kennel Club, 1955, under Mrs. M. Hartley Dodge, Jr., Madison, New Jersey.

The glorious black Miniature bitch, Ch. Fontclair Festoon, owned by Clarence Dillon of Dunwalke Kennels, is handled here by Anne Rogers Clark to a Non-Sporting Group First, Bronx County Kennel Club, 1956. Festoon, an English import, had a fantastic show career which included a Westminster Kennel Club Best in Show, 1959.

Dunwalke concentrated on black Miniatures, and the kennel came to everyone's attention with considerable impact when the lovely imported bitch Champion Fontclair Festoon in 1959 became the second Miniature to win a Westminster Best in Show and the third Poodle within the 1950's to do so. But we'll talk about the Toy Poodle that completed the trio when we discuss Toys in their own separate chapter.

Festoon had an exciting career, throughout which she was handled by Anne Rogers Clark, who had the lead on all Dunwalke winners until after her retirement, when Richard Bauer took over the account. In addition to being a magnificent show bitch, Festoon gave a good accounting of herself as a producer, numbering among her progeny such well-known winners as Champion Dunwalke Garland, Champion Dunwalke Carnatian, Champion Dunwalke Sweetwilliam, and Champion Dunwalke Sweetbriar. Other Poodles who helped make this kennel recognized for quality were Tri-International Champion Montmartre Miranda, Champion Montmartre Marcella, and Braeval Baroness, to name just a few. The Dillons were good breeders, and as the years passed many a lovely champion came from there.

As for Ty-del, Marguerite Tyson had pretty well toured the world looking for good Poodles on which to found her kennel of white Miniatures and Toys, and she made some judicious purchases in England which proved valuable to her plans. It is interesting that the most famous of these—Champion Adastra

Magic Fame—although purchased in England, was a Blakeen-bred dog, having been sired by English Champion Blakeen Oscar of the Waldorf, who had been exported to England by Mrs. Hoyt earlier. In 1955, Ty-del Poodles won most Bests in Show of any kennel in America, these with Champion Blakeen Van Aseltine, Champion Adastra Magic Fame, Champion Estid Snow Storm, and the Toy Champion Blakeen Ding Ding. All four were rich in Blakeen breeding, to which Marguerite Tyson was always quick and eager to give credit. Howard Tyler and Maxine Beam handled these dogs to their successes. Mrs. Tyson was always very much involved and interested in her Poodles, loved dog shows, and was very popular with her fellow fanciers. While she was living in Washington, the dogs lived at Mrs. Winifred Heckmann's spacious and beautiful kennel in Maryland. Then when she moved to Nevada, she had some with her and the rest at Maxine Beam's in Texas. Mrs. Tyson became a breeder of note through her exquisite Toy Champion Ty-del's Dancing Doll, who made spectacular records, and through a number of Miniatures. It is a pity that she died suddenly of a heart attack when only in her fifties, as she was a delightful and charming person who would have remained a true asset to the Poodle Fancy had she lived. Among other honors won by her dogs, Champion Adastra Magic Fame won the Quaker Oats Award in 1957, and Champion Estid Ballet Dancer did so in 1961.

55

Pictured is Miss Maxine Beam holding two of the most famous Poodles of the 1950's. Beside her, the white Miniature, Eng., Am., Can. Ch. Adastra Magic Fame, winner of 53 Bests in Show, Quaker Oats Winner in 1957, the sire of 14 champions. The Toy Poodle, Am., Can. Ch. Ty-Del's Dancing Doll, winner of 10 Bests in Show, grand-dam of several champions. Owner is Mrs. Marguerite S. Tyson.

Ch. Valeway Temptation of Davdon, a Best in Show winner of the mid-1950's, owned by Dr. Donald Davidson and handled by Ben Burwell.

Above: The lovely white Miniature bitch, Ch. Estid Ballet Dancer, bred and owned by Colonel Ernest E. Ferguson, handled by Frank Sabella. This Poodle was a Top-Winning Miniature and a Westminster Group winner. **Above Right:** Ch. Davdon Miss Demeanor, a Best in Show Miniature Poodle bitch owned by Davdon Kennels, Dr. Donald Davidson, handled by Ben Burwell. **Right:** Winners Dog and Reserve at the Interstate Poodle Club, 1954. Puttencove Piper, the black, handled by William J. Trainor, and Loabalo Johnny, the white.

Gorgeous silver Miniature, Ch. Hollycourt La Vedette, photographed in August, 1957. Bred and owned by the Hollycourt Kennels of Miss M. Ruelle Kelchner; handled by Wendell J. Sammet.

Above Left: Ch. Wayne Valley Sir Galahad taking Best in Show at Staten Island in 1957. Jane Forsyth handling. **Center:** Interstate Poodle Club Specialty, 1956. Shown are Forzando Pandora of Gloria, Winners Bitch, left; Douai Carousel Angelique, Reserve, right. Anna Katherine Nicholas judging. **Below Left:** At the Poodle Club of America, 1956, Gaystream Skyrocket was Winners Dog, Wycliffe Coco was Reserve in the Standard Poodle judging under Miss M. Ruelle Kelchner.

Ch. Hollycourt Durandal, black Miniature male, in May 1958. Sired by Ch. Hollycourt Phillipe ex Ch. Hollycourt Dalriada; owned by Miss M. Ruelle Kelchner; handled by Wendell J. Sammet.

Ch. Icarus Duke Otto, stunning white Miniature dog owned by Mrs. Robert Tranchin and handled by Jane Kamp Forsyth, won Best in Show at Rockland County Kennel Club, September 1957.

Above Right: Ch. Douai Carousel Angelique, owned by Mrs. Carol Dewey, handled by Jane Kamp Forsyth, takes a Group First at the Queensboro Kennel Club, December 1956. **Center:** Elm City Kennel Club 1956, Robert S. Forsyth handles the Standard Poodle, Ch. Robinsbrook Noirot to a nice win. **Below Right:** Ch. Beaujeau Hot Chocolate winning Best in Show from Mr. Albert E. Van Court, Minneapolis Kennel Club, 1956. Mrs. Marjorie Tranchin, owner, Dallas, Texas.

Grayarlin Faro of Ricochet is handled by Jane Kamp Forsyth to a good win at the Cavalier Poodle Club Specialty Show, 1958.

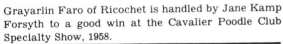

Ch. Miss Nicolette of Don Diablo with her handler, Jane Forsyth, in June 1957.

Ch. Hollycourt Brown Study, a winning Poodle from the 1950's, owned by Miss M. Ruelle Kelchner and handled by Wendell J. Sammet. By Ch. Hollycourt Bronze Knight from Hollycourt Gay of Idlelong.

It was toward the end of the 1950's that International Champion Summercourt Square Dancer of Fircot appeared here in the United States, brought from England by, I believe, Nigel Aubrey Jones. Square Dancer was sold to Mr. and Mrs. Lewis Garlick of Gaylen Kennels, was handled by Anne Rogers Clark to a brilliant career, and sired no less than 61 champions, which kept him at the top of the Producer lists for many years. Among his progeny of that period were the aforementioned Champion Estid Ballet Dancer and the sparkling little dog bred by Ted Young, Jr., Champion Tedwin's Top Billing, who was the Top Eastern Poodle for 1961, climaxing a good youthful career here. He then went to California, where he achieved still further success. He is the fantastic Poodle that returned to the Garden (Westminster) when

ten years old to win the breed as a veteran over all the youthful big-time stars that had been vying for it. Everyone agreed that the decision was entirely correct, and there was not a dry eye at Poodle ringside it was so thrilling! Top Billing was owned in California by Ernest E. Ferguson and later by Frank Sabella.

Another important milestone for Poodles was the beginning of *The Poodle Review,* which first appeared early in the 1950's and still continues to prosper and benefit the breed.

By now the Poodle had fallen into the category of being a "handler" breed, which was and continues to be quite true. For while in the early days our big winning Poodles had been largely owner-handled, gradually the tide had turned. As the coats became bigger, clipping and grooming became more of an art, and competition in-

This handsome little Toy Poodle of the 1950's is Ch. Wayne Valley Prince Regent winning the Group at Richmond, 1957. Jane Kamp Forsyth is handling; judge, Mrs. Warner (Teddy) Hays.

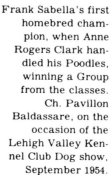

Frank Sabella's first homebred champion, when Anne Rogers Clark handled his Poodles, winning a Group from the classes. Ch. Pavillon Baldassare, on the occasion of the Lehigh Valley Kennel Club Dog show, September 1954.

Mr. and Mrs. William M. Schmick's lovely Standard, Ch. Caledonia Shocking Sandra, was a successful winner in the 1950's. Pictured here with Mr. Schmick in 1956.

creasingly keen, obviously the feeling was that professionals with more time to devote to the dogs could do them better justice. The old days were lamented, for they had certainly been a "glamor period" in the Poodle world, with fashionable ladies, always chic and well-groomed, enjoying the sport of competition. Who could forget Hayes Hoyt, always wearing gloves to match whatever dog she might be showing or her handsome outfits, always the last word and coordinated becomingly to the dogs as well as to herself? Or Ruelle Kelchner, Peggy Githens, and the others who obviously had put thought and good taste into being a credit to their well-turned-out dogs! It had been a lovely era, when dog shows were smaller, more leisurely, and there was always time for a picnic lunch, a pleasant visit, and even becoming acquainted with the dogs!

Quinnipiac Poodle Club, July 1956, Mrs. Olga Hone Rogers passes a judicial eye over the Standard Poodle, Ch. Bel Tor Prenez Moi, being handled by Bill Trainor for Mrs. George Fiig.

Ch. Estid Aristo, bred and owned by the late Colonel Ernest E. Ferguson, a famous Best in Show winner pictured winning the Great Lakes Poodle Club of Chicago Specialty, April 1960, followed by a Non-Sporting Group First that same weekend at Chicago International. Frank Sabella handling.

The great Ch. Tedwin's Top Billing early in his show career, handled by Anne Clark, July 1961.

Above Right: The immortal champion, Tedwin's Top Billing, bred by Ted Young, Jr., was owned during most of his show career by the late Colonel Ernest E. Ferguson who purchased him after judging him to be Best Puppy in Show at the Washington Poodle Club Specialty. He was handled to many ring successes by Anne Rogers, then by later-owner Frank Sabella. Billy's final appearance in the East was his spectacular Best of Variety win at the 1968 Westminster show over younger "stars" when he was 10 years old. **Center:** Belynda of Marcroft taking Winners Bitch at the Wilmington Kennel Club, 1972. Jane Kamp Forsyth handling.

Below Right: The black Miniature, Eng., Am. Ch. Tiopepi Typhoon, a Best in Show winner and the sire of champions in both countries, is owned by Mrs. William H. Ball.

Ch. Crikora Commotion, Mrs. J. Donald Duncan's well known black Miniature, with his handler, Jane Kamp Forsyth, June 1960.

The big winning and very lovely black Standard bitch, Ch. Dassin Naturally High, handled by Michael Hagen for owners, Susan and Robert Fisher.

Ch. Round Table's Loramar's Yeoman winning the Non-Sporting Group at Cincinnati, 1969. John Brennan handling; Mr. and Mrs. Alden V. Keene, owners.

The black Miniature dog, Ch. Crikora Commotion, a Westminster Group winner owned by Mrs. J. Donald Duncan, takes the Non-Sporting Group at the Brooklyn Kennel Club, 1959. Jane Kamp Forsyth handling.

Grand Rapids Kennel Club, May 1975, Luc Boileau handles Edward B. Jenner's white Standard, Ch. Viscara Vagabond King, to Best in Show.

Frank Sabella with Ch. Bel Tor Vintage Wine, Westminster 1962.

62

The well-known dark brown sire of the late 1950's, Ch. Barkhaven Bresette, owned by Ed Weber's Crisward Kennels and handled by Ben Burwell.

As for the "Poodle handlers" that were coming of age in the 1950's, they were fantastic—harder working than anyone who has never done it might realize, conscientious, and very talented. Anne Rogers and Frank Sabella were high on the "masters" list, knowing almost instinctively how to make the most of a dog. Jane Kamp Forsyth had many Poodles in her charge in those days, as did Bob Forsyth and Bill Trainor, too. Ben Burwell, was high on the list for popularity. Tom Crowe (president of Moss Bow Foley Dog Shows), Wendell Sammet, Richard Bauer, Bob Gorman, Howard Nygood, Larry Downey, Cecil Ray, John Brennan, Maxine Beam, Jan Jeffries, Chuck Hamilton, Russell Zimmerman, Henry Stoecker (probably one of the most knowledgeable "dog men" our Fancy has ever known), and so many more gained acclaim. Some of these folks are still handling. Henry Stoecker has become one of our most respected and popular all-breed judges; Annie, Frank, Chuck, and Maxine are all judging successfully.

Ben Burwell with the first Toy Poodle bitch he finished for Carruth Maguire of Carlima Poodles. She is Ch. Black Orchid of Wembley Downs. Photographed here in January 1959.

Others have gone "out of dogs," but all of them played an important role in the development of the show Poodle we know today, and the leaders set the pace for the handlers who would follow, many of whom started out back then as assistants to one or more of the above. We owe them credit and respect for the help they have given their clients, the encouragement, their patience, and their willingness to share their knowledge.

From this point forward, we will let our numerous kennel stories take over the history of the Poodle in the United States, as many of them begin around this period. But prior to doing that we must tell the story of the exciting transition that took place in the transformation from the Toy Poodle to the Poodle (Toy).

Perrevan Kennels' Ch. Perrevan Coupon photographed in 1959 with handler Wendell J. Sammet. By Ch. Hollycourt Platinum ex Ch. Silverette of Ledahof.

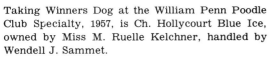

Taking Winners Dog at the William Penn Poodle Club Specialty, 1957, is Ch. Hollycourt Blue Ice, owned by Miss M. Ruelle Kelchner, handled by Wendell J. Sammet.

Ch. Bel Tor Prenez Moi, June 1957. Owned by Mrs. George Fiig, handled by William J. Trainor.

Ch. Chocolate Bit winning a Group for Mrs. Marjorie Tranchin at Longview Kennel Club, 1957.

At Chester Valley Kennel Club, 1965, Richard L. Bauer handles Dunwalke Kennels black Miniature dog, Ch. Dunwalke Sweetwilliam, to a Non-Sporting Group win. Dunwalke Kennels belong to Clarence Dillon, former U.S. Secretary of the Treasury. Sweetwilliam is a son of the Westminster Best in Show bitch, Ch. Fontclair Festoon.

Eng., Am., Can., Mex. Ch. Aspen Bonne Amie going Best in Show at the Beaumont Kennel Club, April 1966, under judge Mr. Vincent Perry, Maxine Beam handling for Mrs. Robert Tranchin.

Ch. Aizbel The Dauphin de Usherson, black Miniature dog, winning the Non-Sporting Group at the Harrisburg Kennel Club, March 1965. Dauphin is owned by Mrs. Elaine Usherson and Mrs. Luis E. Aizcorbe. Handler, Jane Kamp Forsyth.

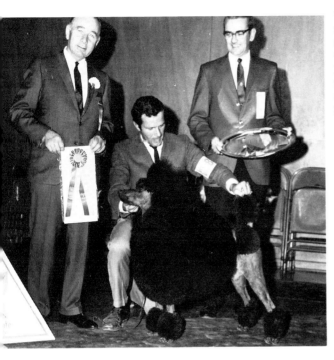

The lovely bitch Ch. De Russy Lollypop winning the Columbine State Poodle Club Specialty, 1967, under judge Henry Stoecker. This bitch was one of the great winning Poodles of the 1960's, widely admired, and the holder of a magnificent show ring record. Owned by Frank and Laura Dale, handled by Frank Sabella.

This is Ch. Icarus Duke Otto, owned by the Beaujeau Kennels of Mrs. Marjorie Tranchin, handled here by Jane K. Forsyth to Best in Show at Rockland County, 1957. Duke Otto was a tremendous favorite of the author for type and elegance.

Richard L. Bauer's first dog show as a professional handler, winning Best in Show with Dunwalke Kennels' Ch. Dunwalke Carnation at Twin Brooks Kennel Club, 1965.

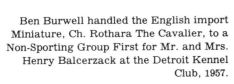

Ben Burwell handled the English import Miniature, Ch. Rothara The Cavalier, to a Non-Sporting Group First for Mr. and Mrs. Henry Balcerzack at the Detroit Kennel Club, 1957.

The head of an elegant Toy Poodle, Ch. Excalibur
Bristol Cream, is the subject of this photo. Owned by
Dave and June Suttie, Wheatridge, Colorado.

CHAPTER THREE

History and Development of the Toy Poodle

Wendell J. Sammet, professional handler and owner of the Carnival Toy Poodles, bred this excellent black Toy dog, Ch. Carlima's J.D., owned by Carruth Maguire. "J.D." was widely acclaimed by Poodle authorities for type and quality. Sired by Ch. Fieldstreams Valentine from Chrisward Tambourine. Photo by Ben Burwell.

As we have previously mentioned, Toy Poodles were in the United States back in the early days of the twentieth century. They were a separate breed of dog, not officially recognized as Poodles, with their own Stud Book and their own Standard of Perfection. Among their earliest breeders were Mr. and Mrs. Hartmann from Philadelphia, who bred and showed large numbers of these dogs prior to World War I and in the 1920's, and Mrs. Bertha Peaster, also of Philadelphia, whose activities as a breeder-exhibitor under the Peaster's and La Rex Doll banners covered a period from the teens into the 1940's with many winners to her credit.

When Toy Poodles were shown for the last time at Westminster in 1943, Leicester Harrison had Champion Leicester's Fidele de Lafferty (by Champion Beau Beau de Muriclar ex Lafferty's Dimples, bred by Minnie Lafferty) and Pruden's Juliette (by Champion Mitor de Muriclar ex Justine de Muriclar), Mrs. Frelinghuysen had La Petite Fille de Muriclar (bred also by Mrs. Charles Clark), Mrs. Austin had Rosbar's Princess Zenadie (bred by Mr. and Mrs. Carl Ross), and Count Alexis Pulaski had representatives of his very popular New York City kennel.

The year 1943 was one in which the American Kennel Club finally recognized these Toy Poodles as a variety of the Poodle breed, where they became Poodles (Toy). Thus the door was thrown open for interbreeding between Toys and Miniatures and the establishment of Toy

Poodles as we know them today, exquisite tiny replicas of the Standards and the Miniatures.

As with the larger Poodles, the antiquity of Toy Poodles has been proved by their appearance in many early works of art. We understand that the Kennel Club in England had its ladies' dining room adorned at one time with a painting entitled "The Dog Stealer," done by Ansell in 1860, depicting a tiny white Poodle being offered to an elegant Victorian lady by a rough-looking man, obviously urging her to give him money for the dog. We have also seen line drawings depicting types of Toy Poodles of the fifteenth and sixteenth centuries as painted by famous masters. General opinion is that the Toy Poodle existed in France and England over a long period of time, and that the original Toys we knew were descendants of the Truffle Poodle of which we have previously written.

Toy Poodles were white dogs here in the United States during the 1930's (the first that I recall personally), so a whole new area was opened for color breeding, as well as closer adherence to Poodle type, when it became legal to merge these little dogs with small, excellent Miniatures. Both here and in Great Britain the advancement and quality produced have been exciting to follow. Actually, I think the Americans undertook the more difficult task as our standard for the breed sets the height limit for Toys at ten inches, while in England 11 inches is acceptable, giving the breeders an extra inch of leeway. However, as we are well aware,

A Group winning Toy of 1950, this picture was unidentified, but if memory serves me correctly the little dog was Ch. Cartlane Once.

the English breeders produce many beautiful dogs that are within the ten-inch limitation. Just look at the records of some that have come from there to the United States!

One more look into the past before we start to contemplate the accomplishments that were to follow. Perhaps it was prophetic of the tremendous popularity they one day would enjoy here in the United States that the first Poodle Champion of Record recognized by the American Kennel Club was a Toy Poodle, Bajone II. The kennel that appears to have had most champions of any in Poodles prior to World War I was that of Mr. and Mrs. Hartmann, again with Toys, no less than 12 bearing their prefix appearing on the early list.

The beautiful brown Toy, Ch. Touchstone Chestnut, handled by Anne Rogers Clark, receives Best of Variety from Poodle breeder-judge William M. Schmick, 1961.

Some of the breeders I recall from the transition period were Gladys Herbel (de Gladville), Mrs. Winfield S. Pruden, Muriel Clark (Muriclar), Leicester Harrison (Leicester's), Mrs. Ross (Rosbars), Mrs. Austin (Catawba), and Mrs. Peaster, all of whom showed Poodles both before and after 1943. The little dog credited with having been the most influential of the pre-1943 period was born in 1932, Champion Happy Chappy, owned by Florence Orsie of California. His descendants are still to be found if one traces back sufficiently far in present pedigrees.

The 1944 Westminster celebrated the new status of Toy Poodles with a nice turnout in the breed, the numbers of which have been steadily

Ch. The Moth, foundation bitch at Lallan Kennels, takes Winners Bitch at the Interstate Poodle Club Specialty, September 1952. Bred and handled by Ben Burwell.

increasing ever since. Leicester Harrison again was in there, as were Bertha Peaster, Esme Davis Matz, Daisy Miller, Lucy Wedge, Count Pulaski, and Mrs. Austin with several, including her future Group winning Champion Powder Puff of Catawba, plus Pruden's Caprice of Catawba and Rosbar's Princess Zenadie.

Now that the light had turned green, everyone was eager to breed colors other than white and to bring type more in line with that demanded by the Poodle Standard. Hayes Hoyt, with her usual foresight, imported an under ten-inch black dog from Switzerland, Vichnou-Labory of Blakeen and Nibroc, that exerted a tremendous influence on the black Toy Poodle here. He was the result of well-planned breeding-down from established black continental Miniature and Standard lines, and through his son, Georgian Black Magic, he stamped his descendants with a remarkable degree of balance and elegance throughout the generations that have followed. Mrs. Hoyt found the Toys a delightful challenge and history points with pride to Champion Blakeen King Doodles, a tiny black dog owned by the Robert Levys, who in 1954, 1955, and 1956 won the Quaker Oats Award, was a Best in Show winner many times, and was the sire of Champion Lime Crest Topper, also a Best in Show winner. The tiny white Champion Blakeen Ding Ding was the first Toy Poo-

Toy Poodle bitch, Ch. Blakeen Ding Ding, born October, 1953, Top All-Breed Winner and Quaker Oats Winner in 1956. Dam of two champions, it is interesting to note that on the sire's side this lovely bitch is entirely Toy bred, while on the dam's side she is descended from Miniatures. Ding Ding was handled for Mrs. Marguerite Tyson, Ty-Del Kennels, by Maxine Beam.

dle to achieve a Top Ten rating in all-breeds category, and Number One at that, the year of becoming America's Top Show dog under Mrs. Tyson's ownership. There were other less spectacular but also highly successful Blakeen Toys, too, that did their bit for the progress of this variety along the way.

Leicester Harrison's name must be a byword wherever Toy Poodles are known, as her knowledge and efforts toward the creation of highest type and quality are recognized and respected world-wide. Champion Leicester's Fidele De Lafferty, through her immortal sons Champion Leicester's Bon Bon and Champion Leicester's Peaches and Cream, led to her claims

An important Toy winner of the early 1960's, Ch. Jonedith's Mary Christmas is handled here by William J. Trainor to a good win for owners Mr. and Mrs. Frank Smith.

An excellent Toy, Ch. Harmony's Easter Parade, here is winning the Toy Group at Long Island Kennel Club, May 1963. Jane Forsyth handling.

of a record unequalled in that more Best in Show all-breed awards had been won by Toy Poodles bred by Leicester or sired by her studs than any Toy Poodles in ring history at that time. The respect in which these studs were held speaks for itself, for back in 1956 way before our present degree of inflation, the stud fees of Champion Leicester's Kid Boots and Champion Leicester's Swan Song's Legacy were raised from $350.00 to $500.00. These dogs, and the two sons of Champion Leicester's Fidele De Lafferty, Champion Leicester's Bon Bon and Champion Leicester's Peaches and Cream, all did their part in type improvement and exquisite quality of our Toy Poodles here.

The Meisen Poodles of Hilda Meisenzahl played an exciting role in breeding Toys of

Joe Glaser owned this attractive Toy, Ch. Meisen Flaming Fella, with which Jane Kamp Forsyth is winning final points to the title at Elm City Kennel Club, February 1965.

magnificent colors. Established around 1940 in California, Meisen was famed for quality Poodles and established a line of marvelous apricot Miniatures among its accomplishments. In 1945 this discerning breeder heard of a black dog in England, Giovanni of Toytown, which she felt would make an ideal outcross for her white silver-bred Meisen Mer-I-Tot (sired by Champion Orsie's Kumsi, a white-bred Toy, from a silver Miniature dam). In due course Giovanni arrived and Meri-I-Tot was bred to him, producing Meisen Bright Knight, an oversize Toy. Champion Sherwood Petite Poupee, a small Miniature sister of one of the Sherwood Hall Toys, was in turn bred to Bright Knight, from which mating Little Sir Echo of Meisen was born in 1952.

Giovanni was from an apricot Toy bitch and thus succeeded in consistently throwing Poodles smaller than himself, making him popular as a stud dog with Toy-thinking breeders. The first pure apricot Meisen Toy was produced in 1953 from two black parents.

Champion Little Sir Echo of Meisen became this kennel's principal stud dog. Throughout the years, he became a Top Producer, siring both Toys and Miniatures, some apricot, some black, but in either case of excellent color. Little Sir Echo was never shown, but none could ever question his importance to establishing apricot Toys. His sons, Meisen Ecru Elf, sired the apricot Toy Meisen Kewpie Doll and in a repeat breeding (to Champion Meisen Paper Doll) sired Champion Meisen Bit O'Gold. Ms. Meisenzahl considered Champion Meisen Golden Gaiete the sire "without which there would be no

Meisen apricots," as he was equally successful siring both Miniatures and Toys of this color. Champion Meisen Frostie Flake, a white Best in Show winner, was another little Poodle from this kennel that gained fame.

Pamela A. B. Ingram's Sassafras Toy Poodles were numerous and very handsome. As of this past year, her Top Producing Sire, the silver Champion Silver Sparkle of Sassafras, had accounted for 84 champions, about double the number of the second most successful Toy Poodle sire, Champion Wilber White Swan. Champion Blackflight of Sassafras, Blackabit of Sassafras, and American and Canadian Champion Silver Fleece of Sassafras are others of her Toy Poodles on the Top Producer lists. Their aggregate number of champion progeny is, to say the least, imposing. Champion Silver Fleece of Sassafras was the Top Winning Toy Poodle Male for 1958. Champion Silver Sparkle of Sassafras was the Top West Coast Toy Poodle in 1959.

Random notes as some of the Poodles we admired then come back to mind. Mrs. Laurence Anthony Slesinger, a famous lady in the Boxer world, discovered Toy Poodles when she decided she would like to have a smaller-sized breed. Her Champion Leicester's Angelo became a Best in Show winner with a goodly number of Group wins to his credit.

One of the lovely Toys from Pamela Ingram's famed kennel, Ch. Gigi of Sassafras is shown here in July 1960. Owner, Mrs. P. Gordon, Miami, Florida.

Ch. Meisen Frostie Flake winning the Progressive Dog Club All Toy Show in 1964 under Mrs. Florence Gamburg. Handler, Jane Kamp Forsyth.

One of my favorite pictures of Ch. Wilber White Swan, Mrs. Bertha Smith's stunning Toy Poodle that contributed so enormously to his breed.

The first Toy dog ever to win Best in Show at Westminster Kennel Club in New York City. Ch. Wilber White Swan took a Group One en route to the finals in 1956, then proceeded to walk off with the Best in Show rosette. "Peanuts" belonged to Mrs. Bertha Smith and was handled by Anne Rogers.

Rosalind Layte of Burlingame Brussels Griffons decided that she too wanted to breed Toy Poodles, which she did, although not with success equal to that which she had attained in Griffons. Marie Medley had a nice "special" out in the early 1950's, Champion Medley's Silver Demon, from Blakeen Hubba Hubba. Mrs. R. Stuyvesant Pierpont of Peapacton Kennels had Champion Silver Dynamo de Gladville. Champion Sir Lancelot de Gladville (by Roi de Argent ex Barnes Little Girl Fluffball) belonged to Mrs. Loretta Geracci, was handled by Ben Burwell, and was bred by Gladys Herbel. Champion Sundance was an early winner bred by Ben Burwell.

Champion Smilestone's Fancy Fee was a black

Toy that I thought quite exceptional. Sired by Vichnou Labory of Blakeen from Champion Smilestone's Fancy Free, she epitomized beautiful Poodle type like a miniature painting. She and Champion Wilber White Swan were both of the same generation, in the early to mid-fifties, and watching the two of them in the ring together would invariably quicken one's pulse. Both were so excellent, yet actually quite different. Fancy Fee was Best Toy Poodle at Westminster in 1952, 1953, 1954, and 1955.

By the mid-1950's, Mrs. C. K. Corbin was sharing her enthusiasm for Poms with the Toy Poodles and had Nibroc Marla, a very nice little black bitch. Beaujeau was also into Toys, Mrs. Tranchin having Champion Highland Sand Star Baby. By early 1956, Champion Wilber White Swan had 15 Bests in Show, including Philadelphia 1955, and in this year he became the first Toy Dog of *any* breed to win a Westminster Best in Show. He was bred and

72

owned by Mrs. Bertha Smith. The European judge Mme. Charles Nizet de Leemans and her daughter Mrs. Elaine Nizet Klein had Toy Poodles.

In 1961, Mrs. Gladys Herbel had a page in the Westminster catalogue listing the Toy champions she had bred. The impressive record included Champion Sir Lancelot de Gladville, Champion Silver Dynamo de Gladville, Champion Princess de Gladville, Champion Dancer de Hayes Gladville, Champion White Cloud de Gladville, Champion Tip Topper de Gladville, Champion Joli Omar de Gladville, Champion Silver Jingle de Gladville, and Champion Page Garcon de Gladville. Need we add that she contributed a great deal to the breed? She was a California breeder, living in West Los Angeles, whose dogs were in demand from all parts of the Country.

Nellie MacAuley had an attractive, successful little dog in Champion MacAuley's White Cygnet (by Champion Wilber White Swan from

Ch. Nibroc Gary, an important Toy of the mid-1950s, handled here by Walter Morris for Mrs. P. H. B. Frelinghuysen.

This is the lovely Ch. Smilestone's Fancy Fee taking Best Toy at Plainfield Kennel Club, May 1954. There was tremendous rivalry between this little dog and Wilber White Swan back in the 1950's, both excellent dogs, each with its devoted fans. An exciting period in Toy Poodle history. Owned by Mrs. Peter Frelinghuysen and handled by Walter Morris.

Ch. Sir Lancelot De Gladville, a consistent winning Toy Poodle, handled by Ben Burwell to Best Toy at the Lorain County Kennel Club, August 1953. Owned by Loretta Geracci.

Champion Bermyth Snow Drop), who was handled by Jane Kamp Forsyth. Emiline Krucker had Champion Sherrode Baby Doll and Champion Sherrode Banker. An apricot Toy owned by Lynn Lund, Champion Lynn's Dry Martini, made her title in 11 days with four majors.

Calvinelle Toys were showing some very nice ones in the early 1960's, among them Champion Calvinelle Dancing Doll and Champion Calvinelle Tipsy Trifle, both by Champion Silhou-Jette's Cream Topping ex Lillie Liante of Trent. Ann and Tom Stevenson were showing Toys in those same days under their Challendon prefix.

Who could forget the adorable pair of Toys belonging to Mrs. George Fiig with which Bill Trainor won Best Toy Brace at Westminster in 1961? And that was the year, too, when Champion Cappoquin Little Sister took Best in Show at Westminster, exactly five years after White Swan had made the breakthrough in 1956. Both

were handled by Anne Hone Rogers, and both had been put up in the Toy Group by Anna Katherine Nicholas, which should prove that lightning most certainly can strike in the same place twice.

Little Sister belonged at this period to Florence Michelson, but you will read all about her in the Cappoquin kennel resume, as her story was unusual and exciting. She herself produced a Best in Show winner when bred, Champion Tropicstar Tequela.

In the Early 1960's, Mr. and Mrs. Frank Dean, Jr., had out a Toy Poodle, Champion Black Sambo of Whitehall.

Above Right: Ch. MacAuley's White Cygnet, a gorgeous little Toy Poodle photographed in 1960. By Ch. Wilber White Swan ex Ch. Bermyth Snow Drop. Nellie MacAuley, owner. **Below Right:** Ch. Arundel Brazin Little Raisin owned by Judith Feinberg and handled by Frank Sabella, a truly lovely Toy Poodle.

Ch. Cappoquin Sugar Bun, Winners Bitch at Westminster Kennel Club in 1966. Owner, Mrs. John P. Berridge, III, Seaford, Delaware.

Ch. Tropicstar Tequela winning the Great Lakes Poodle Club Specialty for Miss Florence Michelson. Richard L. Bauer handling this noted Toy in 1967.

Vernelle Hartman Kendrick winning at Tampa Bay, 1963, with the lovely Toy, Ch. Calvinelle Tipsy Trifle.

Ch. Cappoquin Little Sister shown winning Best in Show at Putnam Kennel Club, 1960. This black Toy bitch blazed a trail of glory throughout her career in the ring, climaxed by winning Best in Show at Westminster—one of only two Toy Poodles ever to have been so honored at the time of this writing. Owned by Miss Florence Michelson, handled by Anne Rogers Clark.

Quinnipiac Poodle Club 1959, judge William M. Schmick, who is now Vice-President of the American Kennel Club, here awards top honors to the incomparable Toy bitch, Ch. Cappoquin Little Sister. Owned by Florence Michelson and handled by Anne Hone Rogers, who is now Mrs. James Edward Clark. A few months later Little Sister set a record in Toy Poodle history by winning Best in Show at Westminster.

Noted professional handler (who later became a highly esteemed judge), the late Larry Downey won Best of Opposite Sex at Westminster, 1960, with Nellie MacAuley's white Toy dog, Ch. MacAuley's White Cygnet.

More history in the making. Anne Rogers has just won the Toy Group en route to Best in Show at Westminster, 1961, with Miss Florence Michelson's famed black Toy Poodle bitch, Ch. Cappoquin Little Sister. This was the second occasion upon which a Toy Poodle took top honors at the Garden.

Pictured here as a puppy is Ch. Regence Sierra, bred and owned by V. Jean Craft and Margaret M. Klotz, handled by Wendell J. Sammet.

The brown Toy male, Ch. Cotian Foot Loose and Fancy Free, takes Best of Winners, still in puppy clip, at Somerset Hills, 1978, under judge Keke Blumberg; handled by Wendell Sammet.

Ch. Peeple's Sahara, one of the truly great Toy Poodles in history, wins the Non-Sporting Group at Westminster, 1974. Judge, Henry Stoecker. Handler, Richard Bauer. Owner, Robert Koeppel.

Ch. Peeple's Sahara on the occasion of her retirement from the show ring, winds up her career with still another Best in Show. Richard Bauer handling for Robert Koeppel at Longshore-Southport Kennel Club, 1976.

Ch. Peeple's Red Head winning the Toy Group at Chicago International. This consistent little Poodle was owned by Joyce Peeples. Vernelle Hartman handling.

The Toy Poodle, Ch. Calvinelle Dancing Democrat, with Vernelle Hartman Kendrick at the Washington Poodle Club Specialty, 1963.

Ch. Regence's Ricochet, the lovely white Toy bred and owned by V. Jean Craft and Margaret M. Klotz. Handled by Wendell J. Sammet.

Winning the Toy Group at Providence County Kennel Club, 1980, is Ch. Hell's A Blazen Fagin's Pride. Richard L. Bauer handling for owner, Mrs. A. C. Pearson.

Ch. Yerbrier Done To Perfection taking Best of Variety at the Creole Poodle Club Specialty, on her way to Group 1, then Best in Show. Handled by F. C. Dickey for owner, Betty Yerington.

The fabulous Toy Poodle, Ch. Peeple's Sahara, taking one of her many Bests of Breed, this time at the Poodle Club of America Specialty, 1976. Richard Bauer is handling for Robert A. Koeppel.

Judge Lydia Hopkins, of Sherwood Hall Poodles, awards a Group One to Ch. Da-Ron-Da's Dark Delight, a lovely Toy well-presented by Ben Burwell.

The Robert Levys of Miami, Florida, really made history with their Toy Poodles, and the nice thing about it is that Bob Levy did the handling almost entirely on his own. A retired retailer, he enjoyed the hobby of the Poodles to the utmost and was a loss to the breed when he passed away of a heart attack. When his little brown Toy Champion Loromar's I'm a Dandy broke the record by becoming the Top Toy Poodle in history (he won the Quaker Oats Award in 1954, 1955, and 1956), the record that he broke was that of his kennel-mate, Champion Blakeen King Doodles, who had held it previously. Another Best in Show winner belonging to the

One of Betty Mahaffy's gorgeous Toy Poodles, homebred Ch. Ashwood's Bit O Trouble, by Ch. Tar's Rebel ex Ch. Ashwood's Bit O Bounce. Wendell Sammet handling.

Levys was Doodles' son, Champion Lime Crest Topper. These dogs made a rousing impact on the breed as you can plainly see.

Ed Jenner had a Best in Show winning Toy "way back when," Champion Kenwood Forest Vodka. Champion Jonedith's Mary Christmas also was a Best in Show winner, owned by Mr. and Mrs. Frank Smith.

A stunning little dog, Champion Tar Baby of Whitehall, by Renrew's Fandango, made a big record on both coasts, first in California with Frank Sabella and then, after coming east to

Ch. St. Anthony's Coco winning the Group at Bronx County, 1964. Handler, Jane Kamp Forsyth. Owned by Mrs. Chris Anthony, Los Angeles, California.

Mrs. Gerald Livingston, with Pat Norwood handling him. He was a Ken-L-Ration Award winner in 1962.

I was a tremendous admirer of the Toy Poodles produced by Audrey Watts Kelch, Champion Fieldstreams Bojangles and Champion Fieldstreams Valentine. To me, they were type and quality every inch of the way. Both were consistent Group winners. Both were exquisite.

Then there was that smashing little dog, Champion Carlima's J.D., that Wendell Sammet bred and that went to Carruth Maguire. Many of us considered him to be the best of all the Toy Poodles we had seen. Interestingly, Champion Carlima's J.D. was sired by Champion Fieldstreams Valentine, who had in turn been sired by Champion Fieldstreams Bojangles. J.D. won Best of Variety at the Poodle Club of

The stunning black Toy, Ch. Fieldstreams Bojangles, winning the Toy Group at Westchester Kennel Club, 1957. Ben Burwell handling for owner, Mrs. Audrey Watts Kelch.

Ben Burwell handling Ch. Fieldstreams Valentine to Best American-bred in Show at Elm City Kennel Club, 1959. This beautifully typey little dog accounted for a long list of important wins under Mr. Burwell's charge for owner Audrey Watts Kelch.

Black Toy male, Ch. Wappo Weatherman, taking a Best in Show under Pat Norwood's handling for Mrs. Gerald M. Livingston. This very enthusiastic fancier also owned another lovely Best in Show Toy, Ch. Tar Baby of Whitehall, along with a Best in Show Pekingese, the Best in Show Miniature Pinscher Ch. Rebel Roc's Fiesta, and some excellent Pugs and sporting dogs.

A famous multi-Group and Best in Show winning Toy of the 1950's. Ch. Fieldstreams Bojangles is handled here by Ben Burwell for owner, Audrey Watts Kelch.

A historic occasion indeed, back in 1961, at the Spartanburg Kennel Club Dog Show, when this little Poodle became the first *Toy* Poodle *puppy* to win a Group. Ch. Wappo Weatherman, owned by Mrs. Gerald Livingston, grew up to become a Best in Show winner under the expert handling of Patrick F. Norwood.

America Specialty in 1963 and 1964 and took Group 2 at Westminster in 1964. These great Poodles trace back to Champion Happy Chappy, whose influence on the breed was mentioned earlier from the 1930's, on both sides of their family. Valentine's dam was the imported Champion Chaman Grouse.

To digress for a moment, we have mentioned the very influential black Toy stud that Mrs. Hoyt brought over in the beginning of Poodle (Toy) development. Champion Cappoquin Little Sister traces directly back to him through her sire, a son of Champion Georgian Black Magic, and it is also noteworthy that these dogs behind Little Sister can be traced right back into the Chieveley line, which started out so many decades ago back in England.

Ch. Laromar's I'm A Dandy, brown Toy multiple Best in Show winner, was owned by Mr. and Mrs. Robert Levy and handled by Bob Levy to many thrilling victories. Here it takes Best in Show at Riverhead Kennel Club, 1967.

Mrs. Audrey Watts Kelch, of Fieldstreams fame, with Chaman Grouse, Best of Winners Toy Poodle at the Interstate Kennel Association, 1956.

Martha Jane Ablett bred some excellent Toys under the Silhou-Jette identification, among them Champion Silhou-Jette's Snow Sprite and Mr. and Mrs. Stevenson's dog (Challendon Kennels) Champion Silhou-Jette's Cream Topping. Mrs. George Dow contributed inestimably through her silvers. Champion Merrymorn Lita was campaigned for Mrs. Erlanger by Anne Rogers Clark.

We know that there are many other dogs and owners who played their part in bringing Toy Poodles to the greatness they achieved here. We have tried, through our kennel stories and the historical chapters, to include them all and regret that in every case it has not been possible to obtain the needed facts from the owners of the dogs. Memory is not always reliable, but at least I've been able to tell you about the special ones that played so important a part.

Ch. Tar Baby of Whitehall pictured winning the Variety at Westminster under Percy Roberts. Owned by Mr. and Mrs. Howard Williams, Stockton, California, during most of his show career; later by Mrs. Gerald M. Livingston, Quitman, Georgia. Frank Sabella, handling.

Pat Norwood handling Mrs. Gerald M. Livingston's many times Best in Show winning Toy Poodle, Ch. Tar Baby of Whitehall, to first in Toy Group at Old Dominion Kennel Club, 1962. Tar Baby was the Quaker Oats Award winner for the Southern Area that same year.

Am., Can. Ch. Syntifny On The Move, a Best in Show son of Ch. Syntifny Piece Of The Rock that is himself producing Best in Show progeny with seven champions thus far. Jane A. Winne, owner. Todd Patterson, handler.

Westminster, 1964, Wendell J. Sammet bred and is handling Martha Jane Ablett's 8½-inch brown Toy bitch, Ch. Carnival Berry Bounce.

Ch. Bel Tor's Sugar Lump was one of the Toys carrying the Bel Tor banner for Mrs. J. A. Mason, 1961.

The black Toy bitch, Ch. Montmartre Minouche, is from the Beaujeau Kennels of Mrs. Marjorie A. Tranchin. Photo by Tauskey, 1968.

The Toy, Aust. Ch. Troymere Sensation, bred and owned by Troy Tanner of Sidney, Australia.

The black Toy, Ch. Fieldstreams Valentine, is awarded Best of Breed at the Washington Poodle Club, 1958. Audrey Watts Kelch, owner. Ben Burwell, handler.

Ch. Peeple's Red Head wins Best of Variety at the Great Lakes Poodle Club Specialty, 1970.

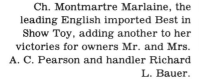

An important Toy, Ch. Cutler's Pop Art, winning a Toy Group award, 1969. Pop Art, a handsome black dog, had specialty shows and many Group Firsts to his credit. Owner, Nancy Cutler.

Pictured is the magnificent white Toy Ch. Syntifny's Piece of The Rock, Top Producer (still living) with 40 champion offspring. Owned by Jane A. Winne, Syntifny.

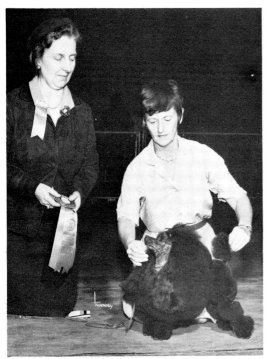

Eng. and Am. Ch. Montmartre Minouche, owned by Mrs. Marjorie Tranchin, handled by Maxine Beam.

Ch. Montmartre Marlaine, the leading English imported Best in Show Toy, adding another to her victories for owners Mr. and Mrs. A. C. Pearson and handler Richard L. Bauer.

Ch. Alekai Oli of Stonebridge, bred by Stonebridge Poodles, owned by Mrs. Henry J. Kaiser, Alekai Poodles. Handled by Wendell J. Sammet.

CHAPTER FOUR

Important Kennels of the Present Day

Ch. Roadcoach Rocket, a Miniature bred and owned by Roadcoach Kennels, handled by Wendell J. Sammet. By Ch. Frenches Vendas Chip of Silver ex Tarquil Zest. Photographed in 1957.

Aizbel

The Aizbel Miniature Poodles, owned by Mr. and Mrs. Luis Aizcorbe, Jr., and located in Miami, Florida, have a proud record of accomplishment in this breed. There has been no period during Luis Aizcorbe's lifetime, since his pre-teen years in Cuba, that at least one Miniature Poodle has not shared his home, including some which he imported to Cuba from the most renowned kennels. In the beginning this hobby was a joint one between Luis and his mother, but a couple of years after the move from Cuba to Miami the senior Mrs. Aizcorbe started becoming less involved with the dogs. By then, however, Mary Jo Aizcorbe, whom Luis had married in 1960, had become quite thoroughly "hooked" on Poodles, too, sharing her husband's enthusiasm every inch of the way. Since then both Luis and Mary Jo Aizcorbe have been equally involved with their dogs.

The beginning of the Aizbel Miniatures, as they are known today, traces back directly to the purchase of Tri-International Champion Chriscrest Jubilee during 1956. Jubilee was not Aizbel's first champion Poodle, but she was the one that provided their breeding program with the sense of direction from which it never has deviated. To Jubilee and her breeder, the late Mrs. Christobel Wakefield, the Aizcorbes give much of the credit for what they have accomplished with their Poodles, since Jubilee provided so solid a foundation upon which the Aizbel breeding program has been built. All Aizbel champions, with no exceptions, are Jubilee's descendants.

While under the Aizcorbes' ownership, Jubilee added Cuban and Mexican Championships to her American title. Specialed at only four shows in the U.S.A. and handled on these occasions by Mr. Aizcorbe's Mother during the late 1950's, Jubilee won two Group Firsts and a Best in Show; the latter was at the Tampa Bay Kennel Club, which made her a Best in Show winner in all three of the countries where she had been in competition. Of still greater significance, however, was her ability to transmit many of the best traits for which the Chriscrest line was recognized as being outstanding. Jubilee produced six champions, including the Group Winning Champion Aizbel Imperial Imp and Champion Aizbel Collector's Item, from a breeding to a Top Ten Producing Best in Show winning nephew, Champion Chriscrest The Fiddler.

Champion Aizbel Collector's Item, a small deep-colored brown, was from the first litter the Aizcorbes bred in the U.S.A. after coming here from Cuba in 1959. A story about this litter is amusing and points out again the fact that one cannot always be certain at too early an age how puppies will mature. From the beginning it was generally conceded that the black puppy which grew up to become Champion Aizbel Imperial Imp would mature into an exceptional dog, and much admiration was expressed for a gorgeously headed brown chosen as "pick of litter" by almost everyone who saw the puppies. The other brown puppy in the litter, called Hector, was Luis Aizcorbes' favorite right from the first, but his admiration for it went almost totally un-

Ch. Aizbel Collector's Item, brown Miniature, has won seven all-breed Bests in Show, a specialty, and 30 Group Firsts. The sire of five champions, including two Best in Show winners, he belongs to Mr. and Mrs. Luis Aizcorbe, Jr., Miami, Florida.

supported, despite the fact that Hector was short backed, moved excellently, and had that cocky selfconfident demeanor one needs in a successful show dog. It had, however, been agreed that only two puppies from the litter would be kept, the black and just one of the browns, and with so much expressed enthusiasm over the *other* brown plus Mrs. Aizcorbe's anxiety to cut down the number (she was taking care of them at that time while Luis and Mary Jo right after their marriage were living in an apartment), it was settled that Hector would be the one going to a pet home. Twice within the month he was given away, somehow managing on both occasions to get himself returned to his breeders. The second time the litter was close to show age, so Luis' mother agreed that the three would stay until after the Florida Circuit where they all would be entered. At Palm Beach, Hector defeated both of his brothers and came away with two points for Winners Dog. At Miami he again placed above both brothers and this time wound up Reserve in a five-point entry. Needless to say, after that future Champion Aizbel Collector's Item was home to stay!

Collector's Item truly justified Luis Aizcorbe's early confidence in his quality. To this day he remains the leading winning dog from his bloodlines, with a total of seven Bests in Show, a Specialty, and 30 times coming away with the Non-Sporting Group blue ribbon. Additionally, in limited use at stud he became a Top Producer with five champions and several other producers of champions among his offspring. Two of his progeny, Champion Aizbel The Dauphin De Usher and Champion Aizbel The One and Only, were multiple Best in Show winners.

One and Only amassed a record of three Bests in Show, three Specialty Bests of Breed, and 20 times took the blue ribbon in the Non-Sporting Group. Later he became a sire of tremendous importance, with 30 champions to his credit, including at least seven Top Producers. His name denoted the fact that he was the only male puppy in a litter of four by Champion Collector's Item from Chriscrest No Trumps.

Two homebreds by Champion Aizbel The One and Only have done more than their share in keeping the Aizbel banner flying high. The multiple Group and specialty Best of Breed winner Champion Aizbel Headstudy In Black is the sire of twelve champions to date, and his sister, the specialty Best of Breed winner Champion Aizbel All About Angels, is the dam of six champions. They collaborated in producing three champions of their own: Champion Aizbel The Knockout, a multiple all-breed and specialty Best in Show winner, Best of Variety at the 1975 Westminster Dog Show; Champion Aizbel On Record, winner of several Non-Sporting Groups and specialty shows for his owner, Marjorie Gans; and Champion Aizbel Slick Chick.

Three of the champions from All About Angels have already become Top Producers, while a fourth, Champion Aizbel On Record, is close to becoming one. Champion Aizbel The Knockout is the sire of 12 champions, with several others approaching their titles as we write this. Champion Aizbel The Imperialist, another from All About Angels, went to Barbara Ireland's Danleri Kennels, where he has sired a dozen champions, including Best in Show and specialty winners. His litter sister, Champion Aizbel Impetuous, a Group winner for her owner, Arlene McKernan, is the Top Producing

Ch. Aizbel The Knockout, a multiple all-breed and specialty Best in Show dog was Best of Variety at Westminster, 1975. Owned by Mr. and Mrs. Luis Aizcorbe, Jr.

Dam of four champions, these including Champion Aizbel The Aristocrat, when bred back to her grandsire, Champion Aizbel The One and Only.

Champion Aizbel The Aristocrat has already reached a record of two all-breed Bests in Show and four Specialty show wins, including the 1978 Poodle Club of America National, plus 20 times Best Non-Sporting Dog. Additionally, he is following in his sire's footsteps as a producer, with a rapidly mounting present count of 22 champions to his credit.

It is interesting to note that of the six different Miniature Poodles to win the variety at the last six Poodle Club of America Specialties, five of them were black. Four of these either have been or were sired by Aizbel dogs. The other black Miniature to win was a granddaughter of Champion Aizbel The Knockout.

By and large, the Aizcorbes' dogs have been owner-handled on the majority of their ring appearances, not only in the classes but to the big wins as well. The fact that all of their all-breed and Specialty Best in Show winners have attained their status owner-handled has been a source of satisfaction and pleasure to these fanciers, adding a special dimension to the enjoyment of each win.

Throughout the years, Mary Jo and Luis Aizcorbe have wisely believed in the importance of not overburdening themselves beyond their capabilities. Accordingly, they have limited themselves to concentrating on black and brown Miniatures which are compatible for breeding. Obviously there is a specific type which they are endeavoring to produce, and they are succeeding admirably. It is not always easy to breed for everything one prefers while remaining within a

Ch. Aizbel The Knockout has been owner-handled to an all-breed Best in Show, two specialties, 10 Group Firsts, and a Best of Variety at Westminster, 1975. Sire of 15 champions.

reasonable framework of genetic purity, which adds to the challenge. The Aizcorbes are strong believers in line-breeding as the way in which to develop and retain consistency of type. But this breeding method, they caution, should be approached with care, responsibility, and the knowledge of the dogs and bloodlines involved. It is also felt by these highly successful breeders that the total picture – the dog as a whole – should never be forsaken in the quest for a particular trait.

The Aizcorbes note that they feel certain that without several strokes of plain *good luck*, such as that which brought Jubilee to them, the Aizbel Poodles probably would not exist today. This author would not be one to underestimate the importance of *luck*, but somehow I feel that the Aizcorbes, with their true determination and dedication to this breed, would have made it even had doing so been more difficult!

This lovely Miniature bitch, the dam of six champions, is Ch. Aizbel All About Angels. A specialty Best in Show winner, she belongs to the Luis Aizcorbes, Miami, Florida.

Ch. Aizbel Headstudy in Black, sire of 13 champions, has won three specialty shows and five Group Firsts, all owner-handled.

Ch. Aldeblou Encore is pictured with handler, Wendell J. Sammet, going Best of Winners at the Durham Kennel Club under Dr. Edward McGough while still a puppy. By Ch. Alekai Argus from Ch. Alekai Aphrodite, this homebred belongs to Mr. and Mrs. Terrence Levy.

Ch. Aldeblou's Carbon Copy, black Standard male, son of Ch. Suffolk Casanova of Joval ex Ch. Alekai Flowers of Mayfair, bred and owned by Mr. and Mrs. Terrence Levy, Huntington, New York. Wendell J. Sammet, handler.

Aldeblou

The Aldeblou Kennels, belonging to Mr. and Mrs. Terrence Levy of Huntington, New York, although relatively new to the Poodle world, has certainly performed with great distinction. As foundation for this venture, handler Wendell Sammet put the Levys off to a splendid start by the selection as their initial purchase of the promising white Standard bitch future Champion Alekai Flowers of Mayfair. Flowers proved herself in the show ring and in the whelping box, as had been hoped would be the case, proving an invaluable asset to her new owners.

Starting her show career with a flourish, she won a specialty show and an all-breed Best in Show from the Open Class her first weekend in the ring. Once retired after an exciting career, she was bred to Champion Alekai Rumble of Stonebridge, a Champion Alekai Luau son. From this litter came the first of the Levys' homebred Best in Show Poodles, Champion Aldeblou Morganna. In a second litter, bred to Champion Puttencove Presentation, she came through with the Group winning black bitch Champion Aldeblou Carbon Copy and the white bitch Champion Aldeblou Mirabai.

In 1976 the Levys purchased the exquisite white bitch Champion Alekai Aphrodite (Champion Alekai Zeus ex Champion Alekai Coconut of Stonebridge). Her show career stands at four all-breed Bests in Show, eight specialty Bests in Show, and 30 times First in the Non-Sporting Group. These wins included such "goodies" as Best in Show at the William Penn Specialty from the Puppy Class and Best of Variety at the Poodle Club of America, both in 1977.

Upon Aphrodite's retirement, it was decided to breed her to Champion Alekai Argus, also owned and campaigned by the Levys. To date one puppy from this litter has finished from the Puppy Class, the white dog Champion Aldeblou Encore.

Champion Alekai Argus is a son of Champion Alekai Ouzo from Alekai Celena. Still being campaigned as this is written, his record currently includes two all-breed Bests in Show and 12 Group Firsts. He has two finished offspring with several others pointed.

Aldeblou Kennels is also the proud owner of Champion Puttencove Presentation, an excellent dog with six champions to his credit. He is a son of Champion Alekai Luau from Puttencove Primrose.

Best in Show for Ch. Aldeblou's Morgana, handled by Wendell J. Sammet; the occasion, Chagrin Valley Kennel Club, 1973. Owned and bred by Mr. and Mrs. Terrence Levy, by Ch. Alekai Rumble of Stonebridge ex Ch. Alekai Flowers of Mayfair.

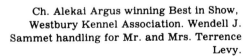

Somerset Hills Kennel Club, 1978, was the scene of a four-point major for future Ch. Aldeblou's Mirabai. Mr. and Mrs. Terrence Levy, breeder-owners; Wendell Sammet, handler. Mirabai is by Ch. Puttencove Presentation from Ch. Alekai Flowers of Mayfair.

Ch. Alekai Argus winning Best in Show, Westbury Kennel Association. Wendell J. Sammet handling for Mr. and Mrs. Terrence Levy.

At home in Hawaii, Mrs. Henry J. Kaiser was snapped informally with one of her gorgeous Alekai Standards.

Alekai

Alekai Kennels originated in the Hawaiian Islands on the estate of Mrs. Henry J. Kaiser (Alyce Kaiser). "Alekai" is a combination of Mrs. Kaiser's first and last names and has become synonymous with quality white Standard Poodles in all parts of the world. It is believed to be the oldest white Standard Poodle kennel consistently breeding and exhibiting in the United States today. Alekai has produced a total of 56 champions, among them 19 All-Breed Best in Show winners, which include 12 bitches and seven males.

The foundation stock for Alekai's breeding program was provided by four white bitches, Champion Ivardon Winter, Champion Davdon Suma Cum Laude, Champion Davdon Captivation, and Champion Tambarine de la Fontaine. Tambarine and Captivation completed their titles under the Alekai banner. These bitches were from the leading producing white males available, namely Champion Hillendale C'est Vrais, Champion Blakeen Bali Hai, Champion Ensarr Glace, and Champion Puttencove Promise. These dogs in turn all trace back to the influential sire, Tri-International Champion Nunsoe Duc de la Terrace of Blakeen, owned and campaigned by Mrs. Sherman R. Hoyt.

The first of these foundation bitches, Champion Davdon Suma Cum Laude, was bred to

Champion Puttencove Promise and produced a litter of five champions. Champion Alekai Kona and Champion Alekai Pikake were the first homebreds to be exhibited in the continental United States. At their first show, the Poodle Club of America 1961 Specialty, they were awarded Reserve Winners Dog and Reserve Winners Bitch. The following year at Poodle Club of America 1962, under judge Mrs. Sherman R. Hoyt of Blakeen fame, Champion Alekai Pikake was Best of Variety and Best of Opposite Sex to Best of Breed. Her litter brother, future champion Alekai Mai Kai, was Best of Winners and Best of Opposite Sex to Best of Variety. Both Pikake and her sister, Champion Alekai Hololaka, went on to become Best in Show winners. The remaining male in this litter was the top producer Champion Alekai Nohea. He became a Group and Specialty winner and produced a total of 12 champion get.

Another of the foundation bitches, Champion Ivardon Winter, was bred to Nohea and produced the top winning Standard Poodle of 1964, Champion Alekai Pokoi. This bitch's show record was outstanding. Her first time shown as a "special," Pokoi captured Best in Show, all-breeds. Her career totaled 16 all-breed Bests in Show, six Specialty Bests in Show, Best of Variety Poodle Club of America 1964, and 48 Group firsts.

Pokoi whelped a total of 16 puppies, ten of which became American champions. Her most famous get, sired by Champion Alekai Ahi, were the brothers Champion Alekai Luau, who

One of Mrs. Henry J. Kaiser's great producing bitches, Ch. Davdon Suma Cum Laude, bred by Dr. Donald Davidson.

went on to become a Best in Show winner and Top Producer, and Champion Alekai Bali, Best Puppy in Show at Poodle Club of America 1967 and a Group winner from the puppy classes. Bali finished at under one year of age.

At this time, Mr. Henry Kaiser became ill and it became necessary for Mrs. Kaiser to devote most of her time to her husband. The kennel in Hawaii was vacated and many of the dogs given away or sold. Alekai maintained a few dogs for future breeding, but on a far smaller scale. These remaining dogs were sent to Massachusetts, where they were kenneled by Alekai's agent and handler, Wendell J. Sammet, and where Alekai remains to this day.

In order that the Alekai line should not suffer from Mrs. Kaiser's temporary curtailment of activities, it was decided that certain friends of Alekai Poodles should continue the breeding program under the advisement of Wendell Sammet. Thanks to the cooperation of Ann Seranne and Barbara Wolferman (of Mayfair Yorkshire Terrier fame), Dorothy Baranowsky (of Stonebridge), and Mr. and Mrs. Terrence Levy (of Aldeblou), the line continued to contribute top winning and producing dogs.

Finished under the Alekai banner, Champion Alekai Luau was acquired by Mayfair Kennels. Luau's show record was phenomenal, totaling 17 Bests in Show, all-breed, eight Specialty Bests in Show (including Best of Breed at Poodle Club of America 1969), and top spot in the Non-Sporting Group 61 times. Luau was also a Top Producer with 14 champion progeny.

Ch. Alekai Mai Kai, breeder-owner Alekai Poodles, went Best of Winners and Best of Opposite Sex to Best of Variety, Poodle Club of America, 1962. Wendell Sammet, handler.

Ch. Alekai Nohea, bred and owned by Alekai; handled by Wendell J. Sammet.

Ch. Alekai Kona, another from the litter by Ch. Puttencove Promise ex Ch. Davdon Suma Cum Laude, bred and owned by Mrs. Henry J. Kaiser. Handled by Wendell J. Sammet.

Ch. Ivardon Winter, whelped November, 1956, by Ch. Puttencove Banner ex Cartlane Collectrice. Owned by Mrs. Henry J. Kaiser; bred by William H. Ivans.

Ch. Alekai Pokoi taking Best of Variety at the Poodle Club of America Specialty, 1964, judged by James Walker Trullinger. Wendell J. Sammet handling for breeder-owner, Mrs. Henry J. Kaiser.

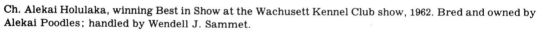

Ch. Alekai Holulaka, winning Best in Show at the Wachusett Kennel Club show, 1962. Bred and owned by Alekai Poodles; handled by Wendell J. Sammet.

Ch. Ivardon Winter, by Ch. Puttencove Banner, was bred by William H. Ivans and owned by Mrs. Henry J. Kaiser. Mr. Robert Zaco is handling here.

Ch. Alekai Bali taking a Group First at Greenwich Kennel Club, 1967, under judge Bob Waters, to finish his championship. Littermate to Ch. Alekai Luau. Handler, Wendell J. Sammet.

Ben Burwell's handsome portrait of the white Standard specialty winner, Ch. Alekai Pokoi, owned by Mrs. Henry J. Kaiser.

Another influential line in the Alekai breeding program comes from those descendants of the foundation bitch Champion Davdon Captivation. She was bred to the homebred Champion Alekai Kila, a Promise grandson and himself the producer of eight champions. This mating resulted in three outstanding champions: litter brothers Champion Alekai Marlin (a Group winner) and Champion Alekai Ahi, and the extraordinary bitch Champion Alekai Marlaine.

Champion Alekai Ahi was Best of Winners at Poodle Club of America 1965. Ahi proved himself a dominant sire, producing 20 champion progeny. His influence as a stud cannot be minimized, as the impact of his children and grandchildren, many of them Best in Show winners and Top Producers themselves, is still being widely felt today.

As for the dynamic Champion Alekai Marlaine, no one who ever saw her could

Ch. Davdon Captivation, photographed in June, 1960. By Ch. Hillandale C'est Vrai ex Ch. Davdon Miss Demeanor. Bred by Dr. Donald Davidson.

possibly refer to white Standards without immediately thinking of her. Marlaine was the epitome of style and elegance, and her presence electrified the ring from the moment she stepped inside it. Marlaine crowned her spectacular record by winning the Non-Sporting Group at Westminster in 1967.

Marlaine was bred only once at five years of age. Bred to Luau, she produced two beautiful bitches, Champion Alekai Maui and Champion Alekai Hula. Maui started off with a Best of Winners at Poodle Club of America 1970 and finished two shows later on the following weekend with a total of three five-point "majors." Champion Alekai Hula was purchased by Mr. and Mrs. James Lester, Longleat Poodles. Hula was outcrossed to a black, Champion Prince Philip of Belle Glen, and produced the black bitch Champion Longleat Hulagan.

Ch. Alekai Kila. By Ivardon Kenilworth of Ensarr from Ch. Puttencove Kaui. Handled by Wendell J. Sammet.

Handled by Wendell Sammet, Hulagan became the Top Standard Poodle in 1974. She also was Best of Variety Westminster 1974, going on to third in the Non-Sporting Group. Her career totaled four All-Breed Bests in Show, four Specialty Shows, and 17 Groups. She is the dam of three champions.

The Prince Philip—Hula breeding was repeated, and from this second litter Alekai purchased the white bitch Longleat White Witch, who was bred to Champion Alekai Luau and produced a male, Champion Alekai Zeus (owned by Mrs. Bernet and handled by Paul Edwards) and a bitch, Champion Alekai Zoe. In her turn Zoe produced a total of five champions, including Champion Alekai Tyrannua (by Longleat Tar and Feathers, black litter brother to Hulagan), who finished as a puppy with Specialty points and was sold to Brazil, where he became a Best in Show winner. Another Best in Show winner, Champion Alekai Ouzo (by Oli), is himself a Best in Show producer.

Zoe also was bred to Champion Puttencove Presentation (Luau from an Ahi daughter), which resulted in the ice-white bitch Champion Alekai Brilliance, sold to Anna Le Blanc who at that time worked for Wendell Sammet. "Brightie" was handled to her title by Wendell and later leased to Alekai for breeding. Bred to Best in Show dog Champion Alekai Argus, she produced Champion Alekai All Together.

The latter, Champion Alekai All Together, was shown once in puppy trim, receiving Best Puppy in Specialty Show at seven months of age. Her first points came at 14 months at the Poodle Club of America 1980 under breed authority Mrs. Rebecca Mason of Bel Tor fame. From the 12-18 month class she went on to

A stunning portrait of the magnificent Standard Poodle bitch, Ch. Alekai Marlaine.

Ch. Alekai Ami, littermate to Ch. Alekai Marlaine, by Ch. Alekai Kila ex Ch. Davdon Captivation. Handled by Wendell J. Sammet.

triumph over 139 class entries to Best of Winners. Following this win she was shown at three more specialties, acquiring three additional "majors" to complete her championship at 18 months of age. Speaking of "Together" in her critique, Mrs. Mason was glowing in her praise of this lovely young Poodle.

The last of the four bitches that were purchased as foundation stock for Alekai Poodles was Champion Tambarine de la Fontaine, bought as a puppy from Canada. She was a beautiful daughter of Champion Puttencove Promise and proved true to her heritage. Shown under Alekai ownership, she finished her title by going Best of Variety from the classes and on to third in the Non-Sporting Group at Westminster 1960. She repeated her Variety win in 1961, placing second that time in the Group. During 1961 she added two all-breed Bests in

Show and 18 Group Firsts to her list. She was the dam of three champions, one of which was English and American Champion Alekai Kalania, by Champion Alekai Kila. After completing her American title, Kalania was sold to Miss Martin of the noted Martindell Poodles in England. Kalania won the Challenge Certificate at Crufts, her first show, then proceeded to win seven more Challenge Certificates.

This brings the Alekai story up to the present time. After twenty-two years of breeding and exhibiting, Alekai has built a legacy of superb quality white Standard Poodles that will ensure the presence of the unmistakable Alekai type in the ring for years to come. The unique partnership between Mrs. Kaiser and her handler, Wendell Sammet, has made a significant contribution to the breed that continues with the presence of each latest young hopeful in the future.

Ch. Tambarine de la Fontaine, bred by Mr. and Mrs. Ken Ellis, Canada. Handled by Wendell J. Sammet. By Ch. Puttencove Promise from Ch. Gillette de la Fontaine.

Ch. Alekai Hula, owned by Mr. and Mrs. James Lester, Longleat Poodles, is shown in September, 1969, taking a **Group One.** Breeder, Mrs. Henry J. Kaiser; handler, Wendell J. Sammet. Sire, Ch. **Alekai Luau;** Dam, Ch. Alekai Marlaine.

Ch. Alekai Brilliance is handled by Wendell J. Sammet to Winners at Central New York, 1978, judged by Mrs. Betty Austin. Owned by Anna LeBlanc, bred by Mrs. Henry J. Kaiser.

Ch. Alekai Maui, littermate to Ch. Alekai Hula, taking Best of Winners at the Poodle Club of America, 1970. Judge, Mrs. Rebecca Mason. Breeder-owner, Mrs. Henry J. Kaiser. Handler, Wendell J. Sammet.

Ch. Alekai Zoe finishing her title at
Queensboro Kennel Club, 1974. By Ch.
Alekai Luau ex Longleat White Witch.

Ch. Alekai Tryannus took Winners Dog and Best of Winners at
the Washington Poodle Club Specialty, 1975, under judge Mrs.
George Dow. Handler, Wendell J. Sammet.

Ch. Alekai Zephyr, black Standard bred and
owned by Alekai Kennels, completing the
title at Northwestern Connecticut Dog Club,
September, 1978. Handled by Wendell J.
Sammet. Sired by Champion Alekai Ouzo
from Montec Lady Hamilton.

98

This is Ch. Alekai Ukelele as a stunning puppy going Best of Winners from one of his earliest dog shows.

An exciting moment at a William Penn Poodle Club Specialty Show. Future Champion Alekai Flowers of Mayfair takes Best in Show from the classes for owner, Mrs. Terrence Levy, and handler Wendell Sammet. Bred by Ann Seranne and Barbara Wolferman, Flowers is a daughter of Champion Alekai Ahi and Champion Alekai Kuke of Mayfair. This same weekend, Flowers also accounted for an all-breed Best in Show from the Open Class.

Alekai-Mayfair

Ann Seranne and Barbara Wolferman became so interested in white Standard Poodles through their beautiful Champion Alekai Luau that they wanted to breed a litter at Mayfair. Mrs. Kaiser consented to lease Champion Alekai Pokoi to them for this purpose, as she was by then retired from the show ring. Mr. Sammct advised that Pokoi be bred to Champion Merrylegs Cetin de la Fontaine, owned in Canada, a fine producing grandson of Champion Puttencove Promise. This litter holds the record for the most champions produced in one litter of any variety of Poodle! It included these champions: Champion Alekai Bikini of Mayfair, Champion Alekai Hauli of Mayfair, Champion Alekai Nahoe of Mayfair, Champion Alekai Tiki of Mayfair, Champion Alekai Umi of Mayfair, and Champion Alekai Kuke of Mayfair. Retired to the luxury of the sofa at the Seranne-Wolferman menage, Pokoi then left it to her daughters to carry on.

Champion Alekai Kuke of Mayfair was Best of Winners at Poodle Club of America 1968 from the puppy class and Best Puppy in Show. She finished her championship still in puppy trim and was bred to Champion Alekai Ahi. This litter resulted in three champions, Alekai Karate of Mayfair, Alekai Ukelele of Mayfair (both male), and Alekai Flowers of Mayfair (a bitch). Flowers was sold to Mr. and Mrs. Terrence Levy of Aldeblou Poodles, became a Best in Show and Specialty winner, and later provided the foundation for the Aldeblou Standards.

Ch. Alekai Luau photographed in November 1971. By Ch. Alekai Ahi ex Ch. Alekai Pokoi. Bred by Alekai, Mrs. Henry J. Kaiser. Owned by Mayfair, Ann Seranne and Barbara Wolferman. Handled by Wendell J. Sammet.

Alekai-Stonebridge

Dorothy Baranowsky, Stonebridge Poodles, was the owner of Champion Alekai Maunalua, a daughter of foundation bitch Champion Tambarine de la Fontaine. She was advised to breed Maunalua to Top Producing Champion Alekai Ahi by Mr. Sammet. The result of this breeding was the bitch Champion Tamara of Stonebridge, many times Best in Show and Group winner. Tamara was bred back to her sire, Ahi, and in turn produced the littermates Champion Alekai Oli of Stonebridge and Champion Alekai Coconut of Stonebridge, both purchased by Alekai Kennels and finished under their banner.

Oli became a Top Producer, siring 13 champions. One of the most outstanding of the latter was Best in Show winning American and Canadian Champion Alekai Ouzo. Purchased as a "special" by Peljo Kennels in Canada, to date he has produced eight champions, including three Group winners and the Best in Show winning Champion Alekai Argus.

Coconut, Oli's sister, also became a producer of Best in Show get, the lovely Champion Alekai Aphrodite, by the Group winning Luau son Champion Alekai Zeus, who was purchased as a "special" by Aldeblou Kennels, and Japanese Champion Alekai Adventure, a Best in Show winner in Japan.

Recognizing the quality in these litter mates, it was decided to breed Tamara again, this time to Best in Show winner Champion Alekai Luau. The resulting offspring were Champion Alekai

Keike of Stonebridge, Champion Alekai Rumble of Stonebridge, and Champion Alekai Ali of Stonebridge.

Ch. Alekai Keiki of Stonebridge en route to the title at Tulare, California, 1972. Martha Fielder handling. Another from the litter by Ch. Alekai Luau ex Ch. Tamara of Stonebridge.

Ch. Akekai Rumble of Stonebridge, by Ch. Alekai Luau ex Ch. Tamara of Stonebridge, breeder Dorothy Baranowsky, owner Janet Abrahams, handler Wendell J. Sammet.

Ch. Alekai Ali of Stonebridge, by Ch. Alekai Luau ex Ch. Tamara of Stonebridge, winning Best in Show at Albany Kennel Club, 1972, under judge John Cook. Owned by Janet Abrahams, bred by Dorothy Baranowsky, handled by Wendell J. Sammet.

Am., Can., Bda., Mex. Ch. Cheerful's Nina Linda of M. This lovely Miniature bitch belongs to Blanche and Rebecca C. Tansil, Andechez Poodles.

Andechez

Andechez Poodles are the result of Rebecca Tansil's meeting in 1951 with a three-month-old white puppy which arrived from Paris as a privileged passenger on the liner *S. S. United States.* The baby Poodle Annette was brought over by the Tansils' good friend John Theadgill, an official of the United States Lines, as a gift for his daughter.

Rebecca says, "Annette and I became fast friends as I trained her, kept her when her family traveled, and later arranged the breeding from which I was to have the puppy of my choice. This union with Champion Happy Felix, U.D.T., gave me Desiree d'Or of St. Dunstans, C.D., C.D.X. Since our first Poodle came from a French import, we followed the French method of registration where each year a letter of the alphabet is taken in sequence. From Annette, 1951, we completed the alphabet in 1976." As this is written, Andechez is in the "D" year of the second time around the alphabet.

The name Andechez was coined from the names of the Tansils' earliest Poodles (An for Anette, de for Desiree, ch for Chelle and Cheerful) with z added to complete the alphabet plan from A to Z. In the early years much time and emphasis was spent on obedience, and every dog earned a degree. Many an Andechez Poodle has won high Obedience honors, and their names are to be found engraved on some of the most coveted Obedience trophies.

The foundation bitch Desiree was bred to Tydel's Hopeful, a grandson of Champion Fircot L'Ballerine of Maryland. From this litter came an exquisite Miniature bitch, Happy

Rochelle of Dunkirk, C.D., called "Chelle." Her owners' full work schedule precluded a ring career for Chelle beyond the puppy classes. Eventually she was bred to a grandson of Ballerine, International Champion Calvinelle Jolly Roger, and started the Andechez line-breeding program. Three bitches were kept from this litter, Cheerful, Poupee, and Petite. The one that was officially named Chelle's Cheerful Cherub of K held particular promise, and hopes were high for her future. Cheerful produced a splendid litter of four bred to a L'Ballerine great grandson, Champion Calvinelle Dandy Gow. When the puppies were two weeks old, Rebecca took Desiree "off on a Mexican safari," from which they returned in late summer.

Upon her return from Mexico, Rebecca Tansil selected the smallest bitch from this litter, which she named Cheerful's Nina Linda of M, the Spanish for "beautiful little girl." At this time Blanche Tansil decided to join her sister in the Poodle venture, so a move was made to the country from the suburbs. This event, we are told, was written up in an article in the Baltimore *News American* as the "Doctors Tansil have gone to the dogs!"

When Cheerful was two years of age, and from all indications ready to start on what had been looked forward to as an exciting career, she met with a sudden and untimely death. Once the shock had abated, the Tansils determined that Nina Linda would carry on for her dam and prove Cheerful's greatness by preserving the

Am., Can. Ch. Andechez Rebel of S, white Miniature male, went Best of Variety from the classes, and on to win the Non-Sporting Group, at the Trio Kennel Club, Canada.

bloodline. Nina made a fine record in the show ring, but more than that, she produced a whole series of magnificent Poodles. In her first litter came American and Canadian Champion Snow Prince of P, American and Canadian Champion Janeene Juno of P, and Canadian Champion Duquesa de Albe. In the second litter were American and Canadian Champion Andechez Stanis, American and Canadian Champion Andechez Linda of S, and American and Canadian Champion Andechez Rebel of S. From her third litter came Champion Andechez Isolde of U. Her grandchildren include American and Canadian Champion Andechez Tristan, Champion Princess Janeene, and Champion Andechez Danse Magnifique.

Through years of careful line-breeding with an occasional out-cross, the Tansils have established an excellent and reliable strain of Poodles. They have about 20 champions, the first of which was finished for them by Wendell Sammet in 1966. They also have twelve Canadian Champions finished by Andrena Brunotte. It has been their ambition to bring a closer relationship between conformation and obedience exhibitors, at which their efforts have proven successful. Andechez Poodles have gained fame in obedience circles, too, four of them holding obedience trial championships. One of these, Champion and Obedience Trial Champion Andechez Zachary Zee, is the only Poodle to date to have both titles, Rebecca Tansil notes with pride.

Above: Ch. Andechez Zenith taking Best of Winners at Virginia Kennel Club, 1979, judged by Howard Tyler. Owned by Andechez Poodles. **Center:** This fine white Miniature, Am., Can. Ch. Andechez Tristan, was handled to her title by Jack Naedell. **Right:** An outstanding moment! Great Lakes Poodle Club Specialty, 1970, judge Alva Rosenberg selects Am., Can. Ch. Janeene Juno of F as Best Miniature. Owners, Rebecca C. and Blanche Tansil; handler, Robert A. Fisher.

Best of Variety at Boardwalk, Am., Can. Ch. Andechez Stanis, owned by Blanche and Rebecca C. Tansil, was handled by Wendell J. Sammet.

Greenspring Poodle Club 1970, Wendell J. Sammet is shown handling Am., Can. Ch. Janeene Juno of F for Blanche and Rebecca C. Tansil, Andechez Poodles, Parkton, Maryland.

Wendell J. Sammet handling Am., Can. Ch. Andechez Rebel of S for Blanche and Rebecca C. Tansil.

Beaufresne

Mrs. Gardner Cassatt owns Beaufresne Miniature Poodles, which specializes in apricots, her greatest favorites. The kennel is located close to Philadelphia, Pennsylvania.

Her lovely bitch, Champion Pixiecroft Sunbeam, was the first truly great winning apricot Poodle and surely made a spectacular record during her show career, including about 20 Bests in Show and a great many Non-Sporting Groups, among them Westminster in 1965. She was the Number Nine Top Dog in the country in 1963. Widely admired for her exquisite color as well as her excellent quality, Sunbeam was bred by Mark Crawford and Ted Doucette and was by Champion Meisen Golden Gamin ex Merrill of Pixiecroft.

Beaufresne Ginger Boy, Champion Beaufresne Gilded Lily, and Champion Beaufresne Cassaba are other lovely Poodles that have represented Mrs. Cassatt well in the show ring. The most recent big-time "star" from here is the glamorous Champion Tiopepi Amber Tanya, imported from England, who has a big Group and Best in Show record in keenest eastern competition under Richard L. Bauer's handling.

Ch. Beaufresne Cassaba, owned by Mrs. Gardner Cassatt, pictured winning the Non-Sporting Group at the First Company Governors Foot Guard, Hartford, Connecticut.

The first of all the Beaujeau Poodles, Ch. Diablotin Kala Jauhar, shown winning at the Lawton-Fort Sill Kennel Club show, 1953. He was purchased when six weeks old from Mrs. Rena Morse of the Diablotin Kennels, Massachusetts, fine producers of truly excellent Miniatures noted for soundness and outstanding heads. Mrs. Robert (Marjorie A.) Tranchin, owner, Beaujeau Kennels, Dallas, Texas.

Beaujeau

The Beaujeau Poodles were founded in 1951 by Mrs. Marjorie A. Tranchin of Dallas, Texas, with the acquisition of Diablotin Kala Jauhar, a black Miniature male, and a year later with the purchase of Diablotin Autumn Leaf, a brown Miniature female. Both Poodles became champions. Bred together they produced Beaujeau Diablesse, a black Miniature that became the dam of seven champions including the top winning black dog Champion Beaujeau Regal.

Next Mrs. Tranchin added a number of American-bred Poodles, mostly from Highland Sand Kennels, and English imports from Braeval, Montfleuri, and as time went on from Montmartre, Aspen, and Tranchant Kennels based on the Braeval bloodlines. The slower maturing English dogs stabilized the quality of the faster maturing American dogs. Beaujeau Meteor, a son of Champion Highland Sand Shooting Star from Champion Desmoulin Delight of Montfleuri and sire of four champions, was an excellent example of the well-balanced, sound dogs produced from the American-English combination.

104

One of the early imported winners from Beaujeau Kennels, the black Miniature bitch Ch. Desmoulin Delight of Montfleuri.

A number of Beaujeau's English imports were of great value to this country as top producers as well as in the show ring. English, American, Canadian, and Mexican Champion Montmartre Bartat By Jingo, a black Miniature male, sired 27 champions; English, American, and Canadian Champion Braeval Boomerang, a black Miniature male, sired 15 champions; Champion Icarus Duke Otto, a white Miniature male, sired ten champions; English, American, Canadian, and Mexican Champion Aspen Bonne Amie, a black Miniature bitch, produced five champions; and Montmartre Minute Man, a black Toy male, sired five champions.

This is the brown Miniature dog, Ch. Highland Sand Shooting Star, one of the noted winners from Mrs. Marjorie A. Tranchin's Beaujeau Kennels.

Notable show records from Beaujeau include that made by English, American, Canadian, and Mexican Champion Montmartre Maria Nina, a black Miniature bitch who gained the Ken-L-Ration Southern Division Award in 1963; and that of English, American, Canadian, Mexican, C.A.C.I.B. Champion Montmartre Super Lad, a black Miniature male who won the Non-Sporting Group at Westminster Kennel Club, Madison Square Garden, New York City, in 1976.

Beaujeau-bred Poodles have also made their contribution. Such homebreds as Beaujeau Diablesse, a black Miniature bitch, produced

Such a pretty Poodle profile is this headstudy of Ch. Highland Sand Shooting Star, a noted brown Miniature dog owned by Mrs. Marjorie A. Tranchin.

seven champions; Beaujeau Meteor, a black Miniature male, sired four champions; Beaujeau Blanchette Chere, a white Miniature bitch, produced four champions; Champion Beaujeau Pride, a black Miniature bitch, produced five champions; and Champion Beaujeau Bittersweet, a brown Miniature female, produced three champions.

Top show winners as well as producers included American and Canadian Champion Beaujeau Regal, a black Miniature male who was a noted Best in Show winner and the sire of seven champions; American, Canadian, Mexican, C.A.C.I.B Champion Beaujeau My Gosh, a black Miniature male who was a Best in Show winner and the sire of five champions; Champion Beaujeau On The Beam, a black Miniature male who was a Best in Show winner and the sire of three champions; and American, Mexican, C.A.C.I.B. Champion Beaujeau Bonnie, a black Miniature bitch who was a Group winner and the producer of three champions. Champion Crikora Commotion, a black Miniature male, was a Best in Show winner and a Westminster Non-Sporting Group winner; he was sired by Champion Beaujeau Regal out of Champion Beaujeau Bittersweet.

Beaujeau has owned numerous Toy Poodles (including the Best in Show winning Champion Chocolate Bit, a brown bitch, and Champion

Langdon Skarda awards a Non-Sporting Group First at Chico Dog Fanciers, May 1976, to Mrs. Marjorie A. Tranchin's Miniature Poodle, Eng., Am., Mex., Bda. C.A.C.I.B. Ch. Montmartre Super Lad, handled by Barbara Humphries.

September, 1970, Am., Can., Mex., and C.A.C.I.B. Ch. Beaujeau My Gosh winning Best in Show at the Lone Star Poodle Club Specialty. Miss Maxine Beam, handler. Mrs. Jesse Mason, judge.

Taking a Non-Sporting Group First at Juarez, Mexico, September 1965, is the Miniature Poodle, Eng., Am. Ch. Montmartre Bartat by Jingo, thus completing his Mexican championship. Owned by Mrs. Marjorie A. Tranchin; handled by Maxine Beam.

Montmartre Minouche, a black bitch) and several Standard Poodles (including Champion Bel Tor Stars In Her Eyes, a black bitch).

Overall, Beaujeau Kennels over the past 30 years has bred 47 champions and owned 64 champions, making a total of 111 champions that have had Beaujeau as their home. However, the past few years have been rather unsettled, necessitating that Mrs. Tranchin curtail her showing and breeding plans. But with English and American Champion Tranchant Mantoman (a black Miniature male) and Champion Aspen Alora (a black Miniature bitch) on the West Coast and Champion Lochranza Rumbaba (a brown Miniature male) and Champion Elizabelle of Tranchant (a black Miniature

C.A.C.I.B. and Mex. Ch. Beaujeau Bonnie winning the Group at Wichita Falls, 1972, under judge Robert C. Hatch, Jr., for Mrs. Marjorie Tranchin.

Palm Valley Kennel club, 1971, Miss Dorothy D. Nickles awards first in the Non-Sporting Group to Am., Can., C.A.C.I.B. Ch. Beaujeau My Gosh owned by Mrs. Robert (Marjorie) Tranchin.

Brown Miniature bitch, Ch. Highland Sand Star of the East, owned by Mrs. Marjorie A. Tranchin.

bitch) on the East Coast, plus Champion Aspen Amorosa, Aspen Ah'm A Doll, and Montmartre Mauna, black Miniature bitches, and Champion Beaujeau Blenheim (no longer young), Champion Aspen Affidavit, and Aspen Amorist, black Miniature males, in her new home with her, Marjorie Tranchin has high hopes for the future.

Others of her famous dogs not included in the above resume are Champion Highland Sand Star Baby, who produced six champions, and Champion Bric A Brac Brag About, who produced nine champions. Both were black Miniature males and both were Best in Show winners.

As a side note, Mrs. Tranchin tells us that there are also some interesting stories behind the dogs in her kennel resume. These involve dogs that never finished their titles although they should have done so, yet contributed enormously to the Beaujeau breeding program. Beaujeau Eng., Am., Mex., and C.A.C.I.B. Miniature Ch. Montmartre Super Lad winning Best of Variety at the Poodle Club of Southern California Specialty, September, 1975.

Meteor was stolen, fenced in for a number of months, and broke off all his teeth chewing the metal fence until he escaped. The next-door neighbors, having seen Mrs. Tranchin's ad for her lost dog, returned him to his home. Beaujeau Diablesse, a little female, had too large a first litter, and subsequently her outline left much to be desired. Montmartre Minute Man, a top Toy producer in England, developed a rare blood disease on the trip to America and would let no one handle him except the woman who had nursed him back to health—but the woman was petrified at being in the ring. Beaujeau Blanchette Chere was sold and never shown, but her progeny were; she produced four champions. Mrs. Tranchin comments, "In any kennel of long standing there are bound to be stories similar to these. Some were very sad, but most, thank goodness, ended happily."

Above: Harbor Cities Kennel Club, 1964, James Walker Trullinger awards a good win to Eng., Am., Can., Mex., Ch. Montmartre Maria Nina owned by Mrs. Tranchin and handled by Miss Beam. **Above Right:** Another lovely headstudy of one of Mrs. Tranchin's great Poodles. This is Ch. Beaujeau On The Beam, a Best in Show winner and sire of three champions. **Center:** Ch. Beaujeau On The Beam winning the Non-Sporting Group at Muskogee Kennel Club, November, 1968. **Below:** Ch. Beaujeau Barnaby, photographed in 1970, a Canadian Group and Best in Show winner owned by Mrs. Tranchin.

A very handsome little Poodle, Ch. Elizabelle of Tranchant, is set up to perfection by Michael Pawasarat for Mrs. Marjorie A. Tranchin.

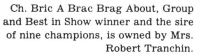

Ch. Bric A Brac Brag About, Group and Best in Show winner and the sire of nine champions, is owned by Mrs. Robert Tranchin.

Ch. Beaujeau Barnaby, Best of Opposite Sex in 1972 at the Creole Poodle Club Specialty, New Orleans. Judge, Mr. Frank Fretwell; handler, Mrs. Ann Hodde; owner, Mrs. Robert Tranchin.

Beaujolais

Beaujolais Kennels is located at Valley Stream, New York, and is owned by Beverly A. Valerio. The foundation stud here, and the dog behind all of the present generation of Beaujolais winners, is Beaujolais' Burnt Sienna, son of De Regis Golden Realm (a Top Producer) from a daughter of Champion Meisen Gram of Gold (a grandson of Champion Meisen Bit O'Gold). "Sunny" himself has what it takes to produce Poodles of real quality, which in turn are happily also reproducing "in the family tradition." As Beverly Valerio says, "A lucky stud—for Beaujolais."

Burnt Sienna had been brought together with his sister via an out-cross, and their daughter

Ch. Beaujolais Double Accent, son of Beaujolais Burnt Sienna, a litter brother to Ch. Beaujolais Brenda Starr, was Winners Bitch at Westminster, 1978. Owned by Beverly A. Valerio, Beaujolais Poodles, Valley Stream, New York.

This 8½ inch Toy dog, Beaujolais Burnt Sienna, belongs to Beaujolais Kennels.

Burnt Sienna is the sire of 14 champions as this is written, with another offspring, Beaujolais' Evil Times Three, now in competition. His champion progeny include Champion Beaujolais' Junior Accent, Champion Beaujolais' Golden Accent, Champion Beaujolais' Sunny Accent, Champion Beaujolais' Accent of Reve, Champion Beaujolais' Exotica, Champion Hermscrest Burnt Orange, Champion Beaujolais' Flaming Madonna (in-bred on Burnt Sienna), Champion Beaujolais' Made in the Shade, Champion Little Bits Manny G., Champion Little Bits Golden Image, Champion Beaujolais' Brenda Starr, Champion Beaujolais' Double Accent, Champion Beaujolais' Fancy Accent, and Champion Beaujolais' Burnt Sienna II.

was bred back to Burnt Sienna, giving the Westminster Winners Bitch in 1978, Champion Beaujolais' Brenda Starr, and also Champion Beaujolais' Double Accent as the result. Both dogs are highly prized by their owner. Burnt Sienna is the sire of many black champions as well as apricot champions. He himself was never shown as he measured only 8½ inches tall and was ultra, ultra refined, which seems to have worked out extremely well in making him a respected stud force!

Ch. Beaujolais' Fancy Accent, apricot Toy, winning the Variety, October 1977. Owned by Beverly A. Valerio, Valley Stream, New York.

Two adorable apricot
Toy babies represent-
ing Beaujolais Poodles.

Another early importa-
tion from England to
Beaujeau Kennels, Ch.
Braeval Montmartre
Sparkle, black Min-
iature male. Mrs. Mar-
jorie A. Tranchin,
owner.

Below: Mrs. Robert
(Marjorie A.) Tranchin
photographed at home
in November 1954 sur-
rounded by some of the
early Beaujeau
Poodles. From left they
are Ch. Highland Sand
Star of the East, Ch.
Highland Sand Shooting
Star, Ch. Beaujeau
Solitaire, Ch. Highland
Sand Star Baby, and
Ch. Braeval Montmartre
Sparkle.

Bel Tor

Bel Tor Poodles came into being as a result of Rebecca (Mrs. J. A.) Mason having received a Standard puppy as a gift for Christmas in 1939. She was just a pet, although "a superior one" according to her owner, and came out of Misty Isles breeding, although Mrs. Byron Rogers was not actually herself the breeder. This Poodle completely converted Mrs. Mason to the breed.

Of her she writes, "She was one of the most extraordinary dogs, both mentally and in character, that I've ever owned, and I've had many dogs of many breeds all my life. Like all people who are deeply involved with dogs, I have found that there are always a few that stay with us in memory more than the others, and this was one of these. Wasn't it lucky that she turned out to be, or I might never have gone into this breed!" With this the author heartily agrees, for if Mrs. Mason had *not* gone into Poodles, the loss to them would have been inestimable.

Having been introduced to Poodles and having bred dogs of other breeds before this, Mrs. Mason decided that she would now branch out into this breed. A black Standard bitch of good quality was purchased from Mary McCreery of the Lowmont Kennels. This was Lowmont Lady Juliette, sired by Champion Blakeen Cyrano (that magnificent brown Standard who was a noted winner of his day) from Barbet Josephine (she by Champion Griseley Labory of Piperscroft ex Champion Blakeen Mira). This was in 1940; owing to the war and to gasoline rationing, Juliette was never shown except for a couple of times locally. Mrs. Mason bred her once, regarding which she comments, "of course, being a novice I did it as wrong as possible. I was living in Florida at the time, and I thought I was doing a great thing when I found a dog named Sunstorm's Merry Messenger, by Marechal of Piperscroft (a son of International Champion Nunsoe Duc de la Terrace of Blakeen ex English Champion Marlene of Piperscroft), and went blithely ahead with this breeding. Only problem was that he was white and my bitch was the product of a brown and black cross."

Today she shudders at the very thought, but actually Mrs. Mason had beginner's luck and there was not a single mismark in the resulting litter of nine puppies. The only problem was that it was necessary to fight the battle of coping with this mixture for a good many following years, as she kept a brown male from this litter, which she named Drambuie, and used him quite extensively at stud. Drambuie was said to bear a very definite resemblance to his grandsire

The most exquisite black Standard Poodle bitch, Ch. Bel Tor Black Helen, finishes her title still in puppy clip. Bred and owned by Bel Tor Kennels, Mrs. J. A. Mason. Helen was handled here by Frank Sabella.

Ch. Bel Tor Marble Faun is handled here by a very young Frank Sabella for Mrs. J. A. Mason, Bel Tor Poodles.

112

Ch. Bel Tor Hussar Busby, one of the many fine Poodles from Bel Tor Kennels.

Exquisite Standard bitch, Ch. Bel Tor Too Good To Be True, was a widely admired campaigner of the early 1960's for Mrs. J. A. Mason.

Cyrano for which reason Mrs. Mason felt that the continued use of her young dog at stud seemed worthwhile. This first Bel Tor litter was whelped on March 26, 1942, and was the start of something really great in the world of Standard Poodles.

In 1943 Mrs. Mason moved north to Connecticut and promptly bought another black Standard bitch, Dubonette (by Champion Intrepid of Misty Isles ex Antoinette of Misty Isles), again from Mrs. Byron Rogers. On April 1, 1945, she had a litter from her by Drambuie. From this she kept a bitch, Black Velvet, who proved somewhat of a disappointment. However, in this litter was another bitch who was sold and subsequently bred to a black male, Lowmont Lord Dion. A brown bitch was purchased by Mrs. Mason from this litter, and she turned out to be Mrs. Mason's first Standard Poodle champion, Beltore Bright Star. She was whelped on February 28, 1948, and finished her championship in March, 1950.

So much for the very beginning. Following it there was not a lot of immediate action on Mrs. Mason's part with the Poodles, as small children occupied the major portion of her time during this period. Actually she was quite content looking at the dogs she had and feeling that she was doing all right without taking them anywhere. However, as things became more relaxed with the children she began to think that perhaps she had better try to get to some shows to see how her Poodles stacked up against the others in competition at the time. Early in the 1950's Bel Tor had branched out into whites as well as

browns by buying a white bitch, Blakeen Bonte (Blakeen White Light ex Champion Blakeen The Swan), from Mrs. Hoyt. This one she had bred to Lowmont Lord Dion and kept a cream bitch, Bel Tor Cotton Candy, from the litter. Subsequently Cotton Candy was bred to Champion White Cockade of Salmagundi, from which two puppies remained at Bel Tor, a bitch and a dog. In 1953 Mrs. Mason tried her luck in the show ring to see what she might be doing and promptly finished the white bitch (who had been named Bel Tor Piaffe) in six shows with five majors under five different judges—all somewhat to her amazement it would seem. She had not really considered Piaffe to be ready for the ring, so had entered her in Novice Class in the first four shows just to gain ring experience. That was Bel Tor's first *homebred* Poodle champion. Subsequently her dam, Cotton Candy, finished and a brown bitch, Bel Tor Cloisonne (Champion Lowmont D'Artagnan ex Black Velvet), got a Group First en route to her title in 1953.

Obviously Mrs. Mason had to have been doing a great deal right. All this made the dog show bug bite very hard, and her enthusiasm has never wavered since. However, Mrs. Mason did not truly feel that this first success proved much of anything about her breeding program, attributing it more or less to luck rather than skill.

She comments, "Mostly I feel that I was pretty lucky all around, plus I had been brought up in dogs so knew something about how they should be built and about such techniques as line-breeding and in-breeding." Whether it has been luck or skill (but in my opinion it takes a generous combination of both to succeed in this field), Mrs. Mason has certainly held the key to a winning combination over the decades, as we will continue to tell.

In 1954 two bitches, Champion Lowmont Lady Cadette (purchased from Miss McCreery) and Champion Bel Tor Hosanna (a stud fee puppy), were bred to Champion Annsown Sir Gay. Each of the litters produced five champions for a total of ten, several of them still as puppies. It was from one of these litters, Cadette's, that Champion Bel Tor Morceau Choisi came. He developed into one of the most prepotent stud dogs Mrs. Mason has bred throughout the years. From Hosanna's litter came Champion Bel Tor Gigadibs, still Number Ten Top Producer of all time in the breed, with 28 champions to his credit. Almost everything produced in Standard Poodles at Bel Tor Kennels since that time has come down from one or the other of these two litters. A son of Morceau Choisi, Champion Bel Tor McCreery, is Number Seven Top Producing Male in the breed with 39 champion get. He was a brown dog and is behind all of the brown stock raised by Mrs. Mason right up to the present day.

The Bel Tor Kennel prefix was registered in 1953, when Mrs. Mason seriously started showing. Prior to this time she had spelled the prefix "Beltore," one word with an "e" on the end, but it was changed at this time to the present form. The name was coined from the names of the Mason children, Belinda and Tobias, and of Mrs. Mason herself, Rebecca. As of November, 1980, 197 Standard Poodles carrying the Bel Tor prefix have become champions, with 142 of them homebred—a fantastic record!

Mrs. Mason had decided to branch out into Miniatures along with the Standards in 1952, purchasing a silver, Cartlane Commotion (Roadcoach Quicksilver ex Venda's Silver Bablon), who finished in 1955. Although she owned this variety for many years, Mrs. Mason found it difficult to like them in comparison to the Standards, and in 1969 when her one and only Miniature homebred champion finished its title, she decided they just were not for her and discontinued working with that variety.

Toys also came to Bel Tor in 1952. The first of these was a brown bitch, Venda's Noisette, an English import. She was oversize but she was in no way "dwarfy" as were so many Toy Poodles

Ch. Bel Tor Black Helen winning at the Poodle Club of America, 1961, handled by John Brennan.

Group winner Ch. Bel Tor Good Faith as a puppy, winning at the Washington Poodle Club Specialty, October 1962.

back in the beginning. To quote Mrs. Mason on the subject, "I had little luck breeding her, for the studs available were the low, heavy-boned kind with Miniature heads which were prevalent. So I tried out-crossing to Miniatures that were known to carry the small gene, and gradually I was reducing size and keeping the type I wanted, which was a true Poodle in outline and balance but of diminutive proportions. This is long, slow work, for the little ones have litters of only one, two, or three puppies, and it seems to take forever to make progress. Also they had problems of slipping stifles, undershot jaws, and lack of testicles, with which to plague us. For ten long years I did my Toy breeding quietly 'behind closed doors,' hoping someday to come up with something worth the effort. If I had not had the Standards at the time to keep me going, this would have put me out of my mind. My hat is off to all those who worked with just the Toys to bring them to what they are today, real Poodles, although tiny." In 1960

Jan Jeffries duPont with Bel Tor Kennels' Ch. Bel Tor Bittersweet.

Her first Group win en route to a highly successful show career, Ch. Bel Tor Xanadu winning under Mr. William L. Kendrick for Mrs. J. A. Mason who is owner-handling. Xanadu became a very famous Best in Show winner.

Mrs. Mason imported a black Toy bitch, Old Timbers Royal Romance, from England who, although slightly oversized, had all the attributes for which Mrs. Mason had been working and who contributed well to the progress of the Bel Tor Toys. The first homebred Toy of Mrs. Mason's to become a champion was Bel Tor Bubbling Over, a granddaughter of Venda's Noisette, in 1962. Her owner describes her as still "dwarfy" but not so much so as many of that period. She had also finished around that time three white Toys of better type which she had bought from a litter belonging to Bertha Plath in California (this purchase made in 1961). The ones she had finished in black had all come down from Romance. To date 17 Toys carrying the Bel Tor prefix have finished, 13 of them homebred.

Ch. Bel Tor Heads I Win of Bibelot at the Poodle Club of America with handler Bob Forsyth, 1969.

The Group winning Standard Poodle, Ch. Torkey To Heaven, from the Bel Tor Poodles of Mrs. J. A. Mason.

The famed Best in Show winner, Ch. Bel Tor Noonday Sun, owned by Mrs. J. A. Mason.

Ch. Bel Tor Where The Action Is, still another splendid Standard Poodle representing Rebecca Mason in the show ring, receives another good win.

In 1975, "beginning to feel my age and not able to find decent help," Mrs. Mason decided that the time had come to cut down drastically on the dogs, keeping only her first love, the Standards. She found good homes for most of the Toys she had left at that time and today has only four of this variety still with her, all champions and "pretty much antiques."

Since 1980 Bel Tor Kennels contains just 11 adult Standards, three of which are over ten years old, and their owner is enjoying it this way as she can take care of them herself if necessary and need not live in perpetual fear that the whole lot of help will walk out without notice, the way

Another of Rebecca Mason's Group winners, Ch. Bel Tor All The Trimmings, winning a Non-Sporting Group First.

they often do these days. She will continue breeding and raising puppies, for that is in her blood, and she will show occasionally when she feels she has something worthy.

In closing this kennel story, one of the greatest in the entire world of Poodles, we again quote the talented lady who has brought it all about.

Says Mrs. Mason, "Now I expect that you are wondering when I am going to mention dogs which have done noteworthy winning, and this is where I am going to fail you. I've had them or bred them, true. But somehow this has never been the important thing to me. I'm a breeder at heart, and what has mattered most all these years is trying to establish a line that bred true so that the difference in the best and the poorest pup-

Ch. Bel Tor Noonday Sun at the Ox Ridge Kennel Club, September 1967. From the famous Bel Tor Kennels of Mrs. J. A. Mason.

pies in a litter was minimal. Some have been fortunate in going to people who wanted the wins, so they were campaigned and made records. Naturally I am pleased that this has happened. But I am not going to say that they were the best because of it. They just had the advantage. I recall too many that never reached the ring that have been just as good in my book. I still go back to my first thought. The main purpose of shows should be to keep us trying to breed the best we can and give us a way of comparing our own dogs to those of other breeders in order that we do not stray too far from the ideal."

Right: Famous littermates from Bel Tor! Nearest the judge is Ch. Bel Tor Trustful; center, Ch. Bel Tor Artful; and Ch. Bel Tor Blissful.
Right Center: Such a pretty white Toy! Ch. Bel Tor Command Module represents the smaller members of the family at Bel Tor Poodles owned by Mrs. J. A. Mason.

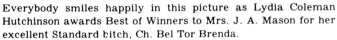

Everybody smiles happily in this picture as Lydia Coleman Hutchinson awards Best of Winners to Mrs. J. A. Mason for her excellent Standard bitch, Ch. Bel Tor Brenda.

The very pretty Ch. Bel Tor Pie In The Sky is another splendid representative of the quality produced at Mrs. J. A. Mason's Bel Tor Kennels, Connecticut.

Foundation bitch behind the Cappoquin Miniatures, Ch. Bric A Brac Bonne Femme was purchased at five months old by Mary Griffin from Ruth Burnette Sayres. Bonne Femme was a Top Producing Bitch according to Phillips System ratings over a period of several years.

Cappoquin

In looking back through Miniature Poodle history, one cannot help being mightily impressed with the success of a small kennel in Pennsylvania known as Cappoquin and owned by Mary Griffin. The kennel prefix was chosen as it was in Cappoquin, County Waterford, in Ireland, that Mrs. Griffin first saw a Poodle, obviously a case of immediate attraction to the breed.

For her foundation bitch, Mrs. Griffin selected a lovely black representing the Bric A Brac breeding owned by Ruth Burnette Sayres, also located in Pennsylvania. This was Bric A Brac Bonne Femme, who Mary Griffin purchased as a five-month-old puppy and who turned out to have been a truly excellent choice.

For her first litter, Bonne Femme was bred to Champion Hollycourt Bronze Knight, which Mrs. Griffin tells us was also the first time that these two highly successful strains had been used together. That this was a wise selection was promptly proven when one of the puppies, an exquisite black dog, from almost the moment of arrival in this world was obviously outstanding. His show training began at an extremely early age, and Mary Griffin was so excited over him that she could hardly wait for him to become six

months old and thus eligible to enter competition. He made his debut in the ring very shortly past his six-month birthday at the first futurity held by the Poodle Club of America, and there Mrs. Griffin's confidence in him was well confirmed as he won Best Puppy All Varieties. The moment he turned 12 months old, Mrs. Griffin took her puppy (with which, owner-handling, she had been winning Puppy Classes quite consistently and in several cases Reserve Winners Dog) to Anne Rogers Clark for serious campaigning. In no time flat, with a Best of Variety from the classes over specials, Alva Rosenberg judging, and a third in the Group, this puppy from the first Poodle litter Mrs. Griffin had bred became Champion Cappoquin Bon Fiston.

As a producer, Bon Fiston more than fulfilled Mrs. Griffin's fondest hopes. He sired at least eight champions, among them the two Best in Show winners Champion Cappoquin Carriage Trade and Champion Moulin's Belle Fleurette.

For her next litter, Bon Fiston's dam, Bonne Femme, was bred again into the Hollycourt line, this time to Champion Hollycourt Calandra. Again Mrs. Griffin had chosen wisely, for this time the resulting litter produced the very famous multiple Best in Show brown dog Champion Cappoquin Bon Jongleur, known far and wide as "Charlie Brown." Bon Jongleur, handled by Anne Rogers Clark, became a champion while still belonging to Mrs. Griffin, taking Best of Variety wins and Group placements from the classes. Then, at less than two years old, he was sold to the late Colonel Ernest E. Ferguson in California, where he was turned over to handler Frank Sabella—the rest is history! Bon Jongleur became a famous and spectacular Group winning and Best in Show dog and did equally as well as a sire, his progeny including several Best in Show winners.

Other noted Cappoquin Miniatures include Champion Cappoquin Creme de la Creme, Champion Cappoquin Guyon, Champion Cappoquin Carriage Trade (a multiple Best in Show winner who went to Mrs. Nancy Cutler of Minneapolis), Champion Ledahof Ballet Master (a Bon Jongleur son co-owned with Mrs. Nathan Allen), Champion Cappoquin Bonne Nuit (owned by James Poag in Greensboro, North Carolina), the Best in Show winning brown dog Champion Cappoquin Railsplitter (who went to Laura Niles' Tilo Poodles), and "Linc's" litter brother, the black Champion Cappoquin Honest Abe (who went to Bel Tor Kennels, Mrs. Rebecca Mason, when only three months old).

Ch. Cappoquin Bon Fiston, a 13½ inch Miniature, was a highly successful show and stud dog with 17 champions to his credit. Bred and owned by Mary Griffin, Cappoquin Poodles, Macungie, Pennsylvania. By Ch. Hollycourt Bronze Knight ex Ch. Bric A Brac Bonne Femme.

Mrs. Griffin became interested in Toy Poodles as well as the Miniatures, and in the 1960's finished Champion Cappoquin Birdie, Champion Cappoquin Sugar Bun, and Champion Cappoquin Davey of Wilcrest.

I am sure that there is no more exciting a "Cinderella story" to be told by any dog fancier than that involving the magnificent and highly successful black Toy bitch that became Champion Cappoquin Little Sister. It was in about 1958 that Mary Griffin started looking for an outstanding Toy Poodle, either black or brown, a dog or a bitch. She had not had much luck finding what she wanted until one day a friend, Mrs. Winifred Heckmann, alerted Mrs. Griffin to the fact that a most beautiful black Toy bitch, as the result of a family tragedy, was up for sale in a commercial kennel. Mrs. Griffin lost no time in getting there to see her, and despite the fact that what greeted her eyes was a dirty, matted, unkempt little Poodle in Dutch trim, the quality was very obvious to one who knew the breed. Mrs. Griffin was so eager to have her that she wrote the purchase check of $200.00 on the hood of her car.

Sister was 14 months old at the time of purchase and still unregistered. As she was related to the Cappoquin Miniatures through Bric A Brac breeding on one side, Little Sister seemed an appropriate name, to which Mrs. Griffin added the Cappoquin prefix.

After a bath and a Continental Clip, Sister was taken to Anne Rogers. A strategy was mapped out to "get her a blue ribbon" at the Old Dominion Kennel Club Show that would qualify her for Westminster (the only requirement then for a Westminster entry) and then to keep her under wraps until that event. The strategy worked out – Sister got her needed "blue" and went to Westminster, where she took Best of Winners. During the year to come she did much Toy Group and Best in Show winning. Her second Westminster appearance, in 1961, left everyone involved with this lovely bitch quite breathless, as Little Sister sailed through Best of Variety, then the Toy Group, and then became the third Toy dog in history to take a Westminster Best in Show. After that she retired to the home of Florence Michelson, the owner who had purchased her from Mrs. Griffin, and produced some lovely puppies.

Ch. Cappoquin Bon Jongleur, the famous brown Miniature known throughout the Poodle world as "Charlie Brown," a record winning Best in Show dog.

Mary Griffin with her future Ch. Cappoquin Bon Fiston
making an early puppy win under judge, Anne Rogers
Clark. From the first litter ever bred at Cappoquin
Kennels.

Ch. Cappoquin Carriage Trade went from Mary Griffin's kennel to become a noted Best in Show winner for
Mrs. Nancy Cutler in Minneapolis.

Ch. Cappoquin Bon Jongleur at the 1959 Poodle Club of
America Specialty, handled by Wendell J. Sammet for
breeder, Mary Griffin.

The great Toy Poodle bitch, Ch. Cappoquin Little Sister, the third Toy dog to win a Westminster Best in Show, belonged to Florence Michelson and was handled by Anne Hone Rogers (now Mrs. James Edward Clark).

Mary Griffin with her Ch. Cappoquin Birdie.

Ch. Cappoquin Bon Fiston finishing at Maryland Kennel Club 1957, going Best of Variety and Group 3rd. Mary Griffin, owner. Anne Rogers Clark, handler.

Ch. Hell's A Blazen Carnival, Toy. Bred by Wendell J. Sammet and Frances Rubinich. Owned by Doris A. Sutton. Handled by Mr. Sammet.

Ch. Hell's A Blazen Carnival Fame, white male Toy bred by Wendell Sammet and Frances Rubinich. By Ch. Silhou-Jette's Sugar Twist ex Branslake Floris. Best of Winners from Bred by Exhibitor Class at Poodle Club of America 1971.

Ch. Trespetite Carnival Caper, black Toy Poodle English import, winning at Sussex Hills Kennel Club 1966. Owned and handled by Wendell J. Sammet, Carnival Toy Poodles. Bred by June Phillips. By Braebeck Achievement ex Tophill Amber Bright.

The English import Ch. Trespetite Carnival Clown (Trespetite Super Toy ex Trespetite Caresse). Owned and handled by Wendell J. Sammet, Carnival Toy Poodles. The judge is Mrs. Krause.

The Group winning Ch. Carnival Idle Chatter, brown Toy male, bred and owned by Wendell J. Sammet, Carnival Toy Poodles. Winning at Quinnipiac Poodle Club under Alva Rosenberg, 1964.

Ch. Carnival Yakkity Yak, black Toy male, bred and owned by Wendell J. Sammet, Carnival Toy Poodles. By Ch. Carnival Idle Chatter ex Burlingame Carnival Molly. Winning in 1966 under judge Mrs. Lauer J. Froelich. Owner-handled by Mr. Sammet.

Chanteclair

Chanteclair silver Miniature Poodles are known throughout the world for excellence and quality. They are owned by Mrs. Lucienne Andre Clement and located at Haverford, Pennsylvania.

To tell the detailed story of Chanteclair would take volumes. We shall therefore confine our remarks to the dogs and the breedings which have produced the type of silvers which have been winning for Mrs. Clement and for other breeders during recent years.

Mrs. Clement pays particular tribute to Champion Brandywine's Beau Brummel, one of the most beautiful and regal silvers it has been her privilege to own. She feels that his impact on silvers still is being strongly felt today, and she expresses gratitude to Mrs. Nancy Cutler, his breeder, from whom she purchased him in January, 1967. He had been named "Le Roi," the King, which indeed he was at Chanteclair, where he was loved and valued not only for his quality but for his ideal temperament.

Mrs. Clement's love for silvers began when her first litter was whelped, back in 1958.

Ch. Brandywine Beau Brummel is typical of the beautiful silver Miniatures owned by Mrs. Lucienne Andre Clement of Haverford, Pennsylvania, whose Chanteclair Poodles played so important a role in the development of outstanding silvers in the United States.

Chanteclair Classi Chassis at 19 months, dam of the Top Producer Ch. Chanteclair Touch of Class, August 1971. "Lucy" was sired by Tophill Silver Glint ex Ch. Chanteclair Nicolette.

Although the puppies were nice, "nice" was not enough for her purpose. In 1959 she purchased a sound platinum bitch, Caline, bred completely differently from the usual available silver bloodlines. She carried a sprinkling of Hollycourt and a double cross to Champion Adastra Magic Fame (white) on her sire's side, while her silver dam had also a combination of the white bloodlines which still represent the foundation of the top white Miniatures in the United States at this moment, they having been Champion Snow Boy of Fircot, Champion Blakeen Snow Flurry, and Champion Blakeen Christabel.

Perhaps this was a gamble at the time, but Mrs. Clement has never regretted her decision to follow this course of action. Caline stood 13.5 inches tall with clear color, a lovely lean head, and a small, correctly shaped eye. Her first litter, born in 1962, was sired by Calvinelle Silver Frost, a grandson on the sire's side of English and American Champion Pita of Manapouri, half brother to Champion Fircot L'Ballerine of Maryland, thus a son of Berinshill Dancing Boy. On his dam's side Silver Frost was a grandson of Berinshill Silver Sequin (sired by English Champion Gypsyheath Silver Wings ex a bitch of Vendas background) and also of Champion Calvinelle Pristine of Trent. It was at this time decided that this would become the foundation litter, and the kennel prefix Chanteclair was selected. One bitch, Chanteclair Petite Fie, was retained. She lived to be almost 16 years of age. Upon the suggestion of Mrs. James Edward Clark she was bred to Champion Freeland's Flashlight. From this litter two girls were kept, and one of them, Chanteclair Honey West, was shown quite successfully in puppy classes but broke her leg in a freak accident. Although it mended well, she never regained quite the same gait. Kimbeney A Gala, a silver bitch from this litter, went to Mrs. Arnold and in time produced Champion Kimbeney Clipper Boy from her litter sired by Mrs. Clement's Champion Brandywine's Beau Brummel.

At about this same time Mrs. Clement approached Mrs. Mildred Imrie with the intention of buying a dog puppy, Frankie of Freeland, which she had offered for sale. Mrs. Clement felt that he would be a definite asset to the Chanteclair breeding program and was greatly disappointed to learn that Mrs. Imrie had decided to keep him for herself. Ironically enough, it was this dog, Frankie of Freeland, that when bred to one of Mrs. Clement's bitches, Chanteclair Classi Chassis, sired what Mrs. Clement tells us is the only living Top Producer silver Miniature Champion, this being Champion Char-K-Touch of Class. Chanteclair Classi Chassis was purchased from Mrs. Clement as an eight-week-old puppy by Kathleen Brown.

The Chanteclair nucleus of stud dogs consisted of Tophill Silver Glint, a small unpretentious dog with beautiful coat texture and fabulous temperament, purchased by Mrs. Clement directly from the Strawsons (owners of Tophill Poodles) during a trip to England in January, 1969. She selected him solely for herself, never realizing that he would become part of the backbone of her kennel. His bloodlines, although a complete out-cross, clicked perfectly with those with which she was working. That same year came the purchase of Champion Calvinelle Snafu, a long-time favorite which she was delighted to finally have, as he had already sired the beautiful bitch Chanteclair Top Billing for her. Snafu was a spectacular platinum silver that had finished his championship with three all-breed Bests in Show and four Group Firsts. He was given to Mrs. Clement's fourteen-year-old daughter Danielle by his owners, Mr. and Mrs. Lockwood. Mrs. Clement remarks, "He was just adored by us, and spoiled." He had been used at stud quite sparingly, mostly by Mrs. Clement, even before he joined the Chanteclair family. One of his last litters produced Champion Sevarre's Chanteclair

Figure, a granddaughter of Tophill Silver Glint and Hostir Silver Charmer. This bitch went to live with Mrs. Herman, who had raised her dam, on breeder's terms with Mrs. Clement, and Mrs. Herman showed her to her title. She now is owned by Mrs. Monique Devine and is the dam of Champion Fontenac Florin, grandson of Champion Brandywine's Beau Brummel and several other pointed progeny that will almost certainly have completed their titles by the time this book appears in print.

Hostir Silver Charmer, mentioned in the preceding paragraph, was purchased in 1967 as an addition to Chanteclair's small group of

This refined and beautiful silver Miniature head belonged to Mrs. Lucienne Clement's Tophill Silver Glint. Photo taken in 1969.

brood bitches. A Touchstone Silver Ducat daughter, she was thus a granddaughter of Champion Freeland's Flashlight. Bred to a young show-prospect male, Chanteclair Oliver, she produced two champions from her litter of four. The bitch was Champion Kimiko de Guadelupe, who, when bred to Champion Char-K-Touch of Class, produced Champion Fanny Glick, U.D., and Champion Chanteclair Man About Town, who went to Mrs. Herms in July, 1972. "Mannix" had been clipped "close as a cucumber" at the time Mrs. Herms took him, as Mrs. Clement had been going to Europe and had not expected to sell this dog, but Mrs. Herms lost no time getting him into magnificent coat and then taking him to his title. Hostir Silver Dollar, his dam, joined Man About Town at

126

Ch. Brandywine Beau Brummel, a silver Miniature, takes five points at the 1964 Heart of America Poodle Club Specialty. Mrs. Lucienne Clement, owner.

Mrs. Herms' kennel in 1973, and she there gained a Top Producer status by becoming the dam of still another champion, Hermscrest Challenger.

Going back to Chanteclair Honey West's daughter, Champion Chanteclair Christmas Joy, this bitch bred to Tophill Silver Glint in 1969 presented Mrs. Clement with two good puppies, one of whom became her first homebred champion, Chanteclair Tale Spinner. The other,

Shown is Ch. Sonata's Joy of Chanteclair who completed the championship with three majors. Handler is Paul Edwards. Whelped 1979, by Ch. Fontenac's Florin ex Ch. Chanteclair Tale Spinner.

Chanteclair Nina Noelle, bred to Champion Brandywine's Beau Brummel, produced the beautiful Champion Chanteclair Cassandra, also purchased by Kathleen Brown, who campaigned her to her title.

Another early member of this kennel deserving of mention here was the pick of litter daughter of Champion Brandywine's Beau Brummel, Chanteclair Classi Chassis and granddam of Champion Char-K-Touch of Class. Co-owned now with Mrs. Janet Madison and bred to a double grandson of Tophill Silver Glint, she produced Champion Blue Heron Windjammer. Chanteclair Silver Belle (another of Mrs. Clement's silver bitches) when bred to her half brother, Canadian Champion Blue Heron Buc-

The Best in Show winning silver Miniature, Ch. Calvinelle Snafu, a fine representative of the Chanteclair silver Miniature Poodles.

caneer, gave Mrs. Madison Champion Blue Heron Tradewind and his litter sister who should also be a champion by now, Blue Heron So Truly Julie.

Just when the Chanteclair breeding program was beginning to show results, tragedy struck in the form of the death of Mrs. Clement's former husband, Marc Andre. It then became necessary that she curtail her breeding program and eventually part with most of her dogs. They went to wonderful breeder-friends, who took them in and gave them loving care. Tophill Silver Glint went to Mrs. Herman, where he joined his daughter, Champion Chanteclair Tale Spinner, and his granddaughter, Champion Sevarre's Chanteclair Figure. But there tragedy struck again, and Mrs. Herman passed away in 1974.

Tophill Silver Glint then went to live with Miss Susan Van Ouwerkerk (Vanwood Poodles), where he was loved and lived out his lifetime until his death in 1980 at the age of 14, leaving behind him a proud heritage.

Now that she is re-married, Mrs. Clement, whose interest has remained extremely active, is returning to the breeding of silver Miniatures and rebuilding her line. Champion Sonata's Joy of Chanteclair, who finished with four majors in six weekends during the early autumn of 1980, represents all of the beloved Chanteclair dogs wrapped up in one. Her dam is Mrs. Clement's first homebred champion, Tale Spinner. All the favorite studs are behind her, as well as the favorite dams tracing back to the foundation bitch Lu-Mar Petite Caline. As she says, though, it makes Mrs. Clement very sad that there is no Beau Brummel to breed her to! She expresses thanks to Mrs. Kathy McLaughlin, Joy's

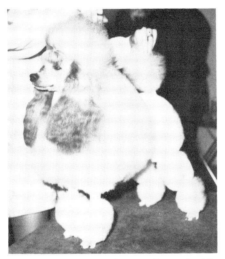

Ch. Chanteclair Cassandra at 19 months old, one of the glorious Chanteclair silver Miniatures.

breeder, for letting her own this bitch, and to Mrs. Monique Devine for all the thought behind the combination of her bloodlines.

Mrs. Clement points out the interesting fact that in the 1980 *Poodle Review* Stud Issue, which lists 18 silver Miniature studs, 13 of them stem directly from Chanteclair-bred bitches or from the champions owned by Chanteclair and their direct blood lines. Also several Miniatures from these same bloodlines are making news in the Scandinavian countries, among them International Champion Char-K-So You Like It (who finished her International Championship (Finish, Norwegian, and Swedish) under James Clark at the Stockholm International Show in November 1980) and the 18-month-old Chanteclair Twelfth of Never, a daughter of

Chanteclair Blue Heron Heir (who just picked up her first C.A.C.I.B. at the Oslo International Show).

Ch. Chanteclair Tale Spinner, a homebred from the Chanteclair silver Miniatures, was sired by Tophill Silver Glint ex Chanteclair Christmas Joy. Photographed at Monmouth County, 1972.

Cin-Don

Beverly Merritt is one of the newer Poodle breeders, but she is a very interested one who is working to establish her own line of black Miniatures and white and silver Toys with which she hopes her prefix, Cin-Don, will one day become famous in the Poodle world.

Currently there is a lovely black Miniature bitch in which Ms. Merritt takes pride, American and Canadian Champion Gregella Pay Attention, a daughter of Temar's Attention Please, and a white Toy male, American and Canadian Champion Wilmar Howlene Stone Broke, a son of the great Champion Syntifny's Piece of the Rock.

We wish this fancier great success as a future breeder.

Champion Faith's Gay Whisper of Clardon, owned by June and Dave Suttie, is handled here to a fine win by June Suttie.

The very justly famous Ch. Excalibur Bristol Cream, is the Top Winning Toy male of the past 10 years. Having been No. One Toy in 1979, he was still holding his own for that position towards the close of 1980. Owners, Dave and June Suttie. Handled by Robert Peebles.

Clardon

Clardon Kennels is owned by Dave and June Suttie and is located at Wheat Ridge, Colorado. The banner of Clardon has been carried by champions in Afghans, West Highland White Terriers, Ibizan Hounds and Poodles, but its most rewarding success has come to the Sutties through Toy Poodles.

The first of the Clardon show Toys finished his championship owner-handled and went on to become Number Eight Toy Poodle in 1975. He is Champion Faith's Gay Whisper of Clardon; this little dog is the foundation stud for the Suttie Toy Poodles.

Gay Whisper and the Sutties' foundation bitch, Clardon's Summer Snow, are from the Hilltop line, Summer being a daughter of the beautiful Champion Hilltop's Das Es Alles.

Working with the Hilltop and Durant lines to help build their own, the Sutties have been tremendously well pleased with the results both in conformation and in temperament of their little friends.

In August, 1978, the Sutties obtained their Champion Excalibur Bristol Cream to introduce into their breeding program, since he also goes back to the old Hilltop line. They are truly delighted with his show record since coming to Clardon. When the Sutties acquired him, Bristol Cream—in the three months remaining of 1978 at that time—reached the position of Number Four Toy Poodle, forging ahead to number one in 1979. With 1980 drawing to a close as this is written, he is still holding the Number One spot for his variety. This record makes Champion Excalibur Bristol Cream the Top Winning Toy Poodle *male* in the United States for the past ten years.

Bristol Cream's show record to date consists of six all-breed Bests in Show, 45 Group Firsts, and numerous additional Group placements. Interestingly, Bristol Cream is the fourth generation of Best in Show winning Toy Poodles.

The Sutties take pride, too, in their homebred Champion Clardon's Sno Foolin, a Best in Show winner, who has been giving Bristol Cream a run for it, as he was rated Number Six Toy Poodle in 1979 and was up to Number Five for the first nine months of 1980.

Although a small kennel, Clardon's owners are justifiably pleased and proud over the excellent, exciting records their dogs have attained, both in all-breed and specialty show competition. Their primary aim for the future is to continue producing sound, quality Toy Poodles that remain within the size limitations.

DaCun

William Cunningham started in dogs in 1964 with a silver Miniature Poodle he took through to a C.D. title in obedience. At that time, he and his ex-wife had also purchased a couple of black Miniature bitches to show. They did not work out as show dogs, but they did make wonderful pets. It was in 1966, when he met Bud Dickey and Ruth Sayres, that Mr. Cunningham really got his enthusiasm going for the dog show world, and he has become a highly competent professional handler and a breeder of several different breeds of dog, including, of course, his first love – Poodles.

Mr. Cunningham traveled with Bud Dickey for one year, learning everything he could. At that time Mr. Dickey was showing Champion Jocelyn Marjorie, and Mr. Cunningham soon knew that he must have a Standard. His partner, Phil Dailey, co-owner of DaCun Kennels, had to have a Standard, too, after some association with the breed, so the first two were purchased from Bud Dickey. These were a male, Dassin's Copy Boy, and a bitch. The latter did not turn out as expected, so Mr. Dickey gave DaCun Poodles a co-ownership on Champion Dassin's Black-Beri Brandy. Bill Cunningham finished her himself in four months of showing, and she became the DaCun foundation bitch.

Black-Beri Brandy was bred to Champion Dassin's Blue Chip, who produced two champions, namely Champion DaCun's Blu Mecca and Champion DaCun's Blu Mascara of Arjon. Mecca has produced five champions, these being Champion Oakview's Sweet Melody, Champion Stemo's Cocky Man of DaCun (who finished as a puppy), Champion Misty Ridges Ever Ready, Champion Brushwood Louis, and Champion Misty Ridges Hot Rocks (Number One male in 1980).

In his handling career, Mr. Cunningham first met Mr. and Mrs. Gregory T. Ross in 1971 and they became his first clients as an American Kennel Club licensed handler. Mr. Cunningham handled Champion Manorhill's Lord Lancelot for the Rosses. Lord Lancelot did well as both a show dog and a sire, having an all-champion litter to his credit.

Mr. Cunningham describes his first Best in Show win as "a great feeling." It all began with a brown Miniature bitch owned by Barbara Powers, Tenpenny Poodles. After going Winners Bitch at the Poodle Club of America from the classes (American-bred) she did the same thing at Bryn Mawr the following day.

Ch. Oakview's Sweet Melody was bred by and is handled here by William Cunningham to a Best of Opposite Sex win. From Ch. DaCun's Blu Mecca.

Ch. Manorhill's Lord Lancelot is the stunning white Miniature dog which Bill Cunningham handled for Mr. and Mrs. Gregory T. Ross, his first Poodle clients. "Lance" was the sire of an entire litter of champions, namely Manorhill's Pacesetter (a Group winner), Manorhill's Talk of Temor and Manorhill's The Gladiator.

129

Poodle Club of America

The Best in Show winning black Standard dog, Ch. Misty Ridge's Hot Rocks, is still in puppy trim as he takes Winners Dog at the Poodle Club of America Specialty, October 1978. William Cunningham handling for Harvey and Doreen Gordin of Carefree, Arizona. Photo courtesy of Mr. Cunningham.

DaCun's Starring Role O'Jamelle, William Cunningham handling, here is taking Best of Winners at the Licking River Kennel Club Dog Show, August 1980.

Champion Villa Cesca Ebony August "kept right on showing her heart out every time we walked into the ring." She became the Second Top Bitch in the United States and finished her career with Best of Opposite Sex at Westminster. Barbara Powers also sent out Champion Broughton Black Legacy, Champion Fontella's Quick Brown Fox, and Champion Vernille Son and Heir.

Bill Cunningham's next Best in Show was the weekend Ebony August retired, this time with a white Standard bitch, Champion Eaton's Filly Buster, bred by Wilmot Salisbury.

Ch. Eaton's Filly Buster, owned by Shirley Yarbrough and handled by William Cunningham, is pictured winning Best Standard Poodle at Asheville Kennel Club, 1976. Photo courtesy of Mr. Cunningham.

Some of the Toy Poodles that Mr. Cunningham mentions having enjoyed campaigning include Champion Bonjos Cajun Fiddler, owned by Dr. Joe and Bonnie Sabo, who won a Specialty Best of Breed from the puppy classes, and the black Toys owned by Jean Holly, including Champion Mannerhill's Janae of Melrose (who finished at eight months), Champion Melrose Billy Boots, and the latest star, Champion Melrose Corky. Judy Goldberg, a silver breeder, owns two of Mr. Cunningham's favorites, Champion Greylocks Ribbon Raider and Champion Greylock's Tia Maria. Judy Feinberg's Champion Arundel Unchained Melody is another whom he mentions with pride.

Others of his charges that Mr. Cunningham lists are the brown Standard finished as a puppy, Champion Mafia of Mayfield, owned by Harriet Laws; the silver Miniatures of Char-K; the black Miniatures of Gadabout (Jo Kew and Bob and Sue Burge); the Morningstar Standards (Harvey and Doreen Gordon); Misty Ridge Standards (Vince and Kathy Champa); the Keri Miniatures (Kathy Rinn Gosser); and so many more.

Bill Cunningham is fortunate in having a family that shares his enthusiasm and interest in the dogs. His oldest son, Bill, and Bill's wife, Deanne, take care of the kennel at times when Mr. Cunningham and Mr. Dailey are on circuits; his youngest son, Troy, and Troy's wife, Debbie, have co-bred and co-owned several dogs who have completed their championships.

Daktari Apogee

Daktari Apogee Poodles represent a partnership of two highly successful kennels, Daktari owned by A. Monroe McIntyre of Atlanta, Georgia, and Apogee owned by Nancy Hafner of Nashville, Tennessee.

The kennels house more than 30 champions and six top producing dogs, among them Champion Gregella Some Spellbinder, the sire of more than ten champions; his sire, Temar's Attention Please, top producing non-champion Miniature in the history of the breed, sire of 24 champions, four of which are Top Producers; the Spellbinder grandson Champion Daktari Apogee Capezio, Best of Winners at the Poodle Club of America Specialty 1979; the English import Champion Lochranza Rumbaba, Best of Winners at the Poodle Club of America Regional in 1978 and a double grandson of English Champion Lochranza Hell For Leather; and Champion Daktari Apogee Macho, a handsome apricot dog.

The producing bitches here make a very impressive list. Included among them we find Champion Aspen Adrienne, now deceased; Champion Daktari Saffron, a Best in Show winner; Champion Daktari Abraxis, a Specialty Winner; Champion Daktari Patina, Specialty Winner; Champion Daktari Apogee Nicole, Specialty Winner; Champion Daktari Passionella; Champion Daktari Apogee Chanel, Specialty Winner; Champion Daktari Apogee Cassini; International, Mexican, and F.C.I. Champion Daktari Apogee Olivia; Apogee Daktari Rebecca; and several others.

Ch. Daktari Apogee Capezio taking Best of Variety at Bryn Mawr, 1980. A truly excellent Miniature owned by Daktari Apogee Kennels, Atlanta, Georgia, and Nashville, Tennessee.

Ch. Apogee Daktari Chanel, brown Miniature, Best of Opposite Sex to Best of Variety, Poodle Club of America, 1978. Owned and bred by A. Monroe McIntyre and Nancy Hafner.

Ch. Gregella Some Spellbinder, Miniature dog, had many Best of Variety wins from the classes over specials as well as two specialty Bests of Breed. The sire of 13 champions to date. Owner, A. Monroe McIntyre. Bred by Mrs. Thomas Hancock of Gregella Kennels.

As a most promising puppy, future Ch. Daktari Apogee Aja is pictured taking Winners Bitch and Best Puppy in Show at the Washington Poodle Club Specialty.

Ch. Daktari Saffron, a brown Miniature, finished from the puppy classes, including Group First en route to the title. Now has three Group victories plus a specialty Best of Breed.

The breeding program is based on one American bloodline, Gregella, and two English bloodlines, Aspen and Lochranza. Primary aims are to produce type, balance and proportion, and useful breed structure without too much emphasis on exaggeration.

On this subject, A. Monroe McIntyre says, "The picture that we work for is that of balance and proportion. In other words, the whole picture. I have found that breeding exaggerated breed characteristics are sometimes esthetically beautiful, but when doing so interferes with usefulness of structure it becomes detrimental to the breed as a whole. Breeding for soundness without regard to breed type is also a detriment. Therefore it is a blending of breed structure to breed type and function that will determine where your priorities lie."

Line-breeding is considered a "must" at Daktari Apogee, that being the way to intensify type and stamp a look of sameness on the puppies. Consequently faults are also intensified, a factor which must be guarded against. Thus it is important that well-made dogs and bitches are selected to breed from, with a strongly line-bred background.

The McIntyre-Hafner combination takes pride in that more than 50 percent of the champions finished by Daktari Apogee have earned one or more of their majors at Poodle specialties.

Champion Aspen Adrienne was really the "grand matriarch" behind the present Daktari Apogee winners. She was imported by A. Monroe McIntyre from the Aspen Kennels of Mrs. MacKenzie-Spencer, then mated to the young English Champion Lochranza Hell for Leather, a dog described as "of balance, style, type, and presence." One bitch from this litter was kept, Daktari Aspen Eugenie.

For her next litter, Adrienne was bred to Champion Gregella Some Spellbinder, a dog that along with his sire, Temar's Attention Please, is now with Nancy Hafner at Apogee. This produced Champion Daktari Saffron and Champion Daktari Passionella. The latter, in her first litter by Champion Gregella Copyright Caliber, is the dam of the brown Champion Daktari Apogee Chanel, Champion Daktari Apogee Cassini, and Champion Daktari Apogee Olivia.

A third bitch from the Spellbinder-Adrienne litter is producing well for Peg Dougherty of Shamrock Poodles.

It is along these lines, from the descendants of these early litters, that Daktari Apogee is producing its finest winners today.

Danleri

Danleri is a very distinguished kennel specializing in black Miniatures. It is owned by Barbara Ireland and is located at Mobile, Alabama.

It was while living in Scotland that Barbara Ireland first was attracted to the breed, and before leaving that country she had purchased for her family a black Miniature who quickly succeeded in making her an ardent enthusiast for Poodles.

Immediately upon having become settled back home in the United States, Barbara started regularly attending dog shows, studying Poodles, familiarizing herself with the different bloodlines, and generally learning everything she could about them. Her first love, black Miniatures, still held, so eventually a call was made to the Aizbel Kennels with the hope of purchasing an excellent one on which to found her kennel.

Aizbel The Imperialist was purchased at seven and a half months of age, turning out as he matured to be everything for which Barbara had sought. At the time of writing he has sired 13 American champions and has indeed become the foundation stud on which the Danleri breeding program has prospered. Currently he has been introduced into the English Hell for Leather line with most pleasing results, producing dogs with type, size, elegance, and refinement.

Among the famous winners already sired by Champion Aizbel The Imperialist are the exquisite multiple Best in Show and Specialty winning bitch Champion Merrimar Queen of the

Above Left: Ch. Daktari Asia taking Best of Opposite Sex at the Great Lakes Poodle Club of Chicago Specialty, 1977. A. Monroe McIntyre, owner. **Above Right:** We love this headstudy of the black Miniature dog, Ch. Danleri's Imperial Wizard, an all-breed Best in Show winner, a specialty Best of Breed and Best Miniature at the Poodle Club of America California Regional. Owned by Barbara Ireland, Mobile, Alabama. **Below:** Ch. Danleri's Afternoon Delight, winning a specialty Best of Breed. A black Miniature, daughter of Ch. Aizbel The Imperialist.

Nile, with which Pat Norwood has done so well for Mrs. Ball. Also Champion Danleri's The Imperial Wizard, an all-breed and specialty Best in Show dog, is a son of his that won the Miniature Variety at the Poodle Club of America Regional in California. Others of his noted progeny include Champion Penchant Paladin (a multiple specialty Best of Breed dog) and Champion Merrimar's Athena and Champion Danleri's Afternoon Delight, both specialty Best of Breed winners.

Dassin

Nowadays when one hears the kennel prefix Dassin the immediate mental association is of magnificent black Standards. Originally, however, it was the whites that had attracted Freeman C. (Bud) Dickey to the breed, and the first Poodle he owned was of this color. Champion Tout D'Argent Fair Fancy by name, she was bred only once and produced five champions in this litter sired by Champion Hallmark Harmony of Windridge.

Soon Mr. Dickey discovered that he really preferred the black Poodle type. Thus it came about that a lovely black bitch was purchased from the Kingsleys' Annveron Kennels. Her name was Annveron Bacardi Peach. Purchased as a puppy, she completed her title in short order under Mr. Dickey's ownership.

Ch. Dassin Butch Cassidy, a splendid homebred from Dassin Farm. Freeman C. Dickey and Joseph P. Vergnetti, Medina, Ohio, owners. Son of Ch. Jocelyene Marjorie.

Ch. Merrimar Athena of Calypso, black Miniature, owned by Virginia and Bill Davis and Bee W. Bassen. Daughter of Ch. Aizbel The Imperialist ex Singing Sheba.

Around this same period, Bud Dickey saw, and lost his heart to, a gorgeous blue bitch named Jocelyene Marjorie. She belonged to a good friend of his, and by the time he had finished persuading her to let him have Marjorie, she had done so and Marjorie was in co-ownership. This lady, Joan Schilke, and Bud owned Marjorie together until Marjorie died in 1979.

Thus the foundation was prepared for future generations of Dassin Poodles. Bud Dickey's plans were to establish a family of dogs by crossing the lines of these two bitches, which perfectly complemented one another. Bacardi Peach was the first to be bred, since Marjorie was to become the show girl.

Champion Wycliffe Thomas was the sire selected for Bacardi Peach's first litter. Among the offspring was the Top Producer Dassin Doubting Thomas. When Bacardi Peach was bred the second time it was to Marjorie's sire, Champion Wycliffe Virgil. This produced the Top Producer black dog named Dassin Daktari, owned by Joan Schilke, and the Best in Show winning black Champion Dassin Kissable of Cardon, who gained this honor under Henry Stoecker.

Bacardi Peach next was bred to Champion Carbon Copy of Bushyrun, by whom she produced Champion Dassin Flitwick Frisco. Then came her last litter, for which she was bred to the black Best in Show winner Champion Winshire's Country Gentleman. From this breeding came Dassin Ruby Begonia and Champion Dassin Lil White Dove. Ruby became the backbone of all the present Dassin Poodles of today. She was destined never to become a cham-

Ch. Dassin Blue Tango of Chalmar winning Best in Show at Pontiac Kennel Club, 1973.

pion due to commitments to clients' dogs. Her contribution to the breed, nevertheless, has made her one of the "greats" in modern Poodle history. On one of her few ring appearances she took Best Puppy in Show at a Poodle Club of America Specialty under Mrs. George Putnam.

Champion Jocelyene Marjorie also won a Best Puppy in Show at Poodle Club of America, in her case from Mrs. Rebecca Mason, and Reserve Winners Bitch in the specialty that same year under Miss Kathleen Staples. She went on to a brilliant show career, being a multiple Best in Show and Group winner; she was also Best of Breed at the Poodle Club of America National Specialty under judge Frances Angela.

It was not until Marjorie was five years old that she was bred, for the first time, to Dassin Doubting Thomas, Ch. Wycliffe Thomas' son from Bacardi Peach. So outstanding were the results that the breeding was repeated for a second litter. The two combined to produce ten champions, one of them the multi (18 times) all-breed Best in Show bitch Champion Dassin Blue Tango O'Chalmar, who had a Best of Breed from the Poodle Club of America Specialty when judged by Francis Fretwell and Mrs. George Dow.

Then Marjorie was bred to the black Best in Show winner Champion Winshire's Country Gentleman. She produced five more champions from this litter. Among the latter are the famous top producing brothers Champion Dassin Broadway Joe, Champion Dassin Sum Buddy, and Champion Dassin Debauchery.

Sum Buddy and Debauchery were multiple Best in Show and specialty winners. Sum Buddy has a Westminster Best of Breed, plus Best of

Breed at a Poodle Club of America Regional in California under judges Mrs. Winifred Heckmann and Mrs. Lauer J. Froelich. Debauchery was Best of Variety at the Poodle Club of America National under Mrs. Jean Lyle. A litter sister, Champion Dassin Sashtie, was also Best of Variety at a Poodle Club of America National under William Kendrick. This litter also contained the Best in Show bitch Champion Dassin Devastation. Champion Dassin Debauchery is now the confirmed sire of 70 American champions.

Ch. Dassin Devastation takes Best in Show at the Progressive Dog Club of Wayne County, 1973.

This is the exquisite Top Producing Standard bitch behind so much of the Dassin Farm quality. Ch. Jocelyene Marjorie, dam of numerous Poodle "greats" including Ch. Dassin Broadway Joe (sire of more than 29 champions) and Ch. Dassin Sum Buddy (sire of more than 20 champions).

136

The magnificent Ch. Dassin Sum Buddy, famous winner and sire of more than 20 champions. Owner-handler, Freeman C. "Bud" Dickey.

Ch. Dassin's Blue Chip, another famous son of Ch. Jocelyene Marjorie, belongs to H. and R. Gordin, Pepper Pike, Ohio.

This splendid Standard is Ch. Dassin's Black Thorn, and she is yet another daughter of Ch. Jocelyene Marjorie. Black Thorn is owned by Shirley Walker, Ravenna, Ohio. Bred and handled by F. C. Dickey.

Ch. Dassin Sashtie en route to her title, handled by F. C. Dickey. Daughter of Ch. Jocelyene Marjorie.

Ch. Dassin Busby Berkley, pictured winning Best of Variety en route to first in the Non-Sporting Group at Staten Island Kennel Club. Mrs. Edward L. Solomon, Jr., Pittsburgh, Pennsylvania, owner.

Ch. Dassin Rose Royce, by Ch. Dassin Broadway Joe from the white bitch, Wiljan Akahai Wahine. Bred by Joseph Vergnetti, handled here by F. C. Dickey.

Ch. Dassin Soul Sister, a Six Pac daughter, taking Best of Opposite Sex.

Ch. Dassin Debussy, black Standard dog, winning Best of Variety at Poodle Club of America. Joseph Vergnetti, handling.

Ch. Dassin Blue With Envy, still another son of Ch. Jocelyene Marjorie.

Ch. Dassin Busby Berkley, one of the excellent Standards, handled by F. C. Dickey for Mrs. Edward L. Solomon, Jr.

Another Dassin winner, Ch. Dassin Rhett Butler.

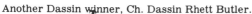

Champion De Russy Nicromancer was the next stud selected for Marjorie. This litter added three more titled offspring to her credit, Champion Dassin Plain Talk, Champion Dassin Six Pac, and Champion Dassin Spartecus.

Carrying on in the family tradition, Champion Dassin Six Pac has produced nine champions to date. Bred to her half brother, Champion Dassin Broadway Joe, she had two that gained titles, with another two when she was bred to Champion Dassin Sum Buddy. Then she was bred to Champion Dassin Debussy, with five more champions the result.

Six Pac and Broadway Joe's litter contained Champion Dassin Soul Sister and Champion Dassin Anheuser Busch. Soul Sister, in her turn, is the dam of the Best in Show winning Champion Candida Soul Music at Delyn and the Group winning Champion Dassin de Cucina. Six Pac and Sum Buddy's litter included Champion Dassin Sum Evidence of Slaton and Champion Dassin Sum Witch of Devone.

And by Debussy she really hit the jackpot, as in that litter Six Pac produced the exquisite Best in Show and specialty winning bitch Champion Dassin Rita La Rose, with many Groups, multiple Bests in Show, and two Poodle Club of

America Specialties to her credit. The latter were the Regional in California, under Mrs. Harriett Laws and Mrs. U.D.E. Walden, and the National in Pennsylvania, under Mrs. Jesse Mason and Mr. Peter Frederico. Also included in this litter are Champion Dassin Busby Berkley (a Group and Specialty winner), Champion Dassin Dancing Daffodil, Champion Dassin Rhett Butler, and Champion Dassin Razzle Dazzle.

Dassin Ruby Begonia (from one of the two foundation bitches, Champion Annveron Bacardi Peach by Champion Winshire's Country Gentleman) has given Dassin Farms its magnificent black Best in Show and specialty winner, Champion Dassin Debussy, who was sired by Champion Dassin Broadway Joe. Debussy was Best of Variety in puppy clip at the Poodle Club of America Regional in Oklahoma under Mrs. Alfred Barrett, then Best of Variety at the Alabama Regional under Dr. Samuel Peacock. He was also Best of Variety at the National under Henry Stoecker. To date, ten of his progeny have finished, with a number more on the way, and his daughter, Champion Dassin Rita La Rose, is making history in Poodle and Best in Show rings for Mrs. Edward Solomon.

Bred a second time to Broadway Joe, Ruby produced the black champion dog named Dassin Dallas. He is young at this point, but hopes are high for his success in the future. Ruby was also bred to Champion Dassin Sum Buddy and produced a white champion bitch, Dassin Daisy Gatsby, who is the dam of two white champions, Dassin Marmolade of Valcopy and Dassin Disco Fever.

Joseph Vergnetti, Bud Dickey's partner in the Dassin Farm Poodles, mentions that Champion Dassin Debussy produces whites. Joseph says, "Hope someday we can produce a white strain from Debussy that will resemble his type and quality. Because I feel that Debussy is the greatest one I've seen, and here at Dassin we have the model of what we consider the correct type of Poodle in Champion Dassin Debussy." Again in deference to the clients' dogs, Debussy, belonging to Mr. Dickey and Mr. Vergnetti, has not been very extensively campaigned, retiring after a short but exciting career.

As of May, 1980, according to the Poodle Club of America listings, Champion Dassin Debauchery is the Top Living Standard Poodle Sire in America, with Champion Dassin Broadway Joe and Champion Dassin Sum Buddy in sixth place and seventh place respectively. What more eloquent comment can we make than this

fact except to add that the champion progeny of these three dogs alone adds up to more than one hundred, without even mentioning those of the younger dogs, the lists for which have been increasing steadily.

Both Bud Dickey and Joseph Vergnetti are dedicated Poodle breeders with considerable talent going for them, judging by the records.

Davaroc

The Davaroc Standard Poodles began in 1954 with the acquisition of a puppy bitch bred by Dr. Samuel Peacock's cousin, Mrs. Tell Schrieber, out of her Best in Show bitch, Champion Fanfaron Lorelei, bred to Fanfaron Pinochio. She was to become Champion Calypso's Miss Timba and the foundation bitch at Davaroc.

Bred to Champion Bel Tor Gigadibs, Miss Timba produced the Group winning bitch Champion Davaroc Star Saphire, Champion Davaroc Careless Love, Davaroc Jolie of Valhalla (retired with fourteen points including her two "majors"), and a very glamorous cream bitch, Davaroc High and Mighty. The latter hated dog shows, but bred to Dr. Peacock's white dog, Champion Ivardon North Star, produced the cream bitch Champion Davaroc Apry. Bred a second time, on this occasion to Champion Jacques Le Noir of Belle Glen, Timba tragically lost her life whelping the litter and only one puppy was saved. This was a black bitch, Davaroc Miss Timba's Stardust, that bred to a Timba grandson, Davaroc King Richard II (Champion Davaroc Star Saphire ex Bel Tor Salad Days), produced Champion Davaroc Vanessa and Davaroc Lucinda.

Lucinda, bred in turn to Champion Bel Tor All The Trimmings, produced Champion Davaroc Harrison and Davaroc Jennifer. The latter bred to Champion Rimskittle Right On produced Davaroc My Dream Come True who bred to her grandsire, Champion Bel Tor Big Picture, produced the Group winning puppy Champion Davaroc J. Kelly Murphy.

In 1974 the marriage of Dr. Peacock and Mrs. Peacock brought to Davaroc the top winning bitch Champion Bel Tor Blissful, acquired two years earlier by Mrs. Peacock from Mrs. J. A. Mason. Blissful was retired in 1977, having won her one hundredth Best of Variety and eighth Best in Show while four weeks in whelp to the brown dog Bel Tor Don't Tread On Me. This dog sadly died at four years of age, needing just one point to finish. The breeding produced a black bitch, Champion Davaroc A Bit of Bliss, and the exquisite brown, Champion Davaroc Bronzed Bliss, U.D.T.

Bred to Champion Dassin Broadway Joe, Blissful produced three Group winning daughters, Champion Davaroc Dazzler, Champion Davaroc Devastation, and Champion Davaroc Disarming, plus a son, Champion Davaroc Desperado. The future of the Davaroc Poodles lies in the subsequent puppies of these "Blissful" offspring.

Dhubne

Although the "doggie" roots at Dhubne Poodles are short in terms of breeding and showing, its owners, John and Elizabeth Campbell, both are from families that always had and loved dogs, and they themselves have followed in the same pattern. When they first were married, two Boxers over a period of years were well-loved pets. When this couple became seriously interested in showing in obedience, their instructor suggested a Poodle. That was the beginning, in 1961, of what has become a deep love of the breed that shows no sign of ever waning.

The Campbells' first Miniature Poodle had the distinction of receiving the first leg on his C.D. degree the same day that he was measured out of the senior puppy class. He completed his obedience title, at the same time whetting his owners' appetite for something to show in the conformation classes. Their first and only Miniature Poodle champion was finished for the Campbells by Mike Shea with a Group 1 from the Open Bitch Class. Unfortunately, she had Progressive Retinal Atrophy and was a half sister to their other two foundation bitches, so Dhubne found itself without a Miniature Poodle breeding program.

About the same time that the Miniature Poodle bitch came to the Campbells, they also acquired their first Standard Poodle, who was to become the Top Producing Champion Wycliffe Martin. Martin was finished by Frank Sabella and specialed only a few times. He totally shifted his owners' interest from Miniature Poodles to Standard Poodles, and to his death at age 11 following surgery for bladder stones, Martin was "king of the hill" at Dhubne. Martin produced well in his limited use at stud. His 16 litters contained 108 pups, which included champions in Canada, Germany, and Holland, as well as in this country, for a total of 22.

Ch. Cade Uhuru, a fine representative of the Dhubne Poodles, is seen here with a Best of Variety win. Owners John and Elizabeth Campbell, Bonita, California. Sire, Ch. Coqan Baccarat. Dam, Ch. Wentworth Bonnie, C.D.

Ch. Wycliffe Martin, the start of the Blacknight-Dhubne Standards. Pictured with Frank Sabella winning his first points at 15 months. Finished at 18 months in nine shows. Top Producer. Genetically a very safe animal. Owned by John Campbell.

Ch. Levade's Audacity, the dam of two American and two Canadian champions, including the Best in Show winning puppy, Can. Ch. Dhubne Candid Cameron, Am. and Can. C.D. Co-owned by A. Reis and Elizabeth Campbell.

Above: A star of the future, Eve Jay You Asked For It, the new brown boy at Dhubne Poodles. **Below:** Ch. Cade Freiheit, a Baccarat son, described by Elizabeth Campbell, Dhubne owner, as "my favorite dog."

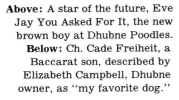
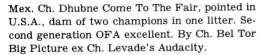

Mex. Ch. Dhubne Come To The Fair, pointed in U.S.A., dam of two champions in one litter. Second generation OFA excellent. By Ch. Bel Tor Big Picture ex Ch. Levade's Audacity.

Both the Dhubne cream and black lines go back to Martin. The Campbells prefer the blacks and have kept only that color for themselves. However, many of Martin's cream offspring have produced well, including the Top Producer Champion Heather of Blacknight, owned until her death by Frank and Laura Dale of Holyoke Poodles. In Heather's two litters, she was the dam of several Best in Show winners, including the black Champion Holyoke Hensley (by Champion Coqan Baccarat) and Champion Star Spangled Debutante (by Champion Acadia Command Performance). Martin was also the sire of the Best in Show winning cream dog Champion Bellepointe Blacknight Joey. Dhubne is proud of the cream family and follows its development with interest.

Ch. Cogan Baccarat, photo courtesy of Dhubne Poodles, John and Elizabeth Campbell.

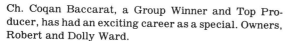

Ch. Coqan Baccarat, a Group Winner and Top Producer, has had an exciting career as a special. Owners, Robert and Dolly Ward.

"We have found that it is fairly easy to breed beautiful Poodles. It is much harder to be sure that their beauty is more than skin deep," to quote Elizabeth Campbell. To this end, Dhubne uses only OFA certified, clear-eyed, non-convulsive stock for breeding. The black line is being concentrated on, along with a new interest here, brown Standard Poodles, as they find the brown color fascinating and the brown temperament delightful. It is hoped that the "brown clowns" will work out well with the Dhubne blacks.

Having an interest in all breeds of dog, the Campbells tell us of their two Greyhounds and the recent acquisition of a delightful English Cocker Spaniel puppy. But this is no threat to Poodle supremacy at Dhubne, for the challenge and the primary interest lies with the Poodles. A Miniature puppy has been added lately, a return to this variety after many years.

The Campbells have been privileged to have a part of several influential producers and show dogs. Included are their foundation bitch, Wycliffe Rowena of Highlane, the dam of ten champions; Champion Wycliffe Martin, as previously mentioned, the Top Producer sire of 22 champions; Best of Breed and Group winning Champion Coqan Baccarat, sire of 12 champions; the cream Best of Breed and Best in Show winner Champion Bellepointe Blacknight Joey; the black Best in Show winners Champion Blacknight Power Play and Champion York of Blacknight; Canadian Champion Dhubne Candid Camera, Canadian and American C.D., owner-handled to Best in Show from the puppy class; Champion Holyoke Hensley; the black Best of Breed winning bitch from the Open Class, Champion Dhubne Bright Thing; the black dog Champion Dhubne Robin Goodfellow, sire of four champions to date; and the multiple Best of Breed and Group winning Champion Dhubne Darth Vader, owned by Carroll Ann Irwin, currently being specialed. While at home at Dhubne the Campbells have the black Martin son Champion Dhubne Robert the Bruce, sire of three champions including a Best of Breed winning daughter, Champion Stygian's Anabel Lee O'Raven, owner-handled to her win from the Open Bitch class. There is high confidence that Robin, Robert, and Darth Vader will make their mark on the breed through the siring of outstanding progeny.

The Campbells began breeding with the kennel prefix Blacknight in honor of their first Miniature Poodle, Cresthaven's Black Knight, C.D., but after the sale of the kennel business that went under the Blacknight name they continued their breeding program with the registered prefix Dhubne, which has become so highly respected wherever Standard Poodles are known. The basic goal at Dhubne is not mere numbers of champions nor of top winning dogs. While the Campbells love it when their dogs do achieve these honors, they are principally concerned with producing sound, typey Poodles with super temperament that will be a joy to their owners and families for all of a very long life.

Ch. Dhubne Robin Goodfellow with Barbara Humphries at one of his first shows. Son of Ch. Wycliffe Martin.

A beautiful Standard Poodle puppy, Blacknight Jeremiah receives the Winners Dog award at the Antelope Valley Kennel Club Dog Show, December 1967. Owned by John and Elizabeth Campbell and handled by Frank Sabella.

Ch. Dhubne Robin Goodfellow, a handsome Standard, is a Specialty Show and Group winner. Janet Cook, owner.

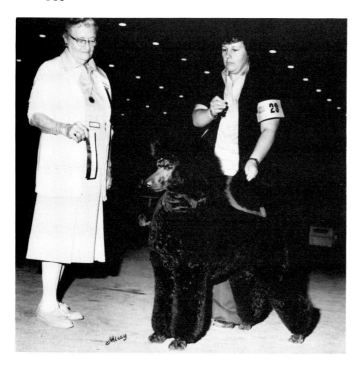

Above Left: Ch. Dhubne King of the Road, an owner-handled Variety winner from the classes. Owned by Leslie Ford. **Left:** Ch. Dhubne Robert The Bruce, sire of several champions. He is a splendid example of how a top quality Standard looks clipped down. **Below left:** Ch. Dhubne Darth Vader, a black Standard, going Best of Breed at the Poodle Specialty Club of British Columbia. Darth became an American and Canadian champion by taking four consecutive shows. Owner, Carroll Ann Irwin, North Hollywood, California.

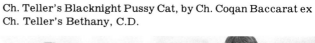

Ch. Teller's Blacknight Pussy Cat, by Ch. Coqan Baccarat ex Ch. Teller's Bethany, C.D.

Am. and Can. Ch. Evanz Lord Happiness Is, the current sire of 25 champions. The owner is Marilyn Pauley, Saline, Michigan.

An Anita McMullen portrait of Ch. Evanz Evening Edition.

Evanz

Evanz Poodles, owned by Marilyn Pauley and located at Saline, Michigan, truly has many exciting records to which they can point with pride. For example, more than 60 of their animals have completed more than 100 championships, and that is a formidable total indeed!

Eleven of the above are International (F.C.I.) Champions, two of which are the only Toy Poodles bred and owned in the United States to hold World Championships. These are a white Toy male, American, Canadian, Mexican, International, and 1978 World Champion Evanz Evening Edition, and a black Toy female, American, Canadian, Mexican, International, and 1978 World Champion Evanz Nuclear Power.

American, Canadian, Mexican, Bermudian, and International Champion Evanz Daring Debutante, a silver Toy female, was the Top Winning Toy Poodle in Canada for 1979. She is a multiple Best in Show winner and was as well the Number Eight Toy Poodle in the United States for '79. While there are no official statistics to be found, Mrs. Pauley believes her also to be the Number One Toy Poodle in Bermuda for that same year.

Top Producers are quite the "order of the day" at Evanz Kennels. In dogs, American and Canadian Champion Evan's Lord Happiness Is, a

Can. and Mex. Ch. Evanz Silver Jubilee, silver Toy male. This tiny dog measures about nine and a half inches.

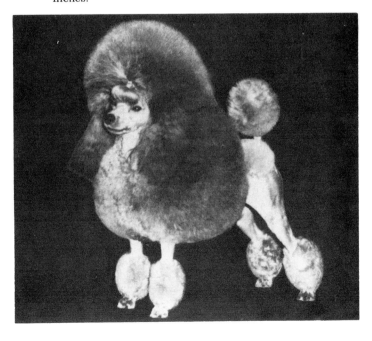

Evanz Double Dealer, by Ch. Lord Happiness Is, is close to championship honors.

Can. Ch. Evanz April Love, owner-handled by Marilyn Pauley. This white Toy female has some good wins to her credit in both the United States and Canada.

silver Toy, now has 25 champions to his credit. Canadian Champion Evanz Sparkling Scimitar and Champion Evanz Simple Simon of Farobs, both silver Toys, have five each. American, Canadian, Mexican, Bermudian, and International Champion Evanz Anchor Man, a white Toy, has six that have finished. American, Canadian, Mexican, International, and 1978 World Champion Evanz Evening Edition, a white Toy, is another with five.

On the distaff side, the silver beige Canadian Obedience Trial Champion Evan's Sassi Minyonnette, American, Canadian, and Bermudian Utility Dog, Mexican P.C.E. (comparable to C.D.X.), is the dam of four champions, as is the white La Joie's Snow Crystal. Evanz Puffenz Pooed D'Naer, silver, is the dam of six champions, and the silver Evanz Tania has three.

Evanz Poodles concentrates primarily on silver, silver beige, and white. Many highly respected names are to be found in the

background of these dogs. For example, Lord Happiness goes back to Champion Thornlea Silver Souvenir on his sire's side, being a grandson of Champion Silver Sparkle of Sassafras. Evening Edition is strong in Sassafras breeding on his dam's side and goes back to Champion Meridian Momentum on his sire's.

Mrs. Pauley has established well her Evanz strain and now has several generations of her own breeding representing her talents in this respect.

Am. and Can. Ch. Evanz Lord Happiness Is, silver Toy male, as a youngster winning his second major at Wheaton, Illinois, 1974.

Informal photo of Bragabout the Chips are Down, silver Toy male. Assumed to be the last Satire son, this young dog has points in both the U.S. and Canada as this is written. Owned by Nancy Dorman and Marilyn Pauley.

Am., Can., Mex., Int. 1978 World Ch. Evanz Nuclear Power, a black Toy female.

Can. Ch. Evanz Sparkling Scimitar winning the Group from the classes. Scimitar finished with three four-point majors, and is a Top Producer.

A lovely "yard shot" by Edward Pauley of Am., Can., Mex., Int. and 1978 World Ch. Evanz Evening Edition. He is currently the sire of five champions with several more close to their titles.

Can. and Mex. Ch. Evanz Sentinal, C.A.C.I.B., silver Toy male, shown taking a major and the Variety in Monroe, Michigan.

Mex. and Int. Ch. Evanz Princess Leia, silver Toy female, shown completing her dual title in four consecutive shows undefeated in her sex.

Can. Ch. Evanz Twist 'N' Twirl, a Group Winner from the classes.

Can. Ch. Evanz Dixie Daisy shown taking Best of Variety as a puppy in 1973.

Bragabout Ante Up doing some of her good puppy winning. "Annie" gained six points in six weekends of puppy showing. She is owned by Nancy Dorman of Orange, Texas (Dawnz Poodles) and Marilyn Pauley, Saline, Michigan (Evanz Poodles). A truly lovely puppy who seems to possess the potential for an exciting future.

Am., Can., Mex., Int., 1978 World Ch. Evanz Evening Edition, completing his International title in Mexico, 1978.

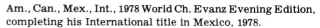

Can. Ch. Evanz Mama Cass O'Lakay, silver-beige Miniature bitch, finishing her title in three weekends with Best of Variety wins from the classes over Best in Show "specials."

Ch. Evanz Anchor Man winning a major en route to winning the Variety and a Group placement.

Am., Can., Mex., Bda. and Int. Ch. Evanz Daring Debutante winning the Group at Forest City Kennel Club, 1979.

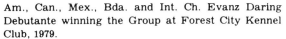

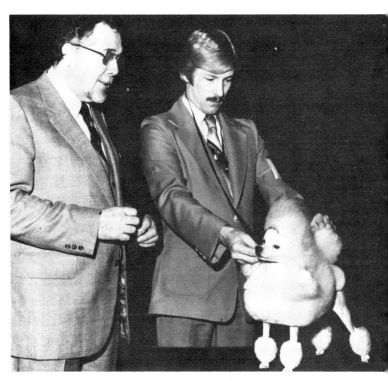

Can. Ch. Evanz City Editor, white Toy male, photographed in Seattle, Washington, where he was Winners Dog.

The very famous Toy bitch, Ch. J. C. Fabulous Fanny, owned by Mrs. A. C. Pearson, Locust Valley, New York.

Ch. Prihim Bobby.

This is Ch. J. C. Fabulous Fanny going Best in Show in 1965. Another fine winning Toy belonging to Mr. and Mrs. A. C. Pearson.

Florian

Florian Poodles belongs to Mrs. A. C. Pearson and is located at Locust Valley, New York. Mrs. Pearson prefers the Toys to the other Poodle Varieties on several counts, and they have a great deal of appeal for her.

Mrs. Pearson says that actually she should not be written about as a successful breeder, as she was not to any extent. She did have the good fortune, however, to purchase some outstanding Toys which have been a source of real pleasure through the years.

Champion J. C. Fabulous Fanny was handled to a long list of exciting wins by Anne Hone Rogers. Unfortunately she was never able to conceive owing to leukemia and died at only four years old, a sad blow indeed to her owner.

Champion Montmartre Marlaine was imported as a puppy from England. Mrs. Pearson first saw her in the Toy Group at Greenwich Kennel Club in 1967 and was reminded so strongly of her late beloved Fabulous Fanny that her immediate reaction was to try to negotiate her purchase. Richard Bauer, Marlaine's handler, succeeded in bringing this about and soon was continuing to campaign Marlaine, but now for Mrs. Pearson under the Florian banner. Marlaine lived to be a good age of 14 years and during her career in the ring accounted for a total of five times Best in Show, two specialty Bests of Breed, 22 Toy Group Firsts, and 70 times Best of Variety.

Champion Chrystal Silver Typhoon, a silver dog, is another to have represented Florian in the Poodle world, and there also was Champion Prihim Bobby, a little fellow of lovely type.

Currently the Florian banner is being carried high by a widely admired sparkling white Toy dog, Champion Hell's A Blazen Fagin's Pride. He is a son of Champion Hell's A Blazen Kinda Kostly from Hell's A Blazen Yes, Yes, and was bred by Frances Rubinich. Mrs. Pearson purchased him at nine and a half months old. He was whelped on December 11, 1976 and has certainly proved Mrs. Pearson's choice to have been a good one. His record, under Richard Bauer's capable handling, now includes Bests in Show and numerous Group honors.

Above Left: Ch. Montmartre Marlaine winning Best in Show, Wallkill, New York, July 1968. Owned by Mr. and Mrs. A. C. Pearson, handled by Richard L. Bauer. **Center:** A Florian Toy puppy that should have finished his championship with ease except for an accident in which the tent was blown down during a violent thunderstorm at an outdoor dog show. Owner, Joyce Peeples. **Below Left:** The leading English imported Best in Show Toy bitch, Ch. Montmartre Marlaine, taking Best in Show at the Putnam Kennel Club, 1968. **Above:** Ch. J. C. Fabulous Fanny, a Toy bitch, going Best of Show at Columbia Kennel Club, 1965. Handled by Richard L. Bauer for Mr. and Mrs. A. C. Pearson.

152

Ch. Freeland's Hi Fi, at seven years old, brings greetings of Christmas 1962. Owner, Monique Devine.

with this dog and instead persuaded Mrs. Devine to take a ten-month-old puppy silver bitch, Freeland's Fair Weather, sired by Champion Freeland's Gone With The Wind (a Flashlight son) out of Merry, a daughter of Champion Hollycourt Vaillant. Thus Monique Devine's silver Miniatures were the result of a marriage between Hollycourt on the dam's side and English breeding on the sire's. This bitch was the foundation for Monique Devine's Ohio branch of the Freeland Kennel. Fair weather was bred to Hi-Fi and produced the well-known Freeland's Fenelon. Although never campaigned, Fenelon sired many quality puppies. He measured 13 inches tall, was short-backed, and had a beautiful eye and expression plus an extremely dense coat. He proved himself a valuable stud dog as he appears in the pedigrees of silvers being currently shown.

Freeland

The Freeland prefix was registered with the American Kennel Club on January 17, 1929 by Mrs. Mildred Vogel Imrie, who throughout the 1930's was highly influential as a breeder of quality Cocker Spaniels.

It was quite a few years later that the silver Miniature Poodles came into being there, with the acquisition of the foundation bitch Meridick Diana, who was bred to the English import Fircot Silvafuzz of Summercourt. From this litter came the first of Mildred Imrie's homebred silver winners, Champion Freeland's Hi-Fi, born in 1955, who lived to the ripe old age of 15 years. A repeat breeding the next year produced Champion Freeland's Flashlight (1956–1972), who was judged Best Miniature and then went on to Best of Opposite Sex to Best in Show at the Poodle Club of America Specialty in June, 1961. A Top Producer, this dog's name appears in most silver Miniature pedigrees of the present day.

It was in October, 1958, that Monique Devine first saw Freeland's Hi-Fi at the Delaware, Ohio show. He certainly kindled the flame of an enthusiast. That very moment she decided she must have him (even before he had won the Non-Sporting Group that day), and, speaking with his handler, she made her admiration of the dog known. His owner, however, refused to part

Happy New Year! Freeland's Fenelon, silver Miniature male, 1964-1978, was sired by Ch. Freeland's Hi Fi ex Freeland's Fair Weather. Bred and owned by Monique Devine.

From 1959 to 1978, Monique Devine bred silver Miniatures in conjunction with Mildred Vogel Imrie, and her Poodles were also registered under the Freeland prefix. Due to retirement, Mildred Imrie transferred her kennel name to Monique Devine on July 14th 1978.

In 1967, Freeland's Finesse (1960 - 1978) came to Columbus to Mrs. Devine. She was the dam of the Top Producer Frankie of Freeland and of the also well-known sires Freeland's Flashaway and Freeland's Flashback and the bitch Freeland's Fille de Joie (11 inches). These were all of platinum color with harsh coat texture and extremely pleasing to the eye.

In the 1970's the need was felt to introduce a new bloodline, so to rekindle the silver Miniatures both Champion Chanteclair Tale Spinner and Champion Sevarre's Chanteclair arrived at Freeland in Ohio in 1975. These two bitches proved themselves not only in the show ring but as producers. It was a complete renovation. Newly acquired bloodlines plus the combination of the original Freeland sires would certainly have beneficial influence on a breeding program, which is exactly how it worked out. The renowned platinum bitch Champion Sevarre's Chanteclair Figure, by Champion Calvinelle Snafu ex Chanteclair Sevarre's New Hope, was bred to Freeland's Fenello, from whom came Freeland's Fairytale (an American and Canadian C.D.) and Freeland's Felicitee, both of whom gained points in conformation competition. Next, Figure was bred to Champion Kimbeney Clipper Boy, a noted sire and grandson of Flashlight, and this time she produced the silver dog Champion Fontenac's Florin. Then she was bred to Champion Manorhill's Classic Touch, from which mating two Poodles presently earning points toward championship were the result, Freeland's Felicia and Freeland's Fernandel.

Combining Chanteclair, Tophill, and Freeland bloodlines in silver has proved gratifyingly successful. Still a very young dog, Champion Fontenac's Florin has distinghished himself by producing type and soundness. A Best of Variety winner, he is the sire of Champion Sonata Joy of Chanteclair, Freeland's Feelings (pointed), and Freeland's Frivole (also pointed), the last two being currently shown. He also sired Freeland's Florine de Sonata (currently in competition), Freeland's Fretwell D'Manorhill, and numerous

Ch. Freeland's Hi Fi, 1955-1971, was bred by Mildred Imrie, New Hope, Pennsylvania.

Ch. Freeland's Flashlight, silver Miniature male, 1956-1972. Bred and owned by Mildred Imrie.

Freeland's Fair Weather, 1959-1967, was Monique Devine's foundation bitch.

Ch. Fontenac's Florin, a silver Miniature male by Ch. Kimbeney Clipper Boy ex Ch. Sevarre's Chanteclair Figure.

Ch. Freeland's Girl Friday, a blue Miniature female owned by Monique Devine, Columbus, Ohio. Photo in Atlanta, Georgia, 1971.

others being readied for competition. Also residing at Freeland Kennels is the three-year-old Fontenac's Falaise, sired by Champion Hauxhurst The Flyer ex Champion Chanteclair Tale Spinner. She was shown and is now doing maternal duties.

The Freeland puppies always have been raised with children, and after the children have grown up, with grandchildren. Intelligence and temperament have shared equally with beauty in Mrs. Devine's breeding plans, as indeed should be the case.

Monique Devine has always acknowledged that one of her good fortunes in life was that of meeting Mildred Imrie, who "adopted" her Poodles and to whom she refers as "mother." Also, she gives much credit to the realization of her ambitions for her silver Miniatures to Joseph Vergnetti who, through his "expertise, handling and instant rapport" has spelled success for this project.

Mrs. Devine makes the following comment: "Considering all the changes in silvers, particularly during the past five years, it seems only natural that the silver Miniature will be viewed again as an excellent specimen of the breed. It is important that we understand the genetics, establish a breeding program, and keep abreast of changes. Introducing another color into silver *is not the answer*. Excellent specimens must be selected as foundation. The success of any breeding program strategy rests on the ability of the breeders who develop and carry out that strategy. Of course, while the whole world is changing, the art and science of breeding better silvers is not standing still. There are more and more silver Miniatures in the show ring today, and we are moving forward in breeding quality, type, and soundness."

Harmo

Perhaps when I refer to the Harmo Poodles belonging to Mrs. Ted Boardman it may not immediately ring a bell, as this is a new name within the past several years for this lady who is so great a Poodle enthusiast. But certainly when I say Anna Mosher it will all fall into place, as that was Mrs. Boardman's name when her dogs were meeting with their most exciting success.

Mrs. Boardman started out in dogs with Doberman Pinschers back in the early 1950's; Bill Trainor handled for her. She then devloped an allergy to dogs which the Dobe hair irritated. So, of course, she thought of Poodles with their non-shed coats as perhaps the ideal solution to her love of dogs and her wanting to remain involved with them. As so many people do, she started out with what developed into an oversized Miniature. Challis, however, remained the love of her life for close to 16 years.

This lady wanted *show* Poodles, however. Bill Trainor, whom she knew and who had been in charge of the Dobes, at that point had been showing Poodles for several well-known breeders in the New England area, so who more logical to help Mrs. Boardman "build up the herd," as it were, with the selection of some good foundation stock?

Harmo started out fairly well, although neither Mr. Trainor nor Mrs. Boardman was entirely satisfied with their earliest purchases. But then came the lucky day when Bill Trainor purchased for his client a brown Miniature from Mrs. Ethel Brough of the Broughton Kennels in

Ch. Harmo Scuffs taking Group One at Salisbury, Maryland. William J. Trainor handling.

Ch. Harmo Butterscotch Sundae at the Greater Miami Dog Club Show, January 1967. Another splendid win for Harmo Kennels.

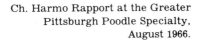

Ch. Harmo Rapport at the Greater Pittsburgh Poodle Specialty, August 1966.

Ch. Harmo Quick As A Wink, white Toy, wins the Variety at Santa Barbara, then proceeds on the way to Group Two. Owner, Harmo Kennels, Amherst, New Hampshire. Bill Trainor is handling.

Ch. Harmo Hi Tor, one of many Best in Show winners from Mrs. Ted Boardman's Harmo Kennels. Handled, as are all Harmo dogs, by William J. Trainor.

Ch. Sudbrook Sunday Go T'Meeting, one of the many fine Poodles owned by Harmo Kennels.

Washington, D.C. This bitch was Broughton's Susan Brown, a sister to Frank Hardy's only Poodle that Howard Tyler had finished for him. Susan lost no time gaining her championship (as her entire family of littermates had done), after which she was bred to an English dog belonging to Mrs. George Putnam, Champion Puttencove Gay Valentino. Susan, following in the paw prints of her dam before her, produced a full litter of champions, too. Champion Harmo Indigo Imp, who won the Poodle Club of America Specialty at about fifteen months of age; Champion Harmo Rough and Ready; and Champion Harmo Intrepid Invader, all Group and special-

Ch. Harmo Rapport and Ch. Harmo Rough 'n' Ready.

ty Best in Show winners. These, in turn, produced specialty and Best in Show winners, a good list of them.

Things continued so, and Harmo had a highly successful breeding program at its gorgeous Amherst, New Hampshire facility until such time, a few years later, that it was discovered that Broughton Susan Brown had progressive retinal atrophy, the dreaded PRA. Bill Trainor's wife, Dr. Betty Trainor, is a well-known veterinarian, and she is the one who first noticed and realized the problem. It was unknown, as she had been retired for awhile at this point, how long Susan had been thus afflicted. Needless to say, with some 25 excitingly promising young Poodles on the place directly descended from this line, all concerned were heartbroken.

Ch. Harmo Gentleman Jim, another Best in Show and Group winning Miniature from Harmo Kennels.

From the moment the discovery was made, Mrs. Boardman refused to allow any of these animals to be purchased, and she literally opened Pandora's Box by publicly making known the presence of this condition, which was already quite prevalent in the breed. Although she would allow no further breeding from any of these dogs, Mrs. Boardman only permitted one of them to be put down owing to the presence of PRA and its associated problems. Champion Harmo Rough and Ready, who eventually became totally blind, lived with the Trainors as their house pet until he died.

In addition to announcing this tragedy in her kennel, Mrs. Boardman was determined to make every effort to help other dogs and their owners. This she had done through large grants to ophthalmologists to finance a study of the condition and the remedy for controlling it.

Ch. Harmo Polaris showing off for the King of Nepal at a dog show arranged by the State Department on Long Island some years back. Mrs. Anna Boardman, owner. William J. Trainor, handler.

Of course this literally destroyed Harmo's black and brown breeding program with which they had, until that time, been so highly successful—a sad, disappointing and frustrating experience.

Fortunately the totally unrelated apricot Miniature line with which Harmo had been working was unaffected by all this, and the dogs being produced from it were having considerable impact in the ring. For instance, there were Champion Gay Prospector, Champion Harmo Gentleman Jim, Champion Harmo Polaris, and Champion Harmo Hi Tor, all outstanding apricots making big records in Group and Best in Show competition.

The white Toy line was also making its presence felt. These included Champion Harmo Willing By George, Champion Sudbrook Sunday Go To Meeting, and Champion Harmo Quick As A Wink, to name a few that did their share of bringing home Best in Show and Toy Group trophies.

The most famous Standard Poodle from Harmo is one that is also very famous throughout the Poodle world: the glorious brown bitch Champion Donna of Westford Ho, bred by Bill Trainor and sold to Sue Chisholm when eight months old, then bought back from her at two years of age. Donna went on to a brilliant career under Harmo ownership with Bill Trainor handling, then was bred to Joy Tongue's Champion Haus Brau Executive of Acadia, from which litter she produced some successful champions.

The experience with PRA was a sad one for Mrs. Boardman, and as a result she is no longer breeding Poodles, although her interest in the breed remains a steady one. For the past 15 years or more, she has had half a dozen or so of them as housepets. Two of these, special favorites of Mr. Boardman as well as of hers, are what Bill Trainor describes as "the last of her geriatrics." These are Champion Harmo Happiness, now 11 years old, and International Champion Harmo Minnimouse, in the same age bracket. Mrs. Boardman is breeding and has established a splendid kennel of Dachshunds, all of which are in Bill Trainor's charge. And as he says, "if we can ever find something decent enough for her, we will try to start again in Poodles." We hope that day will come soon, as Mrs. Boardman is too good a breeder and sincere a lover of the breed not to continue.

Ch. Harmo Rx Joy, a fine white Toy handled by William J. Trainor to a good win.

Ch. Hell's A Blazen Carnival Fame, white Toy female, owned by Frances Rubinich, handled by Wendell Sammet.

Hell's A Blazen

Hell's A Blazen Poodles is, in the minds of the majority of present-day fanciers, associated entirely with outstanding Toys, which is certainly true. However, when Frances and Albert Rubinich first became active in the Fancy, it was with three apricot Standards they purchased back in 1966. Two of these were finished, and Mr. and Mrs. Rubinich went on to breed six more champion Standards.

It was in 1968 that Hell's A Blazen's foundation white Toy bitch was acquired through importation from England. She was Branslake Floris, and from her the first Hell's A Blazen Toy litter was born on October 12, 1969. This consisted of three bitches who grew up to become Champion Hell's A Blazen Carnival Fame, Champion Hell's A Blazen Carnival Fancy, and Champion Hell's A Blazen Carnival Joy.

The next important Hell's A Blazen litter, again from Branslake Floris, was born in March, 1972; this time it was two puppies, and again both finished. They were Champion Hell's A Blazen Kinda Kostly and Champion Hell's A Blazen Kiss A Me. Branslake Floris has become the dam of five champions, of which three are Best in Show dogs, and she is granddam of four Best in Show winners. Floris was a Top Producer, and most of her offspring are following in

her footsteps in this capacity. This bitch has certainly left a firm imprint of outstanding quality on Toy Poodles of the present and for the future.

From their original breeding, Mr. and Mrs. Rubinich have combined several leading English and American bloodlines with the result that they are now producing not only white Toys but silvers, blues, and blacks. Frances Rubinich comments, "I will not go extensively into color breeding, but when I get something of quality, I will show it. My preference, though, is white."

To date, at Hell's A Blazen there have been 32 champions bred, of which seven are Best in Show winners, these being Champion Hell's A Blazen Carnival Fame, Champion Hell's A Blazen Kinda Kostly, Champion Hell's A Blazen Kiss A Me, Champion Hell's A Blazen Fagin's Pride, Champion Hell's A Blazen Hattie Jay, Japanese Champion Hell's A Blazen Elliot, (all Toys), and the Standard Champion Hell's A Blazen She's A Pip.

All Toy Poodles bearing the Hell's A Blazen prefix are directly descended from Branslake Floris. Mr. and Mrs. Rubinich take pride in their dogs and their accomplishments, which are all the more noteworthy as they are small breeders having an average of seven to ten dogs. There is always one coming along, ready to carry on and there is no question that these talented breeders have made a lasting and valuable contribution to Poodles. The Hell's A Blazen kennels are at Oxon Hill, Maryland.

Ch. Hell's A Blazen Fagin's Pride is a Best in Show winner and was Best Toy Poodle at Westminster, 1980. Owned by Mrs. A. C. Pearson.

Ch. Hell's A Blazen Carnival
Fancy at the Washington
Poodle Club Specialty, 1972,
taking Best of Winners.
Wendell Sammet handling for
Frances and Albert Rubinich,
Oxon Hill, Maryland.

Ch. Hell's A Blazen Carnival
Fame, a lovely Toy, pictured
winning Best of Breed at the
Watchung Mountain Poodle
Club Specialty.

The beautiful white Toy
bitch, Ch. Hell's A Blazen
Hattie Jay, is a Best in Show
winner, a Group winner, and
a specialty winner. She is
handled by F. C. Dickey for
owners, Mrs. Ralph Cowan
and Frances Rubinich.

Am. and Can. Ch. Helsonae Dream of Jeannie, one of the multiple Group winning Miniatures at Danville, 1978. Owned by Helsonae Kennels, Detroit, Michigan.

Helsonae

Helsonae Miniature Poodles is owned by Helen and Sonja Petlitzki of Detroit, Michigan, who bought their first Miniature Poodle in August, 1966. She was a white named Winsomore Living Doll. "Gigi," as she was called, was trained by Helen Petlitzki for the obedience ring, and the team was inseparable. "Gigi" attained her American U.D. degree and C.D.X. in Canada and was the top U.D. dog for 1971 at Sportsmen's Dog Training Club of Detroit. Several others have been trained by the Petlitzkis in obedience to their C.D. degree.

While attending the shows, the Petlitzkis became very interested in the breed ring and especially in the black Miniature Poodles. They had the good fortune of meeting F.C. (Bud) Dickey at the time he was specialing Champion Villa Russe Bismark. Through Bud's help a Bismark daughter was purchased by them, Bell Aire's Cara Mia Jewel, from Champion Gregella Faultless Fanny. This bitch quickly became a champion in both the United States and Canada, and the Petlitzkis were on their way. Jewel did some splendid Group winning for them in both the States and in Canada. Eventually it became time to breed her, and Champion Bentwater Aztec was selected as the stud. In great anticipation the litter was whelped on January 11, 1976.

The litter consisted of one puppy, and this is where the Helsonae story truly begins, as the baby became Helsonae Sunday Special (January 11 fell on a Sunday that year). Right from the beginning they knew this to be a very special puppy!

Sunday Special went to Dassin Farm at six months of age to begin his show career. At eight months he won Best Puppy in Show at the Washington Poodle Specialty under Anne Rogers Clark and went Winners Dog for a four point "major" under Edd Bivin. Then he went to the Poodle Club of America Regional Specialty in October, 1976, where "Timmy" was Best Puppy in Show under Marjorie Tranchin. He completed his championship at ten months of age under Mrs. Tom Stevenson with another major. He went on to be campaigned on a limited basis in specials, becoming a multiple Group and Best in Show winner and Number Five Miniature in the United States for 1977.

A Timmy daughter, American and Canadian Champion Tammar Looks Like We Made It, ex Elcoza Honeymoon Sweet, finished on the 1980 Florida circuit with four majors in two weekends at ten and a half months. She was awarded Best Puppy at the Poodle Club of Southern Florida under Peter Frederico.

Am. and Can. Ch. Bell Aire's Cara Mia Jewel, a multiple Group winner, owned by Helen and Sonja Petlitzki, Helsonae Poodles, Detroit, Michigan.

Ch. Helsonae Sunday Special, multiple Group and Best in Show winner, taking the top award at Lexington Kennel Club, 1977.

A son of Timmy, Champion Tammar Take That To the Bank, finished in one weekend with Best of Variety over specials in Canada; he was handled by Carol Hollands. He also has several points in the States. A daughter, Tammar Helsonae Sunday Money, started right out winning points at seven months. Several other Sunday Special youngsters are pointed and also doing well in the obedience ring.

American and Canadian Champion Bell Aire's Cara Mia Jewel was bred to Champion Bentwater Beritas Shiloh. American and Canadian Champion Helsonae Dream of Jeannie is a multiple Group winner. Helsonae Dassin Diversion is being handled by Joseph Vergnetti.

Hermscrest

Hermscrest Poodles was founded by Mrs. Frances M. Herms at Irvington, New York, for the express purpose of breeding top-quality silver Miniature Poodles. To quote Mrs. Herms, "To have succeeded with the black of the midnight sky would have been relatively easy. To have done it with the white of the new snow would have been only a bit more challenging. But to have insisted on doing it with the silver of sterling was to reach for the impossible dream." During the past 26 years that dream has become a reality for the charming and energetic lady who dared to try.

Mrs. Herms would be the first to admit that her first purchase of a silver Miniature back in 1954 and first stud dog selection was based partly on 20 years' experience as a cat show judge and partly on some instinct that kept telling her what she liked. The first puppy she chose was Silver Temple Moquette, bred by Mrs. Jeanne Lawler, well-known silver breeder of that period.

Moquette was shown on a limited basis, and when old enough was taken to the Hollycourt Kennels, owned by M. Ruelle Kelchner. Moquette was bred there to Champion Hollycourt Vaillant, a stud that appears in a great many important silver pedigrees. From this breeding, Mrs. Herms kept a bitch puppy destined to become Champion Hermscrest Vaillantel. "Val" not only gave Mrs. Herms a champion from her first litter, but went on to Winners and Best of Winners at the Westminster Kennel Club Dog Show in 1957. "Val" also took Best of Breed and Best in the Non-Sporting Group at the Bronx County Kennel Club in 1958. "Val" was then retired to become one of Mrs. Herms' most valued companions and her foundation bitch.

Another bitch important to this kennel, Hermscrest Nelida, was responsible for steady progress in the breeding of quality silver Miniatures through the years and produced Champion Hermscrest Harmony, who is a prepotent dam having contributed most significantly to the advancement of Hermscrest Kennels.

The English import, Ch. Tophill Silverbirch, owned by Mrs. Frances M. Herms, Irvington, New York. Handled by Wendell J. Sammet.

Ch. Hermscrest Jamal, with breeder-owner Mrs. Frances M. Herms, wins Best Puppy at a Poodle Club of America Puppy Match.

Mrs. Frances M. Herms with one of her lovely silver Miniatures, Ch. Chanteclair Man About Town.

Ch. Hermscrest Vaillantel winning the Greenspring Poodle Club Specialty, 1958. A puppy from the first litter bred by Mrs. Frances M. Herms.

The silver Miniature bitch, Ch. Hermscrest Harmony, is awarded Best of Winners at the William Penn Poodle Club, 1974. A dam of many top Hermscrest silvers.

To date, Mrs. Herms has eight silver champions to her credit. They are Champion Hermscrest Vaillantel, Champion Hermscrest Lucky Omen, Champion Hermscrest Jamal (Best Puppy at Poodle Club of America Puppy Match, Best of Winners and Best of Breed wins handled by Mrs. Herms, and further Group wins handled by Wendell J. Sammet), Champion Tophill Silverbirch (English), Champion Hermscrest Challenger, Champion Chanteclair Man About Town, Champion Hermscrest Harmony (Best of Winners at William Penn Poodle Club 1974), and Champion Manorhill's Classic Touch, who in 1977 at the Hudson Valley Poodle Club Specialty went Best of Opposite Sex to Best in Show, owner-handled from the American-bred Class, and has numerous other exciting wins handled either by Mrs. Herms or by Wendell J. Sammet, who shows the dogs on most occasions.

Numerous offspring of Champion Manorhill's Classic Touch are currently winning in the show ring, and this dog may well be on the way to becoming a Top Producer. Champion Merene's Silver Calypso by him has already finished, and Mrs. Herms personally is showing some excellent children and grandchildren of his at the present time.

Holly Berry

Holly Berry Toy Poodles is owned by Mr. and Mrs. John P. Berridge of Seaford, Delaware, and consists of a small kennel maintained strictly for the owners' pleasure, enjoyment, and love of the dogs.

Holly Berry was started in 1962 with silver Toys. In 1968, John Berridge presented his wife with their first black Toy as a Christmas gift. This was Berridge's Damview Holly, bred by the late Grace Dinning. Holly became the foundation bitch of the entire black line with which the Berridges are being so successful. Mrs. Berridge comments, "Holly was a 'hard luck' show bitch, still needing a major to finish.

Ch. Holly Berry Center Stage, 8½ inch Toy male, taking Winners Dog at the National Capital Kennel Club Dog Show, March 1976.

The foundation bitch for the black line of Holly Berry Toy Poodles. Berridge's Damview Holly, owned by Mrs. John P. Berridge, Seaford, Delaware.

Ch. Cappoquin's Sugar Bun, photographed in June 1975, groomed and ready to be handled in the Veteran's Class at the Poodle Club of America Specialty.

She has reserves for that major from Westminster and several Specialty shows. Her championship just was not to be." Holly is alive and well, is still jet black except for a graying muzzle, has most of her teeth, and has small tight feet even at age 12 years as this is written.

Joan Scott's line of blacks and those of Holly Berry have blended well, and there are several champions as a result of breedings within them.

Mrs. Berridge seldom keeps a dog, since she and her husband prefer the bitches, who have free run of the house. All are also thoroughly trained to a kennel routine and present no problems when crated or when they go off with a handler. Mr. and Mrs. Berridge consider Toy dogs to be companions first and foremost, so theirs are taught the social graces to make them welcome additions to any household.

Ch. Hell's A Blazen Kiss A Me winning the Tidelands Poodle Club Specialty, late 1970's. Owned by Frances and Albert Rubinich, Oxon Hill, Maryland.

164

Ch. Holly Berry Tempest taking Best of Variety in Toy Poodles at Lancaster Kennel Club, May 1978. Mrs. John P. Berridge, owner-handler.

The black Toy bitch, Ch. Holly Berry Dawn Jay, bred and owned by Mrs. John P. Berridge, handled by Michael Hagen. Shown just starting out as a "special" on what should be an exciting career.

Ch. Holly Berry Tempest taking her first Toy Group at Skyline Kennel Club, 1979. Owner-handled by Mrs. John P. Berridge.

Like all dedicated breeders, the Berridges strive to improve the breed, which is no small task. Their goals are "to breed a Best in Show winner, to try to contribute to the Poodle breed, to try to measure up to some of the 'greats' it has been our privilege to meet in the world of dogs, to learn from them, and to have them as our friends."

The exquisite silver bitch Champion Cappoquin Sugar Bun was one of Mrs. Berridge's early show contenders. She was Winners Bitch and Best of Winners at Westminster 1966 and had come from Mary Griffin's noted kennel. Mrs. Berridge tells us that Sugar Bun stayed in full coat throughout her entire lifetime of 15 years. She loved being bathed and groomed and adored

dog shows, to which she always accompanied her owners. Mrs. Berridge says, "perhaps it was fitting that she died in her sleep during the night at the Warrenton showgrounds."

The Group winning Champion Holly Berry Tempest has been representing the Berridges at shows during the mid to late 1970's. Champion Graclyn Sassafras Maple Sugar, the 8½ inch brown bitch, has Group placements owner-handled as a special, and the current "star" is Champion Holly Berry Dawn Jay, out to the shows with Michael Hagen, where she is attracting considerable attention. She is a daughter of Tempest.

Ch. Graclyn Sassafras Maple Sugar finishing at Carroll County, October 1971. Handled by Lewis Grello.

Ch. Graclyn Sassafras Maple Sugar, 8½ inch brown bitch, owned and handled here by Mrs. John P. Berridge. By Black Light of Sassafras ex Graclyn Hi Style Sassafras.

Kayesett

Kayesett Poodles came into being as the result of Muriel Kaye having received a Standard puppy from her husband as a birthday gift back in October, 1959. Her new owners named the puppy Kaye's Cinderella Abigail, with the call name "Cindy." At five months old, Cindy was started in obedience classes, the hope having been of training her to come when called. Muriel Kaye had to do the training, as Cindy was her dog, but very obviously Herb Kaye wanted to "get into the act," so it was decided to breed Cindy and keep one of her puppies for Herb to enjoy.

Cindy was bred on her second season, and the Kayes raised ten puppies and kept three, which, as they tell us, was when they "went to the dogs." The stud fee puppy from this litter was Hillever Wing Ding, who later became the dam of Champion Bel Tor Sandelwood.

In her second litter, Cindy gave the Kayes their first champion, Kaye's Cocoa Nicole. "Nickie" became a Top Producing Dam, her progeny including Champion Kaye's Ring Master the first time she was bred and three champions in her second litter, Champion Kaye's Trojan Knight, Champion Kaye's Trina Tru, and Champion Kaye's Helen of Troy, the latter owned by Mrs. Peggy De Nuzzi. In her third, and last, litter Nickie gave her owners Champion Kaye's Viva Victoria. She was not bred again, as the Kayes limit the breeding of their bitches to not more than three times.

An exciting win for a gorgeous brown Standard, Ch. Kayesett Xcalabar going from the puppy classes to First in the Non-Sporting Group, Susque-Nango Kennel Club, 1971, Robert S. Forsyth handling for Muriel and Herbert Kaye, Woodbridge, Connecticut.

Ch. Kaye's Trojan Knight, one of the many fine Poodles owned by Kayesett Kennels, handled here to a good win by Jane Kamp Forsyth.

The first homebred champion at Kayesett Kennels. The brown bitch, Ch. Kaye's Cocoa Nicole is handled by Jane Kamp Forsyth.

Ch. Kaye's Ring Master taking Best of Variety at the Quinnipiac Poodle Club Specialty.

The Kayes have gone outside for stud dogs on several occasions, striving always to improve their line and produce the perfect Poodle. They believe good temperament, soundness, and type all are involved in the essentials for a truly fine dog. In 1959 the kennel prefix Kayesett was registered with the American Kennel Club, since which time the dogs have finished under this identification.

The old American and Canadian Champion Trojan Knight is still at Kayesett at 13½ years of age. When he was 11 this dog sired a litter of 14 living puppies. Abby is another of the "old timers" still with the Kayes, approaching 15 years, and their special love and house dog.

When Herbert Kaye retired from business, he took over the running of the kennel, leaving the grooming and breeding to Muriel Kaye with one full time assistant. Mr. Kaye enjoys dog-related activities and thus belongs to numerous dog clubs and is an A.K.C.-approved judge of Poodles.

To date the Kayes have bred 17 American Poodle Champions, five Canadian Champions, and two Poodles that have earned C.D. degrees.

Muriel and Herb Kaye comment, "After many years of breeding and showing our dogs, the joys have far outweighed the sorrows, and we are happy to have given so much love and devotion to such wonderful dogs."

Ch. Kayesett Esperanto, a Standard, winning the Non-Sporting Group at Susque-Nango Kennel Club, 1975.

La Cheri

La Cheri Miniature Poodles began when Mr. and Mrs. James A. Lisano of Pasadena, Texas, learned of a litter from a bitch belonging to one of her close friends, Mrs. Noni Jones. Mrs. Jones, owner of Banjo Poodles, was living in Houston at the time but has since moved to the state of Washington, where she now raises horses. The puppies, born in August, 1968, belonged to their breeder, Richard O. Shelton of Covington, Louisiana, and were sired by Champion Aizbel The One And Only from Banjo's Oh

This outstanding brown Miniature has distinguished himself in both conformation and obedience competition. Ch. Starfire Brandywine, C.D., is owned by Sue Boehm of Houston, Texas, and handled here by Robert Peebles.

You Beautiful Doll, a daughter of Champion Gale's Mardi Gras of Melmar. Deciding that they would enjoy owning one of these puppies, the Lisanos asked another good friend, handler Jimmy Andrews, to look at the litter while at the Louisiana circuit shows and to select one for them. He picked a bitch that grew up to become Champion La Cheri's Bold and Beautiful, and from the day she came home she became very special to all three of them.

Cheri loved the show ring from the very beginning, which was at three months of age when she was entered at the San Jacinto Kennel Club's first fun match, with an entry of more than 500 dogs. Jim Lisano showed her as a puppy, but Jimmy Andrews took over in his usual expert manner during most of her adult show career. Her "majors" were won at the Bluebonnet Specialty Show under William Bergum, where she went on to Best of Opposite Sex to Best of Breed over several Best in Show specials; the following day at the companion show she again got four points, this time from Henry Stoecker. She was held back then for a few shows because Jimmy Andrews wanted to take her to Westminster in the classes, which he did in 1970, where she took Reserve Winners Bitch under Tom Stevenson. Her career was tem-

La Cheri's Bold Streaker is handled here by Jimmy Andrews to a good win for owners Rosalie Lisano and Marcella McGratty.

The late Jimmy Andrews did this sketch of Ch. La Cheri's Bold and Beautiful for Rosalie and Jim Lisano. This young handler was a true friend and a tremendous favorite of the Texas Poodle Fancy.

Ch. La Cheri's Bold and Beautiful, a lovely Miniature bitch.

porarily interrupted following her trip to New York and her appearance on a T.V. show, as she had chewed on an ear fringe. But she wasn't stopped for long, and this lovely bitch completed her title with ease. She went on to win a number of Group placements plus Specialties. It is interesting that at nine and a half years old she returned to the ring "just for the fun of it," adding some Group placements and several Best of Varieties over Group placing Miniatures. She was retired permanently at ten years of age, with some exciting memories for her owners despite the fact that she never had been what is considered "actively campaigned." She won the

Oklahoma Poodle Specialty in 1971 and the Creole Poodle Club Specialty in 1974, along with her other successes.

First and foremost, however, Cheri was, and still is, her family's dearly loved companion. She "rules the roost" at the Lisano household, demanding respect and good manners from the Doberman and the numerous Beagles also living there. Cheri has a second owner, Marcella McGratty, her longtime admirer who wanted to buy her long ago , but even then Rosalie Lisano could not bear the thought of selling her as she had become so important a part of the Lisano's life. So it was decided that the two ladies would become co-owners. Marcella McGratty owns a long-established line of silver Miniatures, one of whom has joined La Cheri at the Lisanos.

Cheri, whose breeding on both sides is strong in the Chriscrest bloodlines, has produced beautiful Poodles as might have been expected. Her son, Cheri's Bold Streaker, earned twenty points toward his title but missed out on the elusive second major due to not especially caring to be a show dog and thus not trying at the crucial moments.

There is a grandson of Cheri, Champion Starfire Brandywine, C.D., who has done well in both conformation and obedience. He finished his championship by winning a Group First while still a puppy and has just completed his C.D. and qualified for the Gaines Regionals. Brandy belongs to Sue Boehm of Houston and is handled by Bobby Peebles.

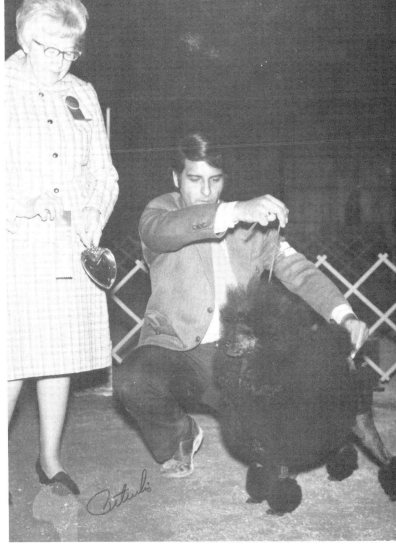

A handsome study of Ch. La Cheri's Bold and Beautiful, handled by Jimmy Andrews for Mrs. James A. Lisano and Marcella C. McGratty of Pasadena, Texas.

Ch. Calvinelle Dandy with Vernelle (Mrs. William) Kendrick at the Greenspring Poodle Club specialty in 1965. Carol Dewey, judge.

Ch. Marney's Goliath, a Standard dog, finished his championship in three consecutive shows. Owned by Mrs. Margaret Durney, San Rafael, California.

Marney

Marney Poodles came into being back in the 1940's when Mrs. Margaret Durney purchased her first show dog, a lovely white Standard bitch, from Mrs. Sherman R. Hoyt. Ma Vielle of Blakeen, shown in the West by Jim McManus and in the East by Mac McBrien, earned her championship with ease and then, working together with her owner, went through obedience competition to become a C.D.X.

Producing but one litter, Ma Vielle nonetheless made a considerable contribution to the future of the breed, for in this litter was a puppy that grew up to be a noted Best in Show dog, Champion Marney's Marquis De Lafayette, the top Non-Sporting Winner for the years 1954 and 1955. Several Best in Show and numerous Group victories were awarded to this dog, and he retired in 1956 on a Best in Show at Sacramento. During his show career he was handled by Ben Brown and occasionally by Margaret Durney.

Over the years, Marney has bred and shown both black and white Miniatures. Champion Darney's Nougat was shown to her title owner-handled. Bred to Champion Tedwin's Top Billing, she produced in one litter Champion Marney's Top Performance, Champion Marney's Magic Eyes, and one other champion. Among the additional champion Miniatures at Marney were Emma Doone of Montfleuri, Champion Ivardon Love Song, Champion Ivardon Harry Hotspur, Champion Blakeen High

Time, English Champion Fury of Montfleuri (who at 14 years old is still going strong as the Durneys' devoted house pet), and American and Canadian Champion Marney's Bonnie Doone (Best Puppy at Poodle Club of America Regional). In brown Miniatures, Marney points with pride to Champion Surrey Sequoia, 1973's Top Winning Miniature Poodle in the United States, Frank Sabella handling, and still the Top Living Brown Sire of Record. Others at this kennel include Champion Jennifer Doone, Canadian Champion Marney's Julia Doone, and Champion Penchant Paladin, the latter co-owned with Betsy A. Leedy. Paladin is a Top Producer as of May, 1980, having ten champion progeny to his credit.

The past two years have been especially rewarding and exciting due to the acquisition of two lovely Standard Poodle "ladies," Champion Rimskittle Bartered Bride and Champion Rimskittle Ruffian, both bred by Mr. and Mrs. James Edward Clark and both handled to perfection by Tim Brazier. These two bitches between them have accumulated a total of more than 50 all-breed Bests in Show, 25 Poodle specialties, and Firsts in 150 Non-Sporting Groups, including such exciting highlights as, for Bartered Bride, Bests in Show at Chicago International, Golden Gate, Lompoc, and Sacramento. During her career she made what at that time was a record of seven consecutive Bests in Show, was Group First at Westchester and twice consecutively at Santa Barbara. As for Ruffian, her prestigious accomplishments have included

Bests in Show at Ox Ridge, Silver Bay, Reno, Silver State (Las Vegas), and Lompac. Notable Group Firsts for Ruffian have come at Chicago International twice, at Philadelphia, Golden Gate, Santa Barbara, and Westminster 1980, to mention just the highlights. Ruffian is co-owned by Mrs. Durney and Edward Jenner.

The Durney family, in addition to the "furry friends," includes two charming daughters, Sharon (DeDe) and Debbie. DeDe became active in Junior Showmanship and had many wins to her credit. Later she worked for Frank Sabella. Debbie is now continuing her education at Wellesley College.

Marney's latest young hopeful is a beautiful white Standard bitch, Graphic Constellation, now starting her show carer with Tim Brazier.

Headstudy of a white Miniature belonging to Mrs. Margaret Durney.

Medrie

Medrie Poodles has done some extremely exciting things for its enthusiastic owner, Mrs. Rita Cloutier of Merrimack, New Hampshire.

It was twelve years ago, in 1968, that Mrs. Cloutier opened Rita's Kennels, which became a highly successful boarding and grooming establishment, and her enthusiasm for everything to do with dogs has remained constant ever since.

One morning in May, 1975, Mrs. Cloutier decided to take the day off in order to attend a dog show, which it turned out was an important occasion in her life. This was the Poodle Club of Massachusetts Specialty, and she went there

with the intention of purchasing a brown Standard show Poodle. There she was introduced to the well-known professional handler Paul Edwards. During their conversation, Paul was busily preparing a nine-month-old apricot Toy bitch for the ring. Her name was Cignet's Gold Medallion, and the longer Rita looked at and played with her, the more she wanted to have her as a gift to herself for her birthday, which was the following day. Rita bought her, Paul finished her to championship, and that was the first of Rita Cloutier's handsome Poodles to gain the title.

Now she was really on her way in dogs, and by the end of 1979, only four short years later, Paul Edwards had made ten of her dogs champions, representing Toy Poodles, Standard Poodles, and Maltese.

In the latter part of 1977, Rita was introduced to J.L.C. Critique, a male white Miniature Paul Edwards had been hired to handle for Round Table Kennels and Jordan Chamberlain. It was love at first sight, and Rita tried desperately to purchase this stunning little dog who had so completely won her heart. But Mrs. Keene, owner of Round Table, and Jordan Chamberlain, kennel manager and handler there, did not want to sell.

Over a year later Rita received the good news that Mrs. Keene and Mr. Chamberlain had decided, if she still was interested, to lease "Tiki" to her. Not only interested, Rita was ecstatic. As she says, "He has given me more pleasure than any other dog I have ever owned."

Ch. Marney Top Performance winning at the Poodle Club of America Specialty, 1964, with Frank Sabella handling for Mrs. Margaret Durney.

Tim Brazier jumps for joy as Ch. Rimskittle Bartered Bride adds another important win to her exciting collection of awards.

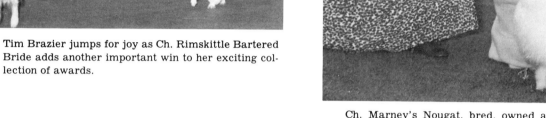

Ch. Marney's Nougat, bred, owned and handled by Mrs. Margaret Durney, taking Winners Bitch at the Del Monte Poodle Club of Central California Specialty judged by Miss Frances Angela.

Ch. Ma Vielle of Blakeen, C.D.X., Margaret Durney's first show dog and the foundation of Marney Poodles.

Headstudy of Ch. Marney Marquis De Lafayette.

Sharon Durney showing Ch. Marney's Top Performance for her mother, Mrs. Margaret Durney. Mrs. L. J. Froelich judge.

Photographed in 1955, Mrs. Margaret Durney with one of her earlier Poodles, the homebred Ch. Marney's Chou Chou.

Ch. Rimskittle Bartered Bride, with Tim Brazier handling, gains the approval of English Poodle authority, Mrs. Philip Howard-Price.

One of the prettiest Standard bitches of all time, Ch. Rimskittle Bartered Bride. She sits proudly with her awards alongside her handler, Tim Brazier, after just winning Best in Show at the International Kennel Club of Chicago, 1977. Mrs. Margaret Durney, owner.

An informal photo of Ch. Ma Vielle of Blakeen, C.D.X., Margaret Durney, and Ma Vielle's famous son, Ch. Marney's Marquis de Lafayette.

Ch. Rimskittle Ruffian making a television guest appearance on the Merv Griffin Show. Shown here with Merv and her handler, Tim Brazier, Ruffian is owned by Mrs. Margaret Durney and Edward Jenner.

This lovely black Standard bitch, Ch. Rimskittle Ruffian, was awarded Best in Show at Reno Kennel Club by Frank Sabella. Tim Brazier handled for owners, Mrs. Margaret Durney and Edward Jenner.

BEST IN SHOW

Critique's show record is a fabulous one. He was under Robert Koeppel's ownership for awhile and was quite extensively campaigned. He became not only a multiple Best in Show winner, but was the nation's Top Miniature Poodle in both 1979 and 1980. Rita Cloutier thought that her most exciting dog show moment of all time had come when Tiki won a star-studded Non-Sporting Group at Westminster in 1979, but she was to learn better two years later when "Tiki" repeated that victory, looking like a sparkling white gem as he paraded around the big ring under Paul Edwards' guidance. Then he came home and is now enjoying life as a family dog and household companion with Rita Cloutier.

During the period when "Tiki" was being shown, Mrs. Cloutier purchased a Maltese puppy which she finished herself. But her greatest interest lies with the Poodles. After the original apricot Toy, Cignet's Gold Medallion, had become a champion, her owner decided that she would become the foundation bitch of the Toy

Rita Cloutier owns this handsome Toy, Ch. Kornel's Memory Lane, handled here by Paul Edwards.

Ch. J.L.C. Critique winning one of his Bests in Show. Owned by Mrs. Rita Cloutier and handled by Paul Edwards.

Poodle part of her kennel and bred her even though she had become so emotionally attached to her owner, never seriously anticipating any problems. Things went very wrong, however, and both the little bitch and her puppies died during whelping. At this point Rita decided that she was getting out of dogs.

Fortunately Paul and Mary Edwards, with whom she had become close friends, persuaded her to reconsider, explaining that breeding champion dogs is not always easy, especially with any of the Toy breeds, which are inclined toward small litters and difficult breedings and whelpings, and that she must not let herself become discouraged. We are very happy that she finally got herself together about it and decided to continue.

As this is written, Medrie Poodles has just finished a homebred white Standard champion in Canada who hopefully is now in route to the title in the United States. There is also a lovely homebred champion bitch.

Rita Cloutier's goal is to produce a champion Miniature Poodle bred by her through Champion J.L.C. Critique and a lovely white Miniature bitch she also owns, and then to personally handle it to championship. We're betting on her to achieve this goal, not just once but repeatedly. After all, with a dog as gorgeous as Tiki to use as a sire, she has a great deal going for her.

Michanda

Michanda Poodles has a slogan that tells the story of its background practically in one sentence. It is, "Our Foundation Is Built On Rock—Champion Syntifny's Piece of the Rock." And that is the way Patricia J. McMullen of Clio, Michigan, has developed her very excellent kennel.

Patricia McMullen started out, as do so many people, with a nice pet and a sincere love of the breed. Then with the third bitch they purchased, the McMullens felt that good fortune really was smiling, as this was a gorgeous Piece of the Rock daughter (purchased from Jane Winne) whom Todd Patterson agreed to campaign. From then on Pat was "bitten by the dog show bug" and, with Jane Winne's, Lee Paul's, and the crew at Todd's help and advice, Michanda was truly on its way.

At this time there are two Top Producers living at Michanda. These are Canadian Champion Yerbrier Fun 'n' Fancy, bred by Betty Yerington, and Canadian Champion Syntifny Snapshot, bred by Jane Winne, both co-owned with the latter.

The goal at Michanda is to breed and love the best possible Toy Poodles. It takes a lot of patience, love, and hard work, but, in Patricia McMullen's words, "when you see the result strutting around the ring, you know that's where it's at."

Ch. Monfret Memory, belonging to Francis P. Fretwell, Monfret Poodles. By Ch. Carillon Dilemma ex Ch. Kah's Kollector's Item, C.D.

Ch. Monfret Spring Flirtation winning Best of Variety at Charleston Kennel Club, 1975. Owner-handled here by Mr. F. P. Fretwell.

Monfret

Mr. Francis P. Fretwell, of Moore, South Carolina, became a Poodle owner in 1948 when he purchased his first member of the breed, a promising black Standard puppy. This youngster grew up to become Champion Colonel Mint Julip of the Nass, C.D., C.D.X., U.D. He was exhibited during the period when it was difficult to find enough competition to make a one-point entry, much less majors, but Mint Julip did get his title, including points from the exciting day at the Greenville Kennel Club in 1953 when he not only gained first place in the Non-Sporting Group, but also was the highest Combined Score Winner in obedience. Two days later he picked up the needed points to become a champion.

Mint Julip made quite a name for himself and for obedience in its early days in the South as a clown, inspiring the foundation of half a dozen or more obedience clubs in the area. He had a regular following or "fan club," and was the subject of several TV shows and appeared also for pre-show publicity to encourage the gate. People still ask Mr. Fretwell about him. He was never shown as a "special" and, regretfully, he has no descendants.

178

Three foundation bitches were Mr. Fretwell's next Poodle acquisitions. These were Champion Roadcoach Fancy Free, C.D., Champion Kah's Kollector's Item, C.D., and Champion Puttencove Spring Song, C.D. We include the pedigrees of these three bitches, feeling them to be of great importance.

Champion Roadcoach Fancy Free, C.D., finished in 11 shows with four "majors" while still a puppy, then as an adult accounted for eight Group placemets. She produced four champions, two by Judge Demitrius of Belle Glen and two by American and Canadian Champion Monfret Merlin.

Champion Kah's Kollector's Item, C.D., was whelped in 1958 (bred by Howard H. Karr) and died in 1969. She was two years old and clipped closely when bought from Howard Tyler. After growing a show coat, she finished in eight shows with five Bests of Variety and one Specialty Best of Opposite Sex to Best of Breed. From five litters she produced 14 champions, to become the Top Producing Poodle Bitch of her day, and she remains even now Number Four in the all-time record. A very good show bitch, an outstanding producer, and a great companion, her number of champions totals 15.

Champion Puttencove Spring Song, C.D., became the dam of three champions, two by Champion Puttencove Jeffery and one by Champion Carillon Jongleur.

Another Poodle who brought fame to Monfret was Champion Monfret Bronzini, the only brown (or Poodle other than black) that Mr. Fretwell ever has owned. He was sold to Joan Schilke Wicklander (while still a puppy) after having won nine points, including a five-point major. He was quickly finished and retired as Mrs. Wicklander was then campaigning Champion Wycliffe Virgil. Bronzini was the sire of five champions, with a large number of title-holding descendants, and he appears on the pedigrees of more Poodles than possibly any other Mr. Fretwell ever has bred. He was a strange shade of dark bright brown which Mr. Fretwell described as a mixture of purples, reds, yellows, etc. To quote, "he looked as though he would glow in the dark." Mr. Fretwell never saw him after he was sold, but Joan Wicklander has assured him that this color did not fade, even at age ten.

American and Canadian Champion Monfret Figaro finished in seven shows and was sold to Mrs. Josanne Larsen, for whom he won several Group Firsts in the United States and Canada

Ch. Monfret Morticia finished with Best of Winners at the Poodle Club of America Specialty, 1966. Francis P. Fretwell owns this lovely Non-Sporting Group and specialty winner.

Ch. Monfret Spring Fashion, by Ch. Jacques le Noir of Belle Glen ex Ch. Monfret Spring Glory.

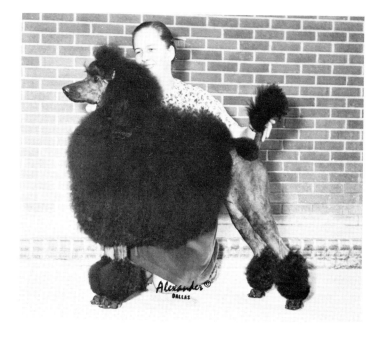

where she also finished him. He was the sire of eight champions.

Champion Monfret Fiorello, C.D.X., finished in nine shows, was Group First after beating his own champion dam at one year of age, and won several more Groups for Mr. Fretwell prior to sale to Mrs. Sally Schaper, for whom he won additional Group Firsts, four of them at least. Fiorello sired four champions.

Champion Monfret Mathieu, considered by some to be the best male Mr. Fretwell had bred, finished in about ten shows with Reserves at "all the best places." Only shown twice as a special, he accounted for a Group First and Second. Mr. Fretwell tells us that this dog was poisoned a few days after these shows by someone "in the game." Understandably, things have never seemed the same to Mr. Fretwell since this experience. Mathieu was the sire of three champions.

Champion Monfret Melanie finished at her eleventh show under Mrs. Jean Lyle, having won Best of Breed earlier at the Southeast Florida Poodle Club Specialty. She was the dam of three champions and a great companion.

Champion Monfret Memory was badly "spooked" at her second show when barely six months old by the rough handling of a still-prominent judge, which made her hand shy for the rest of her life. She finished as a puppy and was still winning Best of Varieties for another four years prior to retiring.

American and Canadian Champion Monfret Merlin won his first "major" at six months of age and finished as a puppy. As a special he won ten Group Firsts and was five years of age when he took his last Best in Show.

Champion Monfret Miranda was a beautiful bitch who, despite having only had two small litters, produced five champions, two of whom became Best in Show winners and two others who became foundation bitches for now-prominent kennels. The two Best in Show bitches, Champion Monfret Mistress Mirth and Champion Monfret Schadracha, finished the same weekend, won Groups the same weekend, and whelped litters on the same days, all totally uncoordinated and in different parts of the country under different ownerships.

Champion Monfret Mistress Mirth finished in nine shows with several Group Firsts and was a Best in Show winner. She was the dam of two champions from her one litter of five puppies.

Champion Monfret Morticia finished with Best of Winners at the Poodle Club of America

Specialty and was twice Best of Breed at Specialty Shows, once Best of Opposite Sex to Best of Breed, and a Group winner. Unfortunately she never had a litter, but Mr. Fretwell comments on her being a great companion and huntress.

American and Canadian Champion Monfret Music Maid was considered by many to be one of the nicest bitches ever bred by Mr. Fretwell. However, he had too many dogs at the time and sold her to Mrs. Josanne Larsen, who put the final points on her and for whom Music Maid won several Non-Sporting Groups both in the United States and in Canada. She also was Reserve Bitch at a Westminster. She was the dam of four champions, three by American and Canadian Champion Monfret Figaro and one by their son, Champion Nesral Dark Brilliance, the sire of six champions. Music Maid was one of six champions and was the only bitch in the only litter from Champion Monfret Melody.

Champion Monfret Music Maestro finished in 11 shows, winning Best of Opposite Sex to Best of Breed at the Greater Pittsburgh Poodle Club Specialty in the process. Sadly, he died very tragically shortly thereafter when in someone else's care, so he was never campaigned. He was the grandsire of Champion Coqan Baccarat.

American and Canadian champion Monfret Music Master was the most successful of all the Monfret stud dogs. He finished in 15 shows in three months. At that time he was overshadowed in looks by his kennel mate Champion Monfret Mathieu, who was a disappointing stud dog. You cannot tell by looks alone! The sire of 16 champions, although little used, Music Master did not like showing for anyone except Mr. Fretwell, and for him the dog was more responsive with less training than most others, seeming almost to read his master's mind.

Champion Monfret Spring Glory, C.D., won all but her final "major" as a puppy in puppy trim, finishing at the first show she competed in after becoming a year old. She was the dam of three champions. Specialed on only 12 occasions, she placed in the Non-Sporting Group on eight of them.

American and Canadian Champion Monfret Master Middleton won a Group Third, First, and Second at his first three shows. In a relatively short career he added several more Group placements and another Group First. Sire of five champions though little used prior to his untimely death, there is now a promising grandson of this dog in the kennel.

180

Mr. Fretwell has never specialed any one dog for any great length of time, showing the champions mostly when he has something going for the classes, too.

"The circumstances of the loss of Champion Monfret Mathieu, coupled with retirement and a kennel full of old champions, has slowed down my breeding program tremendously," Francis Fretwell tells us, and he has done very little showing since the early 1970's. Also, increased activity as a judge cuts back on one's showing, not to mention inflation and dog club work.

There is no questioning the fact that Francis Fretwell's contribution to Standard Poodles has been tremendous. The quality and integrity for which Monfret Poodles stand and the many outstanding dogs raised there or descended from them stand as a tribute to all his efforts.

Pinafore

Pinafore Poodles was established in 1963, when Mrs. Philip J. Harney purchased a black Miniature, Puttencove Dosia, C.D., from Mrs. Katherine Putnam. At that time, as Mrs. Harney says, "I had four children, all under five years of age, and I did not know a thing about coat grooming or breeding." So, once a year

This lovely white Standard puppy grew up to become Champion Mescal Alexis, and is owned by Edward B. Jenner and Barbara Adkins.

Dosia returned to Puttencove to be bred, and Mrs. Putnam evaluated the puppies before they were sold. Through all this, Mrs. Harney discovered that at heart she was really a breeder and that she loved it. Mrs. Putnam was always delighted at the healthy, well socialized puppies in these litters.

In those days the Harneys lived in Boston and Mrs. Harney had many opportunities to see Mrs. Putnam with the big, gorgeous white Standards who seemed always to be with her, so she wanted one of her own. It was arranged that Mrs. Harney would co-own a Champion Puttencove Promise granddaughter, Puttencove Day Lily, C.D. (O.F.A. certified at four years), and she was bred to Champion Alekai Ahi. In the first litter was Mrs. Harney's first champion, Pinafore Panda Bear, C.D., O.F.A. Certified, and a Group winner. When the litter was four months old, the Harneys were transferred to Omaha, Nebraska, with five Standard Poodles, four children, one Siamese cat, and a husband who was not dog crazy, making the trip in their station wagon.

Lily next was bred to Champion Alekai Bali; that litter produced Champion Pinafore Pinocchio, who grew up to become a Group winner.

Ch. Roadcoach Quicksilver, silver Miniature male, is the sire of seven champions and belongs to the Roadcoach Kennels, Dover, Massachusetts. Mary P. Barrett, owner. By Ch. Frenches Vendas Chip of Silver ex Puttencove Tiptoes, 1950.

Karen Meyers with Wentworth George, a Standard from Swag Kennels.

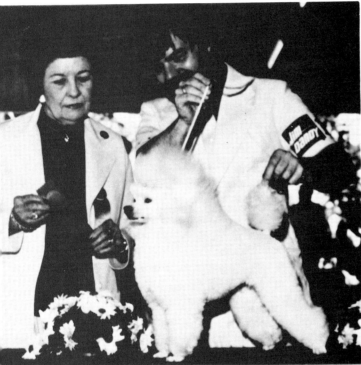

Then Devron's Jennifer, descended from Puttencove breeding, was purchased. She is now a Top Producer. One of her daughters, Pinafore Popcorn, was bred to her litter brother, Pinafore Professor, producing Pinafore Charlie Pirate, who is co-owned with Mrs. H. D. Lindemann of Worthington, Minnesota.

The black dog Champion Pinafore Barrymore was Winners Dog at the Poodle Club of America Regional in 1980, and the white bitch Champion Pinafore Memories of Domino was Winners Bitch there on the same occasion.

Pinafore Poodles is now located in Woodinville, Washington, where it moved in 1976. Mrs. Harney is enjoying raising both black and white Standards at this time.

Ravendune

Ravendune Poodles is owned by the highly successful professional handler Todd Patterson, and is located at Taylor, Michigan. Mr. Patterson breeds black Miniatures and Toys and has some lovely dogs to his credit.

Among the Miniatures, American and Canadian Champion Ravendune Sweet Baby James, born October 11, 1970, is still going strong as this book is being written. He was Todd's fifth homebred champion, and he finished in four consecutive shows in the United States and three consecutive shows in Canada. He went Best in Show at Key To The Sea Poodle Specialty his first time out as a "special," under Robert Sturm, and also was a Group winner from the classes. By Canadian Champion Highlane Bonhomme Richard from American and Canadian Champion Bon Aire Black Temptation, this excellent Top Producing Poodle has 18 Champions thus far to his credit.

Top: Ch. Michanda's Pebble of Sintifny (by Piece of the Rock ex Syntifny Sweettalk), owned by Patricia McMullen. Handled by Todd Patterson. **Center:** Ch. Camelot Rockford Files (by Ch. Syntifny Piece of the Rock) was bred and owned by Paula Smith, Winter Haven, Florida. Finished as a puppy, handled by Todd Patterson. **Bottom:** Ch. Merry Bee Black Ebony, by Janie's Black Dina Mite ex Aldyna's Red Carnatian. Winner of many group placements and other wins. Jeanie Mazza, owner, Wayne, New Jersey; Allen Chambers, handler.

A son of Baby James, Champion Ravendune Prime Time is one of the particularly promising young black Miniatures at Ravendune, and Todd Patterson has high hopes that this dog will follow in the footsteps of his illustrious sire.

Then there is Champion Royal Look Winged Commander, who although not bred at Ravendune is proving an invaluable asset to the breeding program there. Although still very young, he has already sired four champions in his first litters, with several others pointed from the puppy classes, and seems destined to become a Top Producer as time passes. He finished his title in four shows over two weekends.

Among the Toys, half brother-sister blacks Champion Ravendune Ken D Lee Typesetter and Champion Ken D Lee In Dreams are both very exciting. Co-bred by Todd Patterson and Mrs. Geri Kendall, these two have attracted great admiration in the show ring. Typesetter finished his title in five shows, starting under Frank Sabella with a four-point major at Westminster. Shown entirely in Bred-by-Exhibitor Class, he gained two majors from Mr. Sabella (another one following Westminster), the others from Ann Stevenson, Sue Kauffman and Joe Gregory. The sister, In Dreams, became a champion at ten months, also entirely from Bred-by-Exhibitor Class, and was Best of Variety at her very first show.

Ch. Arden Impetuous, by Jeanie's Black Dina-Mite ex Ardyna's Hot Pants. Arden Poodles, B. Wohtruba, Kinnelon, New Jersey.

Ch. Round Table Fan Dancer, by Ch. Summercourt Square Dancer of Fircot ex Round Table Eloise. Bred by Round Table Kennels, owned and handled by Mrs. Samuel F. duPont, Cecilton, Maryland.

Round Table

Round Table Poodles came into being as the result of Mrs. Alden V. Keene having acquired a Miniature Poodle, Seafren Hue and Cry, at the request of her children back in 1942. Prior to then, Mr. and Mrs. Keene had for ten years been breeding Old English Sheepdogs. But Hue and Cry's arrival soon had the entire family converted to the charms of her breed, so Round Table Poodles had its beginning.

Located in Delaware, Round Table had over the past four decades built an impressive record for show dogs who have held important positions in keenest Eastern competition. Blacks, browns, and whites have been especially featured. However, the Keenes also have apricot and silver homebred champions to their credit.

Hue and Cry, described by Mrs. Keene as a sound, good-bodied bitch but lacking in elegance, was bred to Champion Felix of Piperscroft. This first litter of Poodles produced a lovely brown bitch, Champion Round Table's Constance, whom the Keenes sold to a West Coast fancier and who is in the background of many leading browns right up until the present day.

Constance was not the first homebred Round Table Miniature to finish. That distinction goes to Champion Round Table Decollete, also from Hue and Cry but sired by Champion Clairwell Ce Soir and from a litter born the following year. This was a gorgeous black bitch that completed her title in 1946 at the age of 16 months, quite an achievement for Poodles in that period. Mrs. Keene was well satisfied with the fact that her first two litters had each brought forth a champion, and she was filled with enthusiastic plans for the future.

In 1947 the Keenes imported a 13-inch brown dog from Reverend Buchanon in Scotland. He became Champion Bonhomme of Toytown and is to be found behind a large majority of the present Round Table winners. Mrs. Keene describes him as "a squarely built little dog, very sound, with a pleasing head," not the long, lean head of modern times, but a good one from the standpoint of the forties. This was the Round Table foundation stud dog.

Decollete, bred to Bonhomme, produced the brown bitch Champion Round Table's Brown Blossom. At this point the Round Table breeding program was limited to browns and blacks, but Mrs. Keene's interest and enthusiasm were growing and she found herself wanting to acquire some more new blood for the kennel, with the plan of establishing a white line, too.

In the early 1950's, three stud dogs were added who, combined with the bitches retained from the earlier litters, became dogs of tremendous importance from the breeding point of view. During a visit to England, Mrs. Keene saw and lost her heart to a black dog, Harwee of Mannerhead, belonging to Mrs. Campbell Inglis. Unlikely as it might seem, this dog, which she promptly purchased, became the foundation sire of the *white* line at Mrs. Keene's kennel. Harwee could not be shown as he never seemed to carry sufficient coat, no matter how much effort was expended in attempting to improve it. Nonetheless, I am certain that Mrs. Keene never regretted the purchase.

The other two studs purchased were another imported black, Champion Braebeck Esmond of Round Table, and a white, Champion Cricket of the Valley, Mrs. Keene's first Poodle of this color.

Cricket was a Best in Show winner and produced best when bred to a granddaughter of Champion Fircot L'Ballerine of Maryland, by name Heathermaid of Fircot and Round Table. Champion Round Table Cloche de Neige was a result of this combination.

Champion Round Table Elise was a daughter of Esmond and a granddaughter of Mannerhead Diamond, also going back to Champion Bonhomme of Toytown. She was bred to Cloche de Neige—actually it was an accidental mating,

This is the dog Mrs. Alden V. Keene considers the finest she has ever bred, the great white Miniature, Ch. Round Table Cognac. Winner of 24 all-breed Bests in Show, 11 Specialty Shows, and 80 Non-Sporting Groups—including Westminster, 1966.

but it combined all that had preceded at Round Table in one generation. In her litter of all whites came Round Table Eloise and Champion Round Table Conte Blanc. Eloise became the dam of three champions, and Conte Blanc finished under the guidance of Tom and Ann Stevenson in California. Back East he was campaigned by John Brennan and won two All-Breed Bests in Show along with many Groups. He holds a special place in Mrs. Keene's heart as her first homebred Best in Show winner.

In 1959 the opportunity arose for Mrs. Keene to acquire an interest in an especially lovely black bitch she had bred. This was Champion Moulin's Belle Fleurette, sired by a half brother to the great Champion Cappoquin Bon Jongleur, in turn a son of Champion Cappoquin Bon Fiston. Beautifully headed, with an excellent body and strong in both front- and hindquarters, this bitch was everything Mrs. Keene most admired, and she felt would be a tremendous help to her black line. Fleur was shown throughout her career in the ring by Anne Rogers Clark, and she was a show dog every inch of the way, reveling in the big rings where she won many a Group and Best in Show award.

It was planned to breed Fleurette to Champion Dunwalke Boutonniere, owned by Clarence Dillon in New Jersey. While there for the mating, Fleurette escaped and disappeared. This was during a truly bad winter, causing Mrs. Keene added concern for the dog who all her life had been pampered and kept in a warm kennel.

One day Dunwalke had a call that Fleurette had been sighted in the kennel area. One of the girls started off on the double with a lead, and Fleurette came to her quite easily. With the lead around her neck, Fleurette was led back on foot through the snow toward the kennel, but there was a barbed wire fence to be overcome along the way, over which the kennel girl climbed and Fleurette went to follow. But Fleurette's ear caught in the fence. Quite naturally she balked, and in a flash was gone again, with a torn ear. Everyone started to lose hope when Fleurette was not seen again for awhile. Then a little girl living out in the country, who had seen the notice in the local post office about the missing black Poodle, noticed some sort of strange fuzzy black animal entering their barn as the child was preparing for bed. At first her parents were disbelieving, but then they were persuaded to at least go look. And there was Fleurette. Dunwalke was called, and they contacted Richard Bauer, who had made many fruitless

Round Table Allegresse, handled by Frank Sabella for Mr. and Mrs. Alden V. Keene.

Ch. Round Table Danseuse Noel, handled here by Mrs. Anne Rogers Clark for Round Table Kennels. By Ch. Summercourt Square Dancer of Fircot ex Round Table Eloise.

Ch. Round Table Zinnia Noire, owned by Round Table Kennels, Mr. and Mrs. Alden V. Keene. Handled by John Brennan. By Ch. Rocaille Zorro ex Ch. Round Table Fleur Noire.

Ch. Round Table's Loramar Yeoman winning a Best in Show for the Round Table Kennels.

trips to New Jersey, going out on horseback looking for this bitch. He came immediately at the message, in the middle of the night and, to quote Mrs. Keene, "sat quite literally in the snow and talked to this bitch for at least two hours before she overcame her panic and realized this was someone she knew." Then she went wild, licking Richard's face, jumping all over him, ecstatic with happiness and relief. She was not in whelp, for which all concerned were grateful, and her torn ear had healed with no infection, but the torn cartilage remained for the rest of her lifetime. She was bred on three other occasions and is the dam and granddam of several champions.

In the mid-1960's, the Keenes purchased another dog from England, Champion Rocaille Zorro, who became a champion on the West Coast under Frank Sabella's guidance then returned East to be "specialed" by John Brennan, becoming a consistent Best of Variety and Group winner. Two of his progeny were Champion Round Table Zinnia Noire, from a Belle Fleurette daughter, and Champion Round Table Allegresse, who was out of a Belle Fleurette granddaughter.

As a tremendous admirer of Champion Summercourt Square Dancer of Fircot, Mrs. Keene was anxious to have a daughter of his for her white breeding program. This she acquired in the form of Surrey Dancer of Round Table, which Anne Clark owned from one of her own bitches and which she allowed the Keenes to purchase. Dancer was bred to Champion Round Table Conte Blanc, which produced the magnificent Champion Round Table Cognac, born two weeks before Christmas of 1961. Mrs. Keene says that "almost 18 years after my first litter, he was what I had wanted and worked so hard to breed."

Cognac made his show debut in the Open Class by winning first in two Groups, finishing his title in short order. Shown 154 times, his record stands at 146 times Best of Variety, eight times Best of Opposite Sex, 24 All-Breed Bests in Show, 11 Specialty Bests of Breed, and 80 Non-Sporting Group Firsts, including Westminster in 1966. He sired at least 14 champions, among them the Best in Show winners Champion Round Table Loramar Yeoman, Champion Round Table Boucanier, and International Champion Round Table Brandy Sniff (who went to England to Mrs. Rita Price-Jones, where he has gained the amazing total of 25 Challenge Certificates). There must be 50 or more white pedigrees in which Cognac's name appears at least once in the first three generations. He certainly goes down in history as one of the truly dominant, truly magnificent Miniature Poodles of all time.

Swag

Swag Poodles was so named back in the mid-1970's by Barbara Meyers of Brooklyn Park, Minnesota, following a fifteen-year period during which she had been breeding and raising Standards and occasionally Toys.

Now the kennel is jointly owned by Barbara and her daughters, Terri and Nancy. Both girls, along with their sister, Karen, now married and mother of the family's next "junior handler," have been very actively involved with the Poodles at home and in the show ring since the very beginning, and all have a very special love of the breed.

The first Standard the Meyers finished was a big fellow named Champion Meyers Hodgie Ba Ba, who gained his first major under Barbara Meyers' handling, then finished in quite short order when Bob Walberg took over his presentation. This dog and the second of their champions, the homebred Meyers Loreal who became their foundation bitch, are still alive and well and are active members of the family.

The Meyers' next champion was the famed Lou Gin's Kiss Me Kate, who has her own special chapter as "America's Foremost Show Dog" elsewhere in this book. Terri purchased the bitch from breeder Lou Dunston of the Lou Gin Poodles, and she started her career in the ring co-owned by Terri and Barbara.

Then came Katie's brother, Champion Lou Gin's Solitaire, who, like Kate, finished as a puppy; he took Best of Opposite Sex to Best of Breed to Katie when she won the specialty. Solitaire has two champions so far to his credit. One of his offspring has two Puppy Groups back to back in Canada, while another has Best of Breed wins and Group placements. Several of his progeny have major points as well. Solitaire was in the Top Twenty for breed and group placements in 1979. Both Solitaire and Kate have won the Twin Cities Poodle Club Specialty.

A lovely Poodle the Meyers bred and sold, Champion Meyers Dulcinea, finished her title in three days with three five-point majors; she was handled by Nancy Meyers.

As this is written, Wentworth George needs but a major to finish, Swag's Anticipation is also close to the title, Swag's Flicka (being shown by Nancy for her new owners) is on the way to the title, Swag's Born Free will be back in the ring

now following her litter, and Swag's Cat Ballou, Swag's Calamity Jane, and Swag's Belle Star are prospects for the 1981 shows.

Swag was inactive in the Toy variety for awhile, but then a new owner of a Toy the Meyers had bred and sold asked Nancy to campaign it. Swag's Foolish Pleasure has taken the variety and some Group placements since making his debut at six months of age. Another Toy, Swag's Brown Bomber, was a breed winner from the puppy class, and her puppy, Swag's Genuine Risk, will be out in 1981.

When she graduated from school, Terri Meyers was invited to work for Bob Walberg as his assistant, which she is doing very well.

We asked Barbara Meyers to please explain her choice of the kennel name Swag. To this she replied that, after 15 years of raising dogs, she felt that "Swag well describes what it takes – 'Scientific Wild-Ass Guess': Scientific study followed by a wild guess which one hopes will work out right."

Right from the beginning, Swag has been a family enterprise, with the girls every bit as interested and involved as Barbara herself. She says she used to chuckle when, standing at ringside, she listened to herself being criticized

WINNERS DOG

GILBERT PHOTO

for permitting ten- and twelve-year-old girls to take her dogs into the ring, for Barbara felt that as they did so much for the care and correct keeping of the dogs at home, the girls were entitled to enjoy showing them if they wished. It has all worked out very well.

While they sometimes do not agree on the merits of individual Poodles, the Meyers do absolutely agree that the requisites of an excellent example of the breed are movement, good front and rear, shortness of back, and correct angulations.

Barbara's husband, Bud, is a "behind the scenes" supporter of the Swag Poodle venture. Solitaire is his "special" favorite, and we understand that Bud has missed many a leisurely weekend and good golf game to "hold the fort" at home so that Barbara and the girls could go off to the shows.

Syntifny

Mrs. Jane A. Winne, of Syntifny Poodles, located at Three Rivers, Michigan, started her breeding program interested primarily in silver Toys. She remarks that although "it has proved to be a much more difficult color for me to breed the quality for which I strive, I have finished

Ch. Yerbrier Syntifny Shamu, son of Ch. Syntifny Piece Of The Rock, Jane A. Winne, owner, Syntifny Poodles.

Ch. Puttencove Presentation taking Winners Dog at Westminster 1974 under judge Henry Stoecker. By Ch. Alekai Luau ex Puttencove Primrose and handled by Wendell J. Sammet for Mr. and Mrs. Terrence Levy.

nine silver champions." Three of these are Canadian Champions and the other six hold their titles in the U.S.A. The silver homebred American and Canadian Champion Syntifny Silverdrift is the sire of seven champions, three Canadian and four in the U.S.A. Mrs. Winne also co-owns a lovely silver son of Champion Syntifny Piece of The Rock, Champion Leecroft Coined Silver, bred by Lee Paul of Leecroft Poodles and co-owned with her. He is proving to be an outstanding silver sire. Both owners are greatly excited over this dog, looking forward to seeing his name on the Top Producer lists soon. Mrs. Winne feels very definitely that incorporating the Piece of The Rock line with her silvers has improved the latter noticeably.

Champion Syntifny Piece Of The Rock was born on March 31, 1974. Such excitement!—Syntifny's first litter of white puppies and the first litter for the dearly loved Adona, who later became American and Canadian Champion Adona of Aurora. She had been bred by Myrtle Schroeder and came to Syntifny by way of Arlene Mueller, Aurora Kennels.

Very early Jane Winne realized that the little girl in the litter, Syntifny Pebbles, would be too small for the show ring, so the puppy who was going to become Champion Syntifny's Piece of The Rock took over the top spot, which he has never relinquished. In speaking of these puppies Mrs. Winne comments, "Of course I have always admired their dam; she was such a sweet, loving, and affectionate bitch in addition to being a gorgeous one. Many people have told me that their decision to breed to Rocky has been based on their admiration for his dam when they had seen her in the ring." Sadly, this little bitch died when she was three years old.

When Adona's litter was two months old, she went to Todd Patterson to start her show career, and she finished her title in less than three months. Then it was Rocky's turn. "What a happy, bubbly puppy! He was so exuberant, and did so love the show ring. The only trouble Todd ever had with him was getting him to settle down; he wanted to fly. I saw him in the ring very few times, as Todd took him on the Florida Circuit and he returned within a very few points of being finished."

During Rocky's stay with Todd Patterson, Nel Korbijn had bred five of her bitches to him, so it was not long before she had "Rocky kids" ready to make their debut. Mrs. Winne says, "I owe a great deal to her, as my own white breeding program consisted of only Adona and Rocky. Nel Korbijn finished Rocky's first four champion offspring, Champion Kornel's Paradise having been the first, in 1976, then in 1977 the litter mates Champion Kornel's Holiday and Champion Kornel's Hey Day, a Group winner from the classes, owner-handled. Hey Day later was sold to Mavis Dustow and became a Best in Show winner and the Top Winning Toy Poodle in Canada. The fourth one was Champion Kornel's Keeper of the Kastle, a multiple Group and Best in Show winner, later sold to Japan and now the Top Winning Toy Poodle there. Rocky became a Top Producer in 1977, just after his third birthday.

Rocky is the sire of 40 champions to date, four Canadian, one Japanese, and 35 American. He is the Top Living Toy Sire and, at six years old, the youngest of the Top Ten Toy Sires. He has approximately 35 more offspring in the ring now and more youngsters coming but not yet old enough for the show ring, so there would seem to be still a chance of him becoming the All Time Top Producing Toy Sire.

And now we shall quote Jane Winne on the sad and tragic part of this kennel resume. She says, "I cannot end this without a few words about the theft of Rocky and his young son, Shamu, on March 28, 1980. When my boys were stolen, it just took the heart right out of me. I couldn't imagine going on with any kind of breeding program without my Rocky. All of my interest and plans had centered around him. I was so fortunate to have my very dear friends gather around and help me get through that most trying time. I will never be able to understand how anyone could do such a thing. I guess that whoever took them thought that they needed them more than I do. But I will continue to search, and hope that someday whoever has them will let my boys come home. Rocky was stolen just three days before his sixth birthday."

The theft of these two Poodles flashed from coast to coast in the newspapers, on television, and on radio. Everyone who has ever cared about a dog will sympathize with Jane Winne. The dogs were taken from her kennel during a short absence from home. I certainy hope that by the time you are reading this these dogs will be back where they belong, with their owner.

Mrs. Winne has two Top Producing Bitches, Canadian Champion Yerbrier Fun 'N' Fancy, co-owned with Patricia McMullen of Michanda Poodles, and a silver homebred, Syntifny Sweettalk.

Jane Winne's kennel is a small one, and, having limited space, she has made it a policy to sell her Rocky children. "I wanted mainly to keep

Ch. Syntifny Happy Hour, by Ch. Yerbrier Lovem 'N' Leavem from a daughter of Syntifny Pebbles, litter sister to Ch. Syntifny Piece Of The Rock, Jane A. Winne, Syntifny, Three Rivers, Michigan. Todd Patterson handling.

Am., Can. Ch. Adiona of Aurora, the dam of Ch. Syntifny's Piece of The Rock. Owned by Jane A. Winne, Syntifny, Three Rivers, Michigan.

bitches, specifically to breed to him. I am so very fortunate that he had been bred to a number of my bitches just before he was stolen. He left me a lovely legacy. I have three Rocky sons and six daughters coming up, super quality, that will be the foundation of my future breeding stock."

Jane Winne is the breeder of 19 U.S.A. champions, five Canadian champions, one Spanish champion, and two Japanese champions. Additionally she has finished six other champions of which she is not the breeder.

Tilo

Tilo Poodles, owned by Miss Laura Niles of Bayshore, New York, was active and highly successful during the mid- to late 1950's and on into the 1960's. Among the best known winners owned by Miss Niles were Champion Tilo Demi Tasse and Champion Cappoquin Railsplitter, both Best in Show Miniatures.

Ch. Tilo Lin-Ed's Charm pictured in 1972. Richard Bauer handles for owner, Miss Laura Niles.

Ch. Cappoquin Railsplitter, owned by Miss Laura Niles and handled by Robert S. Forsyth, wins Best in Show under Louis J. Murr at Detroit Kennel Club, 1962.

Champion Bric A Brac Black Velvet, C.D.X., did well for her owner as a show bitch, as a producer, and in obedience competition, which has always interested Miss Niles. She produced three noted champions among her other accomplishments.

Cappoquin and Bric A Brac bloodlines made up the foundation stock behind Miss Niles' winners. A dog in which Miss Niles took great pride, Champion Tilo Trade Mark, was another of hers who seemed destined to have a highly successful ring career, but unfortunately the dog died quite suddenly just on the threshold of starting out as a "special."

For a few years when her handlers (Bob and Jane Forsyth) started cutting back on showing Poodles, Miss Niles was inactive in the show ring. But in 1976 she started again, and her Tilo Lin Ed's Charm, by Champion Campbell's Razz-Ma-Tazz out of Lin Ed's Nohi Lalianda, finished for her quickly under Richard Bauer's handling. Now Charm's daughter, Tilo Catherine the great, is being successfully campaigned and should have completed her championship by the time you are reading this.

Valhalla

Valhalla Standard Poodles has carved a niche in Poodle greatness for its owner, Catherine Kish of Tonawanda, New York, who had the foresight and good judgement to select Champion Puttencove Perdita as her foundation bitch and then breed her to Champion Acadia Command Performance. The combination truly hit the jackpot, giving Mrs. Kish her multiple Best in Show and Specialty winning bitch, Champion Valhalla's Critic's Choice, and the Top Producing Dog, also an all-breed Best in Show and Specialty winner, Champion Valhalla's In Command. Critic's Choice has done her share in the production end, too, being the dam of the future young hopeful Champion Valhalla's Main Event, who completed her title from the puppy classes and will soon start out as a "special."

Mrs. Kish has bred six champions at Valhalla, three of which are Best in Show winners, which is indeed a mighty splendid average. Perdita is now eight years old.

Now fully mature, Champion Acadia Xaari steps into the Best in Show winners circle, on this occasion under Mrs. George Dow. Frank Sabella is handling for owner, Edward B. Jenner, Knolland Farm, Richmond, Illinois.

CHAPTER FIVE

Poodles in Australia

For a very long time now I have been increasingly aware of the excellence of Poodles being imported and bred by Australian fanciers. Friends from the U.S. who have gone there to judge have brought back glowing reports of the breed in that country. Some top-flight breeders from America and other countries around the world have been buying Australian-bred Poodles in all varieties to introduce into their own kennels and breeding programs. Of course, when I started making plans for this book I determined that an Australian chapter was a "must" if the book was to give a true picture of what is taking place in Poodles today. The cooperation of the prominent breeders I contacted there has been extremely helpful and is appreciated. We feel that the following pages will bring you a fair perspective on the truly great job being done "down under" in the Poodle world.

John Edwards and Phillip Warburton established the Marsden Kennels in New South Wales back in the early 1960's, starting out with English Cocker Spaniels and then adding American Cockers and Poodles. At about this time a famous English breeder was settling in this country, the lady who owned the Summercourt Kennels from which the immortal American Champion Summercourt Square Dancer of Fircot, Top Producing Miniature Sire for many years in the United States, had come. Her arrival in Australia signaled high excitement in the Poodle world, as she was accompanied by some stunning dogs, mainly of the Toy variety. Unfor-

tunately she passed away only a few years later, indeed a sad loss to the breed.

Friendship with this knowledgeable lady had led John Edwards to becoming interested in Toy Poodles, so he imported an excellent black male, Champion Barsbrae Outward Bound, in partnership with a friend. This little dog became one of the most outstanding winners and producers in Australia, his champion offspring now exceeding 50. To quote Mr. Edwards, "no other Toy Poodle has had such a wide influence on the breed in Australia." Now 16 years old and retired, Outward Bound continues to bask in the reflected glory of his sons and grandsons who are carrying on as leading winners. Mr. Edwards campaigned Outward Bound during his entire show career but did not become interested in breeding until he had become involved with Miniatures.

The first Miniature purchased by Mr. Edwards and Mr. Warburton was Champion Jeunesse Justa Joie, imported from the United Kingdom; he was sired by English Champion Tranchant Philisma Pablo, a leading English sire of the 1970's. Joie won five all-breed Bests in Show and became the dam of five champions, including Australian and American Champion Marsden Indeed I Do, owned by Richard Beauchamp and S. Helgeson of California.

Since then Marsden Kennels has been instrumental in importing several top quality Miniature bitches to Australia from the United Kingdom. Among them is Australian Champion

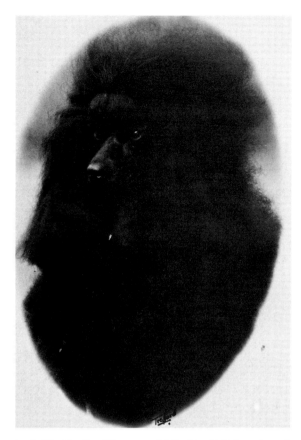

Aust. Ch. Beritas Bianco, exhibited by J. Edwards and P. Warburton, New South Wales, Australia.

Can. and Aust. Ch. Wycliffe Sybil taking first in the Non-Sporting Group at the Australian Royal Dog Show (1200 dogs). Exported to Australia from Wycliffe Poodles in Canada. Mrs. Donald Lyle, owner. Barry Ross, handling.

Beritas Bianco, dam of five champions, who is a daughter of an American Top Producer, Champion Beritas Ronlyn Rockafella. Their exceedingly lovely English and American Champion Black Delinquent of Idadown became Top Winning Miniature of her time in Australia, and was the winner of ten Challenge Certificates in the United Kingdom. To date Delinquent has produced six champions, with three more that are pointed. Her most famed winning daughter, Champion Marsden Black Antics, went Best of Breed at Sydney Royal 1979 under the American judge James Edward Clark; Best of Breed at Melbourne Royal 1979 under another U.S.A. judge, Dr. Lee Huggins; and Best of Breed at the R.A.S. under still another American judge, Mrs. Irene Schlintz. Another daughter, Champion Marsden Black Dilemma, went Best Bitch in Show at Adelaide Royal 1980 under a noted judge from Sweden.

Eng. and Aust. Ch. Black Delinquent of Idedown, winner of eight Royal Challenges and 10 English Kennel Club Challenges, is owned by J. Edwards and P. Warburton, N.S.W., Australia.

Unfortunately, Delinquent's best son, Marsden Black Vandal, went oversize, but he has proved to be a fantastic sire. This is the dog who has been exported to Norway, where his size will not be unacceptable.

One of the most successful of the Marsden Poodles was purchased locally in Australia from the breeder. This is Champion Proudaire By Golly, who became Dog of the Year in New South Wales for 1975-1976. His wins include 20 Bests in Show and nine Royal Challenge Certificates under some outstanding Poodle experts. This is the dog who "Bud" Dickey purchased during a recent visit to Australia; he is already an

Ch. Denise of Piperscroft, a Miniature owned by Helen Thompson, Winelist Kennels, is pictured here with her handler Ben Burwell.

Note the super quality of this Miniature, Aust. Ch. Marsden Black Antics, one of the many splendid Poodles bred by John Edwards and Phillip Warburton, Glenore, New South Wales, Australia. This dog has eight Bests in Show.

U.S.A. Poodle authority, Judge Mrs. Marjorie Tranchin, looks at the winners she has selected at the Poodle Club of Victoria Specialty, March 1977. Best Bitch and Best in Show was the Miniature. Eng., Aust. Ch. Black Delinquent of Idetown; Best Dog in Show, the Standard, Ch. Prowler of Leander.

Aust. and Am. Ch. Proudaire By Golly, one of the most successful dogs with whom John Edwards and Phillip Warburton have been involved. Purchased from a local breeder as a young dog, this outstanding Miniature became New South Wales' Dog of the Year, 1975 and 1976, as winner of 20 Best in Show awards and nine Royal Challenge Certificates. At 4½ years old, he was exported to the United States, having been purchased by Mr. Freeman "Bud" Dickey of Ohio. By Golly gained his American title becoming a Group winner in short order.

American Group Winning champion and evidently is headed for a highly successful stud career.

In total, Marsden has bred 24 Champion Miniatures in the past eight years. Sixteen of these dogs became Best in Show winners. Their oldest Miniature lady, Joie, is still ruler of the pack at nine years of age.

Marsden Black Vandal, the gorgeous Miniature that unfortunately went oversize, has lately been exported to Norway where his quality will be appreciated and size not held against him. An exciting future is anticipated there for this excellent dog, bred by J. Edwards and P. Warburton. Vandal, in 12 months at stud in Australia, produced six champions of whom two are Best in Show winners.

In Standards activity has been limited along with time and space. Nonetheless, Marsden has had considerable impact on this variety, too. They purchased Champion Tandonia A Touch O' Spice, a locally bred black bitch of Acadia and Wycliffe bloodlines who became Top Standard Bitch in Australia, won nine Royal Challenge Certificates and, then took the Group at Melbourne Royal in 1978 under Langdon Skarda from the United States. One litter was bred from a litter sister to Touch O' Spice who produced three champions. Two of these, Champion Marsden Doubting Thomas and Champion Marsden Mindya Manners, are both Best in Show winners. Champion Mindya Manners is currently Queenslands' Top Dog, having had ten Bests in Show during 1980, including two under Dr. Spira and one under the Canadian authority Hans Brunotte.

It was in 1974 that Troy Tanner arrived in

Aust. Ch. Marsden Centrefold, by Marsden Black Vandal, has four Best in Show awards. Bred by John Edwards and Phillip Warburton, Glendore, N.S.W., Australia.

Sydney accompanied by six Poodles, four of them Toys and the other two Miniatures. This young man, a native of Sweden, came to Australia with his parents as a baby. Shortly thereafter, due to a break-up in the family, he went to live in the United States, returning eventually to settle in Australia, the country he had grown to love. While living in the States and pursuing his chosen profession, hairdressing, he had spent his time equally there and in England, working as understudy to the famed Vidal Sassoon. As has been commented, "small wonder his Poodle preparation was faultless."

When he returned to Australia, Troy Tanner settled in Perth, but he soon found that this location was a bit geographically remote for the type of dog show competition he felt he would enjoy. He requested a transfer and soon moved to his present location, Sydney. There he keeps a kennel of about 15 adult Poodles and breeds an occasional litter while at the same time running a highly fashionable beauty salon in the suburb of Gordon, to the north of Sidney.

Champion Toypetite Libra and her dam, Cowan's Tourterelle, who was imported from Bermuda, headed the Troymere show dogs in those earlier days. However, Mr. Tanner soon decided he wanted some new outcross to his breeding stock. Champion Francelle My Felicity was purchased from a local breeder, Mrs. P. Darley, and a stunning little deep chocolate Toy male from England, Champion Montmartre Marmion of Montflair, was also selected. Breedings of these two proved highly successful in that they produced Champion Troymere Achievement and Champion Troymere The Way We Were in successive litters. Between them, these two sisters have indeed made Toy history.

This handsome Standard, Aust. Ch. Marsden Mindya Manners, was bred by John Edwards and Phillip Warburton of New South Wales, Australia. Currently Queensland's top dog as this is written, Mindya Manners had at least 10 Bests in Show during 1980.

Another magnificent Standard owned by Australian breeders J. Edwards and P. Warburton is Aust. Ch. Tandina A Touch O Spice, proudly surrounded by some of her trophies. Bred from Arcadia and Wycliffe stock, Touch O Class won nine Royal Challenge Certificates and the Group at the Melbourne Royal event, 1978.

Aust. Ch. Tranchant Delectabelle, imported from England, is owned by Troy Tanner of Troymere Poodles, Sidney, Australia.

Awards for the Miniature, Aust. Ch. Troymere Heaven On Earth, include: Puppy Class winner, Royal Adelaide, 1978; Best Puppy in Show, Poodle Club of New South Wales, 1978; Reserve Challenge, Poodle Club of New South Wales, 1978 (at 8 months old). Troy Tanner, breeder-owner, Sidney, Australia.

Aust. ch. Miss Brun Fonce of Montflair (imported from the United Kingdom) was a Junior Warrant winner in the U.K. and a Challenge winner at the Adelaide Royal, 1977. Troy Tanner is the owner, Troymere Poodles, Sidney, Australia.

N.Z. and Aust. Ch. Tranchant Actionman, the Top Winning Miniature in New Zealand, 1979. Troymere Poodles, Sidney, Australia.

This is the leading Toy winner ever to be exported to Australia, Eng. and Aust. Ch. Montmartre Marmion of Montflair. He came to Troy Tanner in Sidney with 12 British Challenge Certificates to his credit. A deep chocolate brown, this little dog is an outstanding sire of noted winning Toys. Marmion, although shown sparingly in Australia, is a multiple Group Winner there.

Aust. Ch. Troymere Achievement, winner of the Challenge and Best Toy at the Poodle Club of South Australia, and the challenge at the Royal Melbourne Show. Starting her show career most auspiciously, she gained three Best in Group awards and two Best in Show awards.

Mr. Tanner has been quoted as considering The Way We Were to be the Best Toy Poodle he has owned, bred, or possibly even seen. These are strong words, but then there is a lot on the record to substantiate them, as it includes at least 12 Best in Show wins, among them two Poodle Specialties, Challenge Certificates in 1977 and 1978 from the Royal Adelaide, first in the Non-Sporting Group (where Toy Poodles are classified in Australia) at the huge Melbourne Royal, and – under Irene Schlintz – Best in Show at the Spring Sydney Show the following year. These were just "starters" though, for this lovely bitch's list of wins by now has grown to include Best in Show at numerous other events along with additional Group Firsts and Challenge Certificates.

Meanwhile, Champion Troymere Achievement has been keeping right along with her sister. We understand that Achievement will soon be bred to the young Troymere Systeman, who was born in 1978 and quickly gained his title.

As for The Way We Were, she was bred back to her sire and recently has whelped a super litter by him.

This Miniature, Ch. Troymere High Heritage has two super puppies on the way to the title as this is written. They are Troymere Man About Town and Troymere Main Event. This excellent bitch belongs to Troy Tanner, Troymere Kennels, Sydney, Australia.

Ch. Troymere Mahogany, brown Miniature bitch, Challenge Winner, Royal Melbourne Show, Best Non-Sporting Bitch. Owned by Troy G. Tanner, Troymere Poodles, Sidney, Australia.

Aust. Ch. Flitwick Famous Amos, a Best in Show winner bred and owned by Mr. and Mrs. Robert J. Harrison, New South Wales, Australia. Handled by John Edwards and Phillip Warburton.

Ch. Leecroft Coined Silver, by Ch. Syntifny Piece Of The Rock, bred by Leecroft Poodles and co-owned with Syntifny. Todd Patterson, handler.

Another favorite with the judges is the chocolate bitch Troymere Mahogany (by Champion Grayco Joie de Vivre), who was a Certificate winner while still in the Puppy Classes.

Still another enthusiastic Poodle owner from whom we have heard in Australia is Mrs. R. J. Harrison. A fancier from the United States, Mrs. Harrison and her husband were involved with pure-bred dogs here for more than 20 years (including about five years as superintendents with Moss Bow Dog Shows in the Detroit office). The Harrisons enjoy living in Australia, and they are also doing well with their Poodles there.

This very outstanding Miniature is Flitwich Flash Harry bred and owned by Mr. and Mrs. Robert J. Harrison, handled by John Edwards and Phillip Warburton.

Aust. Ch. Troymere Precocious, a Proudaire-owned bitch. Born in 1978, her list of wins through February 1981 includes: one Best Minor in Show (all breeds), one Best Puppy in Show (all breeds), two Best Junior in Group awards, one Best Junior in Show at a Poodle specialty, and one Best in Show, all breeds, with 2300 dogs competing.

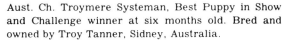

Aust. Ch. Troymere Systeman, Best Puppy in Show and Challenge winner at six months old. Bred and owned by Troy Tanner, Sidney, Australia.

Am. and Can. Ch. Wycliffe Thomas, a multiple Best in
Show winner, is a Top Sire in the breed with 67 cham-
pions to his credit. Mrs. Donald Lyle, owner, Wycliffe
Poodles, Vancouver, Canada.

CHAPTER SIX

Poodles in Canada

A full view of the handsome Dutch Ch. Wycliffe Lord Liege of Fortune imported from Holland to the Wycliffe Poodles in Vancouver, Canada.

It is frequently my pleasure to judge at Canadian dog shows, and when Poodles are part of my assignment that pleasure is increased by the excellence and beauty to be found there in all three varieties of the breed. That Canadian Poodle breeders are doing their work well is very clear, and these accomplishments are being reflected in the records, as Canada must take enormous pride in the fact that one of their own, Mrs. Donald Lyle, holds the position of having bred the second greatest number of Poodle champions produced to date on the North American continent.

There are others, too, who are breeding excellent Poodles and whose achievements have been widely recognized. We wish it were possible to bring you a resume of each, but our space is limited, so we must confine this chapter to just a few.

Wycliffe is an especially interesting kennel, not only due to the records it has maintained but also due to the type of establishment it is and the manner in which it is run. Somehow when one thinks in terms of records one immediately sees visions of a huge very professional kennel operation. This is definitely not the case where Wycliffe Poodles is concerned. Mrs. Lyle refers to it as "The Back Yard Kennel," and, strange as it may seem, this is an accurate description. Something else we like about the Wycliffe operation is that it has been a family project mutually participated in and enjoyed by the Lyles and their three children.

Wycliffe had its beginning back in 1952 when the Lyles had been through one or two experiences with unsuitable pets and were looking for a large, fastidious, bright, and amusing canine companion that could be easily trained. What better than a Standard Poodle? Fortunately they discovered the breed in New York when they encountered a puppy of half-Swiss breeding who, as it turned out, was destined to become their foundation bitch. This puppy grew up to be American and Canadian Champion Carillon Michelle, American C.D.X. and Canadian U.D.T. At the same time that they discovered Poodles, the Lyles also discovered the "wonderful Blanche Saunders" who had bred Michelle and with whom they became close friends.

Michelle found all phases of obedience quick and easy to learn, to the Lyles' great pride. Additionally she was a super "family dog" and very popular in the suburban neighborhood where they lived, learning tricks, playing shortstop at ball games, enjoying hunting, retrieving, swimming, and diving. The Lyles did become irked, however, when they began to hear remarks about obedience being a fine pastime for "pet stock," but that it ruined "show dogs." So they decided to rout this falsehood by taking Michelle out for conformation classes. Quickly she became a champion in both the United States and Canada, despite the Lyles' most amateurish grooming and handling.

Their success with Michelle inevitably led to her owners' wanting a second Poodle for both

Am. and Can. Ch. Wycliffe Nicola, C.D.X. Mrs. Donald Lyle, owner, Vancouver, Canada.

obedience and conformation showing. They found that there was an excellent Standard dog in the same city where they lived, a dog of almost identical bloodlines to Michelle, so she was bred to American and Canadian Champion Petitcote Domino, C.D. As a result of this line-breeding, in their very first litter (of ten!) the Lyles produced their famous and highly successful bitch, American and Canadian Champion Wycliffe Jacqueline, American U.D., Canadian U.D.T., who was a multiple Best in Show and Group winner plus also many times Highest Scoring Dog in Trial. But, as Mrs. Lyle says, "Her best contribution to posterity was her fertility and the remarkable quality of her get."

Jacqueline's five litters produced a total of 41 puppies, 21 of whom became champions, a number becoming top dogs in the breed. These two great bitches (Michelle and Jacqueline) are to be found behind an amazing number of quality Standard Poodles in all parts of the world. They were truly a dominant producing force, and their contribution to Standard Poodle excellence has been enormous.

Numbered among Jacqueline's most noted progeny were American and Canadian Champion Wycliffe Nicola, C.D.X.; American and Canadian Champion Wycliffe Thomas; American and Canadian Champion Wycliffe Timothy; Canadian Champion Wycliffe Theresa; American Champion Wycliffe Veronica; American Champion Wycliffe Virgil; American and Canadian Champion Wycliffe Xavier; and American Champion Wycliffe Xira of Loribon.

Small changes began to occur in the lifestyle of the Lyles. Their back garden acquired a puppy pen, as did their warm basement. On increasing numbers of weekends Mr. and Mrs. Lyle traveled on the dog show route, taking the children to the northern and western shows on both sides of the border and doing so with considerable success. When they took their holiday at Palm Springs over Christmas, so did the Poodles. Almost immediately a pattern emerged of raising two or three litters each year.

The Lyles' first requirement regarding their breeding program was that no Poodle puppy ever was to come into the world unwanted and unspoken for at their behest, which came to mean that a bitch would not be mated until such time as orders were on hand for at least half of a normal litter—trusting that good homes would appear for the remaining half a litter during the four and a half months elapsing between the time of breeding and when the puppies reached ten weeks old, at which age they were ready to leave for new homes. Since the sophisticated, lovely, social, and companionable Wycliffe Poodles were such excellent ambassadors for the breed and their own progeny—plus the rise in Poodle popularity in the 1950's and 60's—placing all puppies well never presented the least problem.

Mrs. Lyle found in raising Poodles that "like breeds like," and that the progeny of a bullying dam were even more quarrelsome, whereas a sweet dam produced dispositions like her own or

Can. Ch. Wycliffe Genevieve at 15 months. Bred and owned by Mrs. Donald Lyle, Vancouver, Canada.

Ch. Wycliffe Delilah, C.D., bred and owned by Mrs. Donald Lyle.

Wycliffe Isabella of Pannovis at nine months old. Mrs. Donald Lyle, owner.

Wycliffe Emma-Elizabetta, winning two points at Duluth for Mrs. Donald Lyle, owner.

better. They became extremely discriminating in selection of the bitches they would keep for breeding, as regards both type and temperament. To quote her, "Though each parent contributes equally the genetic material which controls physique, health, and disposition, it is the dam who environmentally affects her puppies' health, growth, and disposition in those early weeks while she is caring for them." Thus, feeling that the dam makes by far the more important parent, the practice at Wycliffe has been that of pinning one's principal hopes on its long procession of high quality brood bitches.

As the Lyles saw more Poodles, their ambition grew to slightly alter certain things within their line. Of course it was of major importance to retain the high intelligence, fine personality, and working abilities that had distinguished their earliest Poodles, but they wished to increase the size of their dogs more in keeping with the larger English Poodles of the day as opposed to the smaller European ones. Also they eliminated the cream gene which their early dogs carried recessively, feeling that its presence possibly destroyed the depth of black color which they admired. They wanted to be certain that their puppies possessed the correct angulation front and rear to carry their heads high on long, strong necks and their tails set properly to be carried high as the dogs moved strongly with the correct straightforward, easy, light trot. Wanting her Poodles to be so well-constructed that even cut down their profiles would assure their being recognized as poodles from a mile away, Jean

Can. Ch. Wycliffe Tiara of Pannovia winning at the Poodle Club of Southeast Michigan, 1972, for Mrs. Donald Lyle, owner.

Lyle concentrated her breeding efforts on the difficult basic structure so essential to the breed. The results have been most gratifying.

Since Poodles consider themselves people and the Lyles did not want to treat such sensitive and devoted animals other than as family members, the Wycliffe puppies were sold, whether as show stock or pets, only to homes where the owners themselves would care for the dogs. Few ever went to kennels. Mrs. Lyle liked her dogs to be owner-handled for people to better enjoy, and points out that all Poodles shown in the 29 years

Am. and Can. Ch. Wycliffe Genevieve winning the Non-Sporting Group at a Whidbey Island Kennel Club Dog Show. Mrs. Donald Lyle, owner.

of Wycliffe's career have been owner-handled "by me who whelped them," feeling that this is a Poodle's due.

Unavoidably there have been occasions when the Lyles have found themselves unable to accommodate the entire number of Poodles they wished to keep. That has been solved by the placement of these dogs in the homes of close friends or relatives, particularly in the case of young bitch champions, where they could bring pleasure and enjoy family life, and could be brought home for breeding so that Mrs. Lyle could whelp and rear their litters. This was an ideal solution in the opinion of all concerned. It

Ch. Wycliffe Titania going Best of Variety over specials on the way to Group Two at Sioux City Kennel Club, May 1973. Owned by Mrs. Donald Lyle.

has made it possible for the Lyles to retain control over a sufficient number of animals to develop their strain as they wished, at the same time making it possible for them to continue to live in the suburb where they had chosen to raise their children.

Their mentor had said, "Never keep a dog unless he is so good that others as well as you will wish to use him. Otherwise it is better to breed to fine dogs owned by others." This seemed like sound advice, so the Lyles followed it for quite some time. Then, at the start of their sixth year as breeders, Jacqueline produced (on

April 1, 1959) her famous "T" litter, in which was the "beloved and stately gentleman Poodle" who became Champion Wycliffe Thomas. He completed his title on the East Coast mostly owner-handled in three consecutive weekends when he was 13 months old. He soon continued along to win many Groups and Bests in Show, all owner-breeder-handled, and he became the Top Producing Sire in his breed with 67 champions. At home Tom ruled the other Poodles with unvarying kindness but authority. Never during his lifetime, either inside or outside of his home, did any other dog ever question his authority. Of him Mrs. Lyle says, "He was most royal. He was utter joy to live with. And even in his domestic situation he created no problems concerning mixed-sex living."

Glenna Carlson's lovely Standard, Ch. Wycliffe Fanfare of Ascot, age two years, winning Best in Show at the St. Croix Valley Kennel Club, August 1976.

Am., Can. and Mex. Ch. Wycliffe Kenneth, a multiple Best in Show winner, is the sire of 66 champions. Owned by Mrs. Donald Lyle, Wycliffe Poodles, Vancouver, Canada.

When Thomas was four and a half, he produced, from his daughter Zara, a litter which included his son Kenneth, who was so very beautiful that the Lyles had to keep him, too. Father and son lived together harmoniously with several girl Poodles until Thomas' premature death at age eight years. Because he lived with his famous sire so much of his life, Kenneth's stud services were not so widely used as they might otherwise have been. Even so, he managed to sire a total of 66 champions. By coincidence many of Kenneth's offspring were exported to various countries of the world, and as a result of this his influence has been more apparent on a worldwide basis than that of Thomas.

When Kenneth died at age seven, he left an infant son who became American and Canadian Champion Wycliffe Thomas Too. A most impressive dog with slightly more substance than his sire and grandsire, he has sired 16 champions, the most important of them being American and Canadian Champion Wycliffe Xcellente of Shamlot, the sire of 22 champions. Shamlot in turn sired American and Canadian Champion Wycliffe Fitzherbert, who by the age of six years has sired 45 champions. What a magnificent unbroken line of male Top Pro-

Wycliffe Nocturne, handled by Anne Goodwin for Glenna Carlson at Ravenna, 1971, was awarded Winners Bitch for four points. One of the lovely Poodles from Canada's Wycliffe Kennels.

206

Am. and Can. Ch. Wycliffe Thomas Too, the sire of 16 champions. Mrs. Donald Lyle, owner.

ducers, all but one of whom have also won Bests in Show!

As involving as they have found their own Poodle activities, it was inevitable that the Lyles sold to many other fanciers some puppies equally as fine as those they kept. This, of course, has expanded their own interests and they have shared the pride of achievement these dogs and breeders have attained. The successes of other kennels with Wycliffe stock have been phenomenal and have reached as far as England, Holland, Germany, Argentina, Australia, and other distant points. Nearer home there are also many outstanding kennels based strongly on Wycliffe foundation stock. Among them are Acadia, Annveron, Ascot, Clabon, Dassin, Dhubne, Haus Brau, Koronet, Oakgrove and Wentworth.

The lists of Top Producing Standard Poodle sires published in 1980 by the Poodle Club of America contained the names of 20 Wycliffe stud dogs. The numbers they quote are necessarily incomplete, since they counted only American Kennel Club champions, whereas Wycliffe, being Canadian, has many champions in Canada as well as many in other foreign countries. As noted above, the four of these Top Studs that remained at home with the Lyles, Thomas, Kenneth, Thomas Too, and Fitzherbert, produced a total of nearly 200 champions. The other Top Producing Wycliffe Poodles who were sold to other owners include American and

Canadian Champion Wycliffe Virgil (50 champions), American and Canadian Champion Wycliffe Hadrian (25), American and Canadian Champion Wycliffe Xcellente of Shamlot (22), American Champion Wycliffe Martin (19), American and Canadian Champion Wycliffe Timothy (16), American, Canadian, Mexican, Bermudian, and International Champion Wycliffe Varner (15), American Champion Wycliffe LeRoy (13), American Champion Wycliffe Chricton (11), and some half dozen others.

Because of having greatest faith in the benefits of line-breeding, the Lyles have owned the majority of the Wycliffe Top Producing Bitches themselves. These have included American and Canadian Champion Wycliffe Jacqueline, U.D.T. (21 champions), American and Canadian Champion Wycliffe Zandra (15), American and Canadian Champion Wycliffe Genevieve (11), Canadian Champion Wycliffe Theresa (11), and numerous others.

Several lovely bitches, after having produced one litter for the Lyles, were sold to others for whom they became Top Producers, as have numerous puppies that went to new homes at an early age.

Looking at the total picture is very impressive. The Lyles have bred a total of 189 Wycliffe champions in 26 years out of approximately 700

Ch. Wycliffe Fitzherbert, pictured winning one of his Best in Show awards. Mrs. Donald Lyle, owner, West Vancouver, B.C.

puppies. Mrs. Lyle feels that this high proportion of achievement is due equally to the high quality dogs with which Wycliffe started and to the individual attention which each puppy born there has received and continued to receive from loving owners throughout its lifetime.

In the meantime the three small Lyle children have grown to be three almost middle-aged adults and the family has increased to include seven grandchildren. Quoting Jean Lyle, "None of these shows the least inclination to follow in my footsteps in dogs." The Lyles live in western Canada, in Vancouver, British Columbia.

Coming East, we find the glorious Bibelot Poodles at Toronto, owned by Susan Radley Fraser. This kennel began in 1951 with the purchase of a lovely white Standard bitch who became Champion Barlanark Lisette, U.D. She was followed by the black Standard American and Canadian Champion Bel Tor Joshua, American and Canadian C.D., then by the brilliant apricot American, Canadian, and Bermudian Champion Pethmelys Tison of Bibelot, American, Canadian, and Bermudian C.D., the first dog to obtain these six titles.

It was, however, with the acquisition of American and Canadian Champion Lady Joan of Lowmont, American and Canadian C.D., that the Bibelot Poodles made their presence well-known and respected worldwide. Lady Joan

Am., Can. and Bda. Ch. Pethmely's Tison of Bibelot, Am., Can. and Bda., C.D., with his son, Can. Ch. Bibelot's Bouffon d'or. Both belong to Susan Fraser, Poodle Studio, Toronto.

Int.'l. (F.C.I.), Am., Can., Bda. and Mex. Ch. Wycliffe Varner. Mrs. Donald Lyle of Wycliffe Poodles, Vancouver, Canada is the owner.

Bibelot's In Shining Armor, looking very serious. Susan Fraser, owner.

herself produced 12 champions, four of whom went on in turn to produce a total of 90 champions. Lady Joan's most famous son, and one of the great dogs in Poodle history, was English, American, and Canadian Champion Bibelot's Tall Dark and Handsome, C.D.X., who produced a total of 53 champions in nine countries!

Tall Dark and Handsome was the first American and Canadian Champion Poodle ever to go to England. Not only did he quickly gain his championship there, but he earned more Best in Show awards than any other dog in England, to become England's Dog of the Year for 1966. He climaxed his English show career by being runner-up to Best in Show at the

The noted Eng., Am. and Can. Ch. Bibelot's Tall Dark and Handsome owned by Susan Fraser of Toronto, Ontario, Canada.

An excellent rear view of the beautiful Standard, Am. and Can. Ch. Bibelot's Hey Look Me Over, C.D. A top member of Susan Fraser's Bibelot Kennels, Toronto, Canada.

prestigious Crufts event in 1967. Tall Dark and Handsome retired from the show ring with 32 Bests in Show won in three countries!

Champion Bibelot's Rich and Rare was the second Poodle to earn her American and Canadian championships then go to England and gain titular honors there.

Another black Standard who contributed well to the Bibelot success story was American and Canadian Champion Bibelot's Hey Look Me Over, American and Canadian C.D., an All-Breed and Specialty Best in Show winner. This fine bitch has seven champions to her credit, the

It's bath time for Ch. Bibelot's I'm No Angel who is all set to be dried off and groomed.

well-known winners American and Canadian Champion Bibelot's Man's Best Friend, American and Canadian Champion Bibelot's Oh Good Heavens, Champion Bibelot's Word To The Wise, Champion Bibelot's I'm No Angel, Champion Bibelot's Chief Secretariat, Champion Bibelot's In The Best Tradition, and Champion Bibelot's Saturday Night Fever, several of whom were Group and Specialty Show winners.

The current "stars" as this is written are the Best in Show and Specialty winner American

Am. and Can. Ch. Bibelot Oh Good Heavens winning four points (at eight months old) at St. Petersburg, 1979. Bred and owned by Susan Fraser, Bibelot Poodles, Toronto, Canada.

Solid comfort. Ch. Bibelot's I'm No Angel catching "forty winks." Susan Fraser, owner, Bibelot Poodles.

At her beautiful best is Ch. Bibelot's I'm No Angel winning for Susan Fraser, Poodle Studio, Toronto.

This Standard is Am., Can., Dutch, Ger., Lux. and F.C.I. Int'l World Ch. Bibelot's Clean As A Whistle, C.D., on the way to the American title, 1978. Susan Fraser, owner.

Am. and can. Ch. Bibelot's Smart Cut is handled here by Elaine MacDonald for owner, Susan Fraser.

Susan Fraser is particularly proud of the excellent progress she has made in establishing her line of silver Standards. The best-known of these silvers, although sparingly exhibited, have done well for themselves in competition. They include Champion Bibelot's All The Rage, C.D.; Champion Bibelot's Silver Fortunehunter; Dutch, German, Belgian, and F.C.I. International Champion Bibelot's Silver Fleece; Champion Bibelot's Misty Morn; American and Canadian Champion Bibelot's Prosperity In Silver; and currently two youngsters, Bibelot's In Grey Corduroys and Bibelot's With A Silver Spoon.

Bibelot Standard Poodles has set many unbroken world records with a small, consistent

At the head of the class is Ch. Bibelot's Prosperity in Silver.

and Canadian Champion Bibelot's Big Bird and Champion Bibelot's That Hooligan Hariet.

In whites, Susan Fraser has set exciting world records with American, Canadian, Dutch, German, Luxemburg, World, and F.C.I. International Champion Bibelot's Clean As A Whistle, American and Canadian C.D. His titles speak for themselves. As a sire, he has produced more than ten champion offspring.

This very attractive silver Standard is Ch. Bibelot's Prosperity in Silver, owned by Susan Fraser, Poodle Studio, Toronto, Ontario.

breeding program producing quality that competes successfully anywhere in the world.

Griggswood Poodles, owned by Mrs. D. E. Griggs, was started about 20 years ago (around 1960) and is located in Ormstown, Quebec.

Although a small operation where only occasional litters were bred every two or three years during its first decade and which has averaged two, or possibly on rare occasions three, annually since then, this kennel has made its presence felt through some very outstanding Poodles. Mrs. Griggs speaks with justifiable pride of 25 homebred champions plus five others purchased as puppies which she has finished. Show homes until just recently have not been overly plentiful in Mrs. Griggs' area. Consequently, in the past she has kept her best puppies to show herself, the others going to pet homes. Recently the trend is changing, though, and Mrs. Griggs notes with satisfaction that the several most recently finished have belonged to and been shown by other owners.

The first two Poodles Mrs. Griggs purchased, a dog and a bitch, came from the old Petitcote line, which was founded on Carillon. The bitch was a disappointment; she never produced anything worthwhile and unfortunately had to be put down owing to injuries received in an ac-

Can., Am. and Bda. Ch. Griggswood Double Entry is pictured winning a Group, handled by Carol Hollands for Griggswood Poodles. Ann R. Griggs, Ormstown, Quebec is the owner.

Can. and Am. Ch. Griggswood Chrystina, handled by Wendell Sammet at the 1972 Washington Poodle Club where she was awarded Best of Winners. Griggswood Poodles, Mrs. D. E. Griggs, Ormstown, Quebec.

Can. and Am. Ch. Griggswood Kent, shown taking Best of Winners at Mohawk Valley Kennel Club, 1977. Wendell Sammet handling for Griggswood Kennels of Quebec.

cident. The dog, however, became the Griggses' first champion, Petitcote Captain Bim.

The next bitch, who turned out to be the foundation of Griggswood's white line, was also Petitcote breeding from the silver and cream side. She was the first of Mrs. Griggs' Best Puppy in Show winners and produced some handsome offspring. One of these became a champion and was subsequently bred to the white Standard Champion Alekai Oli of Stonebridge. Another bitch from this litter was bred to Champion Park Pledge, and it was her daughter who is the great-granddam of the present day strongly Alekai-bred Griggswood white family.

Can. and Am. Ch. Griggswood Double Entry was Top Winning Poodle in Canada, all varieties, 1975. Griggswood Poodles, Mrs. D. E. Griggs, Ormstown, Quebec.

After losing the original Petitcote bitch, and with the thought of bringing fresh blood to her black line, Mrs. Griggs purchased a beautiful bitch from Joy Tongue of Acadia fame. She, Champion Acadia Upstart, finished quickly and went on to produce seven champions. The two most outstanding of these were Champion Griggswood Chrystina, by Mrs. Griggs' own Champion Griggswood Mannix, and Champion Griggswood Double Entry, by Champion Haus Brau Executive of Acadia, who was Top Winning Poodle, All Varieties, in Canada in 1975. Chrystina did a lot of her winning as a puppy, including 12 times Best Puppy in Show, in approximately two months of showing, and she was extensively campaigned in Canada following completion of her American championship. Both Chrystina and Double Entry were Best in Show winners. Neither of them produced much that was exciting until quite late in their lives, but finally the right combination for them was found and Griggswood has been reaping the benefits since that time. Champion Griggswood Replica is Chrystina's most recent winner, along with a young male exported to Sweden, Champion Griggswood Copyright. Double Entry's daughter, Champion Griggswood Cadenza, who herself never enjoyed showing, produced an outstanding bitch puppy, Champion Griggswood Pizzicato, sired by a homebred grandson of Bel Tor Big Picture, Champion Griggswood

Paco Rabanne. She is to be campaigned in the United States as this book is being written.

Mrs. Griggs is enjoying showing two white daughters of Puttencove Presentation, Champion Griggswood Prelude (another Best in Show winner) and Champion Griggswood Overture. She looks forward with anticipation to their children when they are bred back to the Alekai line.

Mrs. Griggs comments that it was her original intention to concentrate exclusively on her whites, but they have recently produced a couple of young blacks that look so exciting that she just may keep them. Thus they will continue with the black family, too, at Griggswood, at least for awhile, and hopes are high for their future. Mrs. Griggs' ambition is continuing to produce typey Poodles of quality and stamina. Judging by past performance, this would seem to present no problem.

Mrs. Ruth L. Clarkson "started a love affair with apricot Miniatures" in 1965, shortly after she had moved to North Gower, Ontario, from the West Coast, when she saw and purchased an adorable four-month-old male puppy bred by Mrs. Nora Maltby. This dog, Coppermist Red Robin, is now 15 years old and his owner's adored pet. He never liked showing, so he was retired from the ring very early. After this Mrs. Clarkson started looking for a suitable bitch as foundation for what has become Murwyn

Ch. Griggswood Overture, litter sister to Prelude, handled by Carol Hollands to Best in Group at Forest City, 1979. Griggswood Poodles, Ormstown, Quebec.

Poodles, a very well-known and high-quality kennel.

Mrs. Clarkson's ambition was to breed apricots of quality who could stand up in competition against the blacks and whites of that period. She had the good fortune to become acquainted with all-breed judge Margaret Thomas, who had apricots and was breeding her imported bitch to Canadian Champion Puckshill Ambersunsquib, an English import; she offered Mrs. Clarkson the pick of the litter bitch. Needless to say Mrs. Clarkson was delighted, and in due course she purchased Bonfire of Lindenwald, who proved to be an invaluable foundation for the strain she was anxious to develop. Although Bonfire never completed her title (Mrs. Clarkson says this was due to her own inexperience and lack of handling technique), she reproduced the very best of herself and the best qualities of the dog who sired her puppies. She is still with Mrs. Clarkson at 12 years of age, well and husky and enjoying life.

Having spent much time studing pedigrees, Mrs. Clarkson reached the decision that she would like to breed Bonfire to the Adamses' well-known dog, Champion Woodland Burning Bright. The resulting litter was even beyond her fondest hopes and expectations. Unfortunately, at the time the Clarksons were living in an area

Pictured is Ch. Griggswood Crepe de Chine, owned by Mrs. D. E. Griggs, Quebec, Canada.

where there was a limitation on the number of dogs that could be housed, so she kept only one male and one female of the puppies and sold the other three. The male became her invaluable Champion Murwyn's Golden Guardsman, now the sire of seven champions. The bitch is the beautiful Champion Murwyn's October Scarlett, dam of two champions. Scarlett has never been a prolific producer, but she did give Mrs. Clarkson her handsome Murwyn's Golden Scepter and Champion Murwyn's Golden Capricorn, her young stud dog, both of these sired by Guardsman.

It now became apparent that with only Bonfire and Scarlett as her breeding bitches the line was becoming too closely bred, and being very happy with the progeny from her males, Mrs. Clarkson set out to find something either line-bred or a complete out-cross for breeding. She contacted Mrs. Lucille Hooper of Gardencourt in Portland, Oregon, who happened to have a six-week-old puppy available. Mrs. Clarkson purchased her immediately, and she became Gardencourt's Canadian Sunrise, who although not herself a show dog is a marvelous brood bitch. From her first litter, bred to Guardsman, came Champion Murwyn's Lady Tangerine, a large bitch with a long, fine head, good movement, and an exquisite flaming orange color. A puppy sold to Mrs. Joan Butterworth from this same litter became Champion Murwyn's Cinderella Pumpkin.

Can. Ch. Griggswood Pizzicato wins the Best Puppy in Show award, handled by Garret Lambert. Bred by Mrs. D. E. Griggs and owned by Doris Grant.

Ch. Murwyn's October Scarlet completed her championship over two week-ends. Owned and handled by Mrs. Ruth L. Clarkson, North Gower, Ontario.

Can. Ch. Murwyn's Golden Capricorn, miniature apricot dog, pictured here taking Best of Breed over specials. "Cappie" gained his title with five consecutive Bests of Breed. Bred, owned and handled by Mrs. Ruth L. Clarkson, North Gower, Ontario. This exciting young dog is already making a mark as a splendid stud as well as in show competition.

Can. Ch. Murwyn's Golden Scepter, on the day he finished his title, taking Best of Breed over five specials. Mrs. Ruth L. Clarkson is handling her homebred apricot dog.

Mrs. Ruth L. Clarkson handling Murwyn's Flaming Fantasia to a nice breed win over specials at Hochelaga. This handsome apricot Miniature puppy has five points towards championship as a Junior Puppy.

Finishing her title at 13 months old is Can. Ch. Murwyn's Lady Tangerine with her breeder-owner-handler, Mrs. Ruth L. Clarkson of North Gower, Ontario.

Bonfire was now nearing eight years of age, so she was bred for just one more litter, this by her son, Guardsman. One puppy resulted, a bitch (as Mrs. Clarkson had hoped) who became Champion Murwyn's Bonnie Tinkerbelle. Tinker finished at 13 months, then was kept home to mature. After three years she is now out as a "special," doing well for her owner. She will be bred to American, Canadian, and Bermudian Champion Brigalon's Cinnamon Stick, a combination over which Mrs. Clarkson is enormously excited.

So far none of Mrs. Clarkson's dogs have gained their American titles, although several of them are pointed in the States. The reason they have not been more campaigned down here is that when she embarked on this commitment to improving the apricots, it was agreed between Mrs. Clarkson and her husband that doing so would be strictly a hobby, nothing more, and that if she is to go to the dog shows she so dearly loves, it is to handle her own dogs personally, win or lose. Mrs. Clarkson feels that her shortcomings as a groomer and a handler sometimes prevent the dogs from being presented to best advantage, but she is sticking to her bargain.

Murwyn Kennels consists of 13 dogs, as this is written, enjoying a happy, uninhibited life on seven acres of fenced land. The Clarksons enjoy seeing them so healthy and happy. There is great excitement now over an about-to-be-shown puppy by Champion Murwyn's Golden Capricorn ex Champion Murwyn's Lady Tangerine who looks most promising. Mrs. Clarkson speaks with

pride of Guardsman's handsome son, American and Canadian Champion Apropos Burning Challenge, bred and owned by Mrs. Marietta Kahla from her black hybrid daughter of Champion Highland Bonhomme Richard.

Mrs. Clarkson deserves true credit for the beautiful color line she has established.

Traveling to Halifax, Nova Scotia, one finds another small kennel that is also making its presence strongly felt. This is Dawn Messer Poodles, owned by Dawn Attis. This lady's introduction to the breed took place when her future husband brought her a gift from Montreal, Quebec, in the form of a black Standard Poodle puppy. At that time Dawn Attis had no interest in showing, although the puppy was registered.

In 1962 she purchased a Smooth Coated Chihuahua and was persuaded by her veterinarian to show this little dog, which she did to a championship. Need I add that from then on Dawn was "bitten by the bug" for showing dogs? She went on to also finish a second Chihuahua but was unsuccessful with breeding them.

Then in 1963 came the purchase of an imported Toy Poodle bitch puppy who grew up to become a champion. Champion Trollhattan's

Can. Ch. Murwyn's Bonnie Tinkerbelle, age 13 months, is shown the day on which she completed her title. Mrs. Ruth L. Clarkson, breeder-owner, is handling.

Elaine MacDonald here is handling Beverly Merritt's Toy, Am. and Can. Ch. Wilmar Howlene Stone Broke, to a Canadian win.

This lovely white Standard bitch is Ch. Maren's Applause Applause pictured taking Best of Winners at the Poodle Club of America Specialty, January 1981. Owned by Dianne Hopper, Carrington Kennels, Callander, Ontario. Handled by Garrett Lambert. Bred by M. and J. Ahrens, Maren's Pine Tree Kennels.

Amourette had been bred by Mrs. Beatrice Thompson in England and was the foundation bitch for the seven generations of black Toys now at this kennel.

In England for Crufts in 1978, Mrs. Attis brought home with her a beautiful Toy bitch from Mrs. Sheila MacKenzie Spencer's Aspen Kennels. This tiny black is Champion Apoco Deodar Gypsey Rose, and Mrs. Attis is anxious to introduce some of her qualities into the Dawn Messer breeding program.

While attending Poodle Club of America in 1979, Mrs. Attis saw and immediately wanted a beautiful cream Standard puppy dog, Raeann's

Can. Ch. Pomroth Edelson's Diamond, bred by Helen Hamilton, owned by Miss Dina Edelson, of Ottawa, Ontario. Garrett Lambert is handling to a good win.

Timothy, by Champion Oakgrove Captain Midnight ex Champion Raeann's Royal Rose, bred by Mr. Raymond Kauffman of Michigan. She was able to persuade Mr. Kauffman that Timothy really must come to Nova Scotia, and he arrived in August, 1979. As a puppy, he earned six points on his Canadian title, had two Group placements, and four times was Best Puppy in Show. At his first show as an adult, in March, 1980, he went Best in Show from the classes and continued on this season with five

All-Breed Bests in Show and two Specialty Shows. Needless to say, excitement is high over this young dog who should do much to benefit his breed.

A new black Toy Poodle dog imported in August of 1980 from Mary Wilson's Wilinne Kennels will be shown in the future, and a Standard bitch, its first, is about to also join the kennel.

Many of Canada's most beautiful Poodles are presented in the ring by professional handler J. Garrett Lambert, who is also a successful Poodle breeder. We have seen him with many gorgeous dogs over the years and have admired their quali-

Can. Ch. Ramada's Bristol Cream, taking Best of Winners at the Canadian National Sportsmen's Show, 1980. Bred by J. and P. Walter, owned by Diane Hopper, handled by Garrett Lambert.

Can. Ch. 'Afmoon Black Pansy, owned by Garrett Lambert and William and Dot Kniskern, is here taking Best of Winners at Del Otse Nango, 1974. Bred by Mr. Lambert and Joseph R. Repice. Handled by Mr. Lambert.

ty and his good showmanship.

Elaine MacDonald, too, is very active in the breeding and handling of top-flight Poodles, and there are numerous other "Poodle people," both professional and amateur, whom we have seen showing high-quality dogs at the Canadian shows. Our friends in that country have certainly done well by their breed.

A truly magnificent young Poodle, this is Can. Ch. Torbec Carriage Trade taking Best Puppy in Show at Barrie, 1980. Bred and owned by T. G. McIntyre, Torbec Kennels. Handled by Garrett Lambert.

218

Can. Ch. Montec Pomroth Copy Cat, beautifully balanced typey black Toy, owned by Mrs. Helen M. Hamilton, Pomroth Poodles, Schomberg, Ontario. Handled by Garrett Lambert.

This is Can. Ch. Pomroth Bubbling Over, owner-handled by Mrs. Helen M. Hamilton, Pomroth Poodles, Schonberg, Ontario.

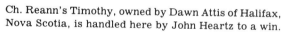

Ch. Reann's Timothy, owned by Dawn Attis of Halifax, Nova Scotia, is handled here by John Heartz to a win.

Can. Ch. Maren's Applause Applause, going Best Puppy in Show. Bred by Marcus and Janice Ahrens, and owned by Dianne Hopper. Garrett Lambert, handler.

Am. Ch. Meridian Memorandum here is taking Best of Variety at the Poodle Club of America from the six-nine month Puppy Class, as well as Best Puppy in Show. A truly thrilling day for everyone concerned with this superb black Toy. Owned by Ruth Winston, and bred and handled by the noted Garrett Lambert.

The Toy puppy, now Ch. Dawn Messer's Nemesia, at 7 months. Owned and bred by Dawn Attis, Halifax, Nova Scotia.

Can. Ch. Doral's Fortune Teller, bred and handled by Garrett Lambert for Mr. and Mrs. D. M. Roberts, owners.

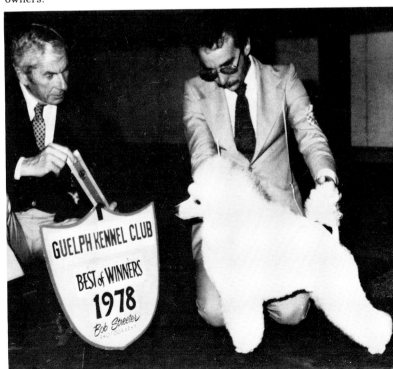

The silver Miniature, Ch. Ardian Silver Osmund, imported from England by Mrs. Hugh Chisholm of Strathgless Kennels, purchased by Roadcoach by Mrs. Mary Barrett. Born October 1955, this lovely Group winning Miniature made a fine show record for Mrs. Barrett and her Roadcoach Miniatures.

CHAPTER SEVEN

English Poodles Of the 1980's

Eng. Ch. Wycliffe Ovation for Vulcan, a Best in Show winner, is one of the famed Standards from Wycliffe Kennels. Mrs. Donald Lyle, West Vancouver, Canada, owner.

Poodle activity in England seems to remain fairly constant over the years, although many of the famous kennels from the past no longer are in operation.

One of the best known still active is Montfleuri, where Mrs. N. Howard Price has raised many a famous and beautiful dog who has succeeded at home and in other parts of the world. Montfleuri Miniatures are no strangers in the United States. We have seen and admired a goodly number of them here and are well aware of their quality.

Currently at the home kennel there is a young dog, Champion Huckalea of Montfleuri, who appears extremely handsome in pictures we have seen of him; another stud dog there, Champion Union Jack of Montfleuri, is evidently carrying on in the family tradition, having out a most attractive son, Clarion of Montfleuri, from the Tweedville Kennels of Mrs. E. R. Lee. Clarion is a Challenge Certificate winner with several reserves to his credit as well, so should be either finished or close to it when you read these words.

Lochranza Miniatures is owned by Miss J. MacMillan and Mrs. J. Gillespie. For many generations there have been champions and other important winners bearing this prefix, and dogs have won fame from this kennel, too, at home and abroad. Champion Lochranza Hell for Leather is a well-known sire and winner here. The black dog Lochranza Moccasins is proving to be an exciting sire of browns, with some beautiful progeny of that color in the ring.

Vulcan Champagne Standard Poodles is breeding Standards of most colors and high quality. Miss Ann Cambray Coppage is the owner.

In silver Miniatures, we have seen some mighty attractive ones pictured bearing the Walditch prefix of Mr. and Mrs. Gundry. One of them, Walditch Silver Cascade, is a winner at championship shows who certainly appears to have a title in his future. Then there is a spectacular silver Toy of whom we have read, Champion Walditch Silver Cassius, a picture of whom has caught our eye.

At Miradel Kennels Mrs. Patricia Rose is raising Miniatures and Toys. Knotrom of Southport, a kennel with some splendid apricots, won two Challenge Certificates during 1980 with Knotrom's Golden Phoenix, an apricot Toy sired by the five-time Challenge Certificate winner Champion Knotrom's Golden Partridge.

Some very outstanding Standards are coming from Mrs. Ann Timson's Kelrarmo Kennels in Surrey. Champion Josato Pink Gin of Kelrarmo was the Junior Warrant *Daily Express* Pup of the Year 1972, becoming a champion in 1974. We admire her handsome head type and quality. As a producer she's done quite a job, too, being the dam of Champion Kelrarmo Lily the Pink, with show credits that include Junior Warrants, eleven Challenge Certificates, eight Bests of Breed including Crufts in 1977, and she is a Championship Best in Show winner. She gained her title in 1976. Then there is Champion

222

Ch. Monfret Miranda, a handsome Standard, is the dam of four champions—two of them Best in Show winners. Owned by Francis Fretwell, Monfret Poodles, Moore, South Carolina.

Kelrarmo Off The Record, a 1980 champion who has won three Challenge Certificates and four Reserves already in his career.

Another of Mrs. Timson's 1980 champions is the lovely young bitch Champion Kelrarmo Call Me Kate, with a Junior Warrant and three Challenge Certificates. She is temporarily retired from the show ring due to maternal duties, but she'll be back.

Kelrarmo Pink Annie is the present young hopeful at this quality kennel. A granddaughter of Pink Gin, she started her career with a good puppy win at the Richmond Championship Show and should be heard from during the 1980's.

Coelegant Poodles is owned by Joan and Bill Atlee and has Standards, Toys, and Miniatures in all colors. This is the home of Champion Tiopepi Star Attraction of Coelegant, a very attractive and well-known black Miniature.

White Miniatures are featured at Jaytor Poodles, belonging to Miss J. M. Coram. Champion Jaytor Mista Softee heads the stud force, which also includes his very lovely son Wharfholm Sauterne of Jaytor, a Junior Warrant win-

ner with two Reserve Challenge Certificates, a very stylish looking young dog.

Pam and Brian Gregory breed Miniatures and Toys under the Snowstar identification. They have a good black Miniature, Snowstar Charles, who at just over two years of age has two Challenge Certificates and six reserves; a lovely silver Toy, Champion Snowstar Ray, who completed his title at 17 months; and a white Toy, Snowstar Johnny, with four Reserve Challenge Certificates.

Mrs. Margaret Boulton has two Challenge Certificates and two reserves on Romar Ringmaster as this is written. Her kennel is noted for Miniatures and Toys of black, white and apricot colors.

Miss J. C. Hawkes owns and operates the Piquant Kennels, long associated with apricot Miniatures, for which she is well-known. Tragapanz, owned by Carole Flatt, specializes in dark chocolate and black Standards. June Rose and Andrew Dunlop specialize in apricot Standards, with which they have succeeded admirably. Their bitch Selzuk Wot A Rhapsody won the reserve Challenge Certificate in her sex at Crufts

Ch. Lorrac Start of It All winning the Non-Sporting Group at the Eastern Dog Club, 1971. Richard Bauer, handling, for Miss Carol Miller.

Gyp de Gillan here is taking Best of Opposite Sex in Toy Poodles at the Quinnipiac Poodle Club Specialty.

Ch. Kendor's Sip of Cointreau, a Toy, handled by Jane Forsyth for Dorris A. Sutton, Kendor Kennels.

Ch. Gaystream Skyrocket, an English import, here is winning at the Poodle Club of America Specialty, May 1956. Handled by Wendell J. Sammet. Owned by Mr. and Mrs. Charles Miles of Eslar Poodles, bred by A. McGuinnes.

The white Toy, Hell's A Blazen Carnival Joy, still in puppy clip, is seen here winning a Toy Group. The handler is Jane Kamp Forsyth, who has loaned us this picture. Kendor Kennels, owner.

A black Miniature of distinction, Eng. Ch. Foreman of Tranchant wins a Group under Bud Dickey's handling, 1976.

Somerset Hills Kennel Club, 1965. Bill Trainor handles Harmo Kennels' fine black Miniature, Ch. Harmo Rough N Ready, to first in the Non-Sporting Group.

Ch. Carliclan First Dancer winning the Group at Monmouth County Kennel Club. Jane Forsyth, handling.

1981, while their young stud dog, Striking Gold for Rosehaven, won his Junior Warrant, multiple firsts at championship shows, and Best of Breed at his three most recent open shows. Camellabois Golden Hello, with three Reserve Challenge Certificates, is another member of this kennel.

Messrs. Roger Stone and Graham Thompson and Miss Vivienne Brown own Vanitonia Poodles, having all three varieties there. They have a mighty impressive black Toy in Vanitonia School for Scandal, with a Junior Warrant and two Reserve Certificates, who was a finalist in the *Dog World*/Spillers Puppy of the Year competition for 1980.

Camellabois Standards has been breeding Poodles since 1953 very successfully with some high-quality Poodles to which they point with pride. Mrs. Warnell is the owner. The gorgeous bitch Champion Camellabois Dream was bred here and is the dam of a promising litter by Champion Montravia Gay Gunner. Camellabois Golden Hello, although owned by June Rose and Andrew Dunlop, was also bred by Mrs. Warnell and was the top winning apricot Standard for 1980. Then Camellabois Lover Boy won his class at Crufts in 1981, and Camellabois Angeles qualified to compete there in 1981.

Meracon Pecan Nut of Clopton, with two Challenge Certificates and a reserve, is a Toy

Poodle to watch in the future. Sired by Champion Clopton Tobago, who has winning progeny both at home and in the United States, he belongs to Miss Penny Jones. Swedish Champion Much Ado of Clopton is an export to that country from this kennel who has just completed championship.

Merrymorn is a name associated with winning Poodles for a goodly number of years, and some exquisite apricot Toys are still carrying the banner nowadays for Lucy Ellis and Honor Sherry. Merrymorn Hot Rod especially seems to be a marvelous little dog. Then there are Champion Merrymorn Golden Sorrell and Hot Rod's exciting son Merrymorn Phoenix. With some

Ch. Lynn's Dry Martini, a Toy that did big winning from 1960-1965. Photo courtesy of Jane Kamp Forsyth, who handled this handsome dog. Lynn Lund, owner.

Ch. Broughton Sweet William II going Winners under William Kendrick. Vernelle Hartman handling for Mr. and Mrs. James Brough.

Eng. and Am. Ch. Alekai Kalania. Owned by Miss Helen Martin, Kenilworth, England. Handled by Wendell J. Sammet in the United States, and by Miss Martin in England.

outstanding young bitches by these dogs just coming into their own, these ladies seem to be well-situated for continued success. You will find reference to a little black Toy from this kennel, Merrymorn Lita, a very successful winner from Mrs. Milton Erlanger in the United States several decades back, in the Toy Poodle chapter of this book.

At Suraliam Kennels there are some very famous, very correct, and typical Miniatures owned by Sue and Ralph Holmes. "Pride of place" here is held by the magnificent Champion Suraliam Rupert, the Top Challenge Certificate winning Miniature Poodle Dog ever in England. Rupert in 1978 won a Junior Warrant and two

Four exquisite white Miniatures belonging to Mr. and Mrs. Alden V. Keene.

jointly by Montravia and Mrs. Warnell. Montravia Gay Amanda is a puppy bitch obviously with a bright future owing to some exciting puppy wins. She is a Gay Gunner daughter.

Among the Miniatures, there is a delightful white Group winner, Champion Montravia Lavinas Snow Blanche, a white named Montravia Shoremei Irish Lad who has attracted some glowing praise among the judges, and a stunning black, Champion Montravia Midnight Marksman, who is a Reserve Group winner. All told (which includes their Afghan Hounds and Bichons Frises as well as the Poodles), Montravia Kennels accounted for 34 Challenge Certificates and Reserve Challenge Certificates in 1980, plus 20 Championship Show Bests of Breed.

Challenge Certificates. In 1979 he became Top Miniature Poodle, gaining an additional 14 Challenge Certificates, and was the Number Fifteen Top Dog of all breeds. In 1980 he was Top Miniature Poodle, had 14 Challenge Certificates, and became number fifteen Top Dog for the year, all breeds. For the future there would seem much to anticipate. A daughter of Rupert, Suraliam Wonder Woman, completed her Junior Warrant and won a Challenge Certificate and a reserve before she had reached 16 months of age and is now doing well in Sweden, where she is owned by Miss A. Stenvell. She is from a repeat breeding of Rupert.

Sudbrook Toys has sent some lovely little Poodles to the States over the years and is still going strong. Mrs. Sheilah Cox is owner. Sudbrook Best Bib 'N' Tucker is siring some exquisite whites there nowadays.

And then there is a distinguished Toy bitch, Champion Grayco Hazelnut, who has won a tremendous number of honors for Mrs. Lesley Howard throughout 1980.

Montravia holds it's position as a force with which to reckon in both Standards and Miniatures. Peter, Pauline, and Marita Gibbs have really made history with their dogs and have much credit due them for the quality with which this prefix has become synonymous. The Standard Montravia Gay Gunner is a Best in Show winner of distinction. Champion Camellabois Dream is a Group winner owned

Opposite Above:

Ch. Ravendune Prime Time, handsome black Miniature male, owned by Todd Patterson. By Am., Can. Ch. Ravendune Sweet Baby James ex Am., Can. Ch. Ravendune Make Mine Roses.

Opposite Below:

Ch. Royal Look winged Commander, bred by Andrew Bidlingmaier and owned by Todd Patterson, Ravendune Poodles, Taylor, Michigan.

Ch. Meisen Frostie Flake winning the Toy Group award at the Westbury Kennel Association, 1964. Jane Forsyth, handling.

228

The Standard bitch Ch. Bel Tor Blissful, a third genera-
tion Top Producer, winner eight times of Best in Show.
Owned by Dr. and Mrs. Samuel Peacock, bred by Mrs.
Rebecca Mason, handled by Pamela Hall.

CHAPTER EIGHT

Poodles in Europe

Dutch Ch. Wycliffe Liege of Fortune belongs to Wycliffe Poodles, Vancouver, Canada. Mrs. Donald Lyle, owner.

A great many Poodles have been exported over the years to various breeders in Europe from the United States and Canada, as you will note in reading our section of kennel stories. European fanciers have bought top-quality stock from the world's leading modern bloodlines with which to enhance their own breeding programs, and there are many truly handsome Poodles to be found there carrying the pedigrees that have made history in Great Britain and in North America.

A very large and active kennel is Del Zarzoso, in Madrid, Spain, belonging to Carlos Fernandez-Renau and Juan Cabrera. All three varieties are featured there. That the owners have really gone all-out to obtain dogs of exceptional quality is clearly evident.

Great pride is taken in the white Standard dog Valhalla Billy Del Zarzoso, imported from Catherine Kish in the United States. This dog is a son of the immortal Champion Acadia Command Performance from the very famous Best in Show winning bitch Champion Valhalla Critic's Choice. Then there is the magnificent white Standard bitch International, Spanish, and Portuguese Champion Leander Star Del Zarzoso who has become Spain's Top Poodle in the history of the breed, with multiple Best in Show wins, who is additionally proving a very exciting producer. From her first litter, by American Champion Valhalla In Command, two bitches have been kept, Del Zarzoso Madrid-New York O.K. and Del Zarzoso Rumbo America, while a litter mate, Del Zarzoso Nuevo Mundo, has

gone to Mario di Vanni in Chile. "Wendy," as Star is called, is a daughter of English, American, and Canadian Champion Leander Stage Door Johnny ex Topaz Mystique.

The Miniatures in this kennel include the very lovely Suraliam The Saint, by Champion Suraliam Rubert, the latter being the Top Winning Miniature Poodle in Great Britain. This dog is delighting his owners with the quality black and brown puppies he is siring, among them Del Zarzoso El Hidalgo and Del Zarzoso Collete, these two being from Champion Vorton Jenny Splendid, Best of Breed at the second Spanish Poodle Club Specialty and a Group winner in Spain and Portugal. Then there is the brown Del Zarzoso Marron Glace by this same young dog from the white Montravia Dearborn Ballerine Doll. The other Miniatures include Berita's Miss Bee, by Champion Beritas Banecheke, with some interesting puppies by The Saint, who is also the sire of some splendid youngsters from Tiopepi Tipsy, a daughter of English and American Champion Tiopepi Typhoon. Another young Miniature of note is Del Zarzoso Alamo, by Aizbel Trouble ex Beritas Boba, who has started out well in puppy competition.

As for the Toys, there is the black dog Suraliam Stop the Press, by Aesthete Secret Edition from Suraliam Jubilee Queen, plus a strong collection of bitches including the brown Suraliam Miss Highlight, Granddaughter of Tuttlebee's Rather Royal and Champion Clopton Tiger Bay, and the black Del Zarzoso Zin-

Ch. Griggswood's Replica at 11½ months, owner-handled to Best Puppy in Show. Bred and owned by Mrs. Ann Griggs.

Ger. Ch. Wycliffe Timoteo, one of Wycliffe Kennels' Best in Show winners. Owned by Mrs. Donald Lyle.

nia, granddaughter of American Champion La Pale's Here Comes Flip. All this gives a detailed picture of why this kennel is bound to become one with which to reckon.

The Top Winning Poodle in Scandinavia in 1979 was International and Nordic Champion Tam O Shanter (by International and Nordic Champion Leander Midnight Cowboy ex Swedish Champion Tragapanz Tick-A-Tee), bred by Eva Valinger of Sweden and owned and handled by Sirkka Salonen of Finland.

Then in Prague there is a white Miniature, International Champion Miradel Cascade, belonging to Mrs. Evelyn Kubska, with a whole impressive list of titles.

Switzerland, too, is the home of some fine current Poodles, brown ones known for being the most successful of that color on the Continent. Lisbeth Mach owns these at Superstar Kennels, where a young dog called Superstar Charly Brown is attracting admiring attention.

Miss A. Stenvall, in Sweden, is doing well there with her Miniature bitch imported from England, Champion Suraliam Mona Lisa, from a repeat of the same breeding that produced English Champion Suraliam Rupert. At the last we heard, she was only two points behind the Top Winning Miniature Poodle there, so who knows what may be the case by now.

Lallan Kennels' Toy, Ch. Leading Man, with his handler Ben Burwell.

A gorgeous Miniature puppy, Pixiecroft Minutemaid, with her handler Jane Forsyth at the Quinnipiac Poodle Club Specialty, 1965. Pixiecroft Kennels, owners.

Int. and F.C.I. Ch. Daktari Apogee Olivia, by Ch. Gregella Copyright Caliber, Top Producer, ex Ch. Daktari Passionella, Top Producer. Owned by Daktari-Apogee Poodles, A. Monroe McIntyre and Nancy Hafner.

Ch. Puttencove Diantha, white Standard, owned by Mr. and Mrs. George Putnam, handled by William J. Trainor. Photographed in 1963.

Mindee's Miss High and Mighty pictured in June 1968 with handler Jane Kamp Forsyth.

Int. Ch. Harlane Hot Shot here is winning a Toy Group in 1961, with Jane Forsyth handling. A beautiful little dog.

Ch. The Magpie, winning a Toy Group at about 10 months old. Owned by Lallan Kennels, handled by Ben Burwell.

Jap. Ch. Alekai Adventure, by Ch. Alekai Luau ex Ch.
Alekai Cocon't of Stonebrae. Owner, Yoshiki Nambu.

CHAPTER NINE

Poodles in Japan

L'ambre Let's Kiss The Sun, daughter of Ch. Kornel's Keeper of the Kastle. From the L'ambree Poodles, Mr. and Mrs. Yukichi Fukazawa, Shizuoka, Japan.

American dog breeders are well aware of the steady increase of interest Japanese dog fanciers have displayed during recent years in importing, owning, and, as their eventual goal, breeding highest quality show dogs. Many of them visit our country each year to see and select fine additions for their kennels or foundation breeding stock, and happily the majority of them are using these purchases to the decided advantage of the breed in their country.

One of the most successful with which we are acquainted is a Toy Poodle kennel, L'ambre, owned and personally managed by Mr. and Mrs. Yukichi Fukazawa of Fujinomiya City, Shizuoa. As they are typical of the Japanese breeders who are anxious to acquire American dogs, we feel that the story of the Fukazawas will prove interesting to our readers. Japan is becoming a country to demand respect in our dog show world, and visitors to that country have brought back glowing accounts of the excellence of their Kennel Club, the dedication of their breeders, and the singleness of purpose with which they proceed in their ambitions to own high quality.

It was in 1969 that the owners of L'ambre became so fascinated with Toy Poodles that the decision was reached to start a kennel of their own. In June, 1970, they traveled to the United States, where they remained for about a month, the purpose being to see the three-day weekend which included the Poodle Club of America Specialty and the two all-breed shows following it that year, Greenwich and Longshore-Southport here in Connecticut. During these days they stayed at a nearby motor lodge, dedicating every moment to seeing and absorbing everything possible about the Poodles shown at these events.

It was over this weekend that the Fukazawas became acquainted with Mrs. Judith Feinberg, owner of the Arundel Toys. Watching judging, they were deeply impressed not only by Champion Arundel Brazen Little Raisin but also by many other fantastic and beautiful Toy Poodles. Growing even more enthusiastic than formerly over the breed, they eventually succeeded in importing several Poodles from Arundel Kennels.

The ambition at L'ambre has been to breed Toy Poodles based on the Hilltop (with which they had started) and Arundel strains. Since importing American Champion Arundel Splash O'Dash, Champion Arundel Shine Little Star, and Champion Arundel A Lovin Spoonful, Arundel has become the more dominant line in the breeding program, but the blending of the two strains has worked out very well, as the Fukazawas had hoped and anticipated, to the point that L'ambre is producing homebred Toy Poodles of outstanding magnificence. They have succeeded in winning Best Toy Poodle in Japan consecutively nine times over a nine-year period, the honors garnered by both their importations and their homebreds.

Like all successful breeders, the Fukazawas are never quite content or satisfied but are constantly seeking to improve. In 1975 a second trip to the States was made to seek advice from friends here, and a third one in 1977.

234

Their attention was drawn to Champion Syntifny's Piece of the Rock and the handsome, elegant, refined Toy Poodles being sired by this little dog. The decision was reached to introduce his bloodlines to still further enhance L'ambre quality. So it was that Champion Kornel's Keeper of the Kastle joined this well-planned kennel, a young dog with a glorious future as his new owners had anticipated. It took a bit of experimentation to hit just the right bitches to which he should be bred, but once this had been accomplished, nine champions were immediately sired by him.

The Toy Poodles preceding those from Arundel imported by the Fukazawas had been, in 1969, future Japanese Champion Challenge in White De Peach and also American and Japanese Champion Hilltop's Man O'Fire. Shortly thereafter these were joined by American, Canadian, and Bermudian Champion Hilltop's Ponderosa Kid. Then came the three already listed Arundels. The latest importation, during 1977, was American Champion Kornel's Keeper of the Kastle.

The Fukazawas tell us that Keeper of the Kastle, or "Casey," in 1979-1980 became Japan's Number One Poodle. With pride his owners claim that he is the "pillar of the Poodle" there. The Fukazawas became so fascinated with this little dog and with his splendid record in the United States prior to his departure for Japan that they begged Mrs. Nel Korbijn, his breeder, to sell him to them, and they were more than happy when finally she consented to do so. Since arriving in Japan, Casey has been chosen the Best in Show whenever exhibited, and Mr. Fukazawa comments that "it is really frustrating to tell, but Keeper of the Kastle can attend only three or four dog shows a year because often I myself go to dog shows as the judge of the show." However, his owners always make it a point to show Casey at the biggest, most important shows, so he may well yet prove himself to be the pillar of the Poodle in Japan. His owner adds, "Anyway, his healthy, sound mind and body, and his cheerful character as a showman, really attract everyone."

Casey has a daughter, Japanese Champion L'ambre Sunshine Augusta, who is also bringing pride to her owners. In 1979 she was Best in Show on three occasions and Reserve Best in Show on several others. Called "Mika," she is gorgeous and graceful, proudly walking into the show ring, tail high, making the most of her every attractive feature.

At the time this is written, American Champion Arundel A Lovin Spoonful is the Top Producer at L'ambre. Famous as the sire of 12 American champions prior to leaving here, he has sired an additional 16 in Japan, of which eight have become Best in Show winners. This record of Raisin's is the best in Japanese Poodle history.

The South Tokyo Poodle Club is a busy one that has evidently been holding Specialty Shows since the late 1960's. The Japanese-bred Toy Poodles from L'ambre have distinguished themselves there with regularity starting in 1972

Am. and Jap. Ch. Kornel's Keeper of the Kastle taking Best of breed at the 1979 Specialty Show of the Poodle Club of Japan. This is Japan's No. 1 Poodle for 1979-1980. Owned by Mr. and Mrs. Yukichi Fukazawa of the famed L'ambre Poodles.

at the Club's fourth event, when Champion L'ambre White Mite was awarded Best of Variety by judge J. Sawabe. The following year Champion L'ambre Spring Sunshine was Best of Breed under judge Y. Nanbu. In 1974 Champion L'ambre White Lotus was Best of Breed, Y. Nanbu again judging. In 1975 Champion L'ambre White Sunshine was Best of Breed under judge Frank Sabella. Champion L'ambre Grand Prix was Best of Breed in 1976, judge T. Kamemoto; Champion L'ambre White Nancy was Best of Breed 1977, judge T. Uryu; Champion L'ambre Country Sunday was Best of

235

Jap. Ch. L'ambre Country Road, a lovely white Toy, owned by Mr. and Mrs. Yukichi Fukazawa, Shizuoka, Japan.

This stunning Toy, Jap. Ch. L'ambre White Sunshine, is a Best in Show winner and Japan's No. 1 Poodle of 1975. He is pictured winning Best in Show at the Tokyo South Poodle Specialty, 1975. L'ambre Poodles, Mr. and Mrs. Yukichi Fukazawa, owners.

The 1980 Tokyo International Dog Show. Am. and Jap. Ch. Kornel's Keeper of the Kastle is winning Reserve Best in Show for his owners, Mr. and Mrs. Fukazawa.

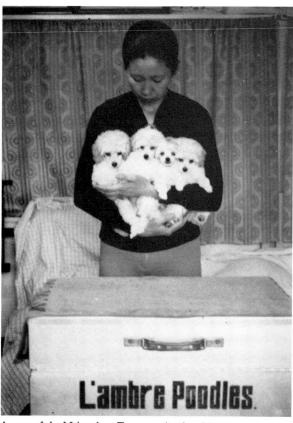

An armful of L'ambre Toy puppies bred in Japan.

Breed 1979, judge Anne Rogers Clark; in 1980 Best of Breed was Champion L'ambre Mountain View, judge T. Uryu. We think it is quite an achievement to have won Best of Breed so many years at the Specialty with so many different dogs, a testimonial, indeed, to the over-all quality of the L'ambre Toy Poodles!

A dog in which the L'ambre Poodles takes especial pride is Japanese Champion L'ambre Spring Sunshine, son of American and Canadian Champion Hilltop's Man O'Fire. He won the titles of Best in Show and Japan's Number One Poodle in 1973. Also he became Best in Show at the all-breed show four times and was Best of Breed at the Specialty Show twice. He is truly a very special little dog. The Toy Poodles at L'ambre are certainly a credit to the breed, as is the enthusiasm of the owners of this highly successful kennel, to whom we extend congratulations on their breeding accomplishments.

Opposite Above:
Jap. Ch. L'ambre Sunshine Augusta, by Am. Ch. Kornel Keeper of the Kastle, the first of her sire's children to finish in Japan. Her show ring honors include several Bests in Show. Mr. and Mrs. Yukichi Fukazawa, owners. L'ambre Toy Poodles, Japan.

Opposite Below:
Japan Ch. L'ambria Country Sunday winning Best in Show at the 1979 Tokyo South Poodle Club Specialty under Mrs. Anne Rogers Clark. Owned by Mr. and Mrs. Yukichi Fukazawa.

Ch. L'ambre Spring Sunshine, a Best in Show winner and Japan's No. 1 Poodle of 1973. His awards include: four times Best in Show (all-breeds), two Bests in Show at Specialty events, and the second top Best in Show winner, as this is written. Owned by Mr. and Mrs. Yukichi Fukazawa of L'ambre Kennels.

238

Vnz. Ch. Barbizon Little Richard, No. 1 Non-Sporting
Dog in Venezuela, 1976, with owner Richard Guevera.

Latin American Poodles

Can., Mex., Int. Ch. Evanz Chronicle, a Best of Variety winner from the classes, is a white Toy son of Ch. Evening Edition, owned by Marilyn Pauley, Evanz Poodles. This boy is currently with Kay O'Brien in Tulsa, Oklahoma.

Poodles in Mexico

Mexico is another country where outstanding Poodles are to be found. The Petersen Von Bauer Kennels here specializes in black Miniatures. Among their best known winners are Marquis, Vincent, Princess, Lancelot, Ferdinand, and Peyerson—all "von Bauer." Based on imported stock, their stud dog has produced well and contributed fine quality in this area.

Poodles in South America

We have tremendous respect for the dog fanciers of South America, having many close friends among them in numerous breeds. They are highly knowledgeable, deeply interested fanciers dedicated to acquiring the finest dogs of leading bloodlines and then using them to carry out their own breeding programs, the eventual goal being to breed South American dogs of quality enabling them to hold their own against competition anywhere in the world. They are attaining this goal in a number of breeds, among them Poodles.

Richard Guevera, now a very famous international all-breed judge, officiates frequently in the United States, where he enjoys great popularity with the exhibitors, as well as in all parts of the world. He has been a Poodle fancier since an early age and has handled some of the finest in South America to exciting show careers. We are indebted to him for photos of some of these dogs and for information about the kennels from which they have come.

McColl's Kennels in Venezuela was one of the most highly successful; it was owned by the late Mrs. Ria Haas. White Miniatures and Toys were the specialties here, both varieties having represented Mrs. Haas in keenest competition. The foundation stock in Miniatures came basically from the United States, Mrs. Haas having sent several of her bitches to such famed sires as Champion Summercourt Square Dancer of Fircot and Champion Round Table Cognac, her English import, the white Miniature Venezuelan, Colombian, and Dominican Champion Minaret's Court Fable, was the Number One Non-Sporting Dog in Venezuela in 1972. Another of her Miniatures, Venezuelan Champion McColl's Goldy's Nanette gained similar honors in 1973, becoming Venezuela's Top Non-Sporting Dog. The Toy Poodle Venezuelan Champion Lochranza Sugar Daddy of Sudbrook became Venezuela's Top Winning Toy in both 1973 and 1974. This Variety at Mrs. Haas' kennel was based on English stock, mainly Sudbrook.

Richard Guevera's own kennel, Barbizon, also is located in Venezuela, but will be moving soon to Sao Paulo, Brazil. Here the emphasis is on Standards, mostly white ones, descended from American Champion Acadia Command Performance. Venezuelan Champion Barbizon Little Richard was that country's Number One Non-Sporting Dog in 1976. The Venezuelan-bred Bougon of Barbizon, a Best in Show winner from the puppy class, and Venezuelan Champion Barbizon Petite Henrietta are other noted winning Standards owned by Mr. Guevera.

Wycliffe Edward Ethelred winning his first Best of Winners for three points. Handled by M. Thurston for Mr. and Mrs. Glen See, Cedar Crest, New Mexico.

Am., Brz., Int. Ch. Holyoke Hensley winning a Group First under Mr. J.B. Valdez of Argentina. Shown only 15 times in Brazil, "Hensley" won the Non-Sporting Group on each appearance, took all-breed Best in Show 10 times, and was Reserve Best in Show 5 times—certainly a distinguished and remarkable record. Owned by Pent Kennels, Evalina and Jaime Martinelli, Sao Paulo, Brazil.

In Colombia, Sabed's Kennels of stunning black Standards belongs to Mrs. Sabrina de Vargas. Based on foundation stock from the Chalmar Kennels of Mrs. Marjorie Bauman, Sabed's has produced a number of very beautiful and very famous dogs, among them the Best in Show winning Colombian Champion Sabed's Emma and Colombian Champion Sabed's Jesabell.

Mackintosh Kennels is in Rio de Janeiro and is owned by Mr. Jose Carlos Guimaraes Santos. He has produced a series of excellent Best in Show winners based on foundation stock from England and the United States.

In Sao Paulo, the Pent Kennels of Evalina and Jaime Martinelli is noted for outstanding dogs, including Poodles. Mr. and Mrs. Martinelli are

Am., Brz., Int. Ch. Eve Queen of Pent Kennels winning one of her numerous Group Firsts under judge Mrs. Heather Logan. In Brazil, "Eve Queen" was undefeated in the breed competition.

interested in numerous breeds. They visit the United States regularly to see and select dogs to import or from which to breed, and Mr. Martinelli is a famous professional handler.

The Martinellis have the distinction of owning the first Brazilian-bred Poodle, and so far the only one, to have gained championship honors in the United States, in which achievement they quite naturally take tremendous pride. This is a bitch, American, Brazilian, and Bermudian Champion Eve Queen of Pent Kennels. She was

The Venezuelan-bred Standard Poodle, Bougon of Barbizon Tigueshang, Best in Show winner from the puppy class, is pictured winning a Non-Sporting Group under Mrs. Winifred Heckman. Owned and handled by Richard Guevera, Caracas.

Vnz. Ch. McColl's Goldy's Nanette, No. 1 Non-Sporting Dog in Venezuela, 1973, winning a Group under Isidor Schoenberg. Owned by McColl's Kennels, handled by Richard Guevera.

242

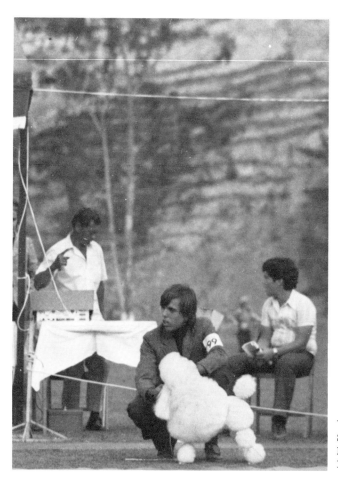

sired by the Martinellis' well-known dog, American, Brazilian, and International Champion Holyoke Hensley, from Canadian and Brazilian Champion Odin Howling Success, and was handled in the United States by Barbara Humphries and while at home and in Bermuda by Mr. Martinelli.

In addition to being a great stud dog, American, Brazilian, and International Champion Holyoke Hensley has also distinguished himself in the show ring, being a multiple Group winner, many times Best in Show dog, and a Specialty Best of Breed winner in both the United States and Brazil.

Canadian and Brazilian Champion Odin Howling Success, the dam of Eve, also is a multiple Best in Show and specialty winner. Based on Standards of such quality, it is easily understandable that the future of Pent Poodles will be a bright one.

Vnz. Ch. McColl's Goldy's Nanette, top-winning Non-Sporting Dog in Venezuela, 1973. Owned by Mrs. Rita Haas, McColl's Kennels, Venezuela. Handled by Richard Guevera.

Can., Brz. Ch. Odin Howling Success winning an all-breed Best in Show under Mr. Langdon Skarda. At the time of this writing, "Mousy" had 10 all-breed Bests in Show and two Specialty Bests of Breed. Owners are Evalina and Jaime Martinelli, Sao Paulo, Brazil.

Vnz., Clm., Dmn. Ch. Minaret's Court Fable is pictured with handler Richard Guevera, now a well known International judge, back in 1972 when "Fable" became the No. 1 Non-Sporting Dog of that year in Venezuela. This English import is owned by Rita Haas, McColl's Kennels, Caracas.

Vnz. Ch. Barbizon Petit Henriette is owned by Richard Guevera, Caracas, Venezuela.

244

Ch. Lou Gin's Kiss Me Kate, her ears in wrappers,
awaiting show time as the judging hour nears. This
famous Poodle has made history for the breed and her
owners, Mr. and Mrs. Jack Phelan and Terri Meyers.

CHAPTER ELEVEN

America's Top Winning Best in Show Dog

Ch. Lou Gin's Kiss Me Kate steals a kiss from her handler, Bob Walberg, while waiting to be gaited in the ring. "Miss Kate," America's Top Best in Show Winning Dog of All Breeds, is owned by Paul-Ann and Jack Phelan and Terri Meyers, bred by Lou Dunston.

It was June 1980, at the Paducah Kennel Club Dog Show, that American show ring history was made. For on that occasion a Standard Poodle bitch, Champion Lou Gin's Kiss Me Kate, broke a record that had stood unchallenged at American Kennel Club Dog Shows since the early 1960's. With that win, "Miss Kate," as she is known, won her 127th Best in Show, bringing her string of such successes to one more than had been attained by the spectacular Pekingese Champion Chik Tsun of Caversham late in the 1950's and into 1960. Jubilation was high, and the immediate question asked was, "Will she be retired now?". But Kate was still very much in her prime, so it was decided to continue a bit longer, possibly through the year or at least until a bit wider margin had been placed between her and the Pekingese.

On November 2, 1980, Champion Lou Gin's Kiss Me Kate won her 140th Best in Show, on which occasion she retired, having broken a whole string of records. To me one of the most noteworthy things about Kate's record is that it was made by a bitch, for one of the most frequently heard laments among people who exhibit is that "bitches can seldom beat the males." Kate could, however, as she proved quite handily, and, we might add, her elegance and refinement are among her most admired assets.

Champion Lou Gin's Kiss Me Kate was born on May 23, 1976, by Champion Ilex Barclay, C.D., from Champion Lou Gin's Chateau Chalon. She was bred by Lou Dunston. She is not only a fantastic show winner, she is also a marvelous personality, so, rather than just giv-

ing you cold statistics, I have asked her co-owner, Miss Terri Meyers, to tell you in her own words about Kate.

"In September of 1976, Louis Dunston brought five white Standard puppy bitches down to the Louisville show, where Bob and Jean Walberg and I were exhibiting. Lou had been telling me about the litter before they had been born, as he was so excited about the breeding. Bob and Lou had gone out to look at the girls and picked out the puppy they thought I should have. She was a cute puppy, but very stubborn and set in her ways.

"If you did not put a leash on her, everything was fine, but put the leash on and everything stiffened up. She was not going to be led around. Since she was only four months old, she couldn't be shown yet, so I sent her home to my family. At the house she ate Mother's plants, used her living room for an ex-pen, and pretty much got her own way.

"My sister Nancy kept the puppy bathed and brushed, while my Mother tried to leash-break her.

"Kate started her show career at seven months, when Charles Hamilton put her up for two points, Best of Winners and Best of Opposite Sex, at Wheaton, Illinois. A couple of weeks afterwards she won the Grand Sweepstakes under Steven Hurt and Best of Opposite Sex to Best of Breed under James Edward Clark at the Greater Milwaukee Poodle Club. Two or three weeks after that she finished down in Georgia under Ann Stevenson.

Bob Walberg smiles happily as Mrs. James Edward Clark awards the Best in Show rosette to the Standard Poodle, Ch. Lou Gin's Kiss Me Kate at Montgomery Kennel Club. Bred by Lou Dunston, this great bitch is co-owned by Mr. and Mrs. Jack Phelan and Miss Terri Meyers.

Best in Show weekend, and not yet a year old! Not very many Poodle puppies go all the way to the top before they are out of puppy clip, but Ch. Lou Gin's Kiss Me Kate has proven herself to be a very special Poodle! This award, at Oshkosh Kennel Club on May 21, 1977, is being made by Haworth Hoch.

"Kate is a strong minded dog. Many times I would leave her on the grooming table, and off the table to find me she would go, with Bob or Jean Walberg after her. We tried tying her to the table, but she would drag it along with her.

"As a 'special' she was entered in Chicago. Here she won the big Sweepstakes under Pat Hancock. The following week we were in Kansas, where she won her first Non-Sporting Group, this under Hayden Martin. Two days later she received her first Best in Show under Dr. Rex Foster, with a standing ovation and lots of tears from us. That is one Best in Show that I will never forget, as Kate stood there on the end of the lead with her tail flapping back and forth as if saying to Bob 'Love this! Isn't it fun!'.

"Kate never moved as the judge walked from

Ch. Lou Gin's Kiss Me Kate, at ten months old and still in puppy clip, wins her first Non-Sporting Group, under judge Hayden Martin at the Hutchinson Kennel Club on April 8, 1977. Handled by Bob Walberg for Terri and Barbara Meyers, who owned her at that time.

one side to the other out in the middle of the ring.

"She has always been full of surprises. I believe that's how she got her nickname, 'Brains.' She never stops thinking. She is a fascinating creature and one not to be denied.

"Kate received her second Best in Show the following weekend under Ruttlege Gilliland. The weekend before she turned one year old she earned back-to-back Bests in Show. She watched the judge walk up and down the line as if she were saying, 'I'm up here. What are you doing back there?' She was awarded the Bests in Show by Haworth Hoch and James Bennett. She also won the Wichita Specialty under Barbara Hussin in puppy trim.

"When Kate went into pattern, she had a total of six times Best Non-Sporting Dog, four Bests in Show, and a Specialty Best of Breed.

"To prove she could keep going, the following weekend she won two more Groups and a Best in Show.

"Kate had proven herself to have become very dependable in the ring, or so we thought. Down in Oklahoma she made a flying leap for the examination table while in the Best in Show ring. I think that Haworth Hoch thought it was funny. But Bob did not. There were many times when either Jean or I would cough or laugh outside the ring when Kate would zero in on us. She would come out of the ring following judging and leap to the floor on her front legs with her butt in the air and look at me as if she were saying, 'Work's over. Now let's play.' Then she would make her flying leap in the air, and I would get smothered with kisses.

"Kate loves to tear around the back yard. She has her tennis ball and an orange hedge-hog squeaker she always plays with. We tell her to get her ball or her toy, and she does. She also likes to chase people, barking all the way. If you were lucky you didn't get playfully nipped.

"Kate also is very good at using the Walbergs' couch as a trampoline. When she gets tired of bouncing, she will lie down and watch everyone. She likes to know where her family is at all times. If someone goes outside, she goes outside. If everyone is inside, she must be, too. She has a skillful way of training people to do what she wants.

"We never, ever got tired of watching Kate show. In fact if anything it became more exciting. There were a lot of tears at a lot of shows. We took every win as it came, one step at a time. We never, ever thought we had any in the bag.

"The most exciting Best in Show to me, and I believe that some of the rest of us feel as I do about this, was the Chicago International under Henry Stoecker. When he sent Kate and Bob around the ring, they started down the long mat and the crowd started chanting 'go, go, go.' The louder they got, the faster Kate went. It looked like she never touched the ground, almost as if she had shifted into a higher gear. It was absolutely breathtaking. As we all clapped and watched, tears began to fall. That is the way Kate affected us.

The Best in Show award with which the white Standard Poodle bitch, Ch. Lou Gin's Kiss Me Kate, broke the All Time Best in Show Record for any dog of any breed in the United States. This, her 127th such award, was made by judge Charles Hamilton at the Paducah Kennel Club Dog Show in June 1980. Bob Walberg, as always, is handling Kate for her owners, Terri Meyers and Mr. and Mrs. Jack Phelan.

Henry Stoecker has just awarded Best in Show to Ch. Lou Gin's Kiss Me Kate at the Chicago International, April 1979. Kate is shown surrounded by her owners, right to left, Terri Meyers, Paul-Ann Phelan, and Jack Phelan. Bob Walberg is handling.

248

"We won!" Ch. Lou Gin's Kiss Me Kate, literally jumping from joy as she is signaled to a Best in Show with her friend and handler, Bob Walberg.

"There were two shows she won that I really wished I could have attended [Terry was seriously injured in a motor-home crash during Kate's show career, spending many weeks hospitalized and convalescing] in Detroit and Louisville, as I understand she was really going strong at them. Another show where she was remarkable was Santa Barbara, where she seemed to float around the ring.

"Kate always knows when to turn on that extra special quality of hers, whether it's speed or daring the judge or trying to catch the crowd's attention. The bitch is really remarkably intelligent. I believe that's one reason she had so many followers during her career. Wherever we went, she attracted her own cheering section.

"Kate is a snob, or a bitch, or whatever you want to call her. If she doesn't want to be touched, she turns away. She is very good at turning her back on people. Don't misunderstand me about her personality. She is extremely affectionate to the people close to her. She likes to stand on her hind legs and tuck her head under my chin and just be hugged for a minute. She has earned her name well. If you say 'Kiss Me Kate' you are bound to get a kiss or two.

"In the motor-home Kate always tried to see if she could get away with lying on the couch. If she had won that day, she would put up an argu-

ment about going into her crate. You could tell she was thinking, 'I won today, I deserve to stay here.' If she had not won, she rarely put up a protest about the crate.

"A lot of people got a big kick out of Kate in the ring when she won. As the judge pointed, it was almost like she knew before Bob did, as she leaped in the air several times. As a puppy she would get a little carried away because she knew she had to get to the platform to earn a big hand and have her picture taken. So while moving on her individual gaiting, she would head for the platform. It was very frustrating for us, but Kate had fun.

"Kate never seemed to tire of showing. She loves the applause, the pictures, and especially the hugs and happy times afterwards. She showed through rain and thunderstorms, ungodly heat, cold—you name it, Kate took it in her stride.

"We were at an outside show once when the black clouds moved in and the thunder was really cracking. The louder it got, the higher Kate's head went up, and you could tell how excited she was. She started leaping and spinning circles, and even barked a few times. She thought it was the greatest thing she ever heard.

During the Best in Show judging, Kate's eye always remains on the judge. One of her prettiest pictures!

"Kate is the type bitch that if you do something she doesn't like, she lets you know it. When I would bring her up to ringside, if Bob was in with an Open bitch, she would never take her eyes off of him, stomping her feet and whining to let him know that he had some nerve to be in there with someone else.

"Many records have been broken by Kate. When we would get close to one, I would go back to be there (I was home recuperating from my accident), and be attacked by Miss Kate as if to say 'Glad you're back, Mom.'

"In 1979 Kate broke most of the existing records. She won the most Bests in Show in a year (66); the most Group Wins in a year (101); she had 46 consecutive Groups; she became Top Non-Sporting Dog Of All Time; Top Winning Poodle of All Time (102 Bests in Show); Top Winning Bitch of All Time, *Kennel Review* System. She has won in all parts of the country, East, West, North, and South. Whenever there was a decision to be made, we all gave our opinion, after which the matter was decided.

Ch. Lou Gin's Kiss Me Kate sits up tall in her director's chair as she and Bob Walberg contemplate the Best in Show they have just won at Michiana Kennel Club, June 1980. The Phelans and Terri Meyers are owners of this famous bitch. Lou Dunston is the breeder.

The rear view you like of a Standard Poodle! Ch. Lou Gin's Kiss Me Kate in the show ring with her handler, Bob Walberg.

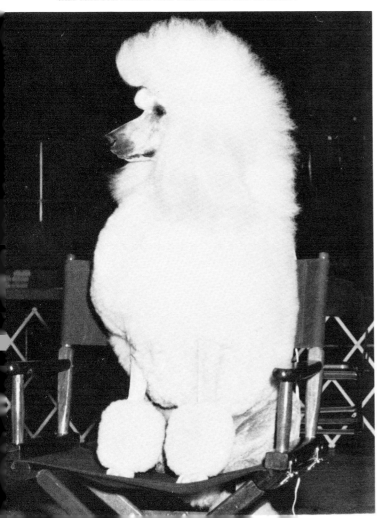

"When Kate was put on a plane, it was to go to California or New York. It is not as though she were a dog we just were showing now and then or here and there. She had a chance to be the Top Winning Dog of All Time, and thanks to my Mother and Dad in the beginning, for the first year and a half, and to Jack and Paulann Phelan, who became her co-owners at that time, and to Jean and Bob Walberg all the way, she made it.

"Kate has won the Quaker Oats Award three times; the *Canine Chronicle* Award twice; Top Non-Sporting Dog Award twice for the *Kennel Review* Award; and the Top All-Breed Best in Show Award from *Kennel Review,* climaxing it all with the total of 140 times Best Dog in Show All-Breeds.

"I often sit back and visualize Kate and Bob flying around the ring without a care in the world and nothing to stop them. Bob did a tremendous job with Kate. If you watched them, they worked so beautifully together. Kate adored him. We did let Bob make the decision on when and where her final show would be. It was down in Oklahoma with Vincent Perry. When she broke the Pekingese's record in Kentucky, it was under Charles Hamilton, who gave her her first two points. It was a tear-jerker at both of these shows.

250

"It is hard to even hold the thought in our minds about going to a show and not taking Kate, getting her ready for the ring with her looking back at Bob saying 'Hurry up Bob, isn't it fun!'"

This story is not only about a great *winning* Poodle, it is a very familiar story of Poodle personality, their intelligence, the rapport they establish with the people close to them. It is also a very real presentation of the way dog show handlers feel about their charges, and the love and pleasure felt by true fanciers for their dogs.

We salute Champion Lou Gin's Kiss Me Kate as a magnificently beautiful Poodle, but also as the true epitome of all the things that have made Poodles so popular as canine friends with so many people all over the world.

To Kate. May you enjoy a long and happy retirement. We understand that there are puppies in your future. Who knows, perhaps one of them may attain big records also in the ring.

Opposite:
The final show for Ch. Lou Gin's Kiss Me Kate marks the occasion of her 140th Best in Show award. The judge is Vincent Perry, Bob Walberg handling. "Kate" was bred by Lou Dunston of Lou Gin Poodles, and is owned by Paul-Ann and Jack Phelan and Terri Meyers.

Repeating her 1979 victory, Ch. Lou Gin's Kiss Me Kate takes a Chicago International Best in Show on October 12, 1980. This is one of America's biggest, most prestigious dog shows, and winning here even once is a great achievement. Doing so twice is a singular honor indeed. The judge is Fred Hunt, handler is Bob Walberg, and owners are Terri Meyers and Mr. and Mrs. Jack Phelan.

The start of something big! Ch. Lou Gin's Kiss Me Kate, the Top Winning Best in Show Dog of All Breeds in the United States. "Kate" is pictured at eight months of age, winning her first Best of Variety from the puppy class under judge James Edward Clark. Bob Walberg handling.

BEST OF VARIETY
C.S.C OF GR.MILW
FEBRUARY 5. 1977
OLSON PHOTO

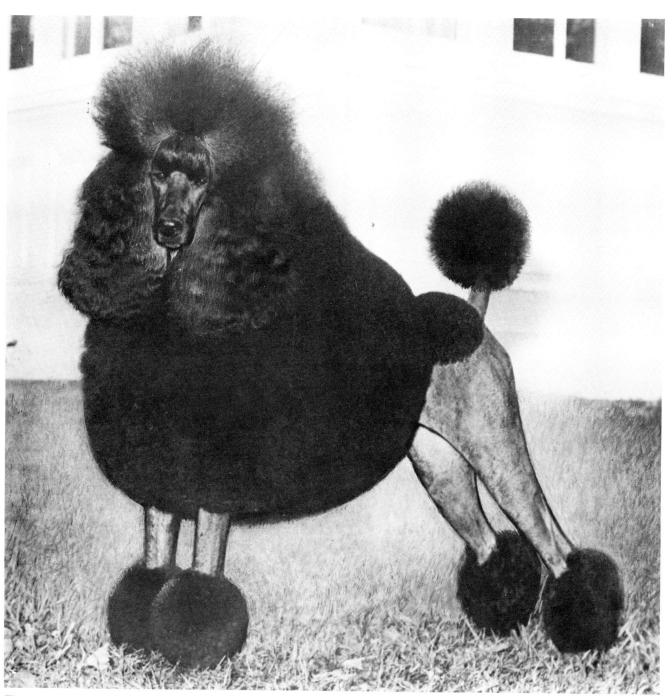

The well known Standard Poodle Ch. Longleat
Hulagan, by Ch. Acadia Command Performance ex
Ch. Alekai Hula, is owned by M. J. Lester. Photo
courtesy of Alisia Duffy.

CHAPTER TWELVE

Official Standard For the Poodle

A magnificent Poodle sculpture of Am., Can. Ch. Dhubhne Darth Vader, as done by the noted sculptress Leslie Lord. "Darth" belongs to Carroll Ann Irwin of North Hollywood, California.

(Compiled by the Poodle Club of America and approved by the American Kennel Club, November, 1978)

GENERAL APPEARANCE, CARRIAGE, AND CONDITION. That of a very active, intelligent, and elegant-appearing dog, squarely built, well proportioned, moving soundly, and carrying himself proudly. Properly clipped in the traditional fashion and carefully groomed, the Poodle has about him an air of distinction and dignity peculiar to himself.

HEAD AND EXPRESSION. (a) SKULL. Moderately rounded, with a slight but definite stop. Cheekbones and muscles flat. Length from occiput to stop about the same as length of muzzle. (b) MUZZLE. Long, straight, and fine with slight chiseling under the eyes. Strong without lippiness. The chin definite enough to preclude snipiness. Teeth white, strong, and with a scissors bite. (c) EYES. Very dark, oval in shape, and set far enough apart and positioned to create an alert intelligent expression. (d) EARS. Hanging close to the head, set at or slightly below eye level. The ear leather is long, wide, and thickly feathered; however, the ear fringe should not be of excessive length.

NECK AND SHOULDERS. Neck well proportioned, strong, and long enough to permit the head to be carried high and with dignity. Skin snug at throat. The neck rises from strong, smoothly muscled shoulders. The shoulder blade is well laid back and approximately the same length as the upper forearm.

BODY. To insure the desirable squarely-built appearance, the length of body measured from the breastbone to the point of the rump approximates the height from the highest point of the shoulders to the ground. (a) CHEST. Deep and moderately wide with well sprung ribs. (b) BACK. The topline is level, neither sloping nor roached, from the highest point of the shoulder blade to the base of the tail, with the exception of a slight hollow just behind the shoulder. The loin is short, broad, and muscular.

TAIL. Straight, set on high and carried up, docked of sufficient length to insure a balanced outline.

LEGS. (a) FORELEGS. Straight and parallel when viewed from the front. When viewed from the side the elbow is directly below the highest point of the shoulder. The pasterns are strong. Bone and muscle of both forelegs and hindlegs are in proportion to size of dog. (b) HINDLEGS. Straight and parallel when viewed from the rear. Muscular with width in the region of the stifles, which are well bent; femur and tibia are about equal in length; hock to heel short and perpendicular to the ground. When standing, the rear toes are only slightly behind the point of rump. The angulation of the hindquarters balances that of the forequarters.

FEET. The feet are rather small, oval in shape, with toes well arched and cushioned on thick firm pads. Nails short but not excessively shortened. The feet turn neither in nor out. Dewclaws may be removed.

This beautiful Miniature is Ch. Surrey Sequioa, winner of ten Bests in Show. Bred by Mr. and Mrs. James Edward Clark, owned by Mrs. Margaret Durney, handled by Frank T. Sabella.

COAT (a) QUALITY. (1) Curly. Of natural harsh texture, dense throughout. (2) Corded. Hanging in tight, even cords of varying length; longer on mane of body coat, head, and ears; shorter on puffs, bracelets, and pompons.

(b) CLIP. A Poodle under twelve months may be shown in the "Puppy" clip. In all regular classes, Poodles twelve months or over must be shown in the "English Saddle" or "Continental" clip. In the Stud Dog and Brood Bitch classes and in a non-competitive Parade of Champions, Poodles may be shown in the "Sporting" clip. A Poodle shown in any other type of clip shall be disqualified.

(1) "Puppy": – A Poodle under a year old may be shown in the "Puppy" clip with the coat long. The face, throat, feet, and base of the tail are shaved. The entire shaven foot is visible. There is a pompon on the end of the tail. In order to give a neat appearance and a smooth unbroken line, shaping of the coat is permissible.

(2) "English Saddle": – In the "English Saddle" clip, the face, throat, feet, forelegs, and base of the tail are shaved, leaving puffs on the forelegs and a pompon at the end of the tail. The hindquarters are covered with a short blanket of hair except for a curved shaved area on each flank and two shaved bands on each hindleg. The entire shaven foot and a portion of the shaven leg above the puff are visible. The rest of the body is

left in full coat but may be shaped in order to insure overall balance.

(3) "Continental": – In the "Continental" clip the face, throat, feet, and base of the tail are shaved. The hindquarters are shaved with pompons (optional) on the hips. The legs are shaved, leaving bracelets on the hindlegs and puffs on the forelegs. There is a pompon on the end of the tail. The entire shaven foot and a portion of the shaven foreleg above the puff are visible. The rest of the body is left in full coat but may be shaped to insure overall balance.

(4) "Sporting": – In the "Sporting" clip a Poodle shall be shown with face, feet, throat, and base of tail shaved, leaving a scissored cap on the top of the head and a pompon on the end of the tail. The rest of the body and legs are clipped or scissored to follow the outline of the dog, leaving a short blanket of coat no longer than one inch in length. The hair on the legs may be slightly longer than that on the body.

In all clips the hair of the topknot may be left free or held in place by no more than three elastic bands. The hair is only of sufficient length to present a smooth outline.

COLOR. The coat is an even and solid color at the skin. In blues, grays, silvers, browns, cafe-au-laits, apricots, and creams the coat may show varying shades of the same color. This is frequently present in the somewhat darker feather-

Ch. Juniper's Truly Yours, by Ch. Highlane's Helmsman ex Ch. Mifwin Happidaze, pictured taking Winners Bitch at Westminster, 1977. Maxine Beam, judge. Wendell J. Sammet handling for owner, June Bierwas, Ringwood, New Jersey.

North Country Kennel Club, September 1976. Ashwood's Sunny Hunny, by Ch. Meridian Memorandum ex Ashwood's Holiday Cheer, bred and owned by Betty Mahaffy.

Ch. Nicolat's Syntifny Starkist, a Silverdrift daughter, here winning the Toy Group at Genesee Valley, 1978. Owned by Jane A. Winne, handled by Todd Patterson.

At the Poodle Club of America Specialty in 1962, Wendell J. Sammet handled Ch. Alekai Pikake to Best of Variety and Best of Opposite Sex to Best of Breed for Mrs. Henry J. Kaiser. Mrs. George putnam (left), owner of Puttencove Poodles, is presenting the trophy as Mrs. Mildred Imrie of Freelands Poodles makes the award.

This magnificent Standard is Ch. Haus Brau Executive of Acadia, owned by Joy Tongue and handled by Frank Sabella, making one of many Best in Show wins. Photo courtesy of Mr. Sabella.

ing of the ears and in the tipping of the ruff. While clear colors are definitely preferred, such natural variation the shading of the coat is not to be considered a fault. Brown and cafe-au-lait Poodles have liver-colored noses, eye rims and lips, dark toenails, and dark amber eyes. Black, blue, gray, silver, cream, and white Poodles have black noses, eye rims and lips, black or self colored toenails, and very dark eyes. In the apricots while the foregoing coloring is preferred, liver-colored noses, eye rims and lips, and amber eyes are permitted but are not desirable.

Parti-colored dogs shall be disqualified. The coat of a parti-colored dog is not an even, solid color at the skin, but is of two or more colors.

GAIT. A straightforward trot with light springy action and strong hindquarters drive. Head and tail carried up. Sound, effortless movement is essential.

SIZE.

THE STANDARD POODLE is over 15 inches at the highest point of the shoulders. Any Poodle which is 15 inches or less in height shall be disqualified from competition as a Standard Poodle.

THE MINIATURE POODLE is 15 inches or under at the highest point of the shoulders, with a minimum height in excess of 10 inches. Any Poodle which is over 15 inches or which is 10 inches or less at the highest point of the shoulders shall be disqualified from competition as a Miniature Poodle.

THE TOY POODLE is 10 inches or under at the highest point of the shoulders. Any Poodle which is more than 10 inches at the highest point of the shoulders shall be disqualified from competition as a Toy Poodle.

An outstanding white Miniature moving in the manner that has won him many high honors including two Westminster Non-Sporting Groups. Paul Edwards has the lead on Ch. J.L.C. Critique, back home again now with Mrs. Rita Cloutier after an exciting career under Robert Koeppel's ownership.

VALUE OF POINTS

General appearance, temperament, carriage, and condition 30
Head, expression, ears, eyes, and teeth 20
Body, neck, legs, feet, and tail 20
Gait 20
Coat, color and texture 10

MAJOR FAULTS. Any distinct deviation from the desired characteristics described in the Breed Standard, with particular attention to the following:

Temperament—Shyness or sharpness.

Muzzle—Undershot, overshot, wry mouth, lack of chin.

Eyes—Round, protruding, large, or very light.

Pigment—Color of nose, lips, and eye rims incomplete or of wrong color for color of dog.

Neck and Shoulders—Ewe neck, steep shoulders.

Tail—Set low, curled, or carried over the back.

Hindquarters—Cow hocks.

Feet—Paper or splayfoot.

DISQUALIFICATIONS.

Clip—A dog in any type of clip other than those listed under Coat shall be disqualified.

Parti-Colors—The coat of a parti-colored dog is not an even, solid color at the skin but of two or more colors. Parti-colored dogs shall be disqualified.

Size—A dog over or under the height limits shall be disqualified.

Approved November 14, 1978

A great favorite of the author during his ring career, Ch. Cappoquin Railsplitter. "Linc" won two Bests in Show, ten Group Firsts, and 24 additional Group placements in 1962. Bred by Cappoquin Kennels, owned by Tilo Kennels, handled by Bob Forsyth.

This stunning white Standard bitch, Ch. Mike Mar's Super Star, is the one that created a sensation at Westminster in 1972 by going through from the classes to take Best of Variety over a magnificent collection of the country's most famous winners. Owned by Mrs. Walter Jeffords, Mr. Michael Wolf, and Miss Pamela Hall. "Super Star" is handled here by the latter.

258

Other Disqualifications For Poodles

The Standard of Perfection has already brought you a listing of the disqualifications which apply to the Poodle breed, and we explain in the next section how a Poodle is measured. But there are some other disqualifications as well to which Poodles are subject, in common with all other breeds of dog, at shows held under American Kennel Club rules and regulations.

A dog which is blind, deaf, castrated, spayed, or which has been changed in appearance by artificial means beyond those specified in the Standard of its breed may not be shown. Nor may a dog which is monorchid (with but one testicle normally located in the scrotum) or cryptorchid (with neither testicle normally located in the scrotum). All such dogs are disqualified from competition, except that a spayed bitch may be shown as a brood bitch in the Brood Bitch Class and a castrated dog may be entered in the Stud Dog Class. Removal of dewclaws or docking of tails in a breed where these acts are customary and in accordance with the Standard will not be considered as artificial changes of appearance.

A dog that is lame in the ring at a show cannot receive an award and must be excused from competition for that day. A dog that appears to have any foreign substances in it's coat (Poodle exhibitors note with care), whether for cleaning purposes or otherwise, *may not be judged and must be excused from the ring.*

If you know that your Poodle is under or over the size limit, do not show it. You may get away with it on that day, but sooner or later some judge will catch the situation and the reflection on the exhibitor is not pleasant.

Do not show your dog if it is lame, in hopes that perhaps the judge may not notice or it may not happen to limp while he is making the examination. Do not show a monorchid or a cryptorchid, either, nor a dog with any of the other listed disqualifications. And, last but not least, never bring your Poodle into the ring loaded down with chalk, powder, hair spray, or any other such preparation, causing yourself and the judge the embarrassment of dismissing you from competition. A reputation for honesty and fair play is vital if one is to succeed in the Fancy and it should be guarded zealously.

If your dog should be disqualified for any reason at a show, you then may appeal to the American Kennel Club for reinstatement. An

Poodle Club of America, May 17, 1957. Ch. Fieldstreams Bojangles, a Toy, handled by Ben Burwell for Audrey Watts Kelch. Ch. Hollycourt Florazel, a Miniature, handled by Wendell J. Sammet for M. Ruelle Kelchner. Ch. Puttencove Promise, a Standard and the Best in Show winner, handled by Bob Gorman for Mr. and Mrs. George Putnam. Judging by Mrs. Flora Bonney.

Poodle Club of America, 1959. Ch. Fieldstreams Valentine, Toy Best of Variety, is handled by Ben Burwell. Ch. Cappoquin Bon Jongleur, Miniature Best of Variety, is handled by Wendell J. Sammet. Ch. Puttencove Moonshine, Standard Best of Variety, is handled by Bob Gorman.

appointment will be arranged for examination of the dog, at which time a decision will be reached as to whether or not the dog can again become eligible for competition. Should this happen to you, speak with the American Kennel Club Field Representative at the show, who will instruct you regarding the course to be followed.

Measuring The Poodle

Knowing how a Poodle is correctly measured is a "must" for those either handling or judging the breed. Since there is a size disqualification involved, there is always the chance that a necessity for doing so may arise.

As a judge, if you notice that a dog in your Toy or Miniature ring looks conspicuously larger than the others in an average class, it is your duty, in upholding the Standard, to take a measurement of that dog. Or if, during the course of your judging a class, an exhibitor requests that you call a measurement on a specific dog, it again is your duty to do so, provided that the request is made prior to your having marked the judges' book for awards in that class.

The procedure is really not all that difficult.

When the need arises, the judge sends his steward to the superintendent or show secretary to request that a wicket be sent to the ring. In due course this arrives and is handed to the person judging, who then examines it and if necessary sets the wicket to the applicable height—in the case of Poodles, ten inches for Toys, 15 inches for Miniatures. This is done quite easily, as the wicket, made of stainless steel and similar in shape to the old fashioned wickets used in playing croquet, has a solid extension leg that slides in and out of each of the hollow legs of the wicket. The hollow legs are calibrated at every half inch. A set screw at the base of each leg is tightened to lock the extension legs at the desired height. Each leg of the wicket is set separately, and the height is read separately on each leg. Before loosening the set screw the judge should turn the wicket so that one leg does not entirely drop out. When both legs have been set at the desired height the wicket is ready for use. Setting the wicket is a very simple operation that is quick and easy to perform.

Meanwhile the exhibitor places the dog on the table, if that is where it was being judged, or on

260

the ground as originally done for the judge's examination. The dog belongs in a natural position with the head up but not stretched upwards (nor grasped around the ears and pulled forward as some exhibitors have been seen doing), feet set squarely with forelegs vertical as forepaws belong well under the dog. In the case of a Poodle, the exhibitor parts the hair over the dog's shoulders with the fingers in order that the judge can locate the highest point of structure, but placing the wicket in a manner so as not to get added height from any of the coat. The judge must have no part in positioning the dog beyond giving instructions which are to be followed explicitly by the exhibitor.

When all is ready, the judge approaches the dog with the wicket held low at his side. With the fingers he touches the dog's shoulders to determine their highest point, then brings the wicket up quickly from behind the dog and lowers it so that the crosspiece comes down directly on the predetermined highest point.

Both legs of the wicket will touch the floor, ground or table if the dog is within the height limit for a Miniature. If the wicket swings across the shoulders or only one leg at a time goes down, the dog is oversized. The same is true of a Toy Poodle with the difference being that for the Miniature a wicket set at 15 inches is used, while for the Toy the setting of the wicket is 10 inches.

The judge must then mark his findings in the judges' book. If all went well, he simply states, "Measured in," and places his initials beneath the notation. If the dog exceeds the limit, the notation reads, "Measured out—disqualified under breed Standard," and in this case, too, the note must be initialed.

Note to judges: Even if the dog measures in, it is important not to overlook noting this fact in your judges' book, as no dog once measured "in" at a show may have further height determination made on him at that show.

A dog disqualified on measurement is not eligible to again be shown until such time as an official measurement has been made by the American Kennel Club.

Poodle breeders or others planning to show Poodles would do well to invest in a wicket for home use, both to keep track of the height of their dogs as they mature and to accustom the dogs to the measuring procedure.

Wickets of the type used officially are available through the American Kennel Club. Permanently set wickets for use by Specialty Clubs and adjustable wickets which can be used for several breeds are both available.

Do not panic if someone calls for a measurement or if the judge requests one on your dog. Very frequently a heavy mane can make the dog appear taller than actually is the case. With a disqualification involved, the judge particularly cannot afford to take a chance if he considers there will be any question.

Ch. Longleat Alima's Raisin Cane winning Best Standard Puppy under Mrs. Rebecca Mason at the Poodle Club of America, 1980. Richard L. Bauer is handling for Alisia A. Duffy.

Am., Can. Ch. Ravendune Sweet Baby James is owned by Todd Patterson, Ravendune Kennels, Taylor, Michigan. By Can. Ch. Highlane Bonhomme Richard ex Am., Can. Ch. Bon Aire Black Temptation.

Winning the Variety Group at Pensacola's 1980 spring event is Ch. Jay-En Egnite of Storytell, black Standard dog owned by Mrs. William H. Ball and handled by Pat Norwood.

Am., Can. Ch. Monfret Music Master is a Group winner
and the sire of 16 champions. By Ch. Wycliffe Thomas
ex Monfret Melody.

CHAPTER THIRTEEN

Mrs. Hoyt Discusses The Poodle

Hayes Blake Hoyt

A Tribute To Hayes Blake Hoyt

It is with boundless pride and pleasure that we have the honor of bringing you, as a special feature of this book, some most knowledgeable and interesting discussions of the breed written by that eminent authority Hayes Blake Hoyt. Mrs. Hoyt's name has been practically a household word in the Poodle world for the past half century. She and her late husband, Sherman Reese Hoyt, attained success and the admiration of the whole dog show world with the quality Poodles they raised for many, many years at Blakeen. When the breed was in the formative stage, the Hoyts imported the best from Europe and from England to breed with the finest American stock. Their original Standards are still to be found far back in the pedigrees of the majority of leading Standards today. From the smaller of these Standards and excellent Miniature stock, they were ready for the popularity explosion in that variety with imported and homebred dogs accomplishing all sorts of "firsts" for their variety in at least several colors.

With the acceptance of the Toys as a variety of Poodle, again the Hoyts were quick to do the right thing. They imported a little dog with a tremendous impact on the colored Toys, and by combining him with small-sized Miniatures, soon Blakeen Toys had joined the other two Poodle sizes in the forefront of keenest competition.

It would be difficult to say to which of the Blakeen dogs most credit is due! Perhaps you can decide for yourself, having by now read the historical chapters of Poodle development in the 1930's and 1940's, which is almost like a kennel history of Blakeen. Their dogs were behind so many of the greatest owned by other fanciers, too! This was not just what was contained within the home kennel; it was what dogs and bitches had produced and sent out from there to other kennels and what they, in turn, had produced, carrying on the family line.

There are those who say that the fabulous white Standards were Blakeen's greatest Poodles, Duc, Jung Frau, Eiger, and later on Bali Hai. Anyone who ever saw them could never forget the two immortal Miniatures Snow Boy and Eldorado and all the fantastic dogs and bitches by Snow Boy and his progeny who swept the record boards from coast to coast. Mrs. Tyson, Ernie Ferguson, and the Hoyts themselves won literally hundreds of prestigious honors each with them.

And then in Toys, again it was Blakeen: King Doodles with a whole array of Best in Show honors and Ding Ding with an impressive display of "Rating Certificates." Both Hayes and Sherman Hoyt loved and enjoyed the Poodles. Sherman for years always insisted on putting the patterns on the show dogs, which he did "second to none," and Hayes personally did the major portion of the handling, except when Norman McBrien, kennel manager at Blakeen, helped out in this regard. It was Henry Stoecker who campaigned Snow Boy during an exciting part of

Headstudy of the great Ch. Snow Boy of Fircot of Blakeen, owned by Mr. and Mrs. Sherman R. Hoyt, Blakeen Poodles.

The grey Miniature, Ch. Blakeen Lustre, born March 18, 1940, owned by Blakeen Poodles, Mr. and Mrs. Sherman R. Hoyt. By Ch. Cheri of Misty Isles ex Ch. Lady in Waiting of Misty Isles.

his career. Both of the Hoyts were popular and respected judges. Sherman would only do Poodles, and it took lots of persuasion before he could be talked into accepting an assignment, as he really did not care that much about it. Hayes was a multiple breed and Group judge and a *good* one, but eventually other interests caused her to resign her license due to lack of time.

Blakeen Poodles were far from being the Hoyts' only activity in the Dog Fancy. Hayes has always been a prolific and talented writer and has several earlier books on dogs to her credit along with some award-winning poetry. For the dog magazines, she has been Poodle columnist for the leading ones over the years when she was active in the breed, was very famous for her "Sauntering Along" column in *Popular Dogs,* did excellent feature columns for *Kennel Review* and other publications, and was involved with the publication of a most beautiful Poodle magazine (very correctly named *Poodle Showcase*) with Mark Crawford some years back.

The Hoyts hosted one of the best of all outdoor dog shows, the North Westchester Kennel Club Annual Event, when they lived at Katonah, New York, on their magnificent estate there—a show very much in the Morris and Essex tradition. They were instrumental in the formation and success of the Interstate Poodle Club.

But probably Hayes Hoyt's greatest service to pure-bred dogs has been through her television broadcasts. She was the first commentator on the Westminster Kennel Club telecasts back when the show was televised live for the general public. Then she created The Dog Show of Champions, a half-hour weekly program on Channel 5 that New York dog fanciers truly loved. Each week she would bring together famous show dogs and their owners, discussing the breeds, letting the people see that show dogs are intelligent, stable, well-tempered, happy animals, not the strange neurotic creatures those who have never known one first-hand believe. The show was successful and popular and did so much to create better understanding of our show dogs.

Later Hayes Hoyt did a series of guest appearances on the Arlene Francis program, again successfully, along the same lines of letting the public see what show dogs are *really* like and teaching them something of the characteristics of the various breeds.

The "Discussions With Mrs. Hoyt" which follow were originally done for use in a book she had been planning to write but never got around to finishing. Most of them were written in the 1960's, but the knowledge, expert advice, and Poodle observations they contain are just as correct and just as applicable now as they were then. We are especially thrilled with the color chapters and those on type, conformation, and character of the breed. This is a lady who enjoyed her Poodles first hand, worked with the dogs herself, and grew to personally know and love each of them. One can only add to one's own knowledge by absorbing that which she shares here with us.

Mrs. Hoyt Discusses Color

WHAT IS COLOR?

When the breeder decides to work only with one certain color, he will benefit if he can learn about the colors behind the Poodles he proposes to use, as well as about the nature of color itself. Also, when the breeder plans to cross colors it would be wise to study the pedigrees of his stock very carefully. The following are some important facts about inheritance and color itself.

What is the color in Poodle hair? When Poodle hair is examined under a high-powered microscope we find that all the colors are caused by minute granules of pigment, with the exception of apricot and cream. Since the apricot and cream hairs have no discernible pigment granules, we cannot be sure whether the color is caused by even smaller pigment granules or a substance so evenly spread throughout the hair that each particle is only one molecule.

The color in black Poodle hair is caused by round black granules of pigment. In a good black they are so tightly packed that a microscope light can hardly shine through them. Blue Poodle hair has the same pigment as the black but more loosely packed.

There are two kinds of brown Poodle hair. The first in its most perfect state is a deep mahogany brown. I have seen many Poodles of this color in France and a few in America. The pigment in this hair is composed of oval brown granules quite closely packed with some round black granules. The browns we usually see in America are this same brown, but the pigment is more loosely packed. Many of these browns take on a silvery appearance due to the black granules in the hair. Of course their shade is much lighter than that of the browns with the closely packed pigment. The second brown is pure red, the color of a horse chestnut. It is a rare color now but was prevalent among the old Whippendells and I

A front view of Mrs. Sherman R. Hoyt's owner-handled brown Miniature dog, Ch. Blakeen Eldorado, at the Tuxedo Kennel Club in 1946.

The lovely white Standard bitch, Ch. Blakeen Aigrette, winning Best in Show in 1943 at Arlington, Virginia. Owner-handler is Mrs. Sherman R. Hoyt, Blakeen Kennels, Stamford, Connecticut.

Mrs. George Marmer owned this handsome brace of Poodles with which handler William J. Trainor is winning at Westminster in 1959.

believe in the Hill Hurst stock. The Rufus line and the beginning of the Leila family were also of this color. Most of the dogs that carry this color today are descendants of Champion Blakeen Eldorado (Miniature) or Champion Blakeen Colorado (Standard), who were true red browns. I have had trouble obtaining hair samples of this color, but I believe it is entirely composed of the brown oval pigment granules with none of the black granules. The red brown does not fade as easily as the other brown and of course shows no tendency to silver.

Gray Poodle hair is filled with loosely packed black pigment granules and some brown ones. However, the coat of a gray Poodle is seldom composed totally of gray hair. There are usually some black hairs and often brown and white ones sprinkled throughout the coat.

The pigment in cafe-au-lait Poodle hair is a very loosely packed mixture of black and brown pigment granules. They give the hair a true silver-beige tone. However, do not let this lead you to believe that you will get cafe-au-laits by crossing silvers and browns.

As I have mentioned before, no pigment granules are visible in either apricot or cream Poodle hair. Apricot and cream may be caused by a gene which promotes a chemical change in black or gray Poodle hair.

As in brown Poodle hair, there are at least two kinds of white. The first kind has a few black pigment granules in the hair. The skin of such a

Poodle is silver, and the nose, eyerims, and lips are black. I believe that Nature intended these Poodles to be black, but the presence of recessive genes which blocked the black color made this impossible. The second white is, I believe, also derived from black. The difference between the two is that in the second white the skin is more apt to be pink, and fewer black pigment granules can be found in the hair. Do not confuse these with albinos. An albino has pink eyes, nose, eye rims, and lips, while those of a white Poodle of either kind are black. Occasionally we do see partial albinism in white Poodles. You are probably wondering about Poodles with spotted skins. I believe they have evolved from crosses with other colors.

Before proceeding any further in our study of coat color, we must ask a very important question: *What is inheritance?* Inheritance is the transmission of unacquired characteristics from one generation to the next. To clarify this let us look at a basic tenet of Mendel's Law: "Characteristics of living organisms which are inherited are controlled by genes which exist in most of the cells in pairs, each parent having contributed one of each pair. When both black and white genes are present in one animal the animal will be a hybrid black. That is it appears black but is able to transmit white as well as black."

Mrs. Sherman R. Hoyt with her sensational brown Miniature dog, Ch. Blakeen Eldorado, winning Best in Show at the Interstate Kennel Association in 1945. W. Ross Procter, judge. Anna Katherine Nicholas, club president.

Ch. Encore Jester, a splendid black Toy male owned by Mrs. Jane Fitts, was shown during the 1950's. Photo courtesy of Pat Norwood.

The brown Standard Poodle, Ch. Blakeen Colorado, born May 30, 1943. Shown only 19 times, this stunning dog had 10 Bests of Variety, 6 Non-Sporting Groups, and 3 times was Best American-bred in Show. Bred and owned by Mr. and Mrs. Sherman R. Hoyt, Blakeen Poodles. By Ch. Berkham Isaac of Sunstorm ex Broadrun Cinnamon.

An excellent photo of Mrs. Edward Solomon's Ch. Dassin Busby Berkley taken at Trenton Kennel Club, 1979.

In Poodles color is controlled by an unknown number of pairs of genes. Therefore we cannot draw clearcut diagrams of Poodle color inheritance. Here are some additional facts which the conscientious breeder should keep in mind.

1. Poodle colors are governed not only by genes which produce color and those which block color, but by modifying genes. Modifying genes control the degree of a color. It is the modifying genes that turn black to blue, gray, or silver, depending on their strength.

2. Thus far we have spoken of genes being either dominant or recessive. However, they can be partially dominant. For example, in some instances silver is only partially dominant when bred to brown and the result is badly colored brownish silvers. These are the cafe-au-laits.

Now let us give you a description of each ideal color, followed by some usual faults apt to be found in that color and the answers to frequent questions in regard to color-breeding.

Black

A deep intense glowing black that in the sun gives off an almost metallic blue-black tone. Eyes very dark, not necessarily as black as those of a white, but so dark as to be described as a "black brown," not just brown. Eyerims, lips, nose, and toenails black.

Common Faults: Such dogs may have a few silvery or white hairs throughout the coat. Provided that they are not so numerous as to cause streaks or spots this is no fault.

268

Ch. Jolero Black Sunday, black Standard bitch owned by the William Tows of Hartsdale, New York.

Such dogs may have a white spot on the chest. This is a show fault, provided it is noticeable, but no breeding fault.

Such dogs may have a brownish or rusty tinge on the top of the coat. This is a show fault, and the breeder must look into the animal's background. Is this tinge caused by weather, or an unhealthy coat, or is the color always like this? In other words, a poor black? This fault can be eliminated in the offspring by proper breeding.

Such dogs may have a grayish tinge about the muzzle or ears. This can be old age. It is a show fault but need not worry the breeder. If the dog has gray blotches or the coat is rust-colored down to the skin, it is a bad black and should not be used.

Such dogs may have a truly brown eye rather than the very dark brown. This is a minor fault, not much penalized in the ring, but the breeder may wonder how much mixed color is behind such a dog.

Question: Will breeding blacks to browns hurt the black?

Answer: The black will not be hurt if only one brown cross is made. If, however, a second brown cross is made into the black line, light eyes may be the result.

Question: Will breeding black to white improve the black coat?

Answer: It may, but why not breed to a good-coated black from a line of good-coated blacks? Most blacks are more refined in type than the whites. Why risk hurting your type when there ARE good-coated blacks, not to mention mixing up the color heritage.

Question: Will breeding to a gray improve an open black coat?

Answer: It may. It is better breeding than to a white or a brown. It would be best to select a gray related to your bitch on the gray's black side. Here is an example: Champion Blakeen Roulette of Misty Isles was a black Standard female with excellent type, good temperament, good quality coat, but a decided tinge of brown. Roulette's sire, Nymphaea Pice, was a black of only fair type with a large white splash on his chest. He could not be shown. Pice came from a mixed heritage of brown, black, and white. His dam, Ranee, was a brown of better type than Pice, but had a very poor temperament, timid, high-strung, etc. Roulette's dam, Anita v Lutterspring, was a black of excellent type and temperament, German bred. Roulette bred to Champion Harpendale Monty, an English black of fair type, and produced an all-black litter, no

Ch. Valhalla's Critics Choice is a multiple all-breed Best in Show and specialty winner. A daughter of Ch. Acadia Command Performance from Ch. Puttencove Perdita, she is owned by Catherine Kish and Dennis McCoy. Handled by Richard Koester.

brown tinge, fair type, and excellent temperament. Monty had a most aggressive temperament, which was inherited. Roulette bred to Eric Labory, who went back to German breeding as did Anita and was a black of excellent type and coat but had a very poor, timid temperament, produced all-black puppies with excellent coat and type. Two became champions. They were not as timid as Eric, but not perfect in temperament. Roulette bred to Champion Griseley Labory of Piperscroft of Blakeen, C.D., (an imported Swiss gray nephew of Eric on his sire's side) produced coal-black puppies. These puppies were even blacker than the Eric puppies and had excellent coats and perfect temperaments. The one I kept (I did not keep any from her other litters) became a well-known winner and stud, champion Blakeen Mirandello. He won Best Brace in Show with his kennel mate Champion Blakeen Michael Mont at Westminster one year. He never sired a brown or a gray, and his black offspring were very black.

This last had been the *right* mating for Roulette. If Griseley had been a black, it might have been even better. When Roulette was bred to brown she produced some browns. Bred to Duc (white Tri-International Champion Nunsoe Duc de la Terrace of Blakeen) she produced an excellent brown bitch with a white chest. This bitch bred to blacks produced blacks and often one or two browns.

Question: Is black a popular color in the show ring and with the public?

A highly successful Standard of the late 1960's. Ch. Black Rogue of Belle Glen, C.D., owned by Janet and Jim Hobbs and handled by Robert S. Forsyth to win the Group at Canadian National Sportsmen's Dog Show, 1968.

Ch. Lin Ed's Mystoria, owned by Ed Jenner, winning the Non-Sporting Group at Lawrence Jayhawk with her handler, Peggy Hogg. A beautiful black Miniature that accounted for great show ring success.

Answer: In the show ring, next to white, it is the most popular. It is difficult, however, for a good black to defeat an equally good white, as good whites are very appealing and glamorous. With the public it is the most popular color of all. Black puppies are the easiest to sell. Black is therefore the easiest color to breed successfully as to money as well as type. A clue to black breeding: remember the most glamorous thing about a black, besides good type and temperament, is *blackness.*

Blue

A dark gray, somewhat the color of steel, the color of a good blue Chow. No brown, rust, light gray or black should appear in the coat. Do not confuse this color with the color that the English breeders called blue until about twenty years ago. That "blue" was a light gray. Eyes are very dark, almost black; eyerims, lips, nose, and toenails black; skin dark gray or almost black.

Common Faults: Such dogs may have large amounts of black and light gray throughout the coat. This is a major show fault, but not to be entirely condemned by the breeder, although the latter must remember that the true blue Poodle is not an excuse for a bad black or gray, but that the color blue can be safely bred to a black and produce good blacks.

Such dogs often turn a lighter gray with age. Provided there are no streaks or splotches this is acceptable in the ring and to the breeder.

Such dogs may have a brown or rusty tinge. This is a major fault in the show ring and should arouse a breeder's suspicion. Is the dog just a mismarked one, unsuitable even to mate with a black?

Question: Is blue a real color or a bad gray?

Answer: It is a real color, a form of gray.

Question: Is it a hard color to obtain in breeding?

Answer: Yes. The offspring are usually darker, i.e., black, or lighter.

Question: Is it recessive?

Answer: To black, yes.

Question: Could a line of blues be started?

Answer: Yes.

Question: What are the best colors to mate with blues?

Answer: Blues from gray or gray and black breeding, blacks, grays, and white-bred whites.

Question: What colors are inadvisable to breed with a blue?

Answer: Brown, white of mixed color ancestry, apricot, and cream—in this order. Whites and creams of mixed color ancestry when mated to blues have produced apricots. The rest of such a litter, however, is usually mismarked or even parti-colored.

Question: Is this color popular in the show ring and with the public?

Answer: No. It is often considered a bad black by inexperienced judges. It shows up very poorly at night under electric light. It is so indefinite that the good type of a blue is often missed. Blue puppies are hard to sell. The average buyer does not want a blue, considering it a poor gray or a bad black.

Question: Is it easy to breed out the color blue?

Answer: Very. Breed to a black, particularly a black related to the blue on it's black side.

Question: Has a blue line ever been established?

Answer: Yes. Leicester Harrison established a line of blue Toys stemming from the blue Miniature Leicester's Alouette. Alouette was crossed with the white Toy Champion Leicester's Bonbon. The best known of the dogs from this breeding is Champion Leicester's Bonbon's Swan Song, a blue Toy. This blue line also produces blacks, grays, and whites.

Grey

A solid, even gray, lighter than an elephant but darker than a Bedlington Terrier. The lighter shades of gray are often called "silver."

Ch. Hollycourt Poppet, one of the lovely Miniatures for which Miss M. Ruelle Kelchner's Hollycourt Poodles were famous. This silver Toy bitch took Winners over 24 bitches at Westminster, 1957. Wendell J. Sammet, handler. By Leicester's Zig of Hollycourt ex Ch. Round Tables Alberta.

One of the beautiful silver Poodles bred and owned by Miss M. Ruelle Kelchner. Ch. Hollycourt Talent of Silver, photographed in 1958. Sired by Ch. Hollycourt Valliant. Handler, Wendell J. Sammet.

Ch. Hollycourt Toison D'Or, silver beige male, photographed in February 1955. Owned by Hollycourt Poodles, Miss M. Ruelle Kelchner. Bred by Miss Marjorie Siebern. Handled by Wendell J. Sammet. By Ch. Hollycourt Platinum ex Seybourne's Majolica.

Ch. Eslar Silver Ki-Ora, silver Standard bitch, at the William Penn Poodle Club Specialty, 1958. Owner, Mrs. Elizabeth Davis. Breeder, Rondelay Kennels. Handler, Wendell J. Sammet. Judge, Mrs. George Putnam. By Ch. Gaystream Skyrocket ex Rondelay's Spring Mist.

The eyes are very dark, almost as dark as the eyes of a white. Eyerims, lips, nose, and toenails are black. Skin compatible with the tone of the hair, a gray tone, but can be almost black.

Common Faults: Such dogs vary in color. Some are quite dark, others very light. These tones, if even, are not a fault.

Such dogs can be almost white, an oyster-white in color. This is a fault in the ring, and the breeder should breed away from it. That is, never breed a gray dog of this color to one of a similar color.

Such dogs may have these oyster-white areas on the inside of the legs, above the eyes, under the chin, on the inside of the ears, and under the tail. This is a form of the black and tan pattern. Unfortunately it is quite common. It is a very serious fault, and it is to be condemned by the breeder.

Such dogs may have many darker hairs throughout the coat, particularly on the back and ears. This is a minor show fault, provided the black is not so numerous as to constitute streaks and patches. If the latter, it is a disqualification. This is also a fault from the breeder's angle, but not serious.

Such dogs may have brown hairs scattered throughout the coat. If there are enough to give a "pepper and salt" appearance, this is a fault in the show ring, but not to the breeder. If, however, there is enough tan to cause spots (in other words, a parti-color) this is a fault to the breeder. Such a dog is better not used, for the color gray may not be inherited by the puppies.

Such a dog may have darker colored ears. This is a very minor fault and should not be penalized in the ring or by the breeder.

Such a dog may have a dark, almost black, spot back of the ears, or if it has had skin trouble or an injury such as to cause loss of hair, a black spot will appear where the new hair grows in. In fact this is the new hair. This must, if noticeable, be considered a fault in the show ring, but it need not trouble the breeder. Such a spot will eventually turn gray.

Such dogs, particularly if they are a very light gray, may have brown or hazel eyes. This is a fault and must be penalized in the ring and somewhat, although not as much, by the breeder. Remember that although it can be done, it is not always easy to breed out light eyes in light-colored dogs.

Some grays are whelped gray with gray eyes, eyerims, nose, lips, and toenails. The coat color of these dogs is extremely solid and even, as well as being quite beautiful—a pale blue tone somewhat like a platinum mink. It is not a correct color, however, and should be penalized in the show ring. The breeder need not condemn this color, but should realize that it is so recessive that it will probably not reproduce bred to an ordinary gray. Bred to a relative of this same color, the offspring will probably be oyster-white with blue or pale gray eyes. Such dogs should be bred to a true, unrelated gray or to a related black.

Question: Can gray be obtained by breeding whites with blacks?

Answer: Not unless the whites carry the modifying genes necessary to produce gray. The Labory grays are a good example of this. Remember, colors in living creatures are not like paint to be mixed in a palette!

Question: How can one obtain this color?

Answer: Breed gray to gray or even to a black relation related on the gray side.

Question: Is it easy to breed grays?

Answer: With Miniatures, yes. There are so many related grays. In a number of these, however, the type could be improved. It is a little more difficult to breed good Standard grays, as there are not as many available. In Toys both the type and color are still mixed and uncertain. It would be advisable to stick to type, and the

best is to be found in the whites and the blacks. If one can find an excellent type gray Toy and an excellent black related to the gray—you're off!

Question: Is it easy to breed away from gray?

Answer: Very. Gray is recessive to black. Breed to blacks unrelated to gray or even related on the black side.

Question: What colors should not be used with gray?

Answer: In-bred browns, apricots, and creams—in this order.

Question: What colors can be bred with gray?

Answer: Besides gray and black, white has produced some lovely creams, apricots, and even grays when the white has gray behind it. Yet one often obtains in the same litter mismarked and parti-colored puppies. For the sake of future generations it is not advisable to use white.

Question: What is meant by "clearing"?

Answer: A gray is born black, not a deep intense black, but a rather mousy tone. In about three to four weeks the hair about the muzzle

Ch. Edrita's Phull-O-Sass, silver Toy bitch, winning from the classes, Lancaster Kennel Club, 1966, judged by Melbourne Downing and handled by Wendell Sammet. This handsome little Poodle, by Ch. Silver Sparkle of Sassafras ex Edrita's Phull-O-Pholly, was bred and owned Ed and Rita Perko.

WINNERS

TROY

KENNEL CLUB

OCTOBER 1979

ASHBEY

The famous little Toy, Ch. Silver Souvenir, owned by
Mrs. George Dow and handled by William J. Trainor.
The judge is Mrs. Lyle.

and around the eyes turns gray at the roots. In
about six weeks the roots of all the hair should
be gray. The last to turn gray is the hair along
the top of the back. At two months of age even
this hair should show gray at the roots. If it does
not, do not consider such a puppy for show purposes or for breeding grays. If the color around
the eyes, muzzle, and other parts of the body is
brown rather than gray, or even if there is some
brown in it, do not purchase the puppy for it
may never clear to a proper color. Of course this
advice applies only to the novice buyer or
breeder. The experienced will know from their
own stock and the considered puppy's pedigree
just how much chance can be afforded. By six
months the good colored gray may be still
somewhat streaky in color, that is dark hairs still
in the gray, but it will be a definite gray. At one
year it should have "cleared" completely. That
is, have become a *solid*, even shade of gray.

Question: In buying a gray puppy as young as
two months, can one be sure that it will clear?

Answer: If the gray around the muzzle and
eyes is a clear true shade of gray, if the gray is
already showing vividly on the legs, if there are
some faint signs at the roots of the body coat of
this same color, and furthermore if the black col-
or of the coat is not a rich, true black but a
mousey tone, the puppy will clear.

Question: Should a gray Poodle be more expensive than a black or a white of equally good type
and breeding?

Answer: Yes, if it already is equally good,
because grays are harder to breed. But very few
grays are as good in type as the good blacks and
whites.

Question: Are grays popular in the show ring
and with the public?

Answer: The public, as a rule, loves this color.
Next to black, it is the most popular. But this is
not true in the show ring. A good black, white,
or even brown will usually defeat an equally
good gray, for the latter is not a dramatic color.

Question: Are there good gray lines?

Answer: There are several. The most influential in Miniatures is the family stemming from
Whippendell Mouflon Bleu. Here is a line of
grays that has endured for over 60 years. Among
the famous Poodles which have come from this
line are English Champion The Silver Gnome,
Champion Blakeen Invincible, and Vendas Blue
Masterpiece, to mention just a few.

Overleaf:
Ch. Valkyrie's Bold Challenge, Standard Poodle, taking Winners at the Troy Kennel Club in 1979. The
judge is Howard Tyler, the handler Jane Forsyth.

Betty Mahaffy's first Miniature Poodle, Ch. Lawnfield Chocolate Cricket, by Champion Montfleuri Sans Souci of Willomead ex Champion Lawnfield's Presentation, lived to be 17 years old. Bred by Marguerite Crosby.

Brown

As previously mentioned, there are two kinds of brown Poodles: a deep, rich mahogany or dark walnut in its perfect state, but usually seen in a lighter tone, and a brilliant shade of chestnut, redder in tone than mahogany or walnut, but just as strong in tone and even right down to the roots of the hair. In both browns, the eyes, eyerims, etc., are the same—the eyes brown, dark amber, sometimes a golden brown, sometimes a reddish brown; eyerims, lips, nose, and toenails all brown to match the tone of the coat. Sometimes the toenails are black, but never the lips, nose, and eyerims. The skin should match the tone of the coat in a lighter shade.

Common Faults: Dogs of the first brown may have some silvery hairs throughout the coat. Provided these are not so numerous as to cause streaks or spots, this is not a serious fault.

Such dogs may have a small white or silver patch on the chest or belly. If noticeable this is a show fault, and the breeder may wonder how much mixed color is behind the dog. If very little, the breeder need not worry.

Such dogs, particularly the first mentioned brown, frequently fade in color, leaving the ears, and often a dark streak down the back, the original color. This is a show fault but should not affect the breeder.

Such dogs, due to hair loss through disease or injury, may grow hair back in the original dark shade causing (especially if the coat has faded with age) an appearance of a dark spot or patch. This is a show fault but need not effect the breeder. These "spots" in time usually fade to the present coat color.

Such dogs often have a pack lighter in tone than the main coat or the "ruff." Provided there is not a profound difference in tone, this is not a serious fault.

Such dogs may have light yellow or almost green eyes. This is a major fault in the ring and is frequently hard to eliminate in breeding.

Question: Does black combined with brown improve the color of the brown?

Answer: No. The brown color is not affected by the introduction of black. The superbly colored French browns have often been brown-bred for many generations. However, breeding to black does not harm brown, but there may be no brown puppies in the first generation of the cross. Also there have been many excellent browns from two black parents.

Question: Does brown crossed with brown tend to produce cafe-au-lait?

Answer: No, not unless both brown parents carry the cafe-au-lait gene transmitted to them from a cafe-au-lait ancestor.

Question: Does brown bred to brown produce brown puppies?

Answer: If dogs of the same color brown are bred to one another, the answer is yes. However, there have been many instances where brown bred to brown has produced black, gray, or blue. The following explanation is only theoretical and has not been proved. Brown can carry black, gray, and blue. This coloring is blocked by two recessive genes. The brown blocking genes in the two brown colors are different, and since it takes two like recessive genes to produce a visible effect, the black, gray and blue are not blocked when the colors we shall refer to as brown 1 and brown 2 are bred together. Therefore black, gray, or blue puppies will result. This happens only when one or both parents carry black, gray, or blue. If they do not, the puppies will be brown because the action of the blocking genes is not needed. If the parents are hybrid for the black, gray, and blue genes, part of the litter will be brown and part the other colors. The reason that we cannot be more definite about this and some of the other color theories is that we do not know exactly how the Poodle color genes are paired or how many there are for each color. We think that brown is caused by a recessive color gene and a blocking gene when necessary, but there may be more.

Overleaf:
Ch. Dassin Dancing Daffodil, daughter of Six Pac and sister to Ch. Dassin Rita La Rose, taking Winners Bitch at the Greater Pittsburgh Specialty 1979 handled by Joe Vergnetti.

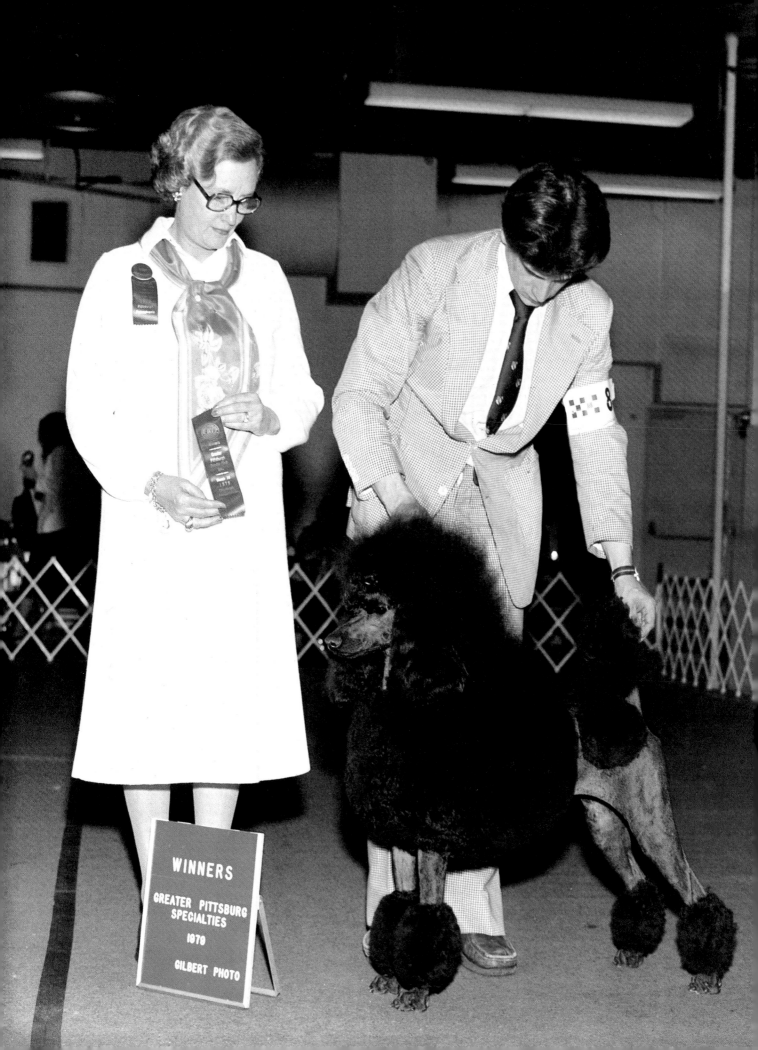

WINNERS

GREATER PITTSBURG
SPECIALTIES

1979

GILBERT PHOTO

BEST OF BREED
OR VARIETY
WESTERN RESERVE
POODLE CLUB
AUGUST 1978
PHOTO BY *Graham*

Question: Are browns more nervous and high-strung than blacks or whites?

Answer: They often seem to be, and this may come from too much in-breeding to preserve this recessive color. The grays started out with better temperaments than the blacks, but now in the Miniature, due to in-breeding, they have often become high-strung and nervous. The Standard grays are beginning to be in-bred and some nervous temperaments are appearing. They started with extra good temperaments. The gray Toys have as yet not been much in-bred.

Question: Are the browns popular in the show ring and with the public?

Answer: They do as well in the show ring as the blacks and almost as well as the whites. They do much better than the grays and creams. A good brown is very dramatic, either indoors or out. They are not as popular with the buying public. Brown puppies are definitely harder to sell, which may be because many browns have light eyes, usually the ones for sale, and this gives them a hard, unappealing expression.

Question: What are the best brown lines in Standards, Miniatures, and Toys for color?

Answer: The French and German lines in all three varieties. There are good browns in England and America, too, but these come from basically black lines. There are two exceptions to this, but they are very old lines. The Rufus line in combination with the base of the Leila line produced deep red browns. The Loubet line was the brown 1 color.

Cafe-Au-Lait

Beige, a tan with a gray overtone, the color of khaki. These French words mean coffee mixed with milk. The eyes are dark brown, amber, sometimes a reddish brown. Eyerims, lips, nose, and toenails are a liver-brown; sometimes the toenails are black. The skin is light pinky gray or tan to match the hair in a lighter tone.

Common Faults: Such dogs may have almost black noses, eyes, and eye rims. This is not correct, but it is, and should be, acceptable in the show ring, but not to the breeder wanting true cafe-au-lait or brown.

Such dogs may have darker brown ears and even streaks of dark brown thoughout the body. This is a show fault but does not need to trouble the breeder.

Such dogs may have light yellow or even green eyes, a definite fault both in the ring and to the breeder.

Such dogs will often turn a strange shade of gray with age, usually a solid color. If solid, this is not a fault.

Such dogs, as in browns or grays, may have dark spots in the coat which appear after coat loss due to disease or injury. The only difference

Ch. Lawnfield's Presentation, brown Miniature bitch winning under Miss Kathleen Staples at Ladies Kennel Association of America, May 1961. Handled by Wendell J. Sammet for owner-breeder Marguerite Crosby, this lovely Poodle was by Ch. Valeway Tilo Presentation ex Valeway Loving Cup.

Overleaf:
Ch. Misty Ridge's Hot Stuff, handled by William Cunningham, was Best of Breed at the Western Reserve Poodle Club Specialty, August, 1978.

is that the dark spot on cafe-au-laits will not return to cafe-au-lait.

Question: Is cafe-au-lait a true color or a bad brown?

Answer: It is a true color more closely related to gray than brown. The puppies are born a dark brown and "clear" as gray puppies do.

Question: Could one establish a line of this color?

Answer: We would think that one could, but with much effort. The line would have to be started with gray stock which carried the cafe-au-lait gene, and it would be necessary to do considerable in-breeding. Since grays have already been in-bred with a loss of type and tempera-

Ch. Cappoquin Creme de la Creme was born June 8, 1957. By Ch. Hollycourt Platinum ex Cappoquin Rikiki. This lovely cafe-au-lait Poodle was bred and owned by Mary Griffin.

ment, your cafe-au-laits would probably be of a type and temperament not as good as that of the grays.

Question: Is there any line at present of cafe-au-laits?

Answer: Not that we know of, because it is not a popular color.

Question: Have there been any great cafe-au-lait Poodles?

Answer: There have been some very worthy champions, both here and in England. One was Champion Cajus v Sadowa. Miss M. Ruelle Kelchner's Champion Hollycourt Toisin d'Or was a true cafe-au-lait in color. He came from Miss Kelchner's gray line, which has produced several other cafe-au-laits.

Question: Is this color at all popular?

Answer: Some people really like it, but the majority do not, considering it a bad brown. It does not do well in the show ring, and dogs of this color must win on good type and personality.

Question: What is the best color to breed away from this color?

Answer: A good deep brown related, if possible, to the cafe-au-lait through a deep brown ancestor.

Question: What is the best color to breed in order to preserve the cafe-au-lait?

Answer: Another cafe-au-lait or a gray known to produce cafe-au-laits.

Question: What are the colors that should not be used with a cafe-au-lait?

Answer: Black, white, apricot, and cream, in this order.

Apricot

A vivid bright color on the tone of the actual fruit, but usually lighter by several degrees; a brilliant tan with an overlay of pink. *Not to be confused with cafe-au-lait.* Eyes are dark brown, but may be almost black or a dark reddish brown. Eyerims, nose, lips, and toenails are black. Skin is a matching shade of pinky tan several degrees darker than the coat. Sometimes the skin is blue or gray.

Common Faults: Such dogs may have blue or black hairs throughout the coat, a minor fault that need not trouble the breeder. If there are real black patches and spots the breeder may be doubtful about the color in future puppies.

Such dogs may have ears much darker than the body coat, almost rust-colored. Provided they are in tone with the body coat, this is a very minor fault.

Such dogs may have dark gray or blue ears. This is a definite show fault but need not trouble the breeder. My apricot Champion Vendas Sunkista of Blakeen had blue ears, but her apricot daughter, Champion Vendas Winter Sunshine of Blakeen, did not.

Such dogs are often darker in the ruff or main coat than in the saddle or pack. This is hardly a fault because this color is most inclined to fade.

Such dogs may show lighter, almost white, at the roots of the hair. This is a minor fault which indicates that the dog will not long hold its color.

Overleaf:
Am., Aust. Ch. Lemeole Le Charbonnier (Daniel to his friends), here is going Best of Variety at Cornhusker Kennel Club, Lincoln, Nebraska, handled by Diane Arhgner. He is owned by Dr. Elian Robinson.

Hayes Hoyt with her fabulous brown Miniature, Ch. Blakeen Eldorado. Judging is the late Anton Rost.

Such dogs often fade to a strange pinky cream, almost a white but not a good white. If the tone is even this is not a fault, but it does not look well in the show ring. It need not trouble the breeder.

Such dogs are sometimes streaked with darker tones and light, almost white, tones. This is a major fault, although such an apricot is still useful for breeding.

Question: Is this a true color?

Answer: Yes, and the puppies are whelped this color. It must not be confused with brown or cream.

Question: In this color, which is preferable, brown or black eyes, eyerims, nose, lips, and toenails?

Answer: We consider black eyerims, nose, lips, and toenails and dark brown, almost black, eyes to be correct. The lighter pigment is acceptable in the show ring, but the darker is to be preferred. When an apricot has brown points, it indicates that brown or cafe-au-lait crosses have been used in its background and it is not as true an apricot.

Question: Is it easy to establish a line of apricots?

Answer: We do not think so, and very often in such a line the type is sacrificed for the color. The Honorable Mrs. Nellie Ionides and Miss Jane Lane produced some excellent Standard apricots of good type and color in England. These apricots, however, did not establish a line. That is, their apricot progeny could not be counted upon to produce this color. In this country apricots are apt to fade to a very poor tone. I have had several whole litters of apricots in my kennel, the Miniatures, and I did not keep any. The type was not good enough, and I was afraid that they would fade at two or three years old.

Question: Is this color popular in the show ring and with the public?

Answer: When not faded it is sensational in the show ring. In fact, apricots of second-rate type, and even sometimes mismarked, have won on coloring alone. My apricot Miniature Champion Vendas Sunkista of Blakeen had blue ears, but the first time shown she went Best of Winners at Westminster under an excellent judge. She did have fine type, was very sound, and was a wonderful little showman. She carried a superb coat of texture. Still there were those blue ears! She never was defeated by one of her own sex and could have done much more winning than she did except that as soon as she gained her title I stopped showing her. The ears embarrassed me. The public also loves this color when it is not faded. But when it fades, as it so often does, the owners are very disappointed. This is because the faded color is not attractive, being a sort of dirty pink or white. Of course the more delicate colored apricot puppies are not popular with the public, as they are just considered a poor white.

Question: What is the best color to use in breeding away from apricots?

Answer: White bred to apricot usually produces true creams and sometimes whites. Brown bred to apricot will produce brown or black unless the brown or black should happen to carry apricot. The black Miniature Champion Vendas The Black Imp of Catawba was bred to the apricot bitch, Champion Vendas Winter Sunshine of Blakeen, and produced the sensational chestnut brown Champion Blakeen Eldorado. Eldorado, of course, produced blacks when bred to blacks and browns when bred to browns. He never produced an apricot, a blue, or a gray, nor did his black brother and sister. Yet Sunshine was a daughter of the apricot Sunkista and a blue, but Imp and Sunshine were related on their brown and black side.

Overleaf:
This lovely headstudy is of Am. Brz. and Int. Ch. Holyoke Hensley, owned by Evalina and Jaime Martinelli, Pent Kennels, San Paolo, Brazil. Hensley's show record includes an all-breed Best in Show, seven Non-Sporting Groups, a specialty Best of Breed, and many Best of Variety awards in the United States.

Question: What are the least advisable colors to use with apricots?

Answer: Black, blue, or gray of mixed color heritage, and cream. If apricot is bred to black, blue, or gray of mixed color heritage, mismarks and parti-colors may result; also brindle and the black and tan pattern appear frequently in this type of cross. Cream will produce poor whites or streaky creams.

Question: What is the best way to establish an apricot line?

Answer: Most of the best apricots were bred by chance or from at least one apricot parent. In order to start an apricot line we would say that you must have at least one apricot dog. If you have a Standard you should not have too much trouble finding a mate for it of the same color. Try to stick to this color. If you have a Miniature you may have more difficulty. If you must make a cross, use a black, blue, or gray that is known to carry apricot. If you cannot find such a dog, try to find one of as pure as possible color heritage. Breed this to your apricot, then breed one of the progeny back to the apricot parent. In doing the latter you may have to sacrifice type and temperament for color; also you would probably get some mismarks, etc. We would not recommend it.

Best in Show, Agathon Kennel Club, 1969, was the apricot male Toy, Ch. Belonis's Amber Sunshine. Bred and owned by Mr. Belones, handled by Wendell J. Sammet, judged by E. Irving Eldredge. This little dog is by Meisen Bit O'Butterscotch ex Belone's Amber Galore.

Question: Have there been any great apricots?

Answer: There have been at least several worthy champions and a few great ones. Champion Frenches Honeysuckle won numerous Bests in Show in England some years back, prior to importation to the United States, where she continued her winning ways. Miss Cecil A. Ray's Standard Champion Chloe Riccochet, held a deep, true apricot until he died at 13 years of age. When "Rickey" was clipped down all over after his show career his color showed no difference. Hilda Meisenzahl established an apricot strain of Miniatures and Toys. One of the results of her efforts was Champion Meisen Bit O'Gold, an apricot Toy. There was also the sensational Miniature Champion Pixiecroft Sunbeam, with Groups and Best in Show, and, more recently, Champion Tiopepi Amber Tanya.

Cream

The color of good, rich Jersey cream. Not just tan, more yellow in tone and a lighter color than the lightest tan. The eyes are deep, soft brown; the jet black eye should not appear in a cream, being unbecoming to this color. Eyerims, nose, lips, and toenails are a very dark brown or black. The skin is blue and sometimes a tawny pink; it should not be spotted.

Common Faults: Such dogs may have white toenails. This is a very minor fault and should not worry the breeder.

Such dogs may have liver nose and eyerims. This, too, is a very minor fault and should not worry the breeder.

Such dogs may have lemon colored or pale tan ears. This is a fault in the ring but need not disturb the breeder.

Such dogs may appear streaked in color, such as lemon or pale tan streaks up the back. This is a show fault but need not disturb the breeder.

Such dogs may have light brown eyes, almost yellow in tone. This is a fault in the ring, and the breeder should hesitate before using such a dog. Light eyes are hard to overcome, particularly in light-colored dogs.

Such dogs may fade to almost a pure white and have, nevertheless, brown rather than black eyes and brown rather than black noses. They often do, and this is just unfortunate in the ring, as it destroys their chances. It need not disturb the breeder unless he, too, has considered the dog as a white. The difference between a true white and

Overleaf:
Bud Meyers on his only appearance in the show ring, with Swag Kennel's first champion, Meyer's Hodgie Ba Ba, in the Parade of Champions at the Twin Cities Poodle Club Specialty. Hodgie was 11 years old on this occasion. Barbara Meyers, owner.

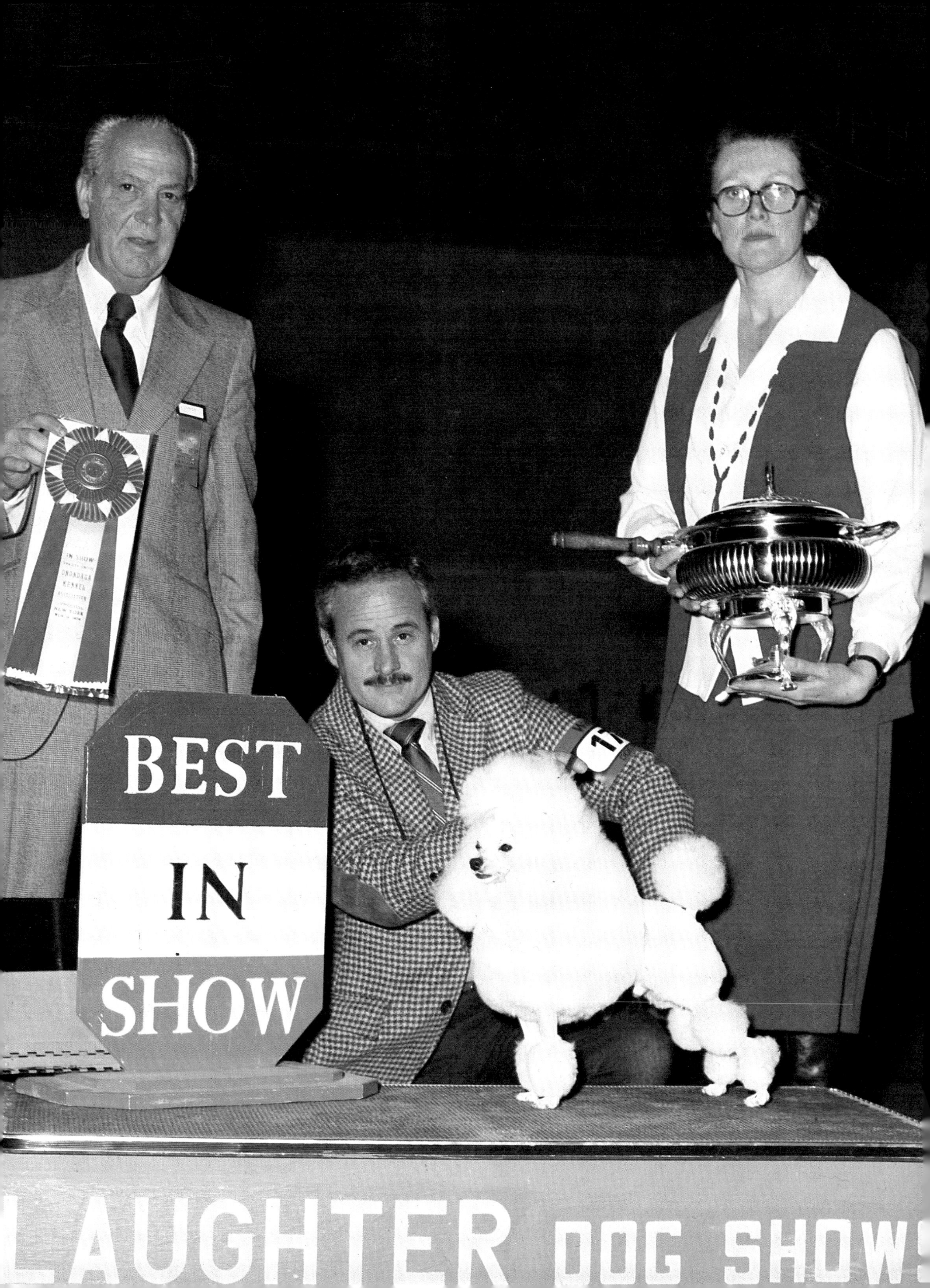
BEST
IN
SHOW
LAUGHTER DOG SHOWS

This is Mrs. Sherman R. Hoyt's "Boysie," Ch. Snow Boy of Fircot, a very famous and very successful Miniature dog of the 1940's. In this 1949 picture he is being handled by Henry Stoecker, prior to the start of Henry's judging career.

a faded cream is as follows: The true white has no lemon or pale tan in the coat. There is no "streakiness" in the coat of a true white, while there is in a faded cream.

Question: Is cream a true color?

Answer: Yes. It is not just a dirty white. The puppies are born cream, sometimes darker than the adult.

Question: Could one establish a cream line?

Answer: We think one could, but it would be difficult because creams seldom reproduce the same shade as themselves. They usually tend toward white. We do not know of a cream line.

Question: What is the best color to preserve cream?

Answer: Another cream related on the cream, not white, side of the pedigree.

Question: What is the best color to breed away from creams?

Answer: White.

Question: What colors are not advisable to breed with creams?

Answer: Black, blue, brown, cafe-au-lait, gray, and apricot, in that order.

Question: Have there ever been any great show winning creams?

Answer: Indeed there have been, both here and in England. Champion Blakeen Osprey was a Group and Best in Show winner. Champion Braevel Biscuit was another.

Question: Is cream a popular color in the show ring and with the public?

This is Ch. Harmo Divot, a fantastic little Toy owned by Harmo Kennels, Amherst, New Hampshire. Handled by William J. Trainor.

Answer: Not particularly, as this color all too often is considered a poor white. it takes an extra good cream to defeat an equally good white, and all too often the inferior white dog defeats the cream. The color is not as dramatic as the pure white. The public often considers a cream a poor white, thus cream puppies do not sell too well

White

Clear and brilliant, with no cream, yellow, or tan. A glistening, startling white. There are at least two kinds of white, white 1 and white 2.

Ch. Ostrom's Snow Man, a winner at the 1960 Greenspring Poodle Club Specialty Show with Ben Burwell handling.

Overleaf:
Ch. Hell's A Blazen Fagin's Pride winning Best in Show for Mrs. A. C. Pearson. Richard L. Bauer, handling.

The only visible difference between the two is that white 2 is more likely to have pink skin rather than a bluish black or silver skin. The eyes are jet black, so dark that one hardly can distinguish the iris from the pupil. Eyerims, nose, and toenails are black. The skin is bluish black or silver, a solid color.

Common Faults: Such dogs may have a pink skin or a pink skin mottled with black or blue spots. This is a very minor fault and only should be counted by the judge if a white dog of equal quality with a black or silver skin is in the ring, or against a colored dog, equally good, with perfect coloring. It should not disturb the breeder.

Such dogs may have white toenails. The same conclusion applies to this as to the skin color above.

Such dogs may have a partially pink eyerim or one whole pink eyerim, or a pink spot on the nose or on the lips, with or without pink eyerims. These are major show faults which the breeder must not ignore, and such dogs should be bred only to a strain carrying very strong black pigment.

Such dogs may have brown eyes rather than the so-called "dead black." This is a fault in the ring, but the breeder can remedy it by proper breeding.

Such dogs may have a small spot of completely black hair, a show fault if the spot is discovered or is in plain sight. The famous Champion Broadrun Cherry had such a spot back of his wide, well feathered ear. No effort was made to disguise it, and no judge ever observed it. We ourselves only discovered it when washing the dog. At any rate, the breeder can overlook such a fault.

Question: Will white bred to white produce white?

Answer: Not always. Again, we cannot be sure of the number of genes responsible for white or how they are paired, but if we go by the theory that white is inherited in a similar manner to brown, we can see why a black or other colored puppy appears in a litter from time to time from white parents. That is, the parents of such a litter are each a different kind of white and when bred together their recessive genes which would

Ch. Alekai Cocon't of Stonebridge, littermate to Ch. Alekai Oli of Stonebridge, by Ch. Alekai Ahi ex Ch. Tamara of Stonebridge. Breeder, Dorothy Baranowsky, Stonebridge Poodles. Owner, Mrs. Henry J. Kaiser, Alekai Poodles. Handler, Wendell J. Sammet. Judge, Mary Barrett, shown here at the Detroit Kennel Club.

Wendell J. Sammet at Westminster, 1962, with Alekai Kennels' Ch. Alekai Holalaka.

Overleaf:
Above: Four generations of outstanding Miniature Poodles (left to right): Ch. Berita's Ronlyn Rockefeller, Top Producer; his son, Ch. Bentwater Berita's Shiloh, Top Producer; Shiloh's son, Ch. Bentwater Aztec, Top Producer; and Aztec's son, Ch. Helsonae Sunday Special. These four individuals represent a very interesting succession of beautiful type, quality, and the ability to reproduce these traits. **Below:** The justly famous Top Producer and Top Winner, Ch. Dassin Sum Buddy, here is winning the Poodle Club of America California Regional Specialty under judge Mrs. Lauer J. Froelich. Breeder-owner F. C. Dickey is handling this son of Ch. Joceleyne Marjorie.

The stunning white Miniature, Champion Tally Ho Tiffany, winning Best in Show. Handled by Frank Sabella for Edward B. Jenner, Knolland Farm, Richmond, Illinois.

Ch. Peeple's Sahara, Best in Show at Eastern Dog Club, 1975. Mrs. Lydia Coleman Hutchinson's very popular choice was Robert A. Koeppel's stunning white Toy, pictured with the judge and Richard L. Bauer, handler.

normally block other colors cannot act. Therefore black puppies can appear. There are probably other genes that we do not know about involved in these crosses. It is these and the introduction of other color crosses which produce the mottled skin.

Question: Will breeding black to white improve the white type?

Answer: Only if there is no other means available and the white is truly inferior in type. As a rule the whites have better coats, better bone, and equally good temperaments. Some of the continental whites are slightly round in the skull and heavy in muzzle. Still, I have seen plenty of blacks like this, too.

Question: What is the best color other than white to breed to white for type?

Gorgeous son of a great sire, Ch. Valhalla in Command, is by Ch. Acadia Command Performance. Owned by Edward B. Jenner and Catherine Kish, handled by Tim Brazier.

Answer: Black.

Question: In breeding white to black to improve type, how can one return safely to white?

Answer: Breed the hybrid offspring of the black and white union to a white-bred white of the same kind of white as the original white.

Question: Will breeding a white and a black produce gray?

Answer: Not unless the white carries the proper modifying genes to produce gray.

Question: Does breeding white to white finally produce albinos?

Answer: No, not unless one "downgrades" one's breeding. For instance, breeding a dog

Overleaf:
Catherine Kish, Joanne Sering and Edward Jenner co-own this lovely Standard Poodle, Ch. Valhalla In Command, handled here by Tim Brazier to a win under James Edward Clark.

with inferior pigment to another relative with poor pigment is downgrading color pigment. One should never use albinos themselves for breeding.

Question: Suppose an albino has perfect type?

Answer: No matter, do not use it. With time, patience, and intelligence one can acquire an equally good type in a sound and healthy animal. Deafness and weak eyes frequently accompany albinism.

Question: Are there any colors which should not be bred to white?

Answer: Whenever white is bred to another color, a risk is taken. Remember that the white color is caused by two recessive blocking genes in combination with other genes. When white is bred to another color which does not carry these recessive blocking genes, any color which these may have blocked in the white may come out. For example, if a white which carries black that is masked by the blocking genes is bred to a brown, very likely the puppies will all be bad blacks. If such a white is bred to gray the color of your gray is not likely to appear in the puppies. If you are lucky, you may get a blue, but most likely you will get poorly colored blacks or grays. This is provided that the silver carries none of the white genes. In that case you may get a white.

Question: Is white popular in the show ring and with the public?

Answer: It is the best color of all, in my opinion, for show purposes. The dazzling purity of white arouses sympathy and admiration, and the color contrast of the black eyes and nose is truly beautiful and dramatic. It is very hard for any color to defeat a good white. On the other hand, white puppies do not sell as well as the darker colored ones. People feel that they will get dirty too easily and be hard to keep as house pets.

Question: Are there many white lines and top winning dogs from these lines?

Answer: There certainly are, in all three varieties. The great winning whites are too numerous to mention. In the 1930's Tri-International Champion Nunsoe Duc de la Terrace of Blakeen won Best in Show at Westminster. Another Standard, Champion Puttencove Promise, a descendent of Duc, did likewise in 1958. A white Toy, Champion Wilber White Swan, became the first Toy Dog to win Best in Show at Westminster, in 1956. All three of these dogs produced many Best in Show winners. All three are behind a great many winners in their varieties. Both Duc and Promise are behind the excellent white Standard line established by Alekai, which includes many famed winners (see Alekai Kennel story). And, of course, it is a white Standard bitch that has just become the all-time Top Winning Best in Show Dog in America, Champion Lou Gin's Kiss Me Kate. There have been many famed white Miniatures, too, from the days of Champion Blakeen Snow Boy of Fircot down to the present, among them Marguerite Tyson's several magnificent Best in Show winners, those of Ernest E. Ferguson, and others including the latest to win the Westminster Non-Sporting Group, Mr. Koeppel's Champion J.L.C.'s Critique. White Toys have been numerous, too, with Champion Blakeen Ding Ding, Champion Peeple's Sahara, and Champion Ty-Del's Dancing Doll among those coming to mind. Indeed, white Poodles have brought many honors to the breed.

Vernelle Hartman, now Mrs. William L. Kendrick, with the handsome Toy Poodle, Ch. Calvinelle Dancing Deacon, February 1965.

Ch. Crikora Commotion, black Miniature dog, winning the Non-Sporting Group at the Westminster Kennel Club Dog Show, 1962. Mrs. J. Donald Duncan, owner. Jane Kamp Forsyth, handler. Miss Iris de la Torre Bueno, judge.

Mrs. Hoyt Discusses Color of the Poodle Skin

The color of any animal's skin, whether solid, parti-colored or spotted, is not the surface effect which it appears, but is rather the result of continuous chemical processes going on within the inner layers of the outer portion of the skin and subject to variations even within an individual animal.

Within the cells of animal tissue there are—among countless others—two chemical processes continuously going on: the building up of protein material and the breaking down or cellular digestion of protein material. Just as an animal's digestive system breaks a food down into component products of digestion, so also in cellular digestion are the proteins broken down into and through a large number of component parts. One of these protein parts (tyrosine), when acted upon by an activating agent (tyrosinase) found in some of the inner cellular strata of the skin, is converted into a pigment which produces skin colors ranging all the way from a slightly shaded pink to brown and black, depending on how much of the pigment

(melanin) is being produced and deposited within the cells. A slight deposition of pigment merely serves to darken the pink color of underlying skin tissue as seen through the outer layers of skin, whereas a heavier deposition hides the underlying pink and gives a brown or even solid black appearance.

An animal inherits, according to the laws of Mendel or chance, a solid skin color or a varied color ("pattern," "markings," etc.). However, there is a broader and more basic way of saying the same thing: any living creature is born with a vast multiplicity of chemical tendencies and characteristics, some of which, for example, contribute to health, some to disposition, and some to external appearance such as color.

Since the pigment-forming (or color) reaction is common to all normal animals, let us now consider it in a little more detail. The protein digestive product tyrosine is normally found in cellular metabolism in all animals (metabolism being defined as "the sum of all the physical and chemical processes by which living organized substance is produced and maintained"). The activating agent or enzyme tyrosinase is normally present in the inner cellular strata of the outer layer of skin of all animals. When tyrosinase acts upon tyrosine the pigment melanin is produced. Two internal conditions therefore obviously affect the amount of pigment formed and the rate of its production: the amounts of both substances present. Heat has been proved to accelerate this chemical reaction, and the radiation effects of sunlight also may contribute, since the pigment is deposited in increased amount in sunburn.

As well as accounting for varying degrees of darkness of the skin, including the nose, lips, and eye rims, this pigment is also present in varying amounts in the colored portion (iris) of the eye, and the concentration of its presence explains ranges of eye color from light yellow-brown to dark brown or "black."

A very interesting freak condition known as albinism is accompanied by the absence of this pigment or the lack in an animal or portion of an animal of the particular chemical sequence necessary to produce it. In fact, albinism has been described as "an inborn error in metabolism." Here one finds the abnormal condition of skin which has no pigment whatever and therefore gives the impression of pure

Overleaf:
Am., Brz., Int. Ch. Eve Queen of Pent Kennels, the first and only Brazilian bred Poodle to earn the American championship title. Bred and owned by Evalina and Jaime Martinelli, San Paolo, Brazil. Handled here by Barbara Humphries.

pinkness, whereas the absence of all pigment in the surface layers really permits one to see the actual color of the underlying tissues which carry the skin's blood supply. Hence, also, the vivid pink of eyes, eye rims, nose, and lips.

Albinism (being a systemic lack of the normally present pigment-forming reaction) often causes severe eye trouble and sometimes deafness; it is a serious weakness in any animal and a trend which should be discouraged in breeding wherever possible. It is, fortunately, a naturally recessive trait.

White animals normally occurring in nature are not albinos but have dark eyes, nose, and lips together with a skin color which, due to the presence of pigment, ranges from darker than albino pink to deeper hues, depending on the concentration of pigment. All these naturally occurring white animals have the darkest portions of their skins at points most exposed to sun and weather and least protected by coat—namely nose, lips, eye rims, and eyes.

Before proceeding to any specific type of animal, let us summarize what has already been discussed.

1. Skin color is an effect chemically produced and chemically maintained and is a function of skin cell metabolism common to all normal animals.

2. The degree of skin color depends upon the amount of pigment deposited within certain cellular skin strata.

3. The rate of pigment production varies with the amount of chemical reactants present and is also subject to variation due to heat.

4. Continuous exposure causes our normal skin to darken.

5. Albinism, an abnormal systemic weakness accompanied by the lack of all pigment-forming processes, produces either generally or locally a completely pink skin.

6. Normal white animals are not albinos, since their skin metabolism produces varying amounts of pigment in the skin.

How does all this apply to Poodles?

It has been claimed that a white Poodle must have a "pink or pinkish skin." In fact, the question of the pink skinned versus the so-called "silver skinned" whites is a favorite old "bone," so why not consider it in the light of history, proven physiological facts, and the Poodle Standard of Perfection?

The most general colors mentioned in early authentic literature (to the best of the writer's knowledge) are black, liver, and pied or spotted (Gervase, 1621). Later we read and see pictures of the "jet black with white feet" (Taplin and Reinagle, 1803), and finally whites, either "pure or crossed" are mentioned (Idstone, about 1865). The dark colors were unquestionably the preponderant variations in the early days of the breed.

Where, then, did the first white feet and "pies" or spots come from? There are three possibilities which readily occur to me. There may have been a northern white strain; there were undoubtedly many "international alliances" between dark-colored Poodles and white or white-marked "foreigners" of other breeds; and there were unquestionably occasional albino freaks.

We must therefore assume that the early "spotted" and "pied" dogs had pigment-bearing skins and that the solid white lines were developed from these by more or less selective breeding. Therefore, based on both normal physiology (as already described) and historical averages, we find pigment-forming characteristics in the skins of white Poodles.

Douai Gay Ghost of Meritor, handled by Jane Forsyth at the Cavalier Poodle Club, 1959.

BEST OF
WINNERS

GILBERT PHOTO

BEST
IN SHOW

FINGER LAKES
KENNEL CLUB INC.
KLEIN APRIL 25 1980

The grey Miniature dog, Ch. Blakeen Invincible, bred by Mary Astor, born August 1943, by Hi Jinks ex Pillicoc Elixir. Owned by Blakeen Poodles, Mr. and Mrs. Sherman R. Hoyt.

Eventually, when dog breeding was taken up as a definite art or occupation, associations were formed and "Standards of Perfection" established as goals for breeders to strive for. The English Poodle Standard, from which ours was taken, to say nothing of the Poodle Standards of all leading dog-breeding countries, calls for black noses, lips, eye rims, and dark eyes in white Poodles, which again confirms the findings of historians and physiologists that normal animals have pigment-forming skin characteristics, for otherwise there could not be dark eyes and black noses, eye rims, and lips in a white dog.

As long as we cannot have black noses and dark eyes without the chemical skin reaction which forms pigment, and since history, science, and all Standards of Perfection demand these "points" in whites, we must prefer the skins of white Poodles to show pigment formation, which will of course be more prominent in the exposed areas. It is about as reasonable to expect to breed a Poodle having an even and unchanging pink skin without any signs of pigment elsewhere than in black nose and lips and dark eyes as to breed one with his clipping design "ready made." Whether this "color" is present in patches of darker pinkish gray or "silver," or whether it appears evenly distributed all over is as yet a matter of more or less breeding chance.

This latter even distribution of "color" in a pinkish skin is the much-discussed "silver." For

while it may be scarcely darker than the albino pink under the coat, it turns a darker grayish or "silver" color where exposed.

Our Standard calls for dark eyes and black nose, lips, and eye rims, and very wisely says nothing about the skin color elsewhere except, without referring to either skin or coat, to call for "any solid color." If this is interpreted, as it sometimes has been, to refer to skin, then anyone who knows the principles of skin coloration or has had any real experience with white animals will realize that the falsely but popularly called "silver skin" is most desirable and that the spotted skin, that is, light skin with dark spots, is far better than all pink.

The Poodle has been described as a "self colored" breed, which we assume to mean a naturally occurring color. Then why object to naturally appearing colors and color reactions in whites and apricots when it is well-known, and not condemned, that the skins of blacks, grays and browns also darken under exposure?

The Standard demands that white Poodles have black nose, lips and eye rims and dark eyes. Nature and science demand with these dark "points" a pigment-bearing skin. If we combine these two we have one of the most beautiful and spectacular animal color combinations conforming to the Standards of Perfection of Poodledom, nature and science.

Mrs. Hoyt Further Discusses Color

"Any good horse is a good color!" says the old adage, and like most sweeping statements it possesses only a fragment of truth. For color itself is a form of beauty which can also be useful, and when it does serve a purpose it must conform to some pattern.

Thus the coloring of most dogs has to do with their purpose as well as appearance, and while throughout the Poodle's history there have always been parti-colors, the solid colors have been preferred. One reason may be that most large retrievers have been solid in color. It could be that a motionless solid color is less easy to observe, particularly in the shadow of a swale and rushes, and by the same token a solid color in motion is easier to spot as a black, brown, or even white head bobbing above the silvery water. A hunter must see his dog in the water to guide him by hand signals. On land the retriever stalks by the side of or behind its master or sits

Overleaf:
Mary Nelson Stephenson making the Best in Show award at the Finger Lakes Kennel Club, April, 1980, to Ch. Dassin Rita La Rose owned by Mrs. Edward Solomon.

beside him hiding in a blind or shrubbery until the game appears.

In appearance the solid-colored Poodle is more attractive than a parti-color; the latter with black, brown, or white patches even unclipped looks common and has a mongrel appearance quite different from the attractive hound markings of a Fox Terrier or the rakish, lovable look of a Sealyham with a black or brown ear.

At any rate the Poodle, since it acquired a Standard, has always been preferred by experts and lovers of the breed as solid color, although we know from pictures and stories that in the breed's past there were many parti-colors. The show Standards of the world, with the exception of a very brief period in England which the top breeders deplored, have insisted that the dog be a solid color.

Yet we would urge the breeder not to establish a line on only a color basis. Type, strength, and temperament come far ahead of color which the breeder can afford to ignore to a much greater degree than the judge. This does not mean that any poorly colored dog of good type is to be preferred or even used. Rather it means that type, heritage, temperament, and above all the correct combination of bloodlines must be considered by the successful breeder, even though his goal is color alone.

Therefore when we say that certain faults in color are not "serious," we mean that they can easily be eliminated by proper breeding, although they may be condemned in the show ring. For instance, an interesting study in breeding for color alone is the development of the Standard grays in this country. We now know that this color was not unusual in Europe but was not well considered. In England it was rare due, we think, to a too frequent use of inbred browns and not many whites, which in some instances carry the modifying genes necessary for gray. As far as we know, when I started raising Poodles in 1931 there were no Standard grays in America, and even the Miniatures of that color were rare. Having established a successful line of white Standards and being aware that there were several good lines of blacks and browns, I wished to see if a gray Standard line could be established.

Although he had done little winning in England, Mrs. Grace Boyd of Piperscroft did not wish to sell Griseley Labory of Piperscroft for the very reason that I wished to purchase him. He was the first good Standard gray both of us had ever seen, he was of the well-known Labory line, and he had a superb temperament. I am inclined to think Madame Reichenbach sold him to Mrs. Boyd because the former did not like grays. The only colors permitted at that time in the continental show ring were white, black, and brown. At any rate I paid very little for Griseley's two sisters, about $200.00 apiece, whereas I paid Mrs. Boyd $3,000.00 for Griseley.

One of these sisters, Manon Labory, was black and of fine quality, very sound, quite large, with a nice head and eye, a good coat, and a superb temperament. She, however, always threw black puppies, even when bred to her relatives, so I eventually sold her to Mrs. W. French Githens, for whom she did very well. The other, Mascotte du Labory, was gray, a bit heavier-boned than Griseley, a bit coarser in head, not as straight behind, with good feet, very sound, and the same perfect temperament. Bred to Griseley's offspring, she produced grays. Bred to the German-born silver-brown Champion Cajus v Sadowa she produced grays. These two families crossed together were the foundation of my gray line.

Griseley himself was a lovely even shade. His coat was dense and "steel wool" in texture. His eyes, eye rims, nose, lips, and toenails were black. His ears were low-set and long. His muzzle was rather short but refined and tight-lipped; his skull was slightly broad and his cheeks rather full. He was almost too short-backed and quite straight behind. His front was beautiful and his feet superb, although the arched toes were very short. He was the most happy-natured and intelligent dog I have ever owned. He won his championship in four consecutive shows, starting with Westminster, but he never won a Group and I soon ceased showing him. His head and his straight hindquarters which caused him to pace went against him in the ring, but nevertheless he exerted the most profound and excellent effect on American breeding. Combined with our lighter-boned, long-headed, and often long-backed nervous bitches, his substance, harsh coat, and glorious temperament produced Poodles vastly superior to their dame, and usually to Griseley himself.

I bred Griseley to his black daughter, Peeress of Piperscroft, and the result was a litter of gray puppies, two definitely the correct shade of gray.

Overleaf:
Ch. Griggswood Pizzacato, by Ch. Griggswood Paco Rabanne ex Ch. Griggswood Cadenzo, owner handled by Doris Grant to Best of Winners at Bald Eagle, 1980, under judge Peter Thomson.

BEST OF
VARIETY

BALD EAGLE
KENNEL CLUB

1980

ASHBEY

BEST OF
WINNERS

GREATER PITTSBURG
SPECIALTIES

1980

ASHBEY

302

Ch. Hollycourt Valentina, blue Miniature bitch, bred and owned by Miss M. Ruelle Kelchner, handled by Wendell J. Sammet. By Barrack Hill Troubador ex Ch. Hollycourt Fleure Noire. From the 1950's.

One of these, Champion Ashridge of Blakeen, I used with Mascotte and also Mascotte's children by Cajus. I also bred Mascotte's daughters by Cajus to Griseley and to Griseley's children. Soon I was getting all gray litters which would "clear" completely before the age of six months. While the coat and coat color of these youngsters were excellent and they were large, sound dogs of perfect temperament, their type was too coarse and too heavy for show. Their heads were usually heavier than Griseley's, their hind-quarters were often straight, and they lacked elegance. They also were often short on the fourth or outside toe of each front foot, so that when standing the foot, without it's proper toe support, would actually roll over. This did not affect their gait but was a definite fault when posing in the ring.

I next tried Griseley with a brown of lovely type and temperament, the dam of Champion Blakeen Cyrano, namely Blakeen Vigee le Brun. The results were gray puppies with some brown in their coats, not a perfect color, but better type particularly as to feet and heads, and lovely dispositions. I kept two bitches from this breeding, but with good reason I was beginning to be discouraged about the future success of my grays. They sold with ease, as this color was and is very popular with the public, even in it's

"clearing" stage, but their type was far from perfect. I was, in fact, breeding pets not show dogs, making the mistake of breeding for color *only* rather than type!

My best male gray Standards were American and Canadian Champion Blakeen Silver Man of Sante Fe and Blakeen Smog. Silver Man was the better of these two and actually won several strong Bests in Show along with many Groups. In size and type he resembled Champion Blakeen Cyrano, although heavier in bone. He had a magnificent head, perfect in color, the coat of "steel wool" texture. He had a perfect front and feet and was much better "let down" behind than most grays. His almond-shaped eyes were very dark and full of fire and intelligence; his ears were low-set and had immense leather and feathering. His muzzle was only moderate in length but fine and clean; his nose, lips, and toenails were black. If he had been a white or a black he would have been quite sensational. Smog, or "Smokey" as he was called by his devoted owner, lived to be 15, but the owner did not wish to show him and kept him in Dutch trim.

The reason I sold these two top dogs rather than show them is that I had decided gray is a poor color for the show ring. It lacks distinction, particularly at an indoor show under artificial lights which destroy the blue tone of the gray. The best chance for this color is at the outdoor shows where sunlight and green lawns set off the indefinite outline of the shining silvery coat. Yet even here it takes a much better gray to win than a black, white, or even a dark brown. All too often the superior gray does not gain its deserved position. I do not think that there is a prejudice against this color on the part of the judges. It is the *indefinite* quality of this color that blurs the outline and destroys distinction.

Appealing though it is, gray is a poor color for the novice to commence breeding, for it demands a most judicious knowledge of color breeding plus breeding for type. The offspring of grays too closely in-bred tend to turn an oyster-white and are whippety and unsound, as well as nervous in temperament. I have seen many gray Miniatures like this. On the other hand, grays which are much out-bred become coarse and heavy, so that while their vigor and temperament may be excellent, their value as show dogs is gone.

Overleaf:
Ch. Valhalla's Main Event, by Ch. Langcroft Country Pride ex Ch. Valhallas Critics Choice, finished as a puppy and will be campaigned as a special. Owned by Fran Penzimer and Catherine Kish.

In conclusion I might add that Champion Griseley Labory of Piperscroft and Blakeen, C.D., did far more for the improvement of black Standards in America than I did for Poodles in establishing a gray line!

On the other hand, one of the best lines of white Miniatures in the world today had its beginning from a white dog whose litter brother was a parti-color, a white bitch of mixed color breeding, and a poorly colored apricot bitch. None of the offspring were ever mismarked, all were white or light cream, and even from the first mating one became a champion. These same offspring were then bred to a white dog with a black sire and a silver dam, and their descendants established world records in the show ring.

The original male was Champion Arnim of Piperscroft of Blakeen. He was a pure white, right up to size, with the profuse steel wool coat seen in the best whites. He had a splendid body, deep narrow chest, proper shoulders, plenty of neck, and a high tail-set. His hindquarters were too straight, but he had a fine proud, sound way of moving. His skull was short and a trifle round; his muzzle was also short but very clean and fine. His eyes were black; his nose, eye rims, lips, and even toenails were black. His short ears were too high-set although well feathered. His feet were a bit long, but not weak or spread. His front was excellent. I showed him, and he completed his championship with ease, even winning a few strong Groups. His snowy profuse coat, sound gait, proud carriage, and happy disposition contributed to this. All-rounders, particularly Terrier judges, admired him. Poodle breeders, with the exception of myself, did not.

The original mother of this line was a small (about 12 inches at the shoulder) very white bitch, by name Adastra Avalanche of Blakeen, that had some small white English breeding behind her. She had a better head than Arnim, more oval in skull and lower set ears. Her muzzle was short but clean and fine, and her eyes were oval and very dark, as were her eyerims, nose, and lips. She had better feet than Arnim, but not as good a body, her chest having been rather "shelly." Her hindquarters were strong and well let down. She, too, had a short back and a lovely temperament. I did not show her because her coat was soft and cottony. She was

not too good a mover in front, and her ears, while set better than Arnim's, were still far too short for a good expression. She was not a dramatic-looking Poodle.

The third member of this trio was Fifi of Swanhill of Blakeen, who had an exceptionally fine head, long and strong, clean muzzle, low-set ears of extraordinary length and thickness, and dark brown, expressive eyes with dark rims and black nose, lips, and toenails. Like many long-headed dogs, she was also a bit long in body, but her actual construction was excellent: a deep, narrow chest, sloping shoulders, straight front legs, good feet, and perfect hindquarters with plenty of thigh but well let down behind. She had a high-set tail and was a sound, gay mover. In fact she had a wonderful disposition and could have been shown except for her size, which was about 16 inches. Her color, which had been a lovely apricot in England, soon faded to a poor cream, while her ears remained rust colored. Of the three, however, she possessed the best type.

The object in acquiring these three Poodles was to attempt to establish a line of white Miniatures that would equal the best blacks of the day. But as time went on and this ambition was more easily fulfilled than I had anticipated, I set a new goal for Blakeen, namely to produce white Miniatures, the best of which would surpass *all* other colors. The reader may wonder why at the very beginning I used Avalanche rather than a perfect black bitch of which there was an ample supply or why did I not breed a perfect black dog to Avalanche or even Fifi?

The answer is that by using white-bred white with white-bred white I was preserving and intensifying the color. Furthermore, in using Arnim I hoped to preserve the good coats, pigment, and substance already established in German breeding. In breeding Arnim and Avalanche I was also intensifying short backs, which I felt were most necessary to offset my coming efforts to obtain better heads. Once color, strength, substance, and short backs were established, then I could go on toward elegance, and from observation of the best blacks and browns I was fully aware that a long, elegant head too often occurs with a long body.

The six offspring of Arnim and Avalanche were all white with short backs, good feet, and fine temperament. They were better bodied,

306

Ch. Blakeen Flurry, white Miniature born in January 1941, bred and owned by Mr. and Mrs. Sherman R. Hoyt, Blakeen Kennels. By Ch. Blakeen Minnikin ex Fifi of Swanhill of Blakeen.

sounder, and better coated than their dam, and slightly better in head and size than their sire. The best of these, Champion Blakeen Minnikin, I kept and bred to Fifi.

This breeding produced five white Miniatures of exquisite quality, including Champion Blakeen Flurry. These were definitely the best whites of that day, but they were far from perfect. They needed to be shorter in body, heavier in coat, and I was not yet sure if they would throw as good or better offspring than themselves, which is, after all, the test of a good and established line. I kept three bitches from this breeding and by judicious line-breeding, and the introduction of one or two more very short-backed English dogs related to mine, I got closer to the ideal. The arrival of Champion Snowboy of Fircot finalized the stability and perfection of this line.

This beautiful white Miniature was purchased by me in 1946 from his breeder, Mrs. E. G. Thomas of England. He did so much for all Miniatures that no Poodle book could be complete without special mention and praise of him. Every Poodle lover is indebted to him, as well as to the Standard, Duc, for making our favorite breed more popular, emphasizing not only the beauty but the essential goodness, gentleness, intelligence, loyalty, affection, and gaiety. Truly of all breeds the Poodle is the most civilized. The large dazzling white Duc and his equally glamorous small counterpart, Snowboy, were

the embodiment of all that is loved and sought after in the breed. Neither of these dogs was perfect in type, but they were in temperament, and added to this profound virtue was a zest for living and a desire to do well and gladly whatever task was set before them.

Snowboy's pictures hardly give the clues to his greatness. First and foremost, he gave his noble head and expression to all his progeny, regardless of the dams. And second, his own distinction and disposition led him to victory after victory in the show ring, so that in the dog world Miniature Poodles assumed an importance which they never had held before. Shown 64 times in the strongest possible competition at the largest and most prestigious and important shows, he won 60 Best of Varieties, 38 Groups, and 17 Bests in Show.

Yet at the start of his career in England Snowboy was not much admired, nor did he win when Mrs. Thomas first showed him. As far as I can gather, he was out of coat, underweight, and shy at these first shows. He was a most sensitive dog, although not a timid one. A harsh voice appalled him; a jerk on his lead or a blow would have broken his heart. So it is possible that the first times he was shown, the pressure and noises of the crowd and the fact that his owner had other older and more important dogs with her and so did not have time to reassure him may have caused him to appear depressed and anxious. Certainly without his glorious coat Snowboy was a trifle long in back. Furthermore, although he was perfect in front, he was a trifle narrow and straight behind.

This inauspicious beginning does not detract from him or from English judgment. Indeed it is fortunate for us in America that he was not admired at first, for if he had begun with one-eighth of what he finally accomplished, Mrs. Thomas would not have let him go. There was, however, one great English breeder, fortunately for me not interested in whites, who recognized his quality from the start. This was Mrs. Grace Boyd of Piperscroft, who wrote to me at once, telling me that I would like him as much as she did. I shall always be grateful to her for this.

When I first saw Snowboy, I loved his oval, beautifully shaped skull, his long yet strong muzzle, his low-set, wide, feathered ears, his almond-shaped black eyes so full of life and intelligent tenderness. "There is the perfect head," I cried, and I have never changed my opinion.

Overleaf:
The handsome Standard Poodle, Ch. Alekai Zeus, litter brother to Ch. Alekai Zoe. By Ch. Alekai Luau ex Longleat White Witch, bred by Mrs. Henry J. Kaiser, owned by Mrs. Bernet, handled by Paul Edwards.

His neck was long and proudly arched, his sloping shoulders tight at the top, his coat excellent in texture and rather creamy in tone as were his ears. His feet were small and perfect. Although he was a bit narrow across the hips and lacking in second thigh, with that high tail-set, his head always up, and that exquisite happy expression, he was exactly what I wanted. Later I was to have the supreme pleasure of knowing his temperament.

What Snowboy needed then was coat, weight, and experience. I should like all who read this book to know how grateful I am to then professional handler and now famed all-breed judge Henry Stoecker for all he did to give bloom and confidence to one of the great show and stud dogs of America. I am also pleased to add that Boysie, remained an active and cheerful monarch for 16½ years. Time set lightly on his snowy shoulders. My only regret is that I could not tell him what he meant to me, and indeed to all who knew him. Perhaps this is a foolish wish, for Snowboy knew he dwelt with friends who loved him!

Why Snowboy was born white has puzzled many, and why bred to whites he always sired this color has confounded more. For his father, Harwee of Mannerhead, was black, and his mother, Solitaire of Piperscroft, was gray. When one knows more about the bloodlines behind this dog, however, it becomes far easier to comprehend.

Snowboy's mother, Solitaire, came from the Ice Fairy line, which stems from a line of small English whites, the same line from which Fifi of Swanhill also was descended. His paternal grandmother, the Mistress of Mannerhead, a black, was a member of the Harpendale line, and she was also the half sister of the white bitch Whippendell Carte Blanche. The mother of Mistress and Carte Blanche was Harpendale Loretta, and although she herself was a black, she was directly descended from the well-known Harpendale whites and creams, commencing with Binfield Lallie, Pine Lade, etc. Loretta evidently carried their white genes which she passed on to her son Harwee, who in turn passed them on to Snowboy.

Therefore the latter, crossed with the products of Arnim's German and English line of whites to which Snowboy was related and other English whites to which he was also related, was bound to produce whites, actually whiter than himself and frequently better in type. Crossed with grays, as he occasionally was, he produced grays, and he could have produced blacks, if properly bred to do so. But crossed with the correct whites he was at his best. No black or gray of his has equalled his white progeny. It is as if Nature in her mysterious combination of chromosomes and genes in making this wonderful little dog white had gone one step further and enabled him to accomplish more for this color than has ever been done before.

Of course this would not have happened had he been bred to the wrong white bitches, and I tried hard to use him only to his own and the breed's advantage. But by crossing him with the right whites, my line became fine and reliable, breeding true to type so that it continued on as one of the great lines in Poodle history. In America and in England we find most of the top

A Miniature dog of tremendous importance, the great Ch. Snow Boy of Fircot. Owned and handled by Mrs. Sherman R. Hoyt, he is shown winning the Interstate Poodle Club Specialty in 1948

Overleaf:
Joe Vergnetti handles Mrs. Edward Solomon's champion, Dassin Dilly by Dali, to Winners under judge Mary Nelson Stephenson at Worcester County Kennel Club, 1979. Sired by Champion Dassin Debussy.

WINNERS

WORCESTER COUNTY
KENNEL CLUB

DECEMBER 1979

ASHBEY

BEST OF
OPPOSITE SEX

WESTERN RESERVE
KENNEL CLUB SHOW
AUGUST 24 1980
PHOTOS BY ALVERSON

A marvelous informal photo of Pat Norwood with his best friend at the Carolina Kennel Club in 1963.

winning white Miniatures stem directly from these dogs, and many of the best white Toys also trace back to this line.

There are those who maintain that the white Poodle is a dog apart, not only possessing heavier bone, greater size, a coarse and more wiry coat, a square head, and round eyes, but possessed of a different temperament, more placid, less sensitive and intelligent, and even less affectionate than the colored varieties. Nothing would be further from the truth. This claim is based on not only inexperience with whites, but with Poodle history. The facts are that from 1900 on, the English interest, and therefore the American, has been in the development of the colored Poodle! The English developed a finer-boned, longer-headed, and often over-sensitive colored strain of Poodles, and as the latest American revival of interest in the Poodle stemmed from England, we have accepted this type of Poodle as the only correct type. Actually, the British went a little "Haywire" on color to the point of harming type, particularly during World War II years, when they were unable to get European dogs. It was during this period, and even afterward, that their shocking and even careless mixture of color breeding produced a number of flat, almost silky, open coats and, worse yet, a curious sort of terrier coat which shed and could actually be

plucked. This was accompanied by an equal deterioration of type and temperament. Alas, many of us accepted these Poodles as proper, simply because they were English!

No wonder that the superb continental whites, blacks, and browns seemed to have more bone, size, and superior coats! If they had "faults" they were old-fashioned ones based on standards obtained from the knowledge of what the animal was meant to do. In other words, standards of service, such as a certain massiveness of skull and muzzle and occasionally round eyes which were, however, never light or the wrong color. The really great English breeders were well aware of these invaluable European qualities, so while chatting, as good salesmen should, about the "German Coarseness" they frequently (and quietly without attempting to show them) imported these "coarse" dogs to improve their own stock.

Is there, however, such a thing as color temperament? For instance, are the whites more stable, the blacks and browns more sensitive and intelligent? Some of the ancient articles on the Poodle when he was a "water dog" or retriever do maintain that the brown Poodle had the best nose and was therefore the best in the field. At that date, however, it must also be noted that the eyes of a brown were supposed to be a "light, bright yellow," a "keen" eye such as that of a field Pointer.

At this same period, the white was supposed to be the most stable and intelligent. The famous talking Poodle, "Boy," of Prince Rupert was a white.

In those days the black Poodle was not so well considered. It was described as "ordinary," although at least one writer said "it kept the best in health" and recommended crossing blacks with browns to improve the latter's strength! At this early period there was, of course, no mention of other colors.

I have found the creams and browns to be the best performers in the field, but this could have been mere coincidence. I did not train many and had no sort of controls.

The most intelligent Standard I ever owned was the gray Champion Griseley Labory of Piperscroft of Blakeen, C.D., and the most intelligent Miniature a black, Firebrave Alphonse. The most affectionate Poodle I ever owned was a cream Miniature, Berinshill Fredericka, that

Overleaf:
Ch. Misty Ridges Ever Ready, black Standard dog, by Ch. Dacun's Blu Mecca ex Misty Ridges Patti Hot Pants, owned by Dr. and Mrs. Robert Burge, Gadabout Poodles, Broadview Heights, Ohio. Handler, William Cunningham.

besides her touching qualities of loyalty and devotion loved to swim in the ocean, regardless of the weather, after mallard ducks. Furthermore she had a truly remarkable nose and was not at all gun shy. Her size, of course, precluded any idea of training her to actually retrieve game.

I have known so many intelligent, delightful Poodles that I believe it is impossible to generalize about temperament in color.

Mrs. Hoyt Discusses Temperament

Surely there is little need to discuss Poodle temperament with Poodle owners, because this quality should be appreciated by them. It is, in most cases, the reason they own Poodles. Will the reader not agree that the Poodle should be a highly intelligent, cheerful, good-natured, responsive dog whose desires are to live with humans and to please his owners by obedience, affection, and intimate companionship? The Poodle does not possess the same kind of intelligence as the guard dog or the intelligence of a breed that hunts with man and has hunting as a native interest. It is true that a Poodle will bark at strangers, which is a form of guarding, but his bark is almost always a warning, not thought of as an attack. He can learn to retrieve game, but more in a desire to please his owner than in a desire to hunt.

The greatest desire our Poodle has in life is to please, and yet this is neither humble as with some breeds nor withdrawn and somewhat impersonal as with others. For the Poodle is a gay, assertive dog that not only spends much time in responding to his master's moods, but is trying to affect them, to amuse, to comfort, and to entertain. The dog honestly has a sense of fun, he wants to have a good time with life! He is not only a loyal companion, but an entertaining one that wants to get on a very personal basis with his owner. And being human, one must admit that true love, which is always serious, is made more satisfactory seasoned with laughter. The Poodle's affection is enduring and made more endearing by charm.

Any deviation from so delightful a disposition is particularly heartbreaking, because this type of temperament is the very essence of the Poodle.

Yet when one becomes overly engrossed in line-breeding, usually to improve type, the results can sometimes have an adverse effect on temperament. Sadly enough, Poodles do exist that are UNintelligent, nervous, high-strung, and even "silly," a thought the breeder must bear in mind in order to protect against its happening in one's own strain.

Real Poodle character can best be described as: *Intelligent,* meaning quick to comprehend and therefore able to learn; *good natured,* meaning willing to please; *aware* of people and places but not overcome by them; *sensitive,* again very much aware of everything, but unafraid, "a heart at leisure with itself to soothe and sympathize"; *cheerful,* meaning confident, able to deal with the world, and therefore enjoying it; and *loyal,* meaning deeply affectionate, amiable with others, but loving one owner above all else.

Can any of us in Poodles afford poor temperament for long? In breeding for type, temperament, like soundness, can still come first. It does, however, take more time and patience on the part of the breeder. As a first step one should search well in advance for good temperament in the stud, and the owner of a stud should refuse service to a bitch whose temperament is below par.

As one of the black Miniatures from Mrs. Boardman's kennel, Ch. Harmo Little Caeser had many good wins with William J. Trainor's handling.

Overleaf:
Above left: Eng., Am., Can., Ch. Bibelot's Tall Dark and Handsome C.D.X., enjoying life in his retirement. Susan Fraser, Bibelot, Toronto, Canada, owner. **Below left:** Ch. Kayesett Cocoa Nicole, a top producing dam, owned by Mr. and Mrs. J. Herbert Kaye, Woodbridge, Connecticut. This lovely headstudy was made when "Nichie" was 13 years old. **Above right:** Ch. Alekai Zeus relaxing at home with his Pomeranian friend, Twirpy. The intelligence and nobility of this lovely Poodle strike one immediately looking at this picture. **Center right:** An informal pose of a very famous winner. Ch. Bel Tor Big Picture owned by Mrs. J. A. Mason, Branford, Conn. **Below right:** Headstudy of Can. Ch. Evanz Suspense, by Ch. Evanz Simple Simon of Farobs ex Evanz Tania, both Top Producers. Marilyn Pauley of Saline, Michigan, owns this little dog.

LOUISVILLE
KENNEL CLUB
100TH SHOW
FEBRUARY 25 1979

B E S T
I N
S H O W

JUDGE
MR PETER B THOMSON

BOOTH
PHOTO

Best in Show to the black Miniature, Ch. Harmo Little Caesar. Owned by Harmo Kennels, handled by William J. Trainor. At Middlesex County Kennel Club, June 1968, are Mrs. Bradford Torrey, club president; Mr. Dale McMakin, judge; and Mr. William Wood, show chairman.

At all costs, avoid in-breeding to a nervous line, no matter how excellent the type. Yet after out-breeding several times, one can return to the poorer line for type without loss of disposition.

Perhaps the following will illustrate what I mean. In the famed Labory line from Switzerland, to which almost all of our winning Standards go back, there was a strong streak of timidity as well as a good strain of temperament. Sometimes this division would actually occur in one litter. When one bred to or from the timid brother or sisters, the offspring were invariably shy, even if the breeding was a complete outcross. Yet the bold, cheerful brothers and sisters had confident, highly intelligent offspring and, what at first was confusing, *both timid and brave dogs produced beautiful type.* Therefore at first a line started in America of beautiful *looking* show dogs who were not only shy, but sometimes silly, and the males were often difficult to breed.

As an experiment, I purchased a litter of two males and two females. Two of these, Champion Griseley Labory, C.D.X., and Champion Mascotte Labory, C.D., not only won obedience titles, taught at home by myself, a rank amateur, but produced famous offspring with perfect temperaments. The other two were desperately shy. I bred the female to a very bold, assertive, completely unrelated male, and the offspring were quite nice in type, but some, the males mostly, were on the timid side. The most cheerful female puppy, which by the way did not have the best type, I bred to her bold uncle, Griseley. The results were puppies of beautiful type, but here again some, though not completely shy, were not what I liked in character. The best of these females that did have an excellent disposition I bred to a son of their aunt, Mascotte. This dog had a fine disposition but not the best type. His sire had been distantly related to the Labory line on the good side, but there had been several definite out-crosses, all with good dispositions. Now with this last litter I again had perfect type, this time combined with marvelous dispositions. All the puppies were superior in type to their parents, and all grew into top show dogs. Of course this was a great satisfaction to me as a breeder, because it proved that one can breed away from a grave fault and then safely back again for type.

As a further experiment I bred one of these bitches to Griseley's timid brother. The result was a litter of excellent type but uncertain, nervous dispositions. This showed how strong the timid inheritance was, as well as the good type inheritance. I have wondered since if this form of inherited timidity and nervousness could be a chemical or blood lack which started in the embryo? At any rate, I never used the timid dog or bitch again, but I was grateful for all that I had learned from them and found a home for each with a written agreement not to breed them.

There is no doubt that patience is required of the successful breeder. But at least it can be said that dog generations go quickly.

Mrs. Hoyt Discusses, "Is The Poodle Still A Sporting Dog?"

The answer to this question is "Not really," although there are a number of Poodle fanciers who would like to have him considered as such and placed in the Sporting Group at dog shows. Their argument is well taken when they maintain that the Poodle Breed Standard is based on a dog able to retrieve waterfowl and that the few large Poodles trained for this work have acquitted themselves well enough to be moderately acceptable by present-day standards.

There is also sentiment. It is a satisfaction for those who admire the Poodle to know he can still perform those duties for which he was bred. It is a proof that our breed was, and still could be of service to mankind, not that the role of a perfect companion is useless, but it is comforting to realize that in times of trouble or stress he can be more than just a playmate, good company, and sympathetic.

Overleaf: Taking Best in Show at the Louisville Kennel Club in 1979, Ch. Lou Gin's Kiss Me Kate, America's Top Winning Best in Show Dog, added another to her then rapidly growing list of victories. Bob Walberg handles, Lou Dunston bred, and the Jack Phelans with Terri Meyers own this magnificent white Standard Poodle.

It was with this thought in mind that we undertook at Blakeen to train two Poodles for retrieving, a brown female named Blakeen Vigee Le Brun and a cream male, Blakeen Cafe Parfait. Both were royally bred, Vigee being a daughter of Champion Nymphaea Jason out of Sophie, a black bitch going back to the famous Hunnewell line, and Cafe a son of the great Tri-International Champion Nunsoe Duc de la Terrace of Blakeen, from the cream bitch Champion Nunsoe Albricias of Blakeen.

Vigee and Cafe were selected for their strength, vigor, courage, and intelligence. Of the two, Vigee perhaps was the best, although smaller and older than Cafe. She was an ardent and excellent swimmer, yet almost immediately grasped the idea of returning the object she pursued without any by-play or nonsense in which her co-worker occasionally indulged. I also believe that she had the keener nose, although at this time neither one of the dogs was put to any difficult inland tests. They worked first on a soft dummy and then pigeons, first dead and later alive. It was quite easy to accustom them to gunfire, and within about a month both were steady to shot. In fact they loved their work, and the smell of a gun obviously enchanted them. Still these simple preliminaries were nothing compared to the long weeks, in fact months, of training that must be given to a genuine field dog. As we wished to breed Vigee again (she had already produced the famous champions Blakeen Cyrano and Blakeen Durante), we decided to withdraw her from our undertaking. Perhaps from the Field Trial point of view this was not a wise decision, but my ambition to breed good Poodles prevailed over all else.

Cafe was put in the hands of a well-known trainer of Labradors and Chesapeakes, Mr. C. Arthur Smith, and his reports on this young Poodle were interesting and enlightening to us, and I think also to Smith as he later reviewed the dog's career. He found him to be highly intelligent ("almost brilliant" were his words) in comprehending what was wanted of him. He also found him courageous and willing to go out in rough conditions ("not one bit soft" he wrote). On our place Cafe had worked on inland ponds, although occasionally we did take him to the coast; for Smith he worked entirely in salt water, his inland terrain being much the same as ours. Smith declared that our Poodle had "a lovely mouth" and was able to contain his temper with

a wounded struggling bird, a control which could not always be counted on with his Chesapeakes.

He also discovered, as we knew he would, that Cafe was a tireless and powerful swimmer. We had worked our dog on a Muscovy drake, unwounded but with pinioned wings, and those familiar with Muscovies, which are large, ill-tempered, brave, and clever, will appreciate our dog's troubles! This drake was thrown from the other side of a pond and the gun fired, then Cafe seated in the blind with his handler, was ordered to fetch. It was a great trial to the young Poodle when the creature dove as it often did, and for some time Cafe nearly drowned himself in his efforts to dive after it, but eventually, as we had hoped, he discovered the solution. He learned to gauge correctly where it would come up, and there a little to one side he waited ready to grasp it, quickly, firmly, but not harshly, even though the bird savagely attacked him; then holding his head up on his strong neck he would bring the indignant bird proudly back to hand.

So it will be seen that with his new wild ducks, blacks and mallards, much smaller and gentler, wounded or dead, Cafe had no problem at all. In this department he was ahead of his fellow students. What he had to learn were hand signals, to restrain his eagerness, to mark perfectly, and to use his nose. This last ability

This noted black Standard dog is Ch. Prankster Darius, shown winning a Group with Bill Trainor handling. Owned by Prankster Kennels.

Overleaf:
Terri Meyers with Swag Kennel's Ch. Lou Gin's Solitaire, litter brother to Ch. Lou Gin's Kiss Me Kate.

GROUP
1ST

HODGES-JAMES
MCA

BEST OF
OPPOSITE

WESTCHESTER
KENNEL CLUB

SEPTEMBER 1978

ASHBEY

was difficult for Cafe. His power of scent was not equal to his keenness for work, nor to his remarkable eyes and ears, nor was it equal to that of the Labradors and Chesapeakes with which he trained. He tried to compensate with his eyes. No dog ever marked a bird better than Cafe, but on land he would, in spite of commands, rise up on his hind legs like a kangaroo to catch the slightest movement in the brush or swale. He also had very keen hearing, so he would pause, alas not to scent, but to listen for the faint whisper of swale or the smallest crackle of brush from a wounded runner. But of course with a dead bird fallen far off, he was hard put to find it. Nearby and on good scenting days he usually did recover his bird, but both Smith and ourselves realized he could have grave difficulty in formal competition.

Of course as Poodles are not in the Sporting Group, it was only through the good will, generosity, and interest of the Field Trial Associates that Cafe was allowed to compete at all, "unofficially" in an Official Trial. If he placed, and we quite sincerely doubted that he would, he could not have been officially counted. But he was entered at this trial and competed as though he had been an accepted official entry.

One of these sportsmen had even been kind enough to donate a small trophy for the unofficial entry, should it accomplish anything. Both my husband and I were truly grateful and equally worried as to how our Poodle would acquit himself. He had been tried out once before as a puppy in Maryland and had done miserably, simply being playful in the water and chasing fish. At that time he had had no professional training and did not grasp what was expected of him. In fact, I think he missed his Muscovy. At any rate, we had been very disappointed and humiliated, and from then on in the back of our minds was the knowledge of what a long time had gone by without any sort of retrieving for our Poodle—300 years without bird sense or training. We had reason to be worried.

At first we hoped for a passing performance, but not even that when we learned that an International Champion Field Trial Labrador had joined our company, and as lots were drawn for position, we drew ours next behind this champ!

It was a bitterly cold day, the water rough and choppy, and the wind from us out to sea, not the best for duck hunting. Three Chesapeakes and two Irish Water Spaniels performed well on dead ducks, then a fourth Chesapeake went out after his wounded duck and killed it in plain sight of the gallery and the judge's boat which was anchored a good way offshore. The gallery murmured, and the Labrador next to us shivered. Cafe sat motionless. I could see that he had marked every bird that had fallen down. He only trembled for a second as each landed on the water.

It was the champion Labrador's turn, and his bird, flying high and caught by the wind, tumbled through the air to the other side of the judge's boat. It was out of sight of the gallery, and I wondered if it was dead. The Labrador was sent in and took off fast and stylishly. But in spite of every signal, hand and whistle, he would not go beyond that boat. Because of his record and also being an import, the judges gave him considerable time, but finally he was ordered to be called in, his handler muttering that the "light was terrible" (it was a dark day) and that "no dog could mark that sort of a bird."

"Do you want to send your Poodle after *this* bird, or will you wait?" asked the committee chairman with a twinkle. "That bird," I gulped, and nodded to handler Smith, who to my surprise appeared cheerful and confident.

At Smith's signal, Cafe left the blind in one great leap, swimming as he always did, fast and smoothly. On this retrieve he never hesitated. He went straight out and around the boat, and then it was no longer ours, but the judges', opportunity and delight to watch him. The duck was not dead; it was badly wounded but quite able to swim. It dove as Cafe approached and our Poodle remembered Muscovy days. Veering sharply to one side and looking down through the water, he swam with tremendous vigor across the arc of a circle so that the poor bird emerged almost into his mouth. Instantly, but gently, he seized it across the back, and, head held high so that it would not drown, he came back through those choppy waves to the shore and delivered it alive into the hands of Smith.

A ripple of applause broke out and tears rolled down my cheeks. It was a good job, as good as the best; our Poodle had not failed us! "Now we'll give him his own bird," said the chairman matter of factly, and once again Cafe gave a flawless performance, only this time it was almost anticlimactic, for the duck fell on our side

Sire of 13 champions, Ch. Alekai Oli of Stonebridge is handled by Wendell J. Sammet.

of the boat and it was dead. Still he had had two perfect retrieves to one of the others.

I wish that I could say that Cafe won that trial, even unofficially, but he did not, although he did place third. It was growing late, and although the wind had died, it was bitterly cold and so dark that the guns hardly killed one bird, they were all just winged or crippled. Cafe had a runner, a pheasant of course, and it was obvious that while he had marked it, he was not now using his nose as he should. Looking back frequently at Smith he obeyed hand signals perfectly, but to no avail. Finally in despair he rose on his hind legs, a shadowy almost human figure in those dim woods, standing still and upright, listening, of course. Then suddenly he plunged down and was off. He returned a few minutes later, the pheasant alive in his mouth, but oh dear, what form. It wasn't his fault that his nose had been bred out of him, and it was to his credit that he used every ounce of intelligence and courage he possessed to retrieve his bird.

The reader may be interested to know that Cafe not only won his bench show championship, as well as going Best in Show three times at large all-breed events, but that his son did some fairly good retrieving for his breeder, Mrs. Gordon Fisher of Wyetown, Maryland. This dog aroused the great interest that Mr. LeBoutellier, a present-day judge of Poodles and

of obedience, takes in Poodles as retrievers. He and Mrs. Fisher have tried to organize water trials for Poodles, and in water retrieving they do perform well, but not, at least in my opinion, on land.

I have had letters from men who have trained and used Poodles for hunting, and all attest to the dog's eagerness and sense, but only a few remark that the nose is keen. And why should it be? Ever since the Poodle has ceased to work, we have bred away from a hunting head and nose.

Just once have I seen a really excellent Poodle nose. A brown Poodle which I owned some years back, Bucko by name, would not only point grouse and hold his point for quite some time, but we and others have seen him suddenly stop and stiffen head up, looking up at a tree. Following the line of his rigid gaze one invariably sighted, high up on some branch, a ruffled grouse. But Bucko was never trained, for I firmly believe that the Poodle's hunting days are best behind him, retired but not forgotten, because he was never used for sport in the sense we now associate with the word. In fact except for those few individuals who do hunt with Poodles, our breed is not really suited to take its place in the Gun Dog Group for the reasons given below.

Our breed was developed to harry, drive, hold, and retrieve large waterfowl such as ducks, wild geese, and swans which were killed not for sport but for food and feathers. Because of this purpose, the Poodle was limited almost entirely to his own specification. He was purely utilitarian, he was never made adaptable to other forms of work. He worked only in marshes, ponds, rivers, and on the coast. His coat would have rendered his work impractical inland, and this coat was never changed by breeding for inland purposes because there were, even then, sufficient breeds satisfactory for inland and upland hunting.

Therefore, as soon as this purely utilitarian and specialized hunting ended, the Poodle, except in individual cases, ceased to be used as a hunter. Only the dog's superb and unique disposition saved it from the extinction which befell many early breeds or from an amalgamation with others to form new breeds. In fact, in all probability the Poodle was used this way, the most likely new breed being the English Curly Coated Retriever, but it was not used enough to be obliterated. It remained as it was and is—a Poodle.

Overleaf:
A current example of the quality for which Bel Tor has become world famous and esteemed. Bel Tor Special Delivery, handled here by Wendell J. Sammet, excels in all the virtues one looks for in an outstanding member of the breed.

BEST OF WINNERS

KENNEL CLUB OF
NORTHERN NEW JERSEY

KLEIN   MARCH 2 1980

Graham

Therefore, to be honest, besides his cleverness and courage, what has our Poodle to offer as a sporting breed today? He was and is a grand swimmer, but so is the Labrador and the Chesapeake. He was and is hardy and nimble, with a rather original sort of brain, working things out for himself. But this is not particularly necessary today or even always desirable in our present kind of hunting. He once had an excellent nose, but so have all modern gun dogs, and at present they are vastly superior to the Poodle. Against him he has his coat, difficult to care for and difficult to breed away from, since as soon as a Breed Standard was established for the Poodle this coat was emphasized while the excellent hunting dog nose was not. In fact, ever since then Poodle breeders have worked away from the "birdy" head, particularly the English and Americans, who breed the most.

Because of this coat and average lack of nose, the time spent in attempting to develop a line of hunting Poodles would be prodigious, and to what effect? We have excellent gun dogs for both water and land, and as civilization encroaches on every countryside, why develop more? Hunting dogs soon will be a limited luxury, as is almost the case now.

So I say leave our Poodle in the group it so nobly enhances and breed for character, which is the heart of its endurance and success, only remembering how this character was developed and for what, so that time and change shall not distill or weaken one drop if its golden image.

Mrs. Hoyt Discusses Type In Poodles

In dog parlance, one of the most misused words is "type," perhaps because many fanciers and even breeders interpret this word rather than define it. One breeder has referred to type as "moving correctly." Another has written, "type is elegance." Both are assets, but they are not *type*. One can, in the face of all this, understand the bewilderment of the novice Poodle fancier over the simple statement, "That dog has type."

To define this word correctly, one must go back to the origin of the Standard for the breed. The forerunner of a written Standard was undoubtedly a contest among similar kinds of dogs. Those which could run were raced against each other. Those which could fight were pitted against other animals or one another. Those

Puttencove Kennels magnificent black Standard dog, Ch. Carillon Colin of Puttencove, winning the Non-Sporting Group at the Interstate Kennel Association, 1947, under judge Mrs. Sherman R. Hoyt. Puttencove Kennels belongs to Mrs. George Putnam, and has been an important force in the breed, especially Standards, over several decades.

which could herd were given tasks in individual herding. Naturally, the sort of dog that won most consistently was considered the best kind of animal to own for that particular purpose. He was the right "type" of dog.

Just as in modern times, dog owners gathered with their dogs to discuss type, and quite often someone particularly familiar with the dogs' duties as well as the dogs themselves would be called upon to decide which dog present appeared to be best suited to perform its appointed work. Indeed, this was the start of our present day dog shows because the dog even then, was judged on its appearance rather than its actions. In other words, which dog *looked* most suitable to race, to hunt, to fight, to herd.

Of course there were written descriptions of different kinds of dogs, first to help owners and breeders and later to assist the judges, for in time owners allowed their dogs to be judged by men not necessarily owners, breeders, or participants in any dog duties, but simply familiar with the requirements of a breed. This judge had to decide which dog most conformed to its breed description, or Standard, which was an outline of the correct *type*.

Overleaf:
Ch. Carnival Cubby Bear, owned by Margaret M. McQuillen, bred and handled by Wendell J. Sammet, Carnival Toy Poodles. This lovely little brown Toy was sired by Carnival Yakity Yak from Chrisward's Carnival Red Hen.

Today the dog which most closely resembles its Standard in both appearance and disposition is the most *typical* of a certain kind of dog developed for a particular purpose. It has *type*. From this point of view, the Bulldog's roll is as sound as the Shepherd's driving walk, and the bowed forelegs of the Pekingese are as sound as the straight forelegs of the Fox Terrier. For without these various physical and mental conformations, each breed could not fulfill its various services to mankind.

Our own breed, and the subject of this book, is the Poodle. He no longer hunts professionally, but let us study the original Water Dog, of which he is a descendant. Compared to the spaniels of that time, he was shorter in the body and higher on the leg. These characteristics enabled him to climb, to get through swamp lands and heavy mud with greater ease. His chest reminded one of the prow of a ship, deep rather than broad, with moderate spring of ribs. Everything about this dog was effective for work in and out of water.

His hindquarters were unusually well-developed and strong for the purposes of climbing and swimming, and for a similar reason his feet, though well padded, had long, flexible toes with considerable thin membrane between

Ch. Calvinelle Dancing Deacon exemplifies the beautiful type and quality of Poodle owned by Mrs. William L. Kendrick, the former Vernelle Hartman.

them—"webbed feet" the "ancients" called them. In thick mud and in the water, these strong feet spread out most effectively, and on dry land the muscular toes arched well up. It was a strong and useful foot in no way resembling the foot of the terrier. Today when one hears an owner say that his Poodle has "feet just like a terrier," one knows that owner is either ignorant of Poodle type or that he hopes to impress the equally ignorant judge!

The neck and shoulders of the original Poodle were like those of any good hunting dog, the latter sloping and well laid back, the former clean, long, and flexible enough to permit a high head carriage on both land and in water.

The head was oval-shaped with a moderate though definite occiput (the "bird bump"), a moderate but definite stop, and extremely flat cheeks. All told, a head streamlined for sharp marsh grass and actual water diving, yet sufficiently roomy for a calm, unexcitable brain. The muzzle was long, strong, and tight-lipped, as, of course, pendulous lips and open flews could choke or drown a dog carrying a struggling bird through the water. Also, unlike spaniels, the eyes were not in the least prominent, but instead almond-shaped and set far apart. A prominent or protruding eye could be severely damaged in sharp marsh grasses and rough water.

The ears of these early Poodles were spaniel ears, but the length was of small account. The set-on was the important feature; they were to be set low, about on a level with the eye, because highly set ears were not only in the way in thick, rough coverage but did not efficiently protect the actual ear orifice. Today, low-set ears give any Poodle the right expression, regardless of their length.

The coat of the Water Dog was very dense and was inclined to crinkle and curl. It was supposed to be just long enough to freeze on top in bitter weather but remain protectively warm and dry near the skin. The developments of this weather resistant quality was probably what caused the coat to grow almost too long, so the dog was then shaved on the hindquarters and feet to facilitate swimming and water retrieving.

Overleaf:
Above: The famous winning black Standard bitch, Ch. Rimskittle Ruffian, wins Best in Show from judge Langdon Skarda. Tim Brazier handling for owners, Edward B. Jenner and Margo Durney. **Below:** Quinnipiac Poodle Club Specialty Show 1980 with judge, Miss Iris de la Torre Bueno, awarding winner of the Brood Bitch Class to Ch. Alekai Psyche (Champion Alekai Ole of Stonebridge ex Montec Lady Hamilton). Handled by Wendell J. Sammet for owners, Mr. and Mrs. Royal Peterson. Psyche's son, Deryabar Trumpet, the white dog, is handled here by Mr. Peterson while Mrs. Peterson has the lead on the black daughter, Deryabar Dulcet. Both sired by Alekai In Style.

One can comprehend that the fairly short body, long legs, and flexible feet gave this dog an interesting appearance and stylish "springy" action. Certainly the high head carriage, wide-set oval eyes, and low-hung ears gave him a wise and noble expression, but it was the shaved parts of his body, done for purely utilitarian reasons, that gave this powerful hunting dog a reputation for more elegance than actually belonged to him. Any heavily coated dog, or any animal for that matter, which is shorn appears more fragile and slender than people imagine it to be.

Today we find an emphasis on the Poodle coat that would have rendered the Water Dog completely useless. In fact, too often our Poodles are judged on this quality alone, the other equally important parts of the Standard being neglected. One often beholds so-called famous show Poodles with short necks, jowly muzzles, over-wide chests, and round eyes winning on their enormous profusion of coat and good showing dispositions. Such dogs lack type and are a breed detriment.

Then there is the other extreme, the Poodle so delicate in bone, so elegant and fragile that it has no strength at all. The word "sporting" could not possibly be attributed to its kind. Such a dog may be "pretty as a picture," but it certainly lacks *type*. It is not a real Poodle.

More Poodle judges should emphasize the construction of our dog rather than merely general appearance, at least until they learn what that general appearance actually should be. More attention should be paid to the quality of the coat rather than its length, and to the way a Poodle moves rather than its showmanship. On the other hand, dog with spirit can move well, but it can do so in an entirely atypical manner. Color is, of course, important within its limitations. Color alone does not make the dog a *typical* Poodle.

Mrs. Hoyt Discusses Head

In all show dogs the head is of great value as being distinctive of its breed, but in the non-sporting varieties it is of special importance. Working and sporting dogs are still presumed to be useful, and therefore their legs and bodies are of equal value to their heads. In our group,

A lovely Tauskey headstudy of the Miniature Poodle, Am., Can., Mex., C.A.C.I.B. Ch. Beaujeau My Gosh from the Beaujeau Kennels of Mrs. Marjorie A. Tranchin, at Dallas, Texas.

however, the former sporting or working varieties are no longer used for the work for which they were originally bred, and therefore they tend to become more exaggerated in type. Type itself is always most vividly demonstrated in head and general appearance. For instance, the heads of the Bulldog and Chow today are far more exaggerated than when the former really "pinned a bull" or the latter hunted, pulled a sled, or was used for food.

This special development of the Poodle also has occurred since the days when he ceased to retrieve waterfowl. In what way has our Poodle's head changed? What is now the correct head?

The answers can be supplied quickly. Our breed's head has become less broad in skull, less deep and wide in muzzle, and the lips (never pendulous) were once upon a time fuller. The stop is less pronounced, the nose is smaller, and the eye, instead of being somewhat round, is almond-shaped. Needless to say, long ear featherings and a true top knot could not exist on the working Poodle.

Overleaf:
A lovely brown, this is Ch. Bel Tor Carefree with owner, Mrs. J. A. Mason.

The modern Poodle head has become exaggerated in length of muzzle (and possibly lack of strength in the muzzle), length of ear, the flatness of the cheeks, and the shape of the eye. We of course know how much ear feathering and top knot are emphasized, as is expression.

Still, these differences from the ancient Water Dog are comparatively minor. So let us accept them, if possible, without too much over-exaggeration.

The head of today's perfect Poodle is not as large in relation to the body as that of a Chow or a Bulldog, but it is just as impressive. This is due partly to the "top knot" (hair on top of the head which should be long and full) brushed back and fastened up out of the dog's eyes, and partly to the set-on of the ears which, covered with long hair, make a frame for the face which when shaven, with the wide-set remarkable eyes, has a look of human intelligence. In fact, the correct Poodle's head looks something like an English judge with his wig on.

This lovely white Miniature is one of the famous Blakeen champions from the kennels of Mr. and Mrs. Sherman R. Hoyt.

In size, from the tip of the nose to the occiput the head is slightly less than one-half the length of the body, measured from the tip of the shoulder blade to the base of the tail. This measurement, however, is not important. What *is* important is that our dog should not appear to have either a large, long head or a small, short head. It should appear to be an impressive but unexaggerated head. Set on a neck long enough to hold it high, the head should appear in perfect harmony or balance with a massive body coat which is carried on quarters strong and round enough to balance the coat and proud carriage.

Viewed from above, the Poodle skull should appear just moderately but not extremely wide, with a mild but definite protuberance called the occiput or "bird bump." From the profile there should be a mild but definite arch of the bones which form the skull cap; this is to permit brain capacity. The stop or indentation where the forehead rises from the muzzle, while not deep, is *very* definite. All these unexaggerated but definite qualities are necessary not only to the appearance but to the character or individuality of our breed. Here is a head which not only contains room for brain tissue, but which has a "brainy" appearance. With all the outside accouterments in order, such as grooming, clipping, etc., the Poodle *looks* intelligent. An extremely streamlined head, narrow flat skull cap, little stop, and eyes set close together does *not* look intelligent.

If our Poodle must have a fault, the wise judge or knowledgeable breeder will prefer the wide skull to an overly streamlined one. Why? Because while not as refined or pretty it is of sounder construction. The animal with the wider head will probably have a better disposition, certainly will have more sense and poise, and will throw better heads when properly mated than his weaker counterpart would throw if mated to a good-headed dog.

Let us now consider the muzzle. First of all, in length from the tip of the nose to the stop it is usually no longer than the skull from stop to occiput. The lips lie flat and tightly closed just on the outside of the lower jaw. The flews are without excessive folds and are tightly closed.

The nose of this muzzle is of medium size with moderately wide nostrils. Our Poodle once had excellent scenting powers, and a large nose with wide nostrils was necessary to him, but the

BEST OF
OPPOSITE

PENN TREATY
KENNEL CLUB

1980

ASHBEY II

modern Poodle's nose is no longer extra large with flaring nostrils. It is not like that of a Pointer or Springer, and it is not at all upturned. It is not, however, a little nose, which would be incorrect. It is a *moderate* nose.

Lift up the lips of this muzzle and you will find a "scissors bite." That is, the upper front teeth close evenly just over the lower. This correct bite is important, because a strong, level underjaw gives this rather refined muzzle a look of strength. Our Poodle should not have a weak-looking muzzle. Any weakness detracts from the noble, intelligent appearance this dog should possess. The Poodle must never be undershot (the lower teeth extending beyond the upper) and, even more seriously, must never be overshot (upper jaw extending beyond the lower). The latter bite is a particularly serious fault, accompanied as it is by a shark-like appearance with the lower jaw hardly in evidence.

The cheeks, or sides of the face, of the correct Poodle are rather flat with a mild chiseling under the eye.

The eyes are a moderate almond shape, medium in size, neither deep set nor bulging, set rather far apart, with an expression of glowing intelligence. A Poodle's eyes should not be hard and keen, as are those of a good terrier, nor should they be melting and soft as those of a Cocker Spaniel. The Poodle's eyes should make one think of an intelligent, friendly human being. Our breed's glance is *personal,* friendly, and full of comprehension.

There are three common faults in the Poodle eye: one, round eyes which detract somewhat from perfect expression; two, eyes set too close together, usually occurring in a too narrow skull; and three, the light eye. Closely set eyes are a more serious fault than the round eye because they give an expression of silliness or stupidity, whereas the round eye may be quite beautiful in color and expression although not quite as pretty in shape as the almond eye. Eyes set too close together, no matter what color, cannot have a good expression. While the Standard deplores light eyes, I think its seriousness is open to argument depending on how light and on the color of the dog. For instance, yellow eyes in a black or white dog are certainly deplorable, but in a brown or grey they may not be too displeasing, provided they are not a bright yellow or greenish yellow. To me it is all a matter of expression. I

This is a truly gorgeous Miniature head. Note correct eye and beautiful refinement of Ch. Aizbel The Aristocrat, bred and owned by Mr. and Mrs. Luis Aizcorbe, Jr., Miami, Florida.

have seen a rich warm brown eye in a black or white far more expressive and therefore more beautiful than the desired jet black. Still, the present Standard says "the darker the better," so our readers had best go by this for the present.

Last but by no means least, where the ears are hung or set on the head is important. In fact the ear-set is more important than its width or length. The ears should be low-set, if possible on a level with the eye, and of course the longer, wider, and more fully feathered the better. This low ear-set is entirely necessary for the correct expression.

On looking at a Poodle's head, one should be able to tell immediately if it is a dog or a bitch. This quality of sexual definition is important. A dog should not look "bitchy"or a bitch "doggy." If one instinctively keeps referring to a Poodle as a "she" when it is a "he," that dog's type is too refined and his expression too soft. These qualities have nothing to do with the size of the animal. A tiny Toy dog should look as male as the largest Standard!

Overleaf:
Pinafore Pride N Joy of Vodanz, gaining points towards the title while still a puppy, under judge Hayden Martin at Rapid City Kennel Club, October, 1980.

This proper sexual expression has to do with bone structure. The male head is slightly heavier, often slightly longer in actual bone size. Actually it is a slightly more impressive head than the average female's, and it should be. A male's expression, while not at all hard, should not be as yielding as a female's. His gaze is very steady, fearless, intelligent, and noble. The female head, while not quite as dominant as the male's in either length or strength, should have a very touching expression, making one love her at first sight. To the noble intelligence of her glance is added tenderness, a warm, eager desire to please.

Mrs. Hoyt Discusses Body

Few judges or even breeders seriously consider the construction of the Poodle's body. This could be because so much is hidden by the coat, although I believe that most of their disregard is due to the fact that the animal is no longer a working dog. Yet without proper construction the Poodle cannot move freely, so that even in

This exquisite headstudy of Ch. Alekai Ahi was done by Ben Burwell in 1962.

obedience work he cannot perform as he was bred to do, namely run and jump with enormous agility plus grace. Nor can he simply exist under all conditions with endurance and strength.

His ancestors were magnificent untiring workers able to endure extreme wet and cold and long hours climbing over rocky cliffs to retrieve large waterfowl. Their bodies were square; that is, from shoulder tip to base of tail measured the same as from shoulder tip to ground. Their chests were deep rather than wide, to facilitate swimming and running. Their hindquarters were muscled and powerful.

Today our Poodle is shorter in back; that is, the distance from shoulder tip to base of tail is shorter by approximately one-sixth than that from shoulder tip to floor. Although not as powerful, this is a prettier conformation. The chest remains muscular, and the hips set far apart with the thighs broad and muscular. Lacking the proper strength of loin, hips, and hindquarters, the shaved Poodle would appear weak and effeminate. Of course, even more essential than appearance, without a deep chest and strong body the dog cannot function properly.

Looking at the proper body profile of a Poodle, we note the correct depth of chest, which should just reach to the elbow, the very moderately tucked up loin, and the powerful hindquarters. The shoulder of this dog is well laid back, which permits ease and freedom of movement. A straight shoulder is incorrect because this structure causes stilty action. The animal does not cover much ground with its stride because this kind of shoulder is not sufficiently flexible and thus prevents correct reach of the foreleg. Frequently the straight-shouldered Poodle has a high-stepping hackney action simply because while he can lift his leg up and down, he cannot reach forward. The "high stepper" may appear pretty and stylish, but this action is fundamentally unsound.

It is quite usual for the steep- or straight-shouldered Poodle to have a short neck so that the head is carried forward rather than up, a most unfortunate plight for a dog that must carry a live bird while swimming. The Poodle neck is correctly moderately long, not as long as that of a Greyhound, but longer than that of a Chow or Keeshond.

The most common body fault, particularly in Miniatures, is a condition referred to as "shelly,"

WINNERS

HUNTINGDON VALLEY

KENNEL CLUB

1980

ASHBEY II

FEDERACION CANOFILA MEXICANA A.C.
X CIRCUITO INTERNACIONAL = 4-XII-77

MEJOR sexo OPUESTO

Ch. Norgate Too Spicey, of the 1960 era. Photo courtesy of Jane Forsyth.

Ch. Highland Sand Star Baby, a multiple Group and Best in Show winner, owned by Mrs. Marjorie Tranchin, Dallas, Texas. "Star Baby," purchased as a puppy from Mrs. Dorothy Thompson, was sired by her great producing stud, Ch. Highland Sand Magic Star. Highland Sand Poodles were noted for heavy coats and short backs, and Star Baby carried on in the family tradition when she produced six champions.

Overleaf:
Above: Mackintosh's The Mystic Touch, one of the fine Poodles owned by Jose Carlos Gimaraes Santos, Mackintosh Kennels, Rio de Janeiro. Richard Guevera handling. **Below:** Mex., Int. Ch. Evanz Ms. Robinson, platinum silver bitch, obtaining her titles undefeated in her sex, at the end of nine days of showing when just 15 months old. Since no C.A.C.I.B. certificates are awarded until the age of 15 months, her owner believes this lovely bitch to be the youngest girl ever to have gained an International Championship. Handled by Allan Chambers for owner Marilyn Pauley; sired by Ch. Evanz Simple Simon of Farobs.

meaning that there is not enough of the actual rib cage and loin. This sort of dog has no spring of rib, feels rather like a flatfish, and is what is frequently referred to as "slab-sided." The thigh in this construction is usually narrow and unmuscular, and the stifles are usually straight. Yet this Poodle can have a heavy coat which will hide the "shelly" chest, while hair on the thighs and hind legs can be trimmed or clipped so as to make them appear broad and muscular. Of course any expert will discover the absence of chest and thigh as well as the straight stifles by feeling them, and before this he or she will guess the condition because the dog will not gait correctly. He will surely cross over in front while the rear action will lack drive or power. Of course he can still be stylish looking, gay, and "showy," but due to his incorrect body he cannot move as a Poodle should. Therefore, even with the most perfect head, a glorious coat, and sunny disposition, the dog must be severely penalized in the show ring and even at home must be bred with great care, because this type of body is unsound and can be inherited.

Another less common fault, most prevalent in Toys, is too much spring of rib, too wide a chest, too much body for the legs. In Toys this is usually accompanied by bow legs. In Standards, where the fault is again more usual than in Miniatures, the dog travels "wide in front." Such an animal definitely will be hindered in running, jumping, or swimming. Good hindquarters often go with this kind of body. Such a Poodle has a rather dumpy, squatty appearance, and as this type of construction hinders the dog in action, it is entirely wrong and must be severely penalized in the show ring. Yet in the kennel this type of body is not as dangerous to a breeding program.

Another less ordinary, in fact most curious, fault is too short a back. Often this dog has a deep chest, but the distance between shoulder tip to base of tail is so compressed that the animal lacks freedom of movement. Although such a dog often has a very short neck as well, he looks fine standing. It is when he gaits that his action is hampered, usually in the rear. Not only does he lack drive, but he often paces, this gait being the most natural for the compressed construction. This type often has a straight shoulder and is almost always straight in stifle.

Let us again summarize the correct body: it is moderately shorter in length than height, possessing a deep chest with a moderate spring of ribs, a very moderate tuck-up of loin, shoulders well laid back supporting a moderately long neck, hip bones quite far apart, and thighs well developed with muscle. One observes how often the word "moderate" appears.

The actual top-line under the coat is moderate, too, for it is not completely straight but can have a very slight dip in the middle which does not show because of the coat. Another word for moderate can be balance, and the Poodle's correct body *really* is balanced and perfectly constructed for active outdoor work, for jumping, climbing, and walking endurance. It has a very stylish appearance due to the trim, but underneath this grace and elegance lie flexibility and strength.

Mrs. Hoyt Discusses Coat

As all who have studied the history of our breed know, the Poodle's coat is its most unique and distinguishing feature, as it has been for the past 400 years, unlike any other canine coat.

Its chief characteristic is curliness. It has a soft undercoat that is rather cottony in texture, very dense, and curls when wet or exposed to the atmosphere. In noticing the "pack" or closely scissored rear end coat of a Poodle in the English Saddle Clip, one sees that this "pack" or "saddle" resembles a tightly curled caracul coat.

As for the top coat, there are two kinds, both equally correct. The first is called the "soft curly," which is what it is, soft and curly, hanging

in ringlets when wet or unbrushed. Brushed out, this coat looks dense, fluffy, and almost straight, but it gradually falls back into curls. It is the thick undercoat that makes it look fluffy and hold its shape when brushed. The hair on the head of a soft curly coat is equally curly but without much undercoat, and the ear hair or feathering is composed of long curly ringlets, with some undercoat, but without as much undercoat as the body. The soft curly coat unbrushed or brushed out feels dense yet soft to the touch.

This soft curly coat is also the kind that, when allowed to grow long and the ringlets brushed out, oiled, and braided, will grow into the so-called "corded" coat. It is necessary when starting a "corded" to comb out most of the wooly undercoat. Once the "cords" or curls grow into long braids, the undercoat is allowed to grow

Ch. Manorhill's Luck Be A Lady with her handler, William Cunningham, showing the lovely quality that made her a winner. Photo courtesy of Mr. Cunningham.

Overleaf:
Above: Nancy Meyers with the brown Toy, Swag's Brown Bomber, owned by the Meyers of Brooklyn Park, Minnesota, wins Best of Variety at the St. Croix Valley Kennel Club in 1979. **Below:** Ch. Tiopepi Amber Tanya winning the Non-Sporting Group from the author at Taconic Hills Kennel Club 1977. This gorgeous apricot Miniature bitch belongs to Mrs. Gardner Cassatt and is handled by Richard Bauer.

ST. CROIX
VALLEY
KENNEL CLUB
JAN 7, 1979

BEST OF BREED

PHOTO BY
VALENTINE

GROUP
FIRST

GILBERT PHOTO

FEDERACION CANOFILA MEXICANA A.C.
EXPO ESPECIALIZADA · 21 · XI · 79
MEJOR de la RAZA

WINNERS
BITCH

PHOTO
BY
K. BOOTH

The Great Lakes Poodle Club Specialty Show, 1977. Edward B. Jenner's Ch. Penchant Paladin, Peggy Hogg handling, is awarded Best Miniature Poodle. Frank Sabella, judge.

Such a magnificent head along with all her other assets. Eng., Can., Am., Mex., Ch. Montmartre Maria-Nina makes a good win pictured here under judge Isidore Schoenberg, on the right. Marjorie Tranchin, owner.

back, as it gives the coat "body" when they are unbraided and combed out.

Expert Poodle breeders were always aware of how to grow a "corded" coat, but because this coat was such an unusual and impressive sight they kept this process secret. Therefore many historians considered the corded Poodle to be a different kind of Poodle and described it as such. No one has ever denied, then or now, that a corded Poodle was very hard to groom and keep clean. Because of this, most of them had a strong odor like a combination of rancid oil and unwashed dog. Today there are very few corded Poodles. The last one I saw was at Madame Riechenbach's.

The second correct type of coat I like to call the "steel wool" coat. In other words, wool which is soft but has a springiness or crispness about it. The actual hairs of this coat are coarser in fiber than the soft curly. They are just as curly, but as they are coarser and shorter they are more crisp. They fall into kinky curls rather than ringlets.

When brushed out, this coat feels not harsh but *springy* to the touch. Your hand does not flatten it as easily as it does the soft curly coat. In fact, this hair stays in place against your hand. It also stays groomed much longer. It has the same thick, wooly undercoat, and the top knot and ear featherings are composed of long but coarser curly ringlets. This coat takes longer to grow than the soft curly and is much more brittle (easier to break the hairs in grooming), but when it is long and properly groomed it is a more impressive-looking coat, mainly because it holds its groomed or "brushed out" appearance for quite some time. Because it is so slow-growing, shorter, and more brittle, the steel wool coat does not make a satisfactory corded coat. Although the steel wool coat occurs in all colors, it is seen more frequently in whites and grays.

Where did these two types of top coat originate? Was it not the influence of the northern Shepherd on the original Water Dog or Silk Hound? Was it not the kind of coat most useful to a dog retrieving in cold climates? I think so, and it is interesting to see how long these coats have endured.

The coats of new-born Poodle puppies do not appear curly. In fact the new-born puppy's coat is usually straight, although it may have a slight marcel-looking wave that is soft and dense across

Overleaf: **Above:** Am., Int., Ch. Evanz Jose Can U.C., white Toy male, winning the breed at Mexico City handled by Allan Chambers. Jose is sired by Ch. Evanz Anchor Man out of the Top Producing white female, La Joie's Snow Crystal. He was bred by Marilyn Pauley and Lillie Ketchell, La Joie Poodles. **Below:** Ch. Syntifny Shine On Me, a Silverdrift daughter, owned by Jane A. Winne, handled by Todd Patterson, here is taking a Winners Bitch award from judge, Mrs. Ann Stevenson.

the back. Soon this marcel wave appears more definite, and at two months of age, the puppy's coat is bursting into patches of little curls all over.

Additionally there are several coat types occasionally seen which are not correct for the Poodle. First, the straight coat, which is a soft coat that does not curl. This coat may or may not have an undercoat, but a straight-haired coat *cannot* occur in a pure-bred Poodle! So powerful and enduring is the curl in a Poodle's coat that when other breeds are crossed with a Poodle the puppies have curly coats. The Curly Coated Retriever, which is an accepted breed, is one example, but I have seen the offspring of a Labrador and a Poodle *all* of which had curly coats. This same phenomenon occurred in several Cocker Spaniel and Poodle crosses to my knowledge.

Then there is the more common "open coat," a curly coat which may be very long and curly but lacks undercoat. This coat has no body to it, and brushed out it falls apart. It occurred most often during the early 1900's in English and American Poodles. I have never seen it in the continental Poodles.

Last, but no means any better, is the "silky" coat, which is often related to the open coat. The hair of this coat is too fine. It has some curl but no substance and lies limp against the body. Quite often this kind of coat has little or no undercoat. This coat used to be seen most frequently in the Toy variety, but today, I'm happy to relate, it rarely appears.

The "steel wool" coat rarely has the above faults, but some years ago a British breeder introduced terrier blood into her Poodle stock. The ensuing coats were very coarse and appeared full and dense, but they could be "plucked out" as can a terrier's; a Poodle's coat cannot be, due of course to the double coat. On careful examination these impure dogs had no true undercoat, and although their hair would curl when wet, it was rather wiry or "harsh" to the touch. The true steel wool coat is never harsh or wiry. It is simply dense and feels crisp or springy to the touch. Unfortunately quite a few of these impure Poodles came to America, but by now the terrier influence has been bred out.

Both types of the correct Poodle coat are extremely weather resistant. A Poodle's top coat

Ch. Harmo Gay Prospector as a puppy. One of the many fine Poodles belonging to Harmo Kennels, Amherst, Massachusetts, handled in the ring by William J. Trainor. An apricot son of Ch. Summercourt Square Dancer of Fircot.

At the Poodle Club of America Specialty, 1960, judge Derek Rayne awards Best of Variety over many "specials" to Ch. Barkhaven's Exotiquette. Miniature bitch owned by Ed Weber and handled by Ben Burwell.

Overleaf: Above: Ch. Merry Bee Beauty Arden, making the same win as her sire Ch. Arden Award did the previous year, Best of Variety in the Hudson Valley Poodle Club Sweepstakes, June 1979. Owner, Jeanie Mazza. The judge is Joseph Vergnetti. **Below:** Ch. Davaroc Bronzed Bliss, U.D.T. by the brown dog, Tel Tor Don't Tread On Me from the black bitch, Ch. Bel Tor Blissful. Bred and owned by Dr. and Mrs. Samuel Peacock, Davadon Standard Poodles, Chester Springs, Pennsylvania.

BEST OF
VARIETY

SWEEPSTAKES

HUDSON VALLEY
POODLE CLUB

JUNE 1979

ASHBEY

can be really wet, but the wooly undercoat will remain dry and therefore so will the skin. In winter snow flakes can cover it or sleet freeze on it, but the undercoat and skin remain warm, dry, and comfortable. My Poodle trained for retrieving took a long time to get truly wet-through in the water. Time after time when going in for a duck he would return, salt water dripping and crusting his sides and shoulders, yet a hand run through those dense, crisp curls would discover his skin to be unwet and of normal body temperature.

Poodles do not shed, which is of course a delight about the house. If not groomed, however, the coats become matted, a state which can lead to unpleasant odor and skin trouble. This is due to dead hair tangled with the live. In other words, the Poodle's coat should be brushed from the roots out and the dead hair will come out on the brush or in the comb. Although the ancient Water Dog's coat was not nearly as long as the Poodle's coat today, the sportsmen of that time did recommend grooming as well as shaving the coat. Today our breed's coat should be brushed out at least once a week, and for a pet I think the coat should be kept fairly short.

It is an interesting fact that fleas, lice, and ticks are not much attracted to the correct type of Poodle coat. I believe that the wooly undercoat has much to do with this. The insects simply cannot reach the skin, or if they do, there is too little air for them to exist in comfort. Our breed's unique curly coat with its wool undercoat is not only handsome when well-groomed, but a distinct asset in many ways over other canine coats. A weekly brushing is not too high a price to pay for its many advantages, and that keeps the average "family dog" comfortable, clean, and neat.

Mrs. Hoyt Discusses Style in Poodles

Style comes nearer to *type* than any other breed characteristic. It is of great importance to the show dog. Unfortunately, like most breed qualities it is a gift from Heaven and your Poodle is born either with it or without it. You cannot make a dog acquire it. At best you or your handler can present the dog with style as if he, not you, possessed it. This in itself is easier with a showy type of dog like the Poodle than with some of the plainer breeds or very heavily built dogs.

The dictionary defines style as "a manner of conduct or action." It further uses the word "elegant," which it defines elsewhere as "choice, superior, tasteful." In a dog, style might be called conduct or action which emphasizes in a superior manner certain *qualities* of type.

For instance, our breed is supposed to move with a "light, springy action," carrying himself "proudly." Therefore the gait of the stylish Poodle is unusually light and springy and his carriage the very essence of pride. Furthermore, he appears to act this way with intent as well as pleasure, as if his purpose was completely enjoyable. Yet the same dog can be shelly or not move soundly, or he may have a wide head and heavy muzzle, but he presents himself and *acts* as a Poodle should, emphasizing this presentation with happy assurance. Such a dog has style and because of this will be quite hard to defeat in the show ring. He is noticeable, he has distinction, he will impress spectators who exclaim, "What class," "How flashy," etc. Even a judge will be forced to give him added attention.

This quality pertains to all breeds. A Bulldog or a Chow can be equally stylish, but not in the *manner* of a Poodle. Their style will emphasize what is peculiar and proper for a Bulldog or a

Overleaf:
Above left: Christmas morning at Rye Top. Mrs. Joseph Longo's famous obedience winners wait for Santa Claus on the stairs. **Above center:** Typical of the high quality Toy Poodles being bred at L'ambre Kennels in Japan is Ch. L'ambre Texas Kid. Mr. and Mrs. Yukichi Fukazawa, owners. **Above right:** This promising Toy Poodle puppy is L'ambre Fire Bird, son of Am., Jap. Ch. Kornel's Keeper of the Kastle, owned by L'ambre Kennels. **Middle left:** Tobyna of Rye Top, U.D., belongs to Mrs. Joseph Longo, Harrison, New York. **Middle center:** Syntifny Tally Ho and Michanda Cachet, by Ch. Hells A Blazen Kinda Kostly ex Ch. Michanda's Pebble of Syntifny, belong to Patricia McMullen, Michanda Poodles, Clio, Michigan. **Middle right:** Topper of Rye Top, U.D. with scent-hurdle dumbbell in his mouth. One of the obedience "stars" owned, trained and handled by Mrs. Joseph Longo who was a leading scent-hurdle dog until his retirement at the age of 11 years. **Below left:** Two of the senior citizens at Dhubne, Ch. Levade's Ambition (right) and Ch. Levade's Audacity talking things over. John Campbell, owner, Bonita, California. **Bottom right:** This is how a Standard Poodle looks entirely clipped down following retirement from a successful ring career. Ch. Cade Freiheit, litter brother to Ch. Cade Uhuru, was bred by Rich and Carol Kestler, and is a champion in America, Canada and Bermuda. A sire of champions, he is still at Dhubne at ten years of age. John Campbell, owner, Bonita, California.

Chow. The former has a decided roll in its gait plus an added willingness, a definite pleasure in rolling along; the latter has an aloof, proud dignity whether still or moving, the stilted gait very decided and full of vigor yet indifferent to the crowd.

Even with people, a stylish man does not resemble a stylish woman though both possess the same quality. They conform to what is appropriate to each, with special grace and assurance.

Therefore style can be said to be a form of appropriate conduct, emphasized but in no way so exaggerated as to be inappropriate, never in any way a caricature, rather unusually tasteful, elegant, and superior.

Because style is so appropriate, in an animal it must be connected with type, but this connection is based on manner and action, not on physical construction. An unsound dog may be stylish, so may a dog lacking type, and by the same token a sound or typey dog may lack style. The latter will win of course because he is honestly correct and excellent, but he will not "sell himself" as easily or as quickly as if he possessed style, that icing on the cake of excellence, that extra distinction, that perfect presentation!

Mrs. Hoyt Discusses Raising A Poodle Champion

Is there anything, you may ask, different about raising a champion from raising a healthy normal dog? Certainly not in the beginning, when all are puppies in the nest; it is then that you select your champion. It is then that you decide if a certain pup is what you hope he is and just how much you can win with him in the future. Not a mere 15 points, you think, that's for a pet or a brood bitch. But for *your* champion dreams come of Best of Breed the first time out, then Groups and Best in Show at Poodle specialties at Eastern and Chicago International, then even at Westminster! Those are the visions dancing in your mind as you observe the litter. You see, *this* dog is different from the average!

What kind of pup is he in the nest? Right from the start he's lively and aggressive, pushing the others away from the milk table, a pup that bounces and wriggles in your hand, that never cringes or cowers when a shadow falls over the nest or a strange scent assails his nostrils. A bold, strong puppy with plenty of room to grow.

There is no refinement about this one right now, not even in a Toy. He has a good coat for a baby, not silky or thin; soft, to be sure, and thick, lots of it, with marcel waves on his back and sides. If he hasn't all of these qualities, health, courage, room to grow, and a good coat, you don't want him as your great show prospect. He must have all these virtues in the very beginning to win, because you won't have the time to acquire these qualities for him; you have so much to do, so very much with even the best to develop the *kind* of champion you want. You cannot afford to do more than just raise him.

At two months of age, still romping with his brothers and sisters, is he different? Indeed he is! He must be if he is to fulfill your dreams. Like the others, his face, feet, and tail have been clipped, revealing that he has dandy feet, thick little pads, long toes which arch right up as he stands and walks. Also, because he holds himself well and because he's very sound, his strong little body looks short and cobby, and he pounces and trots with great decision. Actually he *is* rather cobby, but not so short, however, that he hasn't got a moderately long neck and a well laid

Ch. Bel Tor Bringin Home The Bacon with owner, Mrs. J. A. Mason, at Poodle Club of America Specialty in 1969. Mrs. Fortune Roberts is the judge.

Overleaf: Canadian Obedience Trial Ch. Evan's Sassy Minyonette, Am., Can., Bda. Utility Dog, and Mexican C.D.X. This silver beige bitch was the foundation of the Evanz silver and silver beige Poodles. She is the dam of four champions, granddam of Ch. Evanz Lord Happiness Is. Marilyn Pauley, owner.

BEST OF
WINNERS
WALLKILL
KENNEL CLUB
JULY 1978
DOUGLAS
1978

Ch. Ashwood's Pop Tart, by Ch. Trespetite Carnival Clown ex Ch. Ashwood's Bit O'Bounce. Owned by Betty Mahaffy. Wendell J. Sammet handling.

shoulder. Right now his head looks a bit too big for his body. This is good—there's still room to grow. His muzzle also looks a bit square, but the tiny lips are firm and tight, and he has a strong underjaw with the perfect scissor bite. This is the correct muzzle for a two-month-old baby. In fact his whole head, although not a wide, square head, is most definitely *not* a long, narrow one. It shouldn't be now if it's to be perfect later on. He has a nice arch on his skull cap, which is wide enough to permit a true "bird bump" at the occiput, and he has a definite stop. His rather broad ears are set low, making a frame for the alert dark eyes already glowing with fun, good nature, and intelligence. Little curls are bursting out all over his body, and somehow he catches your eye the moment you look at the litter. Is it because he's such a sturdy, active baby? Or because he's so responsive? The moment you arrive, he drops what he's doing and tries to attract your attention and love.

From this point on, he still will play and wrestle·with his family. But from now on *every day* he spends some time with people, the more the better. If he lives in a house, he visits different rooms and meets different people, some of them from outside his family. He smells new scents, and above all he hears strange noises. But nothing happens suddenly, and whatever happens is pleasant. People talk to him, pet him, reassure him.

If he lives in a kennel, he visits the house, the kitchen, the living room. He learns to walk up stairs, to ride in a car, to enjoy an increasing number of strange people. There's no harsh scolding, no slaps for him, and no *sudden* violent noises, although there is plenty of noise, voices, radio or television, mild banging of pots and pans, clipper machines, a shovel scraping a pavement, etc. Every day for a short time he poses on a table, on a show crate, on the floor. When he stands quiet and steady even for just a second or two, he's praised and given a delicious tidbit. He begins to enjoy this posing, and you want him to, just as you want him to enjoy everything about show business.

Like his brothers and sisters, he's clipped and groomed. But extra time and care are taken with him, just to make him like it. His coat must never get matted or dirty. He gets good food, plenty of play, exercise, lessons that he enjoys, and lots of sleep. All of this amounts to time and attention on your part which he doesn't realize at all. Much more time, much more attention will be spent on this baby as he matures.

About now come short lessons on the lead, given with care, patience, and imagination so that he may even enjoy them. In fact he is scarcely aware that he has learned to be "lead-broken," for nothing is broken; just a light lead which he scarcely notices dangles beside him on the floor while he eats. Then it follows him around the room, and he would like to play with it, but his owner has some tidbits along so he follows the lead and it leads to a tiny snack. Then he leads his owner on the lead. Fun! Then they go together on what seems like an awfully short walk because it is such fun. All the time he just naturally keeps his tail up while on the lead because he likes walking with his owner and also because his owner seems to carry such good things to eat. He keeps looking up in an expectant manner. Once or twice he discovers that the lead *holds him* and he bounces and starts to struggle, but his owner sits down beside him and talks about it. Then they start off again in a different direction and the pup forgets he is held. Now he knows that he is held, but it doesn't matter for he *likes* going on the lead. Of course although he is lead-broken his spirit is not; it has never even been threatened. To him the world is a place of joyous interest and activity with people around to love and please, because they all seem to love him.

Overleaf:
Ch. Kayesett Douglas as a grown dog. Wendell J. Sammet handling for Muriel P. and J. Herbert Kaye.

Now comes another appraisal. Someone who knows is asked to study this puppy on the lead. How does he move? Gaily we know, but soundly, in the correct manner? If the answer is *no*, he becomes a wonderful pet, definitely a champion, but not *your* champion. If the answer is *yes*, some changes come into his life.

Not too suddenly, because his poise and gaity must never be shaken, his lead lessons continue but with strangers often taking the lead—a neighbor, some member of the family, or different kennel employees. Lessons in posing become a bit longer. Strangers handle him, fondle him, examine him. And he thinks it's fun. Pretty soon strangers pose him, "set him up." He learns to pose for them.

Of course every day there is a lot of exercise, plenty of sleep, and some play. But now he plays only with one or two, the gentlest brother or sister, puppies that do not pull coats. His coat is groomed often and with such care; it must never get matted, but also nothing but dead hair must be removed. If it's winter, he gets vitamins, and on dull rainy days he gaits and poses in a room with a sun lamp overhead.

Sometimes he goes to town in the car. He walks on the streets, in the shops when permissible, on a lead. He sees many strangers and hears many sounds. His owner never hurries him, and as his owner seems to take all these adventures for granted and is so calm and so reassuring, the pup feels quite confident about them. Anyway, at first these experiences were not long, and they happened when he felt at his best and liveliest, and then just at the very first an older dog, like his mother, went along, and she, like the human, took everything for granted, so the pup followed suit.

One day the puppy finds himself going in a circle on a lead, then back and forth, followed by posing on his usual outdoor platform, but this time two or three other dogs, not his brothers or sisters, are also walking around this circle on leads held by other people. Quite unalarmed, the pup bounces and pulls to get at them, but he is gently but very definitely halted by voice and lead. It finally dawns on him that they all must walk around one behind the other without trying to reach each other, that they must also pose quietly side by side, and that they must not smell each other or grab. When he finally understands and goes properly without pulling, the puppy is rewarded with much praise and petting, and when he finally poses quietly when set up, he's not only praised, he gets a tidbit.

They do this strange exercise for a number of days, and then one day people sit or stand around this circle, they talk, and sometimes they shout and clap. The pup is puzzled, but he doesn't mind. The other dogs pay no attention, so he soon follows suit. He doesn't know that this is a homemade show ring, but he feels at home in it because he goes there everyday.

Then comes another experience, a rather unpleasant one, but fortunately people he trusts and loves are right there talking to him. He's put in a wire cage and the door is closed. Of course as it *is* a wire cage he can see out, but it isn't as roomy as his stall and no other puppy is in it. So he fusses a bit and bats at the door with his paw. Still, he's been given a big, coarse, juicy bone to chew and his human friends talk to him, so after a day or two he takes the whole thing for granted. In another week this cage turns into a box with only the front made of wire where he can see out, and not very well at that. It's so much darker than the cage, and being healthy and unafraid, the pup yells loudly and scratches

Kamelot's Cracker Jack, by Ch. Acadia's Command Performance ex Kamelot's Kotton Kandy. Owned by Ray and Ginger Scott, handled by Mike Scott.

Overleaf:
Rye Top Thumbelina, U.D., with a score of 199½ out of a possible 200, takes the High Score in Trial award at Springfield, 1980. Mrs. Joseph Longo, trainer, owner, handler.

HIGH SCORE
OBEDIENCE
SPRINGFIELD
KENNEL CLUB
1980
ASHBEY

PEARSALL'S BLACK
MEMORIAL

hard against the door. Still, he has another equally delectable bone, and anyway he was rather tired when they put him in this box as he'd had an extra long, fine run and romp. His human friends are near and they talk to him, so after a brief spell of weeping, he sighs, puts his face down on his bone, and falls asleep. Now every day after exercise he goes into the box for a nap. It begins to smell of him, it's comfortable, with torn-up paper under which he's buried his bone, and he's beginning to like it.

Sometimes he stays there all night, but mostly he still has his stall in which he now sleeps alone, although other puppies, his friends, are next door, as they are when he sleeps in his box. He also goes out alone in his run, but other youngsters, his friends are near.

He's six months old, he's fearless, he is used to being alone, he gaits well on the lead, he likes to be handled, and he has a gorgeous coat. What does he really look like? Frankly, a beautiful Poodle. His head is now in proportion to his strong, cobby body, and it is a lovely head, strong but refined, chiseled, elegant, yet very masculine. He holds himself proudly and every move he makes is filled with vigor and style. He *is* strong and proud. In fact, clipped or unclipped, starting in the six to nine puppy class, he could go with ease up to Winners, even Best of Winners. But that's not the plan. This youngster has to beat the best of the best for Best of Breed.

So one afternoon or evening he finds himself in a strange unusually crowded place with lots of new people and different dogs milling around. He's not exactly afraid, merely curious and puzzled. Of course his favorite, his owner-handler, is with him talking in a cheerful, reassuring manner, and then some of his canine friends are also with him. He goes into a ring; nothing strange about that. He poses regally white a stranger examines him. He moves again, happy, confident, his muscles rippling under his dense and shining coat. Then he stops, poses again to perfection, and his handler gets a ribbon. He has won his first Match Show, but all he notices is that his owner is pleased. This pleases the pup. They go to several of these shows and he does well, but now at home more time is spent on gaiting.

The pup doesn't realize it, but the owner wants to discover this dog's *best* gait. For when

he does, the dog from now on is going to be moved at this exact propitious pace until he automatically assumes it when put on a lead.

The pup also takes time out now from play to learn a new lesson; he considers it a sort of trick. It's not hard because his owner is intelligent as well as patient. Quite soon he learns to stand on a loose lead, tail up and wagging, feet properly under him facing his handler, a bit away from him, head up, eyes alert and sparkling — a lovely picture although puppy doesn't know it.

They do this at the next Match Show, and everybody claps long and loud, almost a new sound. The pup bounces around, puzzled but not frightened, then returns to his pose. The sound, after all, is somewhat familiar.

Now he has some other experiences. He meets, also on a lead, an older dog that is not friendly. The dog bristles and growls and lunges at the puppy. If, startled, the pup cringes or crawls toward the stranger in a placating manner, his owner kneels by him, pets him, speaks

Ch. Crikora Commotion sits proudly in his cup after winning the Non-Sporting Group at Westminster, 1962. Mrs. J. Donald Duncan owned this very famous and beautiful little dog.

Overleaf:
Am., Can. Ch. Dhubne Darth Vader going Best of Breed at the San Diego Poodle Specialty judged by William Fetner. Tim Brazier is handling here for owner, Carroll Ann Irwin, North Hollywood, California.

reassuringly, then poses him. But if the pup growls back or barks, his owner praises him and lets him prance and pull for a moment. He wants this dog to be bold. The pup now meets quite a few unfriendly dogs, but soon he realizes these growls and lunges don't matter, for the dogs can't reach him on their leads, nor can he reach them. He also realizes, however, that he, too, is important; he doesn't need to be humble, he too has rights. He contents himself with a deep, ominous growl, a steady stare, and a very haughty threatening stance.

His owner takes him out in a thunderstorm. They get soaked to the skin, but they have such fun. They play ball, romp, and the pup gets lots of cheer and petting. He learns to *like* thunderstorms. And as well as thunder and lightning, he learns to like flashbulbs. Someone he knows takes flash pictures of him while his owner stands nearby. Nothing much happens except a flash and a piece of liver.

By this time he's coming into a grand adult coat, for he's had the best of food, plenty of rest, and lots of exercise, not just in his run or loose anywhere, but on the open road or a hard, bare field where he follows his owner or other handlers as they pedal a bicycle. All the pup knows is that he feels grand. But his owner knows that *real* exercise not only builds good muscle, it brings about good metabolism, and that is what makes a beautiful dog. Lots of show dogs lack exercise, so they become "poor doers," and eventually this leads to skin and coat trouble. But this youngster is always ready to eat, and he always gets the best. Real beef, some quality cereal, real butter, stewed onions and tomatoes once in awhile, plus an occasional egg and milk. He feels good all the time, and because he's so well and happy, he wants to please as well as play. He's talked to a lot, so he's learned to listen. He knows now when he's done well and when he hasn't. He doesn't want to fail, being

responsive right from the start; and always having personal contact, he longs for human approbation.

Now if he's going to leave home to go to a professional handler, his present owner-handler begins to let others gait, pose, exercise, and feed him. The young dog just barely notices that he sees less and less of his favorite human being. Somehow even when he does see him their relationship has become less intimate. Still, he doesn't mourn because this transition is gradual, and those who now handle him seem awfully nice; they talk to him a lot and pet him, too.

He has always liked people, so he goes right on finding them delightful. And when he does finally leave home, the new handler finds him equally delightful, in fact quite unusually perfect. There is not much to do with this young dog but keep him just the way he is, with those magnificent quarters rounded out with muscle, perfect feet and legs, stunning head, that glorious coat, and manners to burn. "He's a Best in Show right now. Look how responsive he is, how steady. And boy can he move – seems to strike the right gait the moment you put on the lead." So speaks the handler. But the owner says "Wait, let him work with you a bit; remember he's got to defeat much older, more experienced dogs."

If, however, the pup is going to remain at home and be shown by his owner, their relationship becomes increasingly close. They do lots of things together, go everywhere together, see a lot of people together, and the pup, a young dog by now, is delighted to show off his little trick of posing on a loose lead or no lead at all, waiting for people to examine him. This is partly because he and his human friend have grown so close together about everything that he has become hypersensitive in his desire to please. Every sound of that wonderful voice means something to him; his dog friends are forgotten,

Overleaf:
Above: Winning the Stud Dog Class at the Poodle Club of America Specialty Show, 1980, is Ch. Rimskittle Roue La Russe handled by Catherine Pawasarat and owned by Michael Pawasarat, shown in puppy clip at left. Michael Pawasarat, with the corded bitch, Hasting's Ten, owned by Florence Nimick. Center is Ch. Longleat Alimar Raisin Cane, handled by Richard L. Bauer for Alisia Duffy. The judge is Mrs. J. A. Mason. It is interesting to compare the difference in general appearance between the corded coat and the others. **Below:** Hudson Valley Poodle Club's 1980 Specialty was an exciting occasion for this youngster, Ch. Palowen For the Good Times, who finished by going Winners Bitch and Best of Opposite Sex to Best of Variety that day. The judge was Philip A. Lanard, III. The handler, Wendell J. Sammet. Breeders and owners, Mr. and Mrs. Loring Wentzel. "Meg" also was Best Puppy in Show at this event.

BEST OF
OPPOSITE

HUDSON VALLEY
POODLE CLUB

1980

ASHBEY

BEST OF
VARIETY
GILBERT PHOTO

BEST OF
VARIETY
GILBERT PHOTO

354

this man and himself are one, and because he is a dog, this is all he needs. He realizes that just going on the lead and posing make this dear friend happy, and that this happiness has to do with a *kind* of walking; one, two, three, four, and they are in step together, followed by a complete stillness when he poses. It seems somewhat trivial to the young dog, but if this is what his "beloved" desires, he shall have it.

Then one day he finds himself in one of those places crowded with other dogs and people. Of course he doesn't mind, being quite used to this. The only difference is that his wonderful human friend seems a bit tense and anxious. The youngster senses this because he loves him so much. He looks all around, but can't find anything unusual, so he determines to try extra hard to please. Perhaps that will help. How beautifully he gaits, gazing up every now and then at that familiar, well-loved face. "Good boy" says the man, and the pup is relieved as he recognizes a happy tone of voice. There is a subdued murmur around the ring as they gait; the pup doesn't notice much, but it is in a way an approving sound. Yes, things seem more normal. He wags his tail delightedly and poses with an extra regal dignity and stillness. Then his owner drops the lead and steps away as a stranger comes up, feels his tremendous coat and his firm muscles, opens his mouth, and raises a paw. And the young dog never moves, he just wags his tail and gives that unfamiliar hand a tiny kiss.

Once more the almost grown-up puppy and his owner move, first around, then out of the ring, then in again with different dogs. And each time the youngster performs with military precision as well as happiness. Quite honestly he's doing his best and enjoying it.

Then the last time in, a dog as big as himself lunges at him. The youngster raises his magnificent head even higher, his eyes glow dark and cold, and his tail sets very stiff, but he never breaks pace, one, two, three, four, lightly and precisely as his owner wishes it. "Good boy" whispers the human voice, and the pup is doubly pleased, for that *was* a sacrifice.

Now he poses again, once more off the lead, and a storm of applause breaks out all around the ring, but the young dog never moves, head and tail up, eyes on his owner, a glorious statue.

This well balanced and typical silver Miniature bitch is Ch. Sonata's Joy of Chanteclair, owned by Mr. and Mrs. C. F. Clement of the famed Chanteclair Poodles. "Joy" finished her title in six weekends of showing from September 14 to October 31, 1980, with four majors for a total of 16 points. Handled by Paul Edwards, she here is taking her first major, under Al Maurer, at 16 months of age.

Then his owner picks up the lead and they gait as they have been doing together, one, two, three, four, over to that place marked "No. One," where the man keeps on receiving ribbons. This time a current of joy runs between the owner and his dog. The almost grown pup does not quite understand, but his owner seems awfully pleased. He feels a pat, a very special lingering one, on his head, so he gives a little bounce out of sheer happiness and relief. And so does his owner, for he knows now that he has raised a champion!

Mrs. Hoyt Discusses
Refinement versus sexual quality

In dog parlance, there seems to be some confusion between the words "feminine" and "refined," as if the word "refinement" had a sexual connotation. This is incorrect, as there can be a refined male and a refined female, neither of which resembles the other except in their refinement. There can also be a coarse male and a coarse female which display the proper sexual difference, except for their mutual quality of coarseness. According to the dictionary, the word refined means "a fine or pure state, free

Overleaf: **Above:** Ch. Alekai Ouzo, Best of Variety from the classes, Poodle Club of Massachusetts, 1977. Bred and owned by Alekai Poodles of Mrs. Henry J. Kaiser. Sired by Ch. Alekai Oli of Stonehenge ex Ch. Alekai Zoe. Judge Henry Stoecker is making the award to handler, Wendell J. Sammet. **Below:** The fabulously beautiful Miniature bitch, Ch. Merrimar Queen of the Nile, "Cleo" to her many friends, pictured making one of her numerous important wins, this time under judge Martha Jane Ablett. Always handled by Patrick Norwood for owner, Mrs. William H. Ball, "Cleo" has an impressive list of all-breed Best in Show and Specialty Best of Breed wins, and has been Best of Variety at the Poodle Club of America.

from impurities, minutely precise," whereas the word coarse is defined as "inferior or faulty quality, not pure, crude, lacking delicacy of structure." In the dog world, I believe the words "a pure state, minutely precise" can describe a refined animal, and we can also take from the definition of coarse the words "delicacy of structure." For a coarse dog, the words "crude, lacking delicacy of structure" are certainly correct.

Therefore, would a refined dog be feminine or, in dog parlance, bitchy? Not necessarily, for the quality of maleness is not the quality of refinement; it has to do with expression, action, and temperament as does the quality of femaleness, both of which are the result of the hormones: testosterone for males and estrogen for females. For instance, a "doggy bitch" is a female whose structure as concerns the Standard of Perfection would be better for a dog than a bitch, and these physical qualities are often accompanied by an unusually assertive and vigorous disposition. Such a bitch often has a splendid head, but with an expression lacking the tenderness and gentleness of the female. This head often appears on an unusually short-backed, stocky bitch with extra strong bone. In fact, we behold an excellent specimen except that she lacks feminine quality. This bitch is not coarse at all, she is simply rather masculine. She will easily complete her championship but seldom goes further, because the perfect dog, the great dog, must possess sexual *quality* as well as sex.

The "bitchy dog" is her opposite. His head is almost too small and delicate, particularly in regard to skull. His expression is too gentle, his attitude too subservient, while his body and bone, although perfectly sound, are on the delicate, small side. He is, however, a very pretty dog who can and often does complete his championship without going much further. In fact, a coarse dog that is not pretty can have the same lack of sexual quality; one is tempted to say "she" instead of "he" when speaking of him. Both types, whether coarse or fine, lack sexual quality. Against males equally sound, equally beautiful, or equally coarse, the "bitchy" dog appears too feminine.

The reader will notice the words "too feminine" rather than "refined," because refinement is a desirable attribute in both sexes. It is only when the refined animal lacks soundness, substance, and vigor that he or she can be faulted.

In Poodles a coarse head on either sex has too broad and too deep a muzzle which can be "lippy", too wide a skull in proportion to the muzzle, usually a short, strong neck, and unusually heavy bone. It is, in fact, a rather "crude looking" Poodle, yet it may have excellent sexual expression, while lacking in grace, style, and elegance.

What, then, are the ideal sexual expression and attitudes?

The female not only looks but *is* more gentle and yielding. She usually has far more beautiful eyes. The perfect female head is never as massive, frankly never as impressive, as that of a male. On the other hand, the female should gait just as freely as a male and often more gracefully because her bones are smaller and lighter. In long- or dense-coated breeds, the female lacks the density and amount of the male's coat, although her coat can be just as glowing and full enough to be judged perfect.

The male, no matter how gentle the breed, has a bolder, more assertive expression. He appears more alert, more affected by his surroundings and particularly by other dogs. His head, being more massive, although equally refined in proportion is more impressive, his action is usually more vigorous, and when he stands bold and proud, head up, eyes alert for females or competition, one instinctively knows he's a male. There is no tendency to exclaim "Isn't *she* beautiful."

Perhaps one might conclude from this that the perfect male should always surpass the perfect female, but this is not true. If both were truly perfect, each correct representatives of the Poodle breed and of their sex, it would have to be a tie. The female must be more gentle; she is to care for the young, to endure what is blind, demanding, and helpless. The male must be more dramatic and assertive, for he is there to protect and to provide for his family. Furthermore, according to Nature, only the handsomest and boldest males would win the female, thereby improving the race.

The real answer is, of course, that no dog or bitch is perfect, so the prize goes to whichever most truly represents not only the breed but its sex, to whichever one is the most sound, the most typical, and the most refined.

Overleaf:
Above: Ch. Alekai Zeus delivers a kiss to a good friend. **Below:** The handsome silver Miniature, Ch. Hermscrest Challenger, handled by Wendell J. Sammet for Mrs. Frances M. Herms, Irvington, New York.

BEST OF
WINNERS

ASHBEY PHOTO

Richard L. Bauer puts the typey little white Poodle,
Ch. Hell's A Blazen Fagin's Pride through his paces to
win Best of Opposite Sex to Best of Variety,
Westminster 1979. Mrs. A.C. Pearson, owner.

Overleaf:
Above: A Best in Show goes to Ch. Harmo Quick As A Wink, owned by Harmo Kennels, handled by
William J. Trainor. **Below:** Clardon's Peachy Keen, lovely cream Toy Poodle bitch owned by Dave and
June Suttle, Wheat Ridge, Colorado. Bred by Jean Durant, handled by Dave Suttle.

CHAPTER FOURTEEN

Your Poodle As A Show Dog

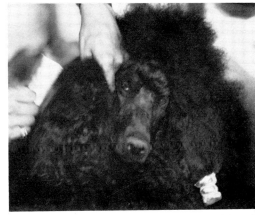

Getting ready for the show ring, Mrs. Edward Solomon's Ch. Dassin Busby Berkley is being groomed prior to judging.

If you have decided to become a Poodle exhibitor, you have accepted a very real and very exciting challenge, for competition in this breed is especially keen, plus the breed is one requiring a great deal of expertise in the clipping, grooming, and presentation of the coat. Mr. Sammet's chapter on the latter should put you off to a good start there. Mrs. Hoyt in "Raising a Poodle Champion" gave sound advice on the selection, rearing, and pre-show preparation of your future "star." Where raising such a dog in the proper way is concerned, Mrs. Hoyt stands as a sterling example of the fact that it can be done, as she has probably made more owner-handled Poodle champions, Group, and Best in Show winners than any other Poodle breeder ever. So you are off to a well-above-average beginning by carefully studying what both she and Mr. Sammet have to say.

The groundwork has been accomplished with the selection of your future show prospect. If it is a puppy you have purchased, we assume that you have gone through all the proper preliminaries to good care, which should be the same if the puppy is a pet or future show dog, with a few added precautions.

Remember that a winning dog must be kept in trim, top condition. You want him neither too fat nor too thin, so do not spoil his figure and his appearance, nor his appetite for proper food, by

allowing children and guests to be constantly feeding him goodies. The best "treat" of all is a small wad of ground raw beef or the packaged "dog goodies." To be avoided are ice cream, cookies, cake, potato chips, candy, and other fattening items which will cause the dog to put on weight. A dog in show condition must never be fat, nor must he be painfully thin to the point that you can feel his ribs fairly sticking through the skin. Poodles have a great fondness for "people food," so be very careful not to spoil your dog's taste for a correct diet.

The importance of temperament and showmanship cannot possibly be overestimated. They have put many a mediocre dog across, while lack of them can ruin the career of an otherwise outstanding specimen. So from the day your dog arrives home, socialize him. Keep him accustomed to being with people and to being handled by people. Encourage your friends and relatives to "go over" him as the judges will in the ring so this will not seem a strange and upsetting experience. Practice showing his "bite" (the manner in which his teeth meet) quickly and deftly. It is quite simple to slip the lips apart with your fingers, and the puppy should be willing to accept this from you or the judge without struggle. Some judges ask the exhibitors to do this themselves—the considerate ones who do not want to risk spreading any

Overleaf:
Above: Gorgeous apricot Miniature bitch, Ch. Tiopepi Amber Tanya in the arms of her handler, Richard L. Bauer, receiving a Non-Sporting Group First at Shawnee Kennel Club, 1978, from judge, Mrs. Winifred Heckman. Mrs. Gardner Cassatt, owner. Below: Ch. Beaujolais' Brenda Starr owned by Beverly A. Valerio, Valley Stream, New York. This lovely apricot Toy, a daughter of Beaujolais' Brown Sienna, was Winners Bitch at Westminster, 1978, handled by Wendell J. Sammet.

WINNERS

THE WESTMINSTER
KENNEL CLUB
FEBRUARY 13-14, 1978

ASHBEY

BEST
OF WINNERS

SOUTH JERSEY
KENNEL CLUB INC
JOE C   OCT 1980

possible infection by taking their hands from mouth to mouth—but the old-fashioned ones still persist in doing the latter, so the dog should be ready for either.

Take your future show dog with you in the car so that he will love riding and not become carsick when he travels; he should associate car rides with pleasure and attention. Take him where it is crowded: downtown, to the shops, anywhere you go that dogs are permitted. Make the expeditions fun for him by frequent petting and words of praise; do not just ignore him as you go about your errands or other business.

Do not overly shelter your future show dog. Instinctively you may want to keep him at home where he is safe from germs or danger. This can be foolish on two counts. To begin with, a dog kept away from other dogs builds up no natural immunity against all the things with which he will come in contact at the dog shows, so it is wiser actually to keep him well up to date on all protective "shots" and then let him become accustomed to being among dogs and dog owners. Also, a dog who never goes among people, to strange places, or among strange dogs may grow up with a timidity of spirit that will cause you real problems as his show career draws near. The very essence of a Poodle is gaiety and joy of life, with head and tail erect, and those are the characteristics you wish him to display when he becomes a show dog.

Keep your Poodle's coat in immaculate condition with daily grooming and baths when necessary. Use a mild baby shampoo or whatever the person who bred your puppy may suggest. Several of the "brand name" products do an excellent job. Be sure to rinse thoroughly; it is a wise precaution to put a drop of castor oil in each eye to assure no soap irritation. Use warm water (be sure it is not uncomfortably hot or chillingly cold) and a good spray. A hair dryer is a "must" for Poodle owners. Use it after first blotting off the excess moisture with a turkish towel. Do not let water find its way into the ear cavity.

A Poodle puppy, whether a future show dog or not, should be trimmed and bathed every six weeks at a minimum for his entire lifetime. If he is to become a show dog, though, as he matures the coat care will become more constant and extensive. For the time being, however, as a pre-show-age puppy, thorough brushing daily is a

Overleaf: **Above:** Am., Can., Ch. Kayesett Barbia Doll, brown Standard, finishing her U.S. title at Tidelands Poodle club Specialty, 1975. Mr. and Mrs. J. Herbert Kaye, owners. **Below:** Freeland's Felicia, by Ch. Manorhill's Classic Touch ex Ch. Sevarre's Chanteclair Figure, owned and bred by Monique Devine, handled by Joseph Vergnetti. Pictured winning her first major, under judge Keke Blumberg.

"Blanche," a Group Winner at Santa Barbara for the second time around. A happy day for Ch. Rimskittle Bartered Bride's owner, Mrs. Margaret Durney. Handler is Tim Brazier.

In the exercise pen prior to being brushed out for the ring is Ch. J.L.C. Critique, owned by Mrs. Rita Cloutier.

Wynwood's Favorite Fella, handled by Jane Kamp Forsyth, making a good win at the Poodle Club of America specialty in 1965.

wise schedule and the best way to avoid possible formation of mats. Toenails also should be watched and trimmed every few weeks. It is important not to allow nails to grow long, as they will ruin the appearance of both the feet and pastern.

Assuming that you will be handling the dog personally, or even if he will be professionally handled, a few moments each day of dog show routine is important. Practice "setting him up" as you have seen the exhibitors do at the shows you've attended, and teach him to hold this position once you have him stacked to your satisfaction. Make the learning period pleasant by being firm but lavish in your praise when he behaves correctly. Teach him to gait at your side at a moderate pace on a loose lead. When you have mastered the basic essentials at home, then hunt out and join a training class for future work. Training classes are sponsored by show-giving clubs in many areas, and their popularity is steadily increasing. If you have no other way of locating one, perhaps your veterinarian would know through some of his clients, but if you are sufficiently aware of the dog show world to want a show dog, you must be personally acquainted with other people who will share information of this type with you.

Accustom your show dog to being in a crate (which you should be doing even if the dog is to be only a pet). He should be kept in the crate at shows "between times" for his own well-being and safety.

A show dog's teeth must be kept clean and free of tartar. Hard dog biscuits can help toward this. But if tartar accumulates, see that it is removed promptly by your veterinarian. Bones are not suitable for show dogs as they tend to damage and wear down the tooth enamel.

If yours is a white Poodle, guard against the hairs on the face becoming stained or discolored. The breeder will advise you about precautionary methods or what to do if it has already occurred. Stained faces are extremely unattractive, and a dog in this condition can never possibly look well-groomed.

Beyond these special considerations, your show prospect will thrive under the same treatment as accorded any other well-cared-for family pet. In fact most of the above is applicable to a pet Poodle as well as to a show Poodle, for what it boils down to is simply keeping the dog at its

Overleaf:
Above: Can. Ch. Sonora's Star in the H'Evanz, silver Toy female, completing her title with her third major. This is the 25th champion sired by Ch. Evanz Lord Happiness Is, and she gained her points entirely owner-handled by Marilyn Pauley, who co-owns with Mrs. Peggy Cooper, Sonora Poodles, Glendale, Arizona. **Below:** The lovely brown Toy Poodle Holly Berry Tea Leaf handled by Gina Rubinich for Mrs. John Berridge. Seaford, Delaware.

Sarnia K·C·

Best Opp. Sex

1980

Stonham Photography

WINNERS
BITCH

GILBERT PHOTO

best. Your Poodle takes great pride in a nice appearance. Just notice the difference in demeanor as well as looks following each bath and trim! Even pets should never be neglected.

Match Shows

Your Poodle's first experience in show ring competition should be in match shows for several reasons. First of all, this type of event is intended as a learning experience for both the dog and the exhibitor. You will not feel embarrassed or out of place no matter how poorly your puppy may behave or how inept are your initial attempts at handling. So take the puppy, go, and the two of you learn the ropes.

Only on rare occasions is it necessary to make match show entries in advance, and even those with a "pre-entry" policy will usually accept them at the door as well. Thus you need not plan several weeks ahead, as is the case with point shows. Also there is a vast difference in the cost, as match show entries only run in the area of two or three dollars, while entry fees for the point shows average between $11.00 and $15.00, an amount none of us needs to waste until we have some idea of how the puppy will behave or how much more "pre-show training" is needed.

Match shows very frequently are judged by professional handlers who, in addition to making the awards, are happy to help new exhibitors with comments and advice on their puppies and their presentation of them. So avail yourself of all these opportunities before heading out to the sophisticated world of the point shows.

Entering Your Poodle At A Dog Show

As previously mentioned, entries for American Kennel Club point shows must be made in advance. This must be done on an official entry blank of the show-giving club. The entry must then be filed either personally or by mail with the show superintendent in time to reach the latter's office prior to the published closing date or filling of the quota. These entries must be made carefully, must be signed by the owner of the dog or the owner's agent (your professional handler), and must be accompanied by the entry fee, otherwise they will not be accepted. Remember it is not when the entry

Ch. Bel Tor Morceau Choisi as a young boy earlier in his career, shown here at a match show. Owner is Mrs. J. A. Mason.

Ch. Nikora of Manapori, a handsome Miniature, handled by Jane Kamp Forsyth.

Overleaf:
Above: Joseph Vergnetti handling Ch. Dassin Debussy for himself and F. C. Dickey to a Group First at Delaware, Ohio, 1978. This magnificent Poodle has distinguished himself as a sire as well as in the show ring, and has made an inestimable contribution to the breed. **Below:** Dorian's Griggswood Image, by Ch. Griggswood Double Entry ex Ch. Torbec Soap Opera, nearing championship in November 1980 at age 11 months. Handled by Doris Grant for Griggswood Poodles, Ormstown, Quebec, under judge, Nigel Aubrey Jones.

Ch. Simone's Storm Warning, by Jeanie's Black Dina-Mite, belongs to Ruth Tymezen. Handled by Todd Patterson.

Ch. Longleat Heir Apparent, owned by Terri Simons. Handled here by Robert S. Forsyth.

leaves your hands that counts, but the date of arrival at its destination. If you are relying on the mails, remember that they are not always reliable where time is concerned these days, so get the entry off well in advance of the deadline.

As a future exhibitor, there is a new book out, written by me, which you will find invaluable in many respects. It is SUCCESSFUL DOG SHOW EXHIBITING, also published by T.F.H. and available wherever the one you are reading was purchased.

A dog must be entered at a dog show in the name of the actual owner at the time of entry closing. If a registered dog has been acquired by a new owner, it must be entered in the name of the new owner in any show for which entries close after the date of acquirement, regardless of whether the new owner has or has not actually received the registration certificate indicating that the dog is recorded in his name. State on the entry form whether or not transfer application has been mailed to the American Kennel Club, and it goes without saying that the latter should be attended to promptly when you purchase a registered dog.

In filling out your entry blank, type, print, or write clearly, paying particular attention to the spelling of names, correct registration numbers, etc. Also be sure to indicate the variety of your Poodle, stating that it is Miniature, Standard, or Toy.

In selecting the class in which to enter your Poodle, take the following into consideration.

The Puppy Class is for dogs or bitches who are six months of age and under 12 months, that were whelped in the U.S.A., and that are not champions. The age of a dog shall be calculated up to and inclusive of the first day of a show. For example, a dog whelped on January 1 is eligible to compete in a Puppy Class at a show the first day of which is July 1 of the same year and may continue to compete in Puppy Classes up to and including a show the first day of December 31 of the same year, but is *not* eligible to compete in a Puppy Class at a show the first day of which is January 1 of the following year.

This is the first class in which you should enter your puppy. In it a certain allowance is made for the fact that they *are* puppies, thus an immature dog or one displaying less than perfect showmanship will be less severely penalized

Overleaf:
Above: And on to win the Best of Breed award! Ch. Peeple's Red Head at the Great Lakes Poodle Club, judge, Tom Stevenson. Joyce Peeples owner, Vernelle Hartman Kendrick handling. **Below:** One of the exciting moments in Poodle history! The stunning white Standard, Ch. Acadia Command Performance, shown winning Best in Show at the 1973 Westminster Kennel Club Show under Mrs. Augustus Riggs. Frank Sabella handled for Edward B. Jenner and Joanne Sering.

A portrait shot of Ch. Donna of Westford Ho, bred and handled by William J. Trainor, owned by Harmo Kennels. Born in 1956, by Ch. Prankster Darius ex Petite Poulette of Westford Ho. A multiple Group and Best in Show winner, Donna had a host of admirers among the judges.

Ch. Sherode Carefree Beau, owned by Emiline Krucker, handled by Wendell J. Sammet. Winners Dog at Farmington Valley Kennel Club, 1971, under judge Miss M. Ruelle Kelchner.

Ch. Donna of Westford Ho, owned by Harmo Kennels, taking Best in Show at Wachusett Kennel Club. This lovely brown Standard bitch is surrounded here by Lester Sawyer, Bill Buckley, handler Bill Trainor, and noted judge Alf LePine.

than, for instance, in Open. Also quite likely others in the class will be suffering from these problems, too. In entering a puppy, be sure to check the classification with care, as some shows divide their Puppy Class into a 6-9 months section and 9-12 months section.

The Novice Class is for dogs six months of age and over, whelped in the United States or Canada, which *prior to* the official closing date for entries, have *not* won three first prizes in the Novice Class; or any first prize at all in the Bred-by Exhibitor, American-bred, or Open Classes; or one or more points towards championship. The provisions for this class are confusing to many people, which is probably the reason it is infrequently used. A dog may win any number of first prizes in the Puppy Class and still retain his eligibility for Novice. He may place second, third, or fourth not only in Novice on an unlimited number of occasions, but in Bred-by Exhibitor, American-bred, and Open as well and still remain eligible for Novice. But he may no longer be shown in Novice when he has won three blue ribbons in that class, or when he has won even one blue ribbon in either Bred-by Exhibitor, American-bred, or Open, or a single championship point.

In determining whether or not a dog is eligible for the Novice Class, keep in mind the fact that previous wins are calculated according to the official published date for closing of the entries, not by the date on which you may actually have made the entry. So if in the interim between the time you made the entry and the official closing date your dog makes a win causing it to become ineligible for Novice, change your class IMMEDIATELY to another for which the Poodle still will be eligible. The Novice Class always seems to have the least entries of any and therefore is a splendid "practice ground" for you and your young Poodle while you both are gaining the "feel" of being in the ring.

Bred-by Exhibitor is for dogs whelped in the United States or, if individually registered in the American Kennel Club Stud Book, for dogs whelped in Canada that are six months of age and older, that are not champions, and that are owned wholly or in part by the person or by the spouse of the person who was the breeder or one of the breeders of record. Dogs entered in this class must be handled in the class by an owner or by a member of the immediate family of the

Ch. Ledahof Silverlaine, photographed in July 1959. By Ch. Touchstone Silversmith ex Ledahof Silhouette, bred by Joan Dalton. Owned by Elizabeth Van Sciver and handled by Wendell J. Sammet.

Ch. Hell's A Blazen Kinda Kostly taking Best in Show from the Open Class to finish his title. Handled here by Lewis Grello for owner, Frances Rubinich. Judging was Robert Wills.

←

Bill Cunningham taking the Non-Sporting Group at Erie Kennel Club, 1977, with Ch. Manorhill's Walkin' N Rhythm, one of the excellent Manorhill Miniatures.

owner. Members of an immediate family for this purpose are husband, wife, father, mother, son, daughter, brother, sister. This is the class which is really the "breeders' showcase" and the one in which breeders should enter with special pride to show off their achievements.

The American-bred Class is for all dogs excepting champions, six months of age or older, that were whelped in the United States by reason of a mating which took place in the United States.

The Open Class is for any dog six months of age or older, and without further restrictions. Dogs with championship points compete in it. Dogs which are already champions can do so, as can dogs which are imported, along, of course, with American-bred dogs. This class is, for some strange reason, the favorite of exhibitors who are "out to win". They rush like sheep to enter their dogs with points in it, under the false impression that by doing so they assure themselves of greater attention from the judges. This really is not so, and it is my feeling that to enter in one of the less competitive classes, with a better chance of winning it and then getting a second chance to gain the judge's approval by returning to the ring in the Winners Class, can often be far more effective strategy.

One does not enter for the Winners Class. One earns the right to compete in it by winning first prize in Puppy, Novice, Bred-by Exhibitor, American-bred, or Open. No dog which has been defeated in one of these classes is eligible to compete in Winners, and every dog which has been a blue ribbon winner in one of them MUST do so. Following the selection of the Winners Dog or the Winners Bitch, the dog or bitch receiving that award leaves the ring. Then the dog or bitch which placed *second* in the class to that one, unless previously beaten by another dog or bitch at this same show, re-enters the ring to compete against the remaining first prize winners for Reserve. The latter award means that the dog or bitch receiving it is standing "in reserve" should, through any technicality when the awards are checked at the American Kennel Club, the one that received Winners be disqualified. In that case the one that placed Reserve is moved up to Winners, at the same time receiving the championship points.

Winners Dog and Winners Bitch are the awards which carry points toward championship with them. These are based on the number of dogs or bitches actually in competition, points scaled one through five, the latter being the greatest number available to any dog or bitch at any one show. Three-, four-, or five-point wins are considered "majors." In order to become a champion a dog or bitch must have won two "majors" under two different judges, plus at least one point from a third judge, and the additional points necessary to bring the total to 15. When your dog has gained 15 points as described above, a Certificate of Championship will be issued to you and your Poodle's name will be published in the *American Kennel Gazette — Pure Bred Dogs,* official publication of the American Kennel Club.

The scale of championship points for each breed is worked out by the American Kennel Club and reviewed annually, at which time the number required in competition may be either changed (raised or lowered) or remain the same. The scale of championship points for all breeds is published annually in the May issue of the *Gazette,* and the current ratings for each breed within that area are published in every show catalogue.

When a dog or a bitch is adjudged Best of Winners, its championship points are, for that show, compiled on the basis of which sex had the greater number of points. If there are two points in dogs and four in bitches and the dog goes Best of Winners, then BOTH the dog and the bitch are awarded an equal number of points, in this case four. Should the Winners Dog or the Winners Bitch also go on to win Best of Breed or Best of Variety (in the case of Poodles), additional points are available on the following basis. If your Poodle dog takes Best of Variety and in so doing defeats additional dogs and bitches that were entered for Best of Breed Competition Only (or "specials" as this is generally referred to), your Poodle by so doing gains extra credit for the number of both dogs and bitches he has defeated in this final award in the variety, plus those for Best of Winners, and the championship points allotted for the day are credited accordingly.

If your dog or bitch takes Best of Opposite Sex after going Winners, points are credited according to the number of the same sex defeated in both the regular classes and "specials" competition. If Best of Winners is also won, then

Ann and Jack Arling own Spin To Win With Escapade, a Miniature handled by Jane Kamp Forsyth, in 1975.

Ch. Dassin Dilly by Dali, a daughter of Ch. Dassin Debussy, winning the points at the Poodle Specialty in Detroit, March 1980. Joe Vergnetti handled for Mrs. Edward Solomon, owner.

Marjoe's Sunkist Guy taking Best of Opposite Sex from Anna K. Nicholas, judge. Linda Pizzonia is handling for owner, Marion E. Dagostaro, Sarasota, Florida.

The lovely Ch. Beaujeau Amity finishing her title in 1975 with Best of Winners under Frank Bilger, Jr., at Del Sur Kennel Club. Barbara Humphries, handler. Mrs. Marjorie A. Tranchin, owner.

whatever additional points for each of these awards are available will be credited. Many a one- or two-point win has grown into a "major" this way.

Moving further along, should your Poodle win its Variety Group from the classes (in other words, if it has taken either Winners Dog or Winners Bitch on the day), you then receive points based on the greatest number awarded to any member of any breed included within that Group during the show's competition. And, should the day's winning also include Best in Show, the same rule of thumb applies, and your Poodle receives the highest number of points awarded to any other dog of any breed at that event.

Best of Breed competition consists of the Winners Dog and the Winners Bitch, which automatically compete on the strength of those awards, plus whatever dogs and bitches have been entered specifically for this class, for which Champions of Record are eligible, Poodles that according to their owner's records have completed the required number of points for a championship rating whether or not they have been officially notified at the time entries closed. Since July, 1980, dogs which according to their owners' records have completed the requirements for a championship after closing of entries for the show, but whose championships are unconfirmed, may be transferred from one of the regular classes to the Best of Variety competition, *provided this transfer is made by the show superintendent or show secretary prior to the start of judging at the show.*

This has proved an extremely popular new rule, as under it a dog can finish on Saturday, then be transferred to "specials" and compete as such on Sunday. Note that word of caution, though. The change *must* be made *prior* to the start of the day's judging, which means to the start of *any* judging at the show, not your individual breed.

Best of Variety winners are *entitled* to compete in the Variety Group which includes them. This is not mandatory, but is a privilege which Poodle exhibitors value. The dogs winning *first* in each Variety Group *must* compete for Best in Show.

Non-regular classes are sometimes included at the all-breed shows and almost invariably at specialty shows. These include Stud Dog Class and Brood Bitch Class, which are judged on the basis of the quality of the two offspring accompanying the sire or dam. The quality of the latter is beside the point; it is the youngsters that count, and the qualities of *both* are to be averaged to decide which sire or dam is the best and most consistent producer. Then there is the Brace Class (which at all-breed shows moves up to Best Brace in each Variety Group and Best Brace in Show), these being judged on the similarity and evenness of appearance of the members of the brace. In other words, the Poodles should look like identical twins in size, color, and conformation and should move together almost as a single dog, one person handling, with precision. The same applies to the team competition, except that four dogs are involved and, if necessary, two handlers.

The Veteran's Class is for the older dogs, usually seven years being the minimum age. This class is judged on the quality of the dogs, as the winner competes in Best of Breed competition and has on a good number of occasions been known to win it. So the point is not to pick out necessarily the *oldest* dog, as some seem to think, but the *best specimen of the breed*, exactly as throughout the regular classes.

Then there are Sweepstakes sponsored by many specialty clubs, sometimes as part of their specialty shows and sometimes as separate events, and Futurity Stakes, of which the same also is true. The difference here is that sweepstakes entries usually include dogs from 6-18 months of age, and entries are made at the usual time as others for that show, while for a Futurity the bitches are nominated when bred and the individual puppies entered at or shortly following their birth.

Pre-Show Preparations for Your Poodle and Yourself

Preparation of the things you will need as a Poodle exhibitor should not be left until the last moment. They should be planned and arranged for at least several days before the show in order for you to relax and be calm as the countdown starts.

The importance of the crate has already been mentioned, and we assume it is already in use. Of equal importance is the grooming table, which we are sure you have already acquired for use at home. You should take it along with you, as your dog will need final touches before enter-

Ch. Alekai Maunalua, bred by Mrs. Henry J. Kaiser and owned by Dorothy Baranowsky, is handled by Wendell J. Sammet at the Ladies Dog Club in 1964. By Alekai Roma ex Ch. Tambourine de la Fontaine. Miss Frances Angela is the judge.

Ch. Black Rogue of Belle Glen wins Best Veteran for Janet and Jim Hobbs at the Poodle Club of America Specialty, June 1970. Robert S. Forsyth handling. Mrs. Rebecca Mason judging.

Going through the rigors of "before-the-show grooming," Can., Mex., Bda. Ch. Elenshar's Little Topper is having the finishing touches attended to by owner, Marilyn Pauley. This dog is a Group Winner from the classes in two countries and the sire of two champions.

Interstate Poodle Club Specialty, 1955. Bob Forsyth with Ch. Alfonco v.d. Goldenen Kette, Best Standard. Howard Tyler with Marguerite Tyson's famed Ch. Blakeen Van Aseltine, best Miniature. Anne Rogers Clark with Ch. Wilbur White Swan, best Toy.

ing the ring. If you do not have one yet, folding tables with rubber tops are made specifically for this purpose and can be purchased at most dog shows from the excellent concession booths to be found there. Then you will need a sturdy tack box (also available at the shows) in which to carry your grooming tools and equipment. The latter should include brushes, comb, scissors, nail clippers, whatever you use for last minute clean up jobs, cotton, swab sticks, first aid equipment, and anything else you are in the habit of using on the dog, such as a leash or two of the type you prefer, some well-cooked and dried out liver or any of the small packaged "dog treats" for use as "bait" in the ring, and elastic for the topknot.

Take a large thermos or cooler of ice, the biggest one you can accommodate, for use by "man and beast." Take a jug of water (there are lightweight, inexpensive ones available at all sporting goods shops) and a water dish. If you plan to feed the dog at the show or will be away more than the one day, bring food from home so that he will have the type to which he is accustomed.

You may or may not have an exercise pen. Personally I think one a *must,* even if you only have the one dog. While the shows do provide ex-pen areas for use of the dogs, these are among the best places to come into contact with any illnesses which may be going the rounds, and I feel that having one of your own for your dog's use is excellent protection. Also it can be used in other ways, such as a place to put the dog to relax other than in the crate and at rest areas or motels when you wish to exercise him during your travels. These, too, are available at the show concession stands and come in a variety of heights and sizes.

For the members of your party, bring along folding chairs unless you all are fond of standing, as these are almost never provided anymore by the clubs. Have your name stamped on them, too, so that in case they stray they can be returned. Bring whatever you and your family enjoy for drinks or snacks in a picnic basket or cooler, as dog show food is expensive, usually not great, and extremely indigestible, it would seem. There are exceptions, but I am speaking generally. See that boots, raincoats, and rain hats are always with you (they should remain permanently in your vehicle if you plan to attend shows regularly), also sweaters, warm coats, and a change of shoes. A smock or big cover-up apron will assure that you remain tidy as you prepare the dog for the ring. Your overnight case should include a small sewing kit for emergency repairs, headache and indigestion remedies, hairspray (for yourself), and any medication you normally use.

In your car you should carry maps of the area where you are headed and, also at all times, an assortment of motel directories. Generally speaking, we have found Holiday Inns to be the nicest about taking dogs. Some Ramadas and some Howard Johnsons do so cheerfully. Best Western generally frowns on pets (not all of them, but enough to make it necessary to check). Some of the smaller chains welcome pets. The majority of privately owned motels do not.

Have everything prepared the night before the show to expedite your departure. Decide upon what you will wear and have it out and ready. If there is any question in your mind, try it on then; don't decide to change when morning comes. Be sure that the dog's identification and your judging program and other show information are in your purse or brief case. If you are taking sandwiches, have them ready. Anything that goes into the car the night before will be one thing less to do in the morning. In planning your outfit, make it something simple that will not detract from your Poodle. If he is black, brown, or dark blue, wear a light color against which he will silhouette attractively. If he is white, cream, apricot, or silver, just the opposite applies, as dark colors will do the most as a background for those shades. If you have several Poodles of different colors, try to select something against which they all will stand out to some extent. I have noted numerous well-dressed Poodle exhibitors who blend the color of their outfit with that of the dog, which certainly looks pretty but which does not really call attention to the *dog* as one should wish to do at this point. Sports clothes always seem to look best at a dog show. What you wear on your feet is important, as many types of floors or slippery wet grass can present a hazard. Make it a rule to wear rubber soles and low or flat heels in the ring for your own protection, especially if you are showing a Standard Poodle with which you may have to move right along smartly.

Your final step in pre-show preparation is to leave yourself plenty of time to reach the show

Getting ready for the show ring, Jane Forsyth puts some final touches on a lovely Standard.

Stepping right out alongside Barbara Humphries. Eng., Am., Mex., C.A.C.I.B. Ch. Montmartre Super Lad illustrates that he is handsome in motion as well as when posed. Mrs. Marjorie A. Tranchin, owner.

The lovely Toy Poodle, Ch. Marjoe's Bit O'Topaz, handled by Linda Pizzonia to a Group Two for owners Marion and Joseph Dagostaro, at the Thronateeska Kennel Club, October 1980.

Ch. Aspen Amorosa taking Best of Winners under Tom Stevenson at the San Diego Poodle Club Specialty. Barbara Humphries handled for Mrs. Marjorie Tranchin, owner.

that morning. Traffic can get extremely heavy at the opening of a dog show in the immediate area, finding parking places can be difficult, and other delays may occur. You'll be in better humor if you can take it in your stride without the strain of watching every second because of shortness of time.

You and Your Poodle Go To The Dog Show

From the moment of your arrival at the dog show until after your Poodle has been judged, keep foremost in your mind the fact that he is your purpose for being there. You will need to be there well in advance of the judging to put last minute touches on your Poodle so that he will enter the ring looking his sparkling best. Every hair must be in place, with no rough edges to your scissoring. Brush out the ears and topknot, putting the elastics carefully in place; then let the dog shake himself vigorously and note carefully if all is perfection. Before doing this, give him a chance to exercise and take care of personal matters. A dog arriving in the ring and immediately using it for an ex-pen hardly makes a fond impression on the judge.

When you reach ringside, request your arm-card from the steward and anchor it firmly into place. Make sure that you are *there* when your class is called. The fact that you have picked up your arm card does not guarantee, as some seem to think, that the judge will wait for you, as it is very unlikely that he will unless you appear within a minute or two. Even though nervous, assume an air of cool, collected calm. Remember that this is a hobby to be enjoyed, so approach it in that state of mind. The dog will do better, too, as his attitude is so quick to reflect our own.

If you make mistakes in presenting the dog, don't worry about it—next time you'll do better. Do not be intimidated by the more expert and experienced exhibitors. After all, once they, too, were newcomers.

Always show your Poodle with an air of pride. An apologetic attitude on the part of an exhibitor does little to help the dog win, so wear an appearance of self-confidence as you set up and gait the dog.

Judging routine starts, usually, when the judge asks that the dogs be gaited in a circle around the ring. During this period the judge is watching each dog as it moves along, noting style, topline, reach and drive, head and tail carriage, all in addition to general balance. During this period, keep your mind and your eye on your dog, moving him at his most becoming gait, keeping your place in line without coming in too close on the exhibitor ahead of you. Always keep your dog on the inside of the circle, between yourself and the judge, so that the judge's view of the dog is unobstructed.

Pose the dog calmly when requested to set up for examination. If you are at the head of the line and several or many dogs are in the class, go all the way to the end of the ring before starting to stack the dog; do not stop half way down and begin setting up. Consideration for others demands that sufficient space be left for the other dogs, too, to be lined up along whatever side the judge has requested, so do not be a hog about it. Also space the Poodles so that the judge will have room in which to make his examination from front, rear and the sides, which means there must be sufficient space between each for the judge to move around among the dogs. Time is important when you are setting up your Poodle, as you want him to look *right* when the judge gets there, so practice for dexterity in front of a full-length mirror at home, trying to accustom yourself to "getting it all together" correctly in the least possible length of time. When you set up your Poodle, you want forelegs well under the dog, feet directly below the elbows, toes turning straight ahead, and hindquarters extended *correctly*, not overdone (stretched too far behind) or with the hindfeet more forward than they should be. Hold the dog's head up with the lead or with your hand at the back inner corner of the lips, and with your left hand support the tail. You want the dog to look short-backed, with head carried proudly on a good length of neck, hindquarters nicely angulated, the front straight and true, and the dog standing firmly up on his feet.

Listen carefully as the judge instructs the manner in which the dog is to be gaited, whether it is straight down and straight back; down the ring, across and back; or in a triangle. The latter has become the most popular pattern with most judges. "In a triangle" means down the outer side of the ring to the first corner, across that end of the ring to the second corner, then back to the judge from that corner using the center of the ring in a diagonal line. When you do this pat-

An unretouched photo of Eng., Am. Ch. Orlaine Fonteyn with eyes only for his handler, Pat Norwood, as he stands so beautifully on the judging table. One of Mrs. William H. Ball's successful Miniatures.

Robert S. Forsyth is keeping Ch. Cappoquin Railsplitter "on his toes" in the ring with the help of tasty bit of liver. "Linc" belongs to Tilo Kennels, Miss Laura Niles.

tern please learn to do it without breaking at each corner to twirl the dog around you, a senseless maneuver we sometimes have noted. Judges like to see the dog moved in an *uninterrupted* triangle, as they get a better idea of the dog's gait.

It is impossible to overemphasize that the gait at which you move your Poodle is tremendously important, and considerable thought and study should be given to the matter. Have someone move the dog for you at home at different speeds so that you can tell which shows him off to best advantage. Your Poodle should travel with a light, springy action with topline firm and head and tail held high. Galloping or racing around the ring is out of character for a Poodle and unbecoming to almost any dog. You want the Poodle moving precisely, easily, and lightly in perfect rhythm.

Do not allow the Poodle to sidetrack, flop, or weave as you gait him, or to pull off so he appears to lean on the lead as you are gaiting him. He should move in a straight line, proudly and firmly. That is your goal as you work with him in preparation for his show career.

In baiting your dog, please do it in a manner that will not upset the other Poodles in the ring or cause problems for their handlers. A tasty morsel of well-cooked and dried out liver is fine for keeping your own dog interested, but discarded on the floor it can throw off the behavior of someone else's dog who will attempt to get it. So, please, if you drop liver on the floor or ground, take it away with you when you have finished.

When the awards have been made, accept yours courteously no matter how you may actually feel about it. To argue with a judge is unthinkable and will not change the decision. So be gracious, congratulate the winners if your dog has been defeated, and try not to show your disappointment. By the same token, please be a gracious winner, too, which sometimes seems to be even more difficult.

Good job well done! "Blanche" (Ch. Rimskittle Bartered Bride) relaxed with a stretch after winning the Non-Sporting Group at the Long Beach Kennel Club Dog Show. Mrs. Margaret Durney, owner. Tim Brazier, handler.

380

An exquisite headstudy of the silver Ch. Trumbull's
Silverella made in January 1967. Photo courtesy of
Wendell J. Sammet.

CHAPTER FIFTEEN

Care, Clipping, and Trimming of the Poodle Coat

by Wendell J. Sammet

Ch. Calvinelle Tipsy Trifle, one of the beautiful little Poodles owned by Mrs. William L. Kendrick, Devon, Pennsylvania.

There are three basic trims recognized by the American Kennel Club: the Puppy trim, the Continental, and the English Saddle. This chapter deals with taking your dog from Puppy trim into his adult clip. (See Figure 1.)

To correctly trim the Poodle, you must first read and understand the American Kennel Club Standard of the Poodle. It describes the picture you are trying to create. The introductory paragraph of the Standard explains it all ". . . a very active, intelligent and elegant looking dog, squarely built, well proportioned, moving soundly and carrying himself proudly. Properly clipped in the traditional fashion, and carefully groomed, the Poodle has about him an air of distinction and dignity peculiar to himself." In addition to an understanding of the Standard, it helps to have an eye for balance and proportion and some basic knowledge of anatomy. The latter is very important. You must know what is structurally correct in order to determine your dog's strengths and weaknesses. (Fig. 2)

Your first step is to assemble some basic grooming equipment. A sturdy grooming table with a non-skid top is a must. This will provide a secure surface that your dog will feel comfortable standing on during long grooming sessions. Have an electric clipper with several sharp blades (#40, #30, and #15) and one or two pairs of sharp scissors which you can hold comfortably. Also on hand should be a slicker brush, a

pin brush, and a comb that has both fine and medium spacing. You are now ready to start the actual grooming process.

Brush your dog thoroughly, making sure he is free of all mats. Bathe him, being sure he is completely clean and rinsed free of soap. Never clip or scissor dirty hair as it dulls your equipment. Clean hair is easier to scissor and gives you a more finished appearance.

Blow dry your dog, be certain the hair is dry to the roots, and then brush through the dog once again. Before you begin to trim, let the dog off the table to exercise and shake. He will be standing in one position for some time, and this little respite will help him to relax.

Have someone set your dog up in a show stance while you observe at a distance. Evaluate the profile, front and rear. Pay special attention to the length of leg, length of back, rear angulation, tail set, and length of neck. All this information (good *and* bad) will help you make a better picture when trimming. Remember, you are trimming to emphasize the good and minimize the bad, and no two dogs are exactly alike.

First clip the front feet. They may be clipped with a #40 or a #30. Not all dogs can be clipped with these close blades. Dogs with particularly sensitive skin may have to be clipped with a #15 even though this will not give you the finished appearance of the surgical blades.

With the dog sitting down facing you, pick up either of his front feet and start clipping. Clip against the hair, up the feet toward the pastern. Clip up to where the pastern *starts* or just below where the dewclaw was or is. The easiest way to clip between the toes is to carefully push the flesh up from underneath with your fingers. Don't forget to clip the hair between the pads on the bottom of the feet. Do the other front foot in the same manner. (Fig. 3)

After you have clipped the front feet, remove all loose clipped hairs from the leg furnishings with a slicker. If these clippings are not removed they will cause matting.

Now to the back feet. Clipping against the grain of the hair and up the foot to the start of the pastern, clip both the back feet in the same manner as the front. (Fig. 4)

After the feet are neatly clipped, do the nails. You have a choice of several instruments to use, so use whichever your dog resists the least. A manual nail clipper (blade type) is the easiest but leaves the nails rough and cracked unless the edges are filed. Always have the "Kwik-Stop" handy in case of bleeding. The electric nail file is very good, but you must have someone to hold the dog so that he will not catch his topknot, ears, or tail in the machine. The electric file is relatively painless and leaves the nails very neat and natural looking, but it has to be used more often. Using an old fashioned "bastard" file is a painless and safe method, though a bit more time consuming. You can purchase one of these files in a hardware store. This is an excellent tool for use on the dog that will not tolerate nail clipping by the usual methods.

After the nails have been done, trim the tail. Clip a small circle around the base of the tail and anus. Placing your clipper less than halfway up the tail and moving toward the base, clip the hair from the tail. Try to leave as much of the tail itself in the pompon as you can, as it will help to support the hair and give that jaunty look so typical of the Poodle. (Fig. 5)

Clip the face with a #40, #30, or #15. Providing the dog's skin will stand it, the more elegant and chiseled the face the closer it should be trimmed. Clip away from the eyes toward the nose, leaving a straight line between the inner corners of the eyes. Avoid clipping TOWARD the eyes or topknot, particularly if you or the dog is inexperienced; should your dog move sud-

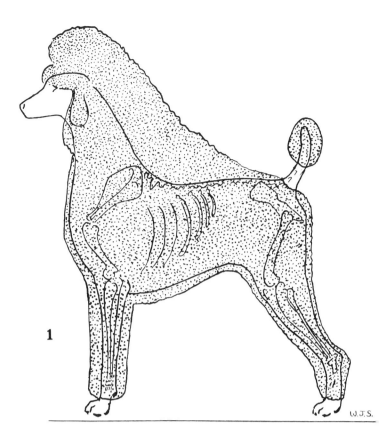

1

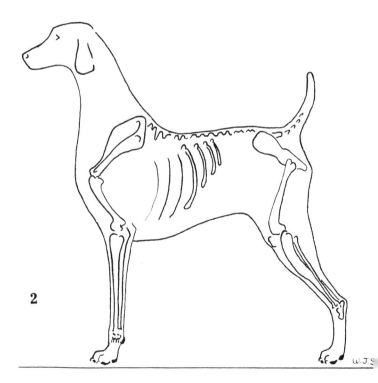

2

These figures are referred to by number within the text of this chapter.

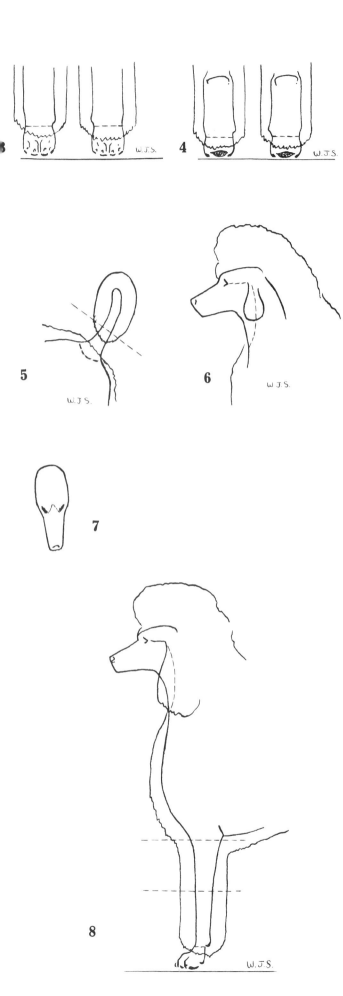

denly the clipper can injure the eye or cut into the topknot.

Clip the sides of the muzzle and the underjaw. To establish the lines of the face, clip in a straight line from slightly under the ear canal opening to the outer corner of the eye. If you are unsure of yourself, lower this line slightly and set a definite line later. After this line is set, clip the cheeks and remaining facial hair up to the lower eye rims. Next clip the throat upward, starting (on a Standard) about 1½ to 2 inches below the Adam's apple. Then clip a *slightly* curved line from the base of the ear canal opening down to the starting point below the Adam's apple. This will form the "necklace." (Fig. 6)

For a finishing touch, go back to your first line set between the inner corners of the eyes. Starting gradually, clip a small, narrow "V" in the forehead, with the vertex pointing toward the back of the skull. This "V" will give a finished appearance to the face as well as emphasizing eye placement and shape. You must gauge the size of the "V" to complement your dog's natural expression. (Fig. 7)

The next step is the placement of the front puffs. Stand so that you are looking at your dog's profile, specifically the front leg and shoulder. Holding your scissors parallel to the ground, scissor a horizontal line in the coat slightly below where the front leg joins the body at the forechest, in a direct line from the elbow. Continue this scissored line around the leg and under the elbow (leaving the hair on the point of the elbow prevents the exposed skin from becoming calloused). Gradually scissor this line horizontally around the leg in a narrow band. This band will serve as one of your guidelines for clipping the front leg. Do not attempt to round off the ruff above the elbow, as you may want to change this line later. (Fig. 8)

Now go to the front of your dog and scissor a similar horizontal line in the coat *slightly less than halfway down the front leg* and well above the pastern joint (on a Standard approximately 1½ to 2 inches above the pastern joint). In the same manner as you did on the elbow, scissor a narrow band on the leg just *above* the line you have made. This will roughly mark the top of the front puff.

Now that your guides are set, clip all the hair from the leg between the two bands, remembering to clip against the hair. Take your slicker and remove all loose clippings from the puff and the bottom of the ruff. You can now do the other leg in the same manner.

Clip the stomach with a #30 or #15. Starting at the navel and working backward, shave the area between the rear legs using the tuck-up as a guide. Now that most of the basic clipping is out of the way, begin the shaping of the front puffs.

About Scissoring

When you scissor, always make sure that the area to be scissored is clean and freshly brushed. Keep in mind that long hair does not naturally stick straight out from the body, but falls down with its own weight. It must be trimmed short enough to give it body while maintaining the fullness of the trim.

Scissoring is as much an instinct as an art. Not everyone can learn to scissor well unless they naturally have that special talent. Everyone has a different style of scissoring that he or she thinks looks best, and practice makes perfect. No matter what the style, the end result should be the same—a well-balanced, finished trim in keeping with the dog.

When scissoring, keep in mind that the dog does not always stand in a show pose. Move the legs in various positions and see how the hair falls. Scissoring is a constant process. Keep combing the area to be scissored, always allowing for the natural movement of the hair. When you scissor the puffs, pick up the foot and shake it, letting the hair fall where it may. Place the foot back on the table in position and scissor again.

Never scissor in one spot too long, as you will distort the proportions. Work over the entire area, constantly shaping a total picture until eventually you get a finished product. Try to visualize that you are working with odd shapes, trying to round the corners and make them smooth and balanced.

When working on the puffs, do not attempt to finish one puff before you start on another. Rough out the first puff, then move to the other puff and rough it out to match. Keep going back and forth in this manner until you have a matching finished product.

The Continental

I will first concentrate on the Continental Clip. This pattern seems to be most popular at this time and does have its advantages. The in-

Ch. Runge's Black Beau. Photo courtesy of Jane and Bob Forsyth.

Ch. Colonel of Westford Ho, bred and handled by William J. Trainor. Owned by Harmo Poodles, Mrs. Anna Boardman.

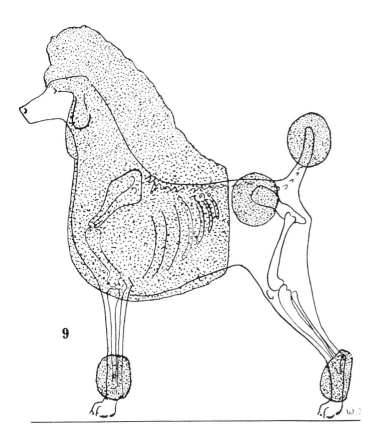

9

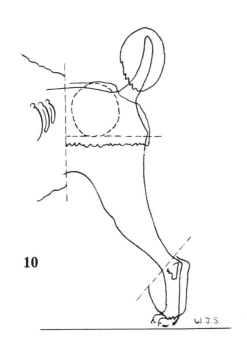

10

dividual owner/exhibitor finds the Continental much easier to scissor and maintain, and most dogs look better in this pattern than in the English Saddle. It takes a real artist to scissor an English Saddle and make the dog look in balance; I am afraid this elegant trim is a thing of the past.

In the Continental, the face, throat, feet, tail, and hindquarters are shaved with optional rosettes left on the hips. Bracelets are left on the hind legs, puffs on the forelegs, and a pompon on the tail. This pattern leaves the legs and rear quarters fully visible, while the body remains in full coat. It is a trim that accentuates soundness and length of back. (Fig. 9)

Trimming the Hindquarters

So far you have clipped the front legs and scissored the puffs. This is basic to both the Continental and the English Saddle. You must now set the lines of the particular pattern on the hindquarters. Again, have someone pose your dog while you observe. Visualize the dog in trim and give yourself a mental picture of where you will locate the ruff.

Facing your dog's profile, begin by scissoring the line of the dog's croup. Even out the hair *slightly* on the top of the croup to give the suggestion of topline. Now locate the last rib with your fingers and continue 2 inches back toward the tail (this applies to a Standard—other varieties will be proportionate). At this point, scissor a line perpendicular to the ground, continuing from the tuck-up on up to the back vertebrae. Do the same on the other side. This will establish the *approximate* border of the ruff.

To set the line of the rear bracelets, scissor a line in the coat a short distance above the ball of the hock. Do not make this a straight line as you did with the front puffs, but slant it slightly downward toward the top of the hock joint in front. Enlarge this line into a band, as you did with the front puffs, to serve as your guideline.

Next, scissor a band in the coat, parallel to the ground, from the start of the ruff at the tuck-up straight across the dog's thigh to just below the point of the rump. Shave between this band and the band above the bracelet, exposing the dog's lower leg and stifle. Before you attempt to shape the rosettes, scissor the remaining hair on the hindquarters *slightly* (to about 2 inches in length on a Standard) to help you define the shape of the dog's quarters. (Fig. 10)

Shaping the Rosettes

Starting at the clipped base of the tail, clip a straight line from the base of the tail between the hip bones to the start of the ruff. This line will divide the two rosettes. On a Standard this line will be approximately the width of a clipper blade and correspondingly smaller on the other varieties. The top of the rosettes should always cover or border on the hip bones.

Using the point of the rump as a reference, imagine a line drawn parallel to the ground from the point of the rump to the ruff. Scissor a band straight across the dog's thigh just slightly below this imaginary line. This line will be the bottom of the rosette. Clip off any hair remaining below this line, thus continuing the shaved line of the lower leg. Once your top and bottom lines have been set, begin to place the rosettes. The rosettes should be centered between the back of the ruff and the point of the rump. Be careful not to place the rosettes too far from the ruff. On a Standard the band between the ruff and the rosette should be about 1½ to 2 inches wide. Using these guidelines, scissor a round rosette in proportion to the dog's size. Be careful not to scissor the rosettes flat. They should have the rounded appearance of a ball. Clip off any hair remaining on the hindquarters around the rosette, and do the other side in the same manner. When placing the rosettes you must also view the dog from the rear to ensure that the rosettes are placed at equal heights. When both rosettes have been scissored, make definite their outline by clipping around them against the grain of the hair. Do the same for the line of the bracelets. Scissor the bracelets as you did the front puffs, giving them a rounded, full appearance. When your scissoring is completed, remember to brush all loose clippings from the dog's ruff and bracelets.

The Tail

The most difficult part of scissoring the tail is in getting the dog to hold his tail up naturally on the table as he would in the ring. Most dogs dislike having their tails worked with, and you will probably have to talk to him and stroke his tail for a few moments until he relaxes and carries it naturally. Being careful not to take too much off, scissor the tail into a neat round pompon in proportion to the dog. Shake the tail occasionally, allowing the hair to fall naturally so that you can trim off any excess.

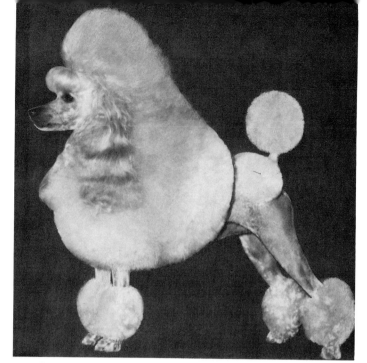

Can. Ch. Murwyb's Golden Guardsman was the sire of seven champions at the time of this writing. Breeder-owner is Mrs. Ruth L. Clarkson, Murwyn Poodles, North Gower, Ontario, Canada.

Am., Can. Ch. Wycliffe Joyous Jacqueline, A Best in Show winner. Bred and owned by Mrs. Jean M. Lyle, Wycliffe, West Vancouver, Canada. Born December 1975, by Am., Can. Ch. Wycliffe Fitzherbert ex Am., Can. Ch. Wycliffe Titania.

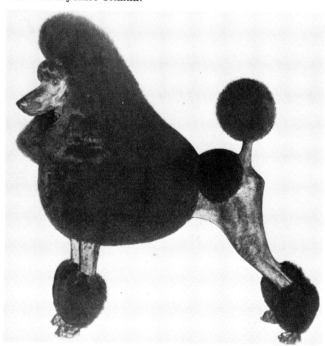

Ch. Rimskittle Roue La Russe, by Rimskittle Mugshot ex Ch. Rimskittle Executant. Bred by Mr. and Mrs. James Edward Clark, owned by Michael Pawasarat, Hastings Farm, Richland Pennsylvania.

This lovely black Miniature bitch is Ch. Merrimar Bathsheba, owned by Mrs. William H. Ball and handled by Patrick Norwood.

Scissoring the Ruff

Brush the entire ruff thoroughly. At this point your dog will have been standing in position quite some time and will, I'm sure, be very happy to lie down and be brushed! After the brushing, allow him off the table to exercise and shake before you resume trimming.

Put the dog's topknot up exactly as you would for show (elastics only—don't spray it). In this way you can estimate the height of the crest when "done up" and scissor the ruff accordingly.

Have someone set your dog up in show pose; look at the ruff and estimate how much hair will have to be removed and where it will have to be removed in order to achieve the correct balance. At the same time examine what you have already scissored and clipped. Make sure the puffs, bracelets, rosettes, and tail look neat and tidy and in balance with the dog. If you find you have taken off too much don't worry. It will grow back, and you can correct your mistakes the next time.

Note the placement of the back of the ruff. Will the ruff appear balanced when scissored to this line, or will it be too far back? In prime condition, the ruff should appear neat and full. Naturally a dog coming out of Puppy trim will not have the amount of coat an older dog would have, but you must visualize his adult coat when you set the lines of the ruff.

When scissoring the ruff you will be constantly rounding it, blending in any "corners" or definite lines that will ruin its contour. Between the front legs the hair should be scissored evenly in line with the elbows, moving up to smoothly rounded shoulders and bib. Do not scissor the bib flat; give it some fullness over the chest. you must also be careful not to remove too much hair from the front at the elbow until you see your dog move. You may want that hair there to compensate for faults in movement.

On the sides, fluff the hair upward with your hands and see how it falls. Without making the ruff appear flat and two-dimensional, remove any excess hair that will flop and "roll" when your dog moves.

The topline should be scissored in accordance with the length of your dog's neck. Ideally the topline should form a diagonal line from the back of the ruff to the top of the crest. However, for a dog lacking in neck you may want to round off the topline slightly over the last ribs in order to give the crest the appearance of more height. Keep in mind always that you want your dog to look elegant and squarely built.

After scissoring on the ruff, have someone move the dog so you can view his movement from the front, rear, and side. Any excess hair that interferes with his movement should be removed.

After scissoring the ruff neatly, you will probably find you will have to scissor the topknot and ears so they do not look thin and untidy.

The English Saddle

The procedure for the English Saddle is very similar to the Continental, except, of course, for the hindquarters. Follow the basic trimming outlined up to and including scissoring the front cuffs. (Fig. 11)

The Hindquarters

Face your dog's profile and scissor a narrow band in the coat above the hock joint on the rear leg, identifying the bracelet in the same manner as has been previously described.

Again, as has been described, locate the start of the ruff approximately two inches back from the last rib and scissor a narrow line defining it. Once you have defined the line of the ruff, round off the back of the ruff slightly in order to facilitate scissoring the pack.

Once the line of the ruff is set you may place the kidney patches. Looking at your dog's profile, scissor a half circle approximately the size of half an orange into the side of the pack (this guideline applies to a Standard). The patch should be placed at equal distances from the back vertebrae and the tuck-up, with the straight side of the half circle bordering the start of the ruff. When you have the patch properly placed on both sides, shave it in. You will probably want to enlarge it later, but for now don't attempt to make it too big.

Placement of the Bands

Before attempting to place the bands, scissor the remaining hair on the legs above the bottom bracelet to a length of about 3 inches. Removing this excess will make it much easier to place the bands.

Before you can scissor the actual pack you must place the band between the pack and the middle bracelet. Where this band is placed will depend directly on the dog's angulation and length of leg. (Fig. 12)

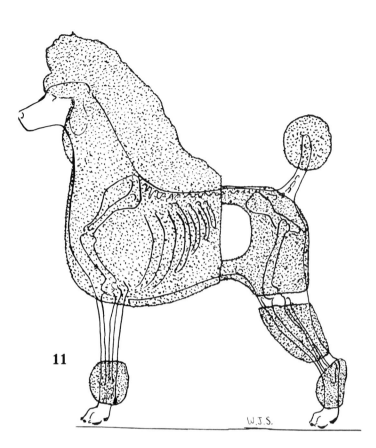

11

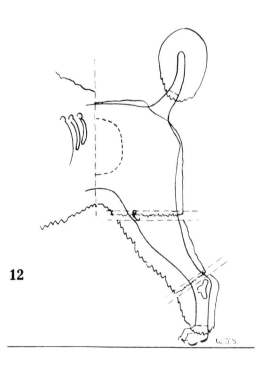

12

Ch. Midcrest Tradewind, owned by Celeste H. Masters and handled by Wendell J. Sammet, winning the Non-Sporting Group at Durham Kennel Club, 1967, under Mr. Heyward Hartley. By Ch. Lawson's High Flyer ex Ch. Miscrest the Camco.

Ch. Braeval Montmartre Sparkle, black Miniature male, sire of two champions including Ch. Beaujeau Hot Chocolate. Mrs. Marjorie A. Tranchin, owner.

First locate the patella (stifle joint). As a rule, the band is placed directly at or slightly above this joint. Again, it will depend on the individual dog. Once you have located the patella, scissor a line parallel to the ground directly across the dog's thigh. When you clip in the final placement, incline this band *slightly* upward toward the rear to emphasize angulation.

Stand back and view your dog's profile, keeping in mind that the size of the middle bracelet must be in proportion to the rest of the pack. If you are happy with the placement of the bands, clip them in. If you are at all unsure, visualize the bands placed at different heights until you are sure the placement is correct. With Miniatures and Toys the width of the two bands will almost always be equal, but because of the greater length of leg on a Standard, the band directly above the bracelet can be made quite a bit wider than the upper band in order to keep the middle bracelet in proportion.

You are now ready to scissor the "pack." Remember that the breed Standard designates a "short blanket of hair." Overloading the pack with hair will drag your dog down, making him look "dumpy" and low on leg.

The pack should appear smooth and plush, largely following the contours of the dog's hindquarters. The topline should be scissored dead level from croup to ruff, with the edges gradually rounded off to blend into the sides of the pack. The line of the dog's croup should be scissored at an angle that places the tail in a one o'clock position. The English Saddle is ideal for correcting faults in these areas; even if your dog's topline and tail-set are not ideal, the pack can be scissored to make them appear that way.

Keep fluffing the pack with your comb until all the excess hair is scissored off and you have a smooth blanket of hair with all the edges neatly rounded. Do not work in any one area for too long; rather view the pack from all angles and scissor the overall picture. When the pack is scissored to your satisfaction, stand back and view it, paying particular attention to the size of the kidney patches in relation to the trim. Change the size if necessary; when they are in proportion, scissor the edges until they blend neatly into the pack.

Move now to the bottom bracelet. Rough it into the approximate size and shape you wish, but do not finish it. Instead, begin work on the middle bracelet. By going back and forth between the two, it will be easier to keep them in proportion.

Any faults in angulation that your dog has can be compensated for by properly trimming the middle bracelet. As a rule, you will take more hair off the back of the bracelet than the front. In other words, the leg itself will not necessarily be at the center of this bracelet as it is in the front puffs and bottom bracelets. It depends entirely on the amount of natural angulation your dog has and how he uses it.

Scissor this bracelet carefully, keeping it in proportion to the bottom bracelet. Step back frequently and view your work from a distance to make sure that you are complementing the dog's angulation and not making him appear out of balance.

When you have roughed in the approximate size and shape of the middle bracelet, go back and finish the bottom bracelet.

Before you return to the middle bracelet, observe your dog while someone moves him. Observe the balance and proportion of the trim. Make note of any weaknesses that can be corrected by trimming. With this picture in mind, finish off the bracelets and pack.

Completing the Trim

Scissor the ruff in the same manner as described for the Continental. With the English Saddle, however, you may find that you will have to leave more hair on the ruff to keep it in balance with the blanket of hair on the hindquarters.

Make the ruff look rounded and full with all excess hair neatly trimmed. When you have finished the ruff, view your dog from a distance. You may have to change the placement of the ruff or take more hair off the pack or bracelets in order to achieve the desired balance. The entire trim should be in proportion, with the pack emphasizing the contours of the dog's body.

In Conclusion

If you are inexperienced, it is a good idea to put your dog in pattern at least two months prior to showing. This will give you time to correct any mistakes you have made in scissoring or clipping.

As your dog matures you will have to change the lines of the trim also. While the basic outlines of the traditional trims never change,

each person's interpretation is different. You will also find that each dog is different, requiring different lines and lengths to make them look their best.

You now have the basics of trimming. What you do with them is up to you. Never be discouraged with your first efforts; the more you scissor the more you will improve. Each person has their own style of trimming, and you will find that styles change with the times. Poodles of even ten years ago would look out of place in the ring today. By practice and observation you will be able to achieve and perfect your *own* style. May you never complete the perfect trim, because then you will have no goal to work for!

The lovely corded Poodle has been attracting considerable attention, being the first with corded coat to compete in the show ring during recent times. She is Hasting's Ten, owned by Florence Nimick of Ligonier, Pennsylvania, bred by Catherine Pawasarat, and sired by Ch. Rimskittle Roue La Russe ex Rimskittle Wineglass Sage. Michael Pawasarat handling.

Ch. Dassin Disco Fever finished in 1978. Handled by "Bud" Dickey for Mrs. Edward Solomon.

Harmo Kennels famed winning Toy, Ch. Harmo Quick As A Wink, made a big record in keenest competition. Handled by William F. Trainor.

Showing what it is that helps her hold her own against the more frequently seen clipped Poodles, Hasting's Ten is moving right out with the excellent reach and drive Poodle experts admire. Bred by Catherine Pawasarat, handled by Michael Pawasarat, owned by Florence Nimick, this bitch has Group placements to her credit. An excellent corded Poodle coat.

Ch. Suntaug Silver Ballet, a Standard dog bred and owned by Mrs. Elizabeth P. Davis and handled by Wendell J. Sammet. By Forzanda Captain Silver ex Ch. Eslar Silver Ki-Ora, March 1961. Madeline Beggs is the judge shown in this picture.

Some typical and adorable puppies of the Deryabar
Kennels, Mr. and Mrs. Royal Peterson, Greenwich,
Connecticut.

CHAPTER SIXTEEN

The Poodle Puppy

The Toy Poodle Ch. Lochmanor's Silver Lace at six months of age. Best Puppy at the Greenspring Poodle Club Specialty. V. Jean Craft owner. Regence Poodles, Vienna, Virginia.

Selecting Your Poodle

Once you have decided that a Poodle is the breed of dog you wish to own, the next step is to prepare yourself to make an intelligent, sensible purchase of one. For, as with any breed of dog, your pleasure and satisfaction as a Poodle owner will be largely dependent on the care, forethought, and time you have put into making your selection.

Even if you wish the dog purely for companionship, to become a family member, with no thoughts of breeding or showing in the future, it is not wise to just rush out and buy. You want to assure yourself of a healthy, properly raised puppy or adult from sturdy, well-bred stock, as this is the only way you can be reasonably certain of a trouble-free future for the dog. The background and early care behind your pet, as well as behind your brood bitch or show dog, will reflect in his or her future health and temperament. The purchase of a dog is a major purchase and one of importance, since with sensible care from you and barring accidents, this dog should share your home for at least a dozen years. So do not buy on impulse and do not buy in haste.

Throughout the pages of this book you have seen the names and locations of many well-

known and well-established kennels in various areas. The address of the American Kennel Club is 51 Madison Avenue, New York, New York 10010; from them you can obtain a list of recognized Poodle breeders in the vicinity of where you live. I cannot too strongly urge you to heed this advice and to follow one of these paths when you start out to purchase your new dog.

Even if you are not looking for a show dog, it is a good idea to see some prior to making your purchase, as in that way you will acquaint yourself with what is considered correct and beautiful within this breed. A Poodle puppy should be active and sturdy, with bright eyes and intelligent expression, friendly and alert, neither hyperactive nor dull and listless. His coat should be clean, soft, and thick. The premises on which he was raised should look tidy and be clean-smelling, making it obvious that the puppies and their surroundings are in capable and particular hands.

Your first step in searching out your puppy is to make appointments at Poodle kennels and inspect the dogs there if there are some nearby (which, considering the popularity of Poodles, almost certainly there will be). If several are in your area, try to visit them all before making your final choice. If there are not any Poodle kennels within a reasonable distance of you, or if you are not pleased with what you see, do not hesitate to contact others at a distance and purchase from them if they have what seems more suitable. Shipping dogs is a regular practice nowadays. A recognized, well-known breeder wants you to be satisfied, thus he will represent the puppy fairly. Should you not be pleased with it upon arrival, certainly a breeder such as I have described will allow its return. A breeder of conscience wants dogs placed where they will bring pleasure, for the sake of both the dog's future and his kennel's reputation.

If your puppy is to be a pet or "family dog," I feel the earlier the age at which it joins your household the better. Puppies are weaned and ready to start out on their own, under care of a sensible new owner, from about six weeks old, and if you take a young one it is often easier to train it to the routine of your household and your requirements than in the case of an older dog which, even though still a puppy, may already be started with habits you will find difficult to change. The younger the puppy usually the less costly, too, as it stands to reason the breeder will not have as much expense invested in it. Obviously, a puppy that has been raised to five or six months old represents a greater expenditure on the breeder's part than one sold earlier and therefore should be priced accordingly.

A word of caution here. Even if you are buying just a pet, do not look for a "cheap" puppy. "Bargain" puppies, cheaply raised purely for sale and profit, can and often do lead to great heartache, with problems and veterinarian expenses which might well have been avoided by paying a more realistic price in the first place. In dogs, as in most other things, one seldom gets more than one pays for. On such a long-range an investment as this, the all-important goal should be to purchase a dog that has been properly reared from well-conditioned, well-cared-for parents and thus has the odds in its favor of being off to a good start in life. One more word on the subject of pets. Bitches make a fine choice for this purpose as they are usually quieter and gentler than the males, easier to housetrain, and more affectionate. If you do select a bitch and have no intention of breeding or showing her, by all means have her spayed for her sake and for yours. The **advantages** to the owner include avoiding the

Standard Poodle puppies just being weaned. This photo is from Alisia Duffy.

Am., Can., Mex., C.A.C.I.B. Ch. Beaujeau My Gosh, still in puppy clip in this 1968 photo, This black Miniature male became a Best in Show winner and the sire of five champions for his owner, Mrs. Marjorie A. Tranchin.

Can anything possibly be more appealing than a Poodle puppy? This one comes from Mrs. Ruth L. Clarkson, Murwyn Poodles.

Mandy loves shopping, especially when she can ride atop the shopping bag. A Murwyn-bred puppy from Mrs. Ruth L. Clarkson's kennel.

Alisia Duffy sent us this picture of a beautiful nine-week-old Standard litter by Ch. Longleat Ruffian and Ch. Rimskittle Roue La Russe.

nuisance of periodic "in season" times which normally occur twice yearly, with the accompanying eager canine swains stampeding your premises in an effort to get to the interesting one, plus, particularly with the Standards due to their size, the unavoidable messiness and spotting at this time, which can be trying if she is a household companion in the habit of sharing your sofa or bed. As for the bitch, she benefits as she grows older from having been spayed, this simple operation almost entirely eliminating the possibility of breast cancer ever occurring. I personally believe that all bitches should be spayed, even those used for show and breeding, when their careers have ended in order that they may enjoy a happier, healthier old age.

Everything we have said about careful selection of your pet puppy and the place where it is purchased applies, but in this case with many further considerations, when you start out to buy a show dog or foundation stock for a kennel you are planning.

Now is the time for "in depth" study. Your first step is to learn everything you possibly can about the Poodle as a breed and about what is considered desirable in a member of this breed for show purposes. For starters, study every word and every picture in this book. The Standard of Perfection now has become your guide, and you must learn not only the words but how to interpret them and how they are applicable to actual dogs before you are equipped to make an intelligent purchase of a show dog.

If you are looking for a show dog, obviously you must have learned about dog shows and must be in the habit of attending them. Fine. Now is the time for you to increase this activity by attending every single dog show within a reasonable distance from your home. Much can be learned about the Poodle at ringside at these events. Talk with the breeders who are exhibiting. Study the dogs who are present. Watch the judging thoughtfully, concentrating seriously on what is taking place and endeavoring to follow the reasons for each award. Note carefully the attributes of the dogs that win and, for your later use, the manner in which they are handled or presented. Close your ears to the ringside "know it alls," usually owners of only a dog or two and very new to the Fancy who have only derogatory remarks to make about each and everything that happens in the ring. This is the type of exhibitor who "comes and goes" through the Fancy and is never satisfied, refusing to realize that their own knowledge is of necessity limited through lack of experience. You, as a fancier whom we hope will last and enjoy Poodles, need to develop independent thinking at this stage and learn to draw your own conclusions about the merits, or lack of them, of the various contenders in order to sharpen your own judgment and prepare yourself to make selections wisely for yourself.

Watch carefully which breeders are campaigning winning dogs, not just an occasional good one, but bringing out homebred winners consistently. It is from one of these people that you would be wise to purchase your future "star."

If you are located in an area where only occasional dog shows take place or where there are long distances involved in getting to them, you will need to find another testing ground for your ability to select a worthy show dog. Hopefully there are some good Poodle kennels easily available. By all means ask permission to visit these, and do so when it is granted—not necessarily to buy, as they may not have what you want for sale right then, but to see the type of dog being raised there and to discuss the dogs with the breeder. Every time you do this, you add to your knowledge. Should one of these kennels you visit have dogs you consider to be truly excellent, you perhaps could reserve a puppy from a coming litter. This is frequently done, and it is often worth waiting unless you have seen something immediately available with which you are truly impressed.

We have already discussed how to approach buying a puppy from department stores or other commercial dealers. Obviously this applies in a far greater degree when the purchase involved is a future show dog. You are in for almost certain disappointment and financial loss if you do not heed these words. The only place at which to purchase a future show dog, especially if you are a novice in the breed, is from a respected and successful breeder, someone who loves Poodles, is dedicated to the breed, and really cares about the dogs as such, not just as a means of quick commercial profit. To such a breeder, the welfare and future of Poodles and of the stock raised in his or her kennel are the all-important things. The reputation for integrity is priceless to such breeders, who almost certainly dedicate a

A Standard puppy with a bright future, Bel Tor Bringin' Home The Bacon at the start of a highly successful career, June 1967. Owner-handled by Mrs. J. A. Mason.

large part of their life to the production of quality Poodles and to their welfare in the world. They consider it essential that their dogs be placed where they will be appreciated, give satisfaction, and have the opportunity to fulfill their highest potential. Such a breeder selling a show dog is every bit as anxious as the buyer for the dog to succeed and will represent the dog to you with truth and honesty. Also, such a breeder does not lose interest the minute a dog leaves the home kennel, but will be right there ready to assist you with beneficial advice and suggestions based on years of experience should it be needed. This type of breeder does not just want to make a sale. A satisfield customer and the bright future of the dog matter far more!

Another point for your consideration is the fact that active show and breeding kennels obviously cannot keep them all. Fine young stock, therefore, usually is readily available which the owner is pleased to sell to the right type of prospective exhibitor.

If there is no such breeder within visiting range or with whom you have become acquainted at dog shows, again do not hesitate to contact one that has been recommended and purchase long distance. Ask for pictures, pedigrees, and a complete description. Heed the breeder's recommendations on what seems most suitable after you have outlined your requirements and ambitions, and be perfectly honest when you state the latter. Do you want a dog with which to just win a few ribbons? Do you want a dog that can complete its championship? Have you the serious campaigning of a dog in mind, with Best of Variety, Non-Sporting Groups, and possibly even Best in Show as your ambition? Consider it all carefully in advance, then *honestly* discuss your plans or write about them with the breeder, as it is only fair. You will be better satisfied with the results if you paint a clear picture of your expectations from the dog.

As you make inquiries of at least several kennels noted for quality show dogs, keep the following facts in mind. Show prospect puppies are less expensive, sometimes considerably so, than fully mature show dogs, the latter often running into four figures and always costing close to $1,000.00. The reason is that with a puppy there is an element of chance, the possibility that it may develop unexpected faults as it matures, failing to develop the excellence

This very pretty apricot Miniature puppy is Can. Ch. Brigalon's Copper Link. He belongs to Mrs. Patricia Palmer.

and quality that earlier had seemed probable. There definitely is a risk factor when one wishing a future show dog chooses a puppy. Sometimes all goes well, but sometimes not, where the eventual matured quality is concerned. So reflect on this as you consider available puppies and young adults, as you might well decide it would be wiser to go for an older dog.

Although initially more expensive, a grown show dog in the long run can be your better bargain. Here you see exactly what you are getting, a dog standing fully matured before you that because it *is* fully matured is not liable to suddenly develop problems or become less excellent, beyond possible changes in coat or condition which are your responsibility to preserve. Another advantage in buying a mature show dog, particularly for a novice fancier, is that a dog of this quality that is already grown is almost certainly trained for the ring, a decided advantage if this is to be your first venture into this area.

Frequently it is possible to purchase a beautiful dog that has completed its championship but which, due to similarity in bloodlines, is not essential to the kennel's breeding program. Here you have the opportunity of owning a champion, usually in the two- to five-year-old range, which you can enjoy campaigning as a "special" (i.e., for Best of Variety competition) and which will be a settled, handsome Poodle that you and your family can own with pride.

If your dog is to be campaigned by a professional handler, by all means let the handler help you locate and select a good dog. Through their numerous clients, handlers have access to a variety of interesting show prospects, and the usual arrangement is that the handler re-sells the dog to you for what his cost has been with the understanding that the dog be campaigned by him for you throughout its career.

If the foundation for a future kennel is what you are planning, concentrate on the acquisition of one or two really excellent bitches. These need not necessarily be top show-quality bitches, but should represent the finest Poodle bloodlines and be noted for producing quality Poodles generation after generation.

A proven matron which already is the dam of show-type puppies is, of course, the ideal answer, but such dogs are also usually difficult to obtain as no one is anxious to part with so valuable an asset. You just might strike it lucky, though, in which case you are off to a flying start. If you cannot find such a matron available, select a young bitch of finest background from Top Producing parents which is herself of decent type, free of obvious faults, and of good substance and quality.

Great attention should be paid to the pedigree of the bitch from which you intend to breed. If not already known to you, try to see the sire and dam. It is generally agreed that someone starting with a breed should concentrate on a fine collection of top-flight bitches and raise a few litters before considering keeping one's own stud dog. The practice of buying a stud and then breeding everything you own or acquire to that dog does not always work out. It is better to take advantage of the many famous Top Producing sires that are available for use at stud, representing all of the leading strains, carefully selecting in each case the one that in type and pedigree seems most compatible to each of your bitches, at least for your first several litters.

In summation, if you want a "family dog" as a companion, it is best to buy it young and raise it to the habits of your household. If you are buying a show dog, the more mature it is the more certain you can be of its future. If you are buying foundation stock for a breeding program, bitches are better, but they must be from the finest *producing* bloodlines.

Prices for pet-grade Poodle puppies range from about $250.00 to $350.00 for a Standard, perhaps about $50.00 less for Miniatures and Toys. Show puppies in all three varieties start around $500.00 at three months old and increase about $100.00 a month as the puppy matures. A grown show dog can run from $1,000.00 on up, depending on its future potential for "specials" winning. There is little difference in price between dog and bitch puppies, if any. A proven brood matron would certainly run over $500.00.

When you buy a pure-bred dog that you are told is eligible for registration with the American Kennel Club, you are entitled to receive from the seller an application form that will enable you to register your dog. If the seller cannot give you the application, you should demand and receive an identification of your dog consisting of the breed, the registered names and numbers of the sire and dam, the name of the breeder and

Meal time! Poodle puppies at the Kayesett Kennels of Muriel and Herbert Kaye.

Ch. Kamelot's Feature Forecast, by Ch. Acadia Command Performance ex Kamelot's Kotton Kandy. Owned and handled by Donald Sturz, Jr., Huntington, Long Island, New York.

An adorable ball of fluff, this tiny Poodle is a daughter of Ch. Wilmar Howlene Stone Broke and belongs to Beverly Merritt.

A lovely Standard puppy, Kaeley Duke Thomas, in 1971 with handler Bob Forsyth, being judged by Edith Hellerman.

your dog's date of birth. If the litter of which your dog is a part has been recorded with the American Kennel Club, then the litter number is sufficient identification.

Do not be misled by promises of "papers" later on. Demand a registration application form or proper identification as described above. If neither is supplied, do not buy the dog. So warns the American Kennel Club, and this is especially important in the purchase of show or breeding stock.

Advance Preparation For Your Poodle Puppy's Arrival

The moment your decision has been reached that you will be the new owner of a Poodle puppy is not one second too soon to start planning. The new family member and you will both find the transition easier if your home is geared in advance for his arrival.

First things to be prepared are a bed for the puppy and a place where you can pen him up for rest periods. I am a firm believer that every dog should have a crate of its own right from the very beginning so that he will come to know and love it as a haven. It is an ideal arrangement, for when you want him to be free the crate stays open. At other times you can securely latch it and know that the puppy is safe and out of mischief. If you travel with him, his crate comes along in the car, and of course in traveling by plane there is no alternative to a crate or, in the case of a Toy Poodle accompanying you on the flight, possibly a carrier alongside you or under your seat. If you show the dog, you will want him upon occasion to be in a crate a good deal of the day. So from every consideration, a crate is a very sensible and sound investment in your puppy's future safety and happiness and your own peace of mind.

The crates I recommend are the wooden ones with removable side panels, which are ideal in cold weather (with the panels in place keeping out drafts) and in hot weather (with the panels removed allowing better air circulation). Wire crates are alright in the summer but give no protection from cold or drafts. Aluminum crates I intensely dislike due to the manner in which aluminum reflects surrounding temperatures. If it is cold, so is the metal of the crate; if the weather is hot, so is the cage. For this reason I consider them neither comfortable nor safe.

When you choose the puppy's crate, be certain that it is roomy enough not to be outgrown. He should have sufficient height to stand up in it as a mature dog and sufficient area to stretch out full length when relaxed. When the puppy is young give him first shredded newspapers, then a mat or turkish towels as a bed. Carpet remnants are great for the bottom of the crate, as they are inexpensive and in case of accidents can be quite easily replaced. As the dog matures and is past the chewing age, a pillow or blanket in the crate is an appreciated comfort—something soft and comfortable.

Sharing importance with the crate is a safe area in which the puppy can exercise and play. If you are an apartment-dweller, a baby's play pen for a small Poodle works out, or, for a larger one, a portable exercise pen which you then can use later if you are planning on taking the dog to shows. If you have a yard, an area should be fenced in so that the dog can be outside in safety. It does not need to be a large area, but it needs to be made safe and secure. If you have close neighbors, stockade fencing works out well as then the neighbors are less aware of the dog and the dog cannot see and bark at everything that passes near the area. If you are out in the country, then just regular chain link fencing is fine. If you only have one dog, however, do not feel that it will get sufficient exercise just sitting in its fenced area, which is what most of them do when they're alone. Two or more dogs will play and move themselves around, but from my own experience, one by itself does little more than make a leisurely tour once around the area and then lie down. So you must include a daily walk or two in your plans if your puppy is to be rugged and well. One more word about the fenced-in area. Have it attended to before you bring the puppy home. Do not wait and risk the possibility of a heartbreaking accident because of not having this protection.

As an absolute guarantee that a dog cannot dig its way out under the fence, an edging of cinder blocks tight against the inside bottom of the fence is very practical. Also if there is an outside gate, provide a padlock and key and strong fastening for it, and use them, so that it could not be opened by others and the dog taken or turned free. The ultimate in convenience in this regard is, of course, a door from the house around which the fenced area can be made, so

Poodle puppies are clever, too, and they know how to be very appealing. This one comes from Mrs. Ruth L. Clarkson's lovely apricot strain.

that all you have to do is open it, and out he goes. It is both safer, as then you need no outside gate, and easier, as then in bad weather you can send the dog out without going yourself. This is not always possible to manage, but if your house is arranged so that you could do it this way, I am sure you will never regret having done so, due to the convenience and added safety thus provided.

The puppy will need a collar (one that fits *now*, not to be grown into) and lead from the moment you take possession of him. Both should be of an appropriate weight and type for his size. Also needed are a feeding dish and a water dish, preferably made of unbreakable material. Your pet supply shop should have an adequate supply of these and other accessories from which you can choose. Then you will need grooming tools like the puppy's breeder recommends (a Poodle coat must have care right from the very beginning) and some toys. One of the best toys is a beef leg or knuckle bone, the type you can purchase as a soup bone, cut to an appropriate size depending on the variety of your Poodle. These are absolutely safe and are great exercise for the teething period, helping get the baby set out of the way quickly and with no problems. Equally as good is Nylabone, a nylon bone that does not chip or splinter, and in addition to providing the pup with necessary chewing activity "frizzles" when it is chewed providing the pup with healthful gum massage. Rawhide chews are safe, too, *if made in the United States.* There was a problem a few years back owing to the chemicals with which some foreign rawhide toys had been treated, so to be sure, avoid those. Also avoid plastics and any sort of rubber toys, *particularly* those with squeakers. If you want a ball for the dog in order to play with him, select one made for the purpose of very hard construction, and even then do not leave it with him to work at chewing. Take it away when the game is over. There are also some "tug of war" type toys which are fun when you and the dog are playing together. But again, do not leave them with the dog.

Too many changes all at once can be difficult for a puppy. Therefore no matter how you may wind up doing it, in the beginning, keep him on the food and feeding schedule to which he is accustomed for at least the first few days you have him. Find out ahead of time from the breeder what he feeds his puppies, how frequently, and

This Toy Poodle, Cin Don's Flower Child, belongs to Beverly Merritt of Newfane, New York.

at what times. Then be prepared by having a supply of this food on hand when the puppy comes home, plus any supplements he has been using and recommends.

One other thing that should precede the puppy's arrival is the selection of a veterinarian, because you should stop there on the way home and have him check out the puppy. If the breeder is from your area, ask him for recommendations. If you have friends who are dog owners, get their opinions and see what experiences they may have had with various local vets. Choose someone whom several of your friends regard highly, then contact him about the puppy; if you like him too, make the appointment to stop in with the puppy on the day of purchase. Be sure to obtain the puppy's health record from the breeder, with information on shots, wormings, etc., the puppy has had.

With these things attended to, you are now prepared and ready to introduce your new Poodle to his future home.

Your Poodle Puppy Joins The Family

Remember that, exciting and happy as it is for you, the puppy's move from his place of birth to your home can be a traumatic experience for him. His mother and litter mates will be missed. He will perhaps be slightly frightened or awed at the change of surrounding. The person he depended on will be gone. Everything should be planned to make it smooth going for him, to give him confidence, and to help his realization that yours is a pretty nice place to be after all.

Never bring a puppy home on a holiday. There just is too much going on, with people and gifts and excitement. If he is commemorating an "occasion," work it out so that his arrival will be a few days before or, perhaps even better, a few days after the big one, when there will be normal routine and you will have your undivided attention with which to greet him. Try not to bring the puppy home in the evening. Early morning is the ideal time, as then he has the opportunity of getting acquainted and the first strangeness wearing off before dark and bedtime. You will find it a more peaceful night that way, I am sure. Allow the puppy to investigate under your watchful eye. If you already have a pet in the household, keep a wary watch that things are going smoothly between them, so that the relationship gets off to a friendly start, or you may quickly have a lasting problem.

Much of the future attitude of each toward the other will depend on what takes place that first day, so keep your mind on what they are doing and let your other activities slide for the moment. Be careful not to let your older pet become jealous by paying more attention to the puppy than to him, as that will build a bad situation immediately.

If you have a child, here again it is important that the relationship starts out well. Hopefully you will have had a talk with the youngster in advance about puppies in general and Poodle puppies in particular so it will be understood that puppies are fragile and to be neither teased, hurt, mauled, nor overly rough-housed. Gentleness from the child toward the puppy should reflect in the dog's attitude toward the child as both mature. Never permit your children's playmates to let loose on the puppy as I have frequently seen happen, tormenting it until the puppy turns on the child in self defense. Children often do not realize how rough is too rough. You, as a responsible adult, are obligated to assure that your puppy's relationship with children is a pleasant one.

A cautionary note. Do not start out by spoiling your puppy. Poodles are extremely smart, and what you had considered to be "just for tonight" may be accepted by the puppy as "for keeps." So be firm with him, strike a routine, and stick to it. The puppy will learn more quickly this way, and everyone will be happier as the result.

Socializing and Training
Your Poodle Puppy

Socialization and training of your new puppy should begin the very day he arrives in your home. Never address him without calling him by name, and you will be amazed how quickly he will learn and respond to that name. A short, simple one is the easiest to teach as it catches the dog's attention quickly, so avoid elaborate call names. Always address the dog by the same name, not a whole series of pet names, as the latter will just cause confusion.

Call the puppy over to you when you see him awake and wandering about, using his name clearly. When he comes, make a big fuss over him being such a good dog. He thus will quickly associate the sound of his name with coming and a pleasant happening.

Several hours after his arrival is not too soon to start accustoming the puppy to the feel of a light collar. He may hardly notice it, or he may struggle, roll over, and try to rub it off his neck. Divert his attention when this occurs, and before long he will not even notice the strange feeling around his neck. Next comes the lead. Attach it, then take the puppy immediately outside, where there will be interesting things to see and places to sniff. He will probably struggle at first, trying to free himself, but in a few moments interest and curiosity should take precedence over resentment, he will forget to continue fighting the lead, and he will start walking.

At first just follow along after the puppy, holding on to the leash. Then when the puppy has seemed to completely relax, try to get him started following after you. Don't be rough or jerk him, just tug gently on the lead in the direction you want him to come. Once that has been accomplished, the next step is teaching him to follow on the left at your side or heel. Of course this will not all be accomplished in one day, but it should be done gradually, making the experience pleasant for him. The length of time it takes will vary with the puppy, but as I have said before, Poodles are smart, so the deed should be accomplished within several days or a week.

During the course of housetraining him, you will need to take your puppy out frequently and at regular intervals: first thing in the morning, directly from the crate; immediately after meals; when the puppy has been napping; or when you notice that the puppy is looking for a spot. Choose more or less the same place to take the puppy each time so that a pattern will be established. If he does not go immediately, do not return him to the house as he probably will do so immediately then. Stay out with him until he is finished, then be lavish with your praise for his good behavior. If you catch the puppy having an accident indoors, grab him firmly and rush him outside, saying sharply *No!* as you pick him up. If you do not see the accident occur, there is little point in doing anything except cleaning it up, as once it has happened and been forgotten, the puppy will most likely not even realize why you are scolding.

With a Toy Poodle or a small Miniature, especially if you live in a big city or are away many hours at a time, having a dog that is

Poodle babies make great bed-fellows. The Currie children with their puppies, sired by Mrs. Ruth L. Clarkson's Can. Ch. Murwyn Golden Guardsman.

These well matched puppies, future champions Harmo Jaunty and Harmo Empress Eugenie, are winning Best Brace at the Poodle Club of Massachusetts, 1957. William J. Trainor is handling for owner, Mrs. Anna Boardman. By Ch. Haus Brau Executive of Acadia ex Ch. Donna of Westford Ho.

trained to go to paper has some very definite advantages. To do this, one proceeds pretty much the same way as taking the puppy outdoors, by placing the puppy on the newspaper at the proper times. The paper always should be kept in the same spot. An easy way to paper-train a puppy if you have a play pen or exercise pen for it is to line the area with newspaper; then gradually, every day or so, take away a section of newspaper until you are down to just one or two. The puppy acquires the habit of using the paper, and as the papered area grows smaller, in the majority of cases the dog will continue to use it. My own experience, especially with Toy dogs, has been that this works out well. It is pleasant, if the dog is alone for any length of time, to be able to feel that if he needs it, the paper is there and will be used.

The puppy should form the habit of spending a certain amount of time in his crate, even when you are home. Sometimes they will do this voluntarily, but if not they should be taught to do so, which is accomplished by leading the puppy over by his collar, gently pushing him inside, and saying firmly "Down" or "Stay." Whatever expression you use to give commands, stick to the very same each time for each act. Repetition is the big thing in training, and so is association with what the dog is expected to do. When you mean "Sit," always say exactly that. "Stay" should mean only that the dog must remain where he receives the command. "Down" means something else again. Do not confuse the dog by shuffling the commands, as you will make yourself a problem by confusing the dog.

As soon as he has had his immunization shots, take your Poodle puppy with you whenever and wherever possible. There is nothing that will build a self-confident, stable dog like socialization, and it is extremely important that you plan and give the time and energy necessary for this, particularly if you are planning on this being a show dog, but even if he is just to be a pleasant family member.

Take your Poodle puppy in the car so that he will learn to enjoy riding and not become carsick as dogs may do if infrequent travelers. Take him anywhere you are going that you are certain he will be welcome: visiting friends and relatives (if they do not have housepets that may resent it), to busy shopping centers (keeping him always on the leash), or just walking around the streets of your town. If someone admires him (as always seems to happen when we are out with puppies), encourage them to pet and talk to him. Socialization of this type brings out the best in your puppy and helps him to grow up with a friendly outlook, liking the world and its inhabitants. The worst thing that can be done to a puppy's personality is to overly shelter the puppy. By keeping him always at home away from things and people unfamiliar to him you may be creating a personality problem for the mature dog that will be a cross for you to bear later on.

Ch. Alekai Kuke of Mayfair at the Poodle Club of America, June 1960. Owned by Ann Seranne and Barbara Wolferman, handled by Wendell J. Sammet. "Kuke" was Best of Winners on that occasion, and Best Puppy in Show under judge Frances Angela.

Brown and black Poodle puppies at Kayesett Kennels,
Mr. and Mrs. J. Herbert Kaye.

Can. Ch. Murwyn's Lady Tangerine, an apricot
Miniature, taking Best of Variety for Mrs. Ruth L.
Clarkson, owner-handling at the Quebec International.
R. Williams Taylor is judging.

Ch. Wissacre Moneysworth, black Toy male, bred and owned by Joan Scott and handled by Wendell J. Sammet, winning the Toy Group at Boardwalk Kennel Club, 1974. Judge, Frank Landgraf.

CHAPTER SEVENTEEN

Feeding Your Poodle

The brown Toy, Ch. AALove Tiffany, handled by Wendell J. Sammet to Group First at Carrol County Kennel Club, 1971, under judge Louis Murr. Mrs. Marge McNelis, owner.

Time was when providing nourishing food for our dogs involved a far more complicated routine than people now feel is necessary. The old school of thought was that the daily rations should consist of fresh beef, vegetables, cereal, egg yolks, and cottage cheese as basics, with such additions as brewer's yeast and vitamin tablets.

During recent years, however, many minds have changed regarding this procedure. We still give eggs, cottage cheese, and supplements to the diet, but the basic methods of feeding dogs have changed, and the changes are, in the opinion of many authorities, definitely for the better. The school of thought now is that you are doing your dogs a service and favor when you feed them some of the fine commercially prepared dog foods in preference to your own home-cooked concoctions.

The reason behind this new outlook is easily understandable. The dog food industry has grown to be a major one, participated in by some of the best known and most respected names in the American way of life. These trusted firms, it is agreed, turn out excellent products, so people are feeding their dog food preparations with confidence and the dogs are thriving. What more could we want?

There are at least half a dozen absolutely top-grade dry foods to be mixed with water or broth and served to your dog according to directions,

there are all sorts of canned meats, and there are several kinds of "convenience foods," those in a packet which you open and dump out into the dog's dish. It is just that simple. The "convenience" foods are neat and easy when you are away from home, but generally speaking we prefer a dry food mixed with hot water or soup and meat. We also feel that the canned meat, with its added fortifications, is more beneficial to the dogs than the fresh meat. However, the two can be alternated or, if you prefer and your dog does well on it, by all means use ground beef. A dog enjoys changes in the meat part of his diet, which is easy with the canned food, since all sorts of beef are available (chunk, ground, stewed, etc.), plus lamb, chicken, and even such concoctions as liver and egg, just plain liver flavor, and a blend of five meats.

There also is prepared food geared to every age bracket of your dog's life, from puppyhood on through old age, with special additions or modifications to make it especially nourishing and beneficial. Our grandparents, and even our parents, never had it so good where the canine dinner hour is concerned, because these foods are tasty and geared to meeting the dog's gastronomic approval.

Additionally, contents and nutrients are clearly listed on the labels, plus careful instructions for feeding just the right amount for the size and weight of each dog.

With these foods we do not feel the addition of vitamins is necessary, but if you do, there are several excellent kinds of those, too, that serve as taste treats as well as being beneficial. Your pet supply shop has a full array of them.

Of course there is no reason not to cook up something for your Poodle if you would feel happier doing so, but it seems to us unnecessary when such truly satisfactory rations are available with so much less trouble and expense.

How often you feed is a matter of how it works out best for you. Many owners prefer to do it once a day. I personally think that two meals in smaller quantity are better on the digestion and more satisfying to the dog, particularly if yours is a household member who stands around and watches preparation of the family meals. Do not overfeed. That is the shortest route to all sorts of problems.

Once your puppies are fully weaned, until they are about twelve weeks old, they should be fed four times daily. A Miniature Poodle, for each of these meals, would need a half to a full cup of puppy kibble soaked in about a half cup of water, broth, or soup, mixed with about one-fourth can of beef or one-fourth pound of ground raw beef morning and evening. At noontime and before bed a half can of evaporated milk with an equal amount of water and some dry kibble added can be given. The amounts would be about double for Standard Poodle puppies or cut in half for Toys.

As the pups grow older, from three to six months, cut to three meals, increasing the kibble to about 1½ cups with three-fourths of a cup water or broth and double the amount of meat for each meal. Again adjust the amounts more or less for Standards and Toys. From six months to a year the pups can switch to one meal daily if you wish, although most people prefer to keep them on two meals until they are a year old. If you do feed just once a day, do so by early afternoon at the latest and give the dog a snack or biscuit at bedtime.

Remember that plenty of fresh, cool water always should be available to your dog. This is of utmost importance to his good health.

Ch. Deryabar Ruffle, bred and owned by Mr. and Mrs. Royal Peterson, Greenwich, Connecticut. Wendell J. Sammet, handler. Miss Virginia Sivori, judge. Ruffle is by Ch. Popcorn of Deryabar.

Poodle Club of America, May 1965. Jane Forsyth handled the well known Ch. Wycliffe Leroy to Best of Variety under judge Mrs. Rebecca Mason.

Ch. Zulu Headdress was handled by Ben Burwell at the Chicago International, 1957.

Ch. Merry Mouse Arden, by Jeanie's Black Dina-Mite from Tiopepe Midnight Saphire, taking Best of Opposite Sex at Paper Cities, 1978. Owned by Shelia Hobson.

Ch. Arden Original, by Jeanie's Black Dina-Mite ex Ardyna's Hot Pants, owned by Bea Schaaf. Photo courtesy of Jeanie Mazza.

Am., Can. Ch. Merrylegs Cetin de la Fontaine taking Best of Breed at the National Sportsman's Show in Canada, judged by Louis Murr. Breeder-Owners, Mr. and Mrs. Ellis. By Calvados de la Fontaine ex Yours Truly de la Fontaine.

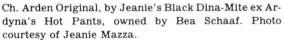

410

Kayesett Anastasie Kerri is all dressed for the party.
Mr. and Mrs. J. Herbert Kaye, owners.

CHAPTEREIGHTEEN

The Poodle As
A Family Companion

A most exquisite Poodle head, that of Ch. Calvinelle Dancing Gow. Owned by Mrs. William L. Kendrick, Devon, Pennsylvania.

Assets

When a breed of dog remains with consistency on or at the top of the popularity list over many years, one can be sure that this breed has something very special to recommend it, making it desirable to people in all situations and many walks of life. Such a breed is the Poodle. For, between its three sizes, its versatility, and its high degree of intelligence, these dogs seem to adapt well with people of all ages, interests, and circumstances.

The breed is known for super intelligence and learning ability. They are quick-witted dogs, easy to teach, that display a highly admirable degree of good sense. A smart dog is surely more fun than a stupid one to have around, and I have yet to see a stupid Poodle. Occasionally a hyper one, yes, but never stupid!

Poodles are pleasant companions. They are gay and cheerful, anxious to please, always devoted to their owners.

Poodles savor sociability. They can accompany you anywhere and seem to enjoy doing so. They are good travelers and, particularly the two smaller sizes, easy to take along in a carrier even on planes or wherever your plans may lead you.

Poodles are excellent watch dogs, even the Toys. I have always been of the opinion that a small dog is just as efficient at sounding the alarm against intruders and helping to "burglar-proof" your house or apartment as a large one and far handier to own when you live in the city or closely developed suburbs. Toy dogs are always especially quick and alert and can bark up quite a storm when disturbed or alarmed. Which, after all, is as good a job as the most enormous family dog can do, short of chewing up the intruder, and attack-trained dogs have their drawbacks, too, except in isolated places and under special situations. A quick-moving, small, barking dog has tremendous nuisance value to those entering your premises for illegitimate purposes, including the fact that they are fast on their feet and can get under or behind the furniture, making it mighty hard for the intruder to get hold of them or aim at them with a silencing blow or with a gun. So if space precludes your having a Standard or any other large dog, give very serious consideration to the fact that a Toy or Miniature Poodle can act very well as a burglar alarm system for you, at the same time persuading the intruder that it would be better to move to a quieter location.

Children and Poodles go well together, too. For a youngster, I think a Standard Poodle or a Miniature is ideal, but for a young child a Toy might be a bit fragile. If the child is properly instructed by his parents as to the way to care for and enjoy a dog, then there should be no problem anyway. It is wrong to allow a child to look upon a dog as a plaything, indestructible and immune to pain.

Of great importance to family members who are allergic to dog hair is the fact that Poodles do not shed. A family Poodle's coat requires care, but not to the extensive degree of the show dog. As a puppy, the coat should be trimmed and shaped when five or six weeks old and then repeated every six to eight weeks throughout his lifetime. A thorough brushing at least twice a week is essential to keep the coat clean and to prevent formation of mats. The hair within the ear canal should be plucked out whenever the dog is bathed and trimmed, and the ear may be wiped out with baby oil or peroxide should cleaning appear necessary. Such precautions will help to avoid ear infections.

If you are handy at that sort of thing, you may well be able to learn to trim, clip, and shape the coat yourself. However, many pet owners find this difficult if not impossible to do, and there are a great many Poodle grooming shops in all areas where you can get it done, usually at a charge of between $12.00 and $20.00, depending on your area. Most professional handlers or people who work on show coats lack the time in which to trim pets, but you will find satisfactory people available almost everywhere. There are all kinds of clips you can put on a pet Poodle, from the legitimate "puppy clip," which is neat, attractive, and serviceable, on into more inventive styles if your tastes run in this direction. So long as the dog will not be shown, your personal satisfaction is all that is necessary.

Another asset of Poodles as family dogs is that they are a breed of excellent longevity, which is important when one considers the shortness of a beloved dog's life as compared to the length of our own. With reasonable care and all the modern ways of feeding and caring for dogs available, your Poodle should reach 14 years or older, barring accidents.

If you enjoy having a dog with a well-learned

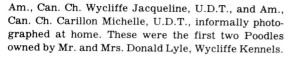

Am., Can. Ch. Wycliffe Jacqueline, U.D.T., and Am., Can. Ch. Carillon Michelle, U.D.T., informally photographed at home. These were the first two Poodles owned by Mr. and Mrs. Donald Lyle, Wycliffe Kennels.

Miniature Poodles and cats can live together very amicably as these are doing, sharing their owner's attention. Toughy of Junkin, Toughy's Chocolate Fancy, and the pussycats all belong to Marcia Foy.

collection of tricks, all it takes with a Poodle is a small degree of patience. Remember that they have excelled in the entertainment world as dancing dogs, acrobatic dogs, and in many feats requiring intelligence and skill. Walking on their hind legs is almost second nature to them and can be encouraged with tidbits and praise if you wish them to "dance." Shaking hands is easy; it is merely done by reaching for the right paw as you say, clearly, "Shake hands." Also it is easy to teach a Poodle to "catch" by attracting its attention with short throwing motions, then tossing a tidbit to it as you repeat the instruction "Catch." If you find the puppy scrambles to grab the "goodie" up off the floor, beat him to it by picking it up quickly, and repeat the process until he gets the idea that he is to catch it in the air.

Another trick Poodles can learn easily is to "carry" a small package or object. The first couple of times you may find it necessary to force

the object into his mouth while repeating the word "carry," but your quick-witted Poodle will soon catch on. If he drops the object, repeat the process, ordering him to "Hold." When he is doing this well, attach a lead and back away, repeating the word "Carry." Soon he should progress to the point of walking toward you on the lead with the object in his mouth. After that he must learn to trot along at your side doing so. Make sure that the object is light enough not to be a burden to him.

To "fetch" or "retrieve" is a natural instinct with Poodles. Remember that they were originally water retrievers, so this is really only "doing what comes naturally" for them.

And please do not forget that your family Poodle will only benefit by even a short course in basic obedience training, for his own safety and to make him a more pleasing companion. Poodles excel in this field, as you will note in

414

studying the pictures in this book. Just notice how many, many Poodles have titles denoting obedience degrees following their names.

Traveling With Your Poodle

When one travels with a dog, it must always be borne in mind that everyone does not necessarily share our love of dogs, and those who feel that way about it (strange creatures though they seem to us) have their rights, too, on which we should not infringe. They include not being disturbed, annoyed, or made uncomfortable by the presence and behavior of other people's dogs. Poodle owners, since they own one of the most intelligent and easily obedience-trained of all breeds, should have their dogs, especially the two larger varieties, well-trained by the time they reach maturity, which is a help. Your dog should not jump enthusiastically on strangers, no matter how playful or friendly his intentions. A sharp "Down" from you should be obeyed, as, for the dog's own protection, should be "Come," "Sit," and "Stay."

If you expect to take your dog on many trips, for your sake and for his he should have a crate of appropriate size if a Standard or Miniature or a sturdy, lightweight carrier if a Toy. In any emergency or accident, a crated dog is far more likely to escape injury than one riding loose in a car. Dogs become accustomed to this quickly, settle down happily, and are far better off when this precautionary measure has been taken. If you do permit the dog to ride loose in the car, for pity's sake *do not* permit him to hang out the window, ears blowing in the breeze. He could become overly excited at something he sees and jump out; he could lose his balance and fall out; and many a dog has suffered an eye injury induced by the strong wind generated by the moving car.

If you are staying at a hotel or motel with your dog, *please* exercise him somewhere other than in the flower beds and the parking lot there. People walking to and from their cars are really not thrilled at "stepping in something" left by your dog, so try to avoid it. Should an accident occur, pick it up with tissues, don't just let it remain

Ch. Prankster Darius, owned by Mrs. George Marmer, a Standard, was handled in the ring by William J. Trainor.

Standard Poodles make great beds for smaller friends! Ch. Alekai Zeus is quite content as Twirpy, a little Pom, cuddles in his thick coat. Mary and Paul Edwards snapped this adorable "informal" for us.

Two of the Wycliffe Poodles enjoying a game of cards. Owned by Mrs. Donald Lyle, Wycliffe Kennels, West Vancouver, British Columbia.

A very informal pose of two Round Table Poodles relaxing at home. Mrs. Alden V. Keene, owner.

there. Usually there are grassy areas off to the sides or behind motels where dogs can be exercised. Use those rather than the more conspicuous areas. If you are becoming a dog show enthusiast, you will need an exercise pen eventually as you acquire two or three show dogs, and these are ideal for use when staying at motels, too.

Never leave your dog unattended in the room of a motel unless you are absolutely, positively certain that he will stay quiet and non-destructive. You do *not* want to return to torn curtains or bedspread, soiled rugs, or other embarrassing evidence. You do not want a long list of irate complaints from other guests, caused by the annoying barking of a lonesome dog in strange surroundings or one over-zealous about barking furiously at every foot-step outside the room. If yours is not a dog used to traveling with you and you are not absolutely certain of its behavior when left alone in the room, it is far better to let him remain in the car until you are ready to retire to the room yourself, when you will be there to know what he is getting into.

When you are traveling with a dog, it is often simpler to take along food and water for him from home. That way he will have the rations to which he is accustomed and there will be no fear of problems due to different drinking water. Feeding is quite easy now, at least for a short trip, with all the splendid dry prepared foods and high quality canned meats available. Many types of lightweight, handy water containers can be bought at all sporting goods stores.

If you are going out of the United States, to Canada for instance, you will need a health certificate from your veterinarian for each dog you are taking, certifying that each has had rabies shots within the required length of time preceding your visit.

Be careful to always leave sufficient openings to ventilate your car when the dog will be alone in it. Remember that in summer the rays of the sun can make an inferno of a closed up car within only a few short minutes, so leave plenty of windows open. Again, if your dog is in a crate, this can be done most safely. The fact that you

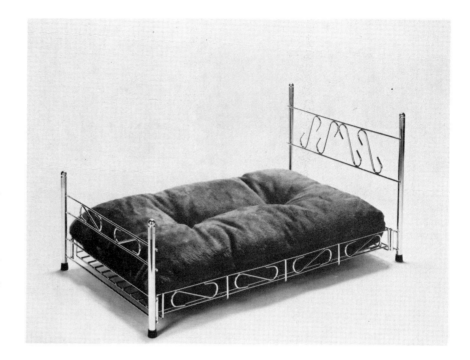

This beautiful dog bed, made by Crown Products Company, is suitable for that Poodle deserving royal treatment. Many accessories from travel carriers to grooming items are available at your local pet store. The proprietor can offer helpful advice on selecting those that are most appropriate for your Poodle.

"To reduce the dog's anxiety when left alone he should also be given a safety outlet such as a toy to play with and chew on. In fact, the dog may be encouraged to develop an oral attachment to this object by playing catch or tug of war with the toy at other times. Indestructible meat-flavored nylon bones are excellent." (Quoted from the 1980 practitioner monograph *Canine Behavior* by Benjamin L. Hart, D.V.M., Ph.D. with other contributors.) Shown in the illustrations at right and below is the ham-flavored Nylabone® , the perfect chewing pacifier for young dogs in their teething stage, or even for older dogs to help satisfy that occasional urge to chew. Unlike many other dog bones on the market today, Nylabone® does not splinter or fall apart. It will last indefinitely and as it is used it frills, becoming a doggie toothbrush that cleans teeth and massages gums.

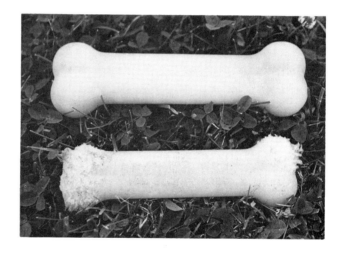

BEST OF BREED
OR VARIETY
PHOTO
BY *Graham*

CHINTIMINI K.C.
NON-SPORTING
GROUP

have left the car in a shady spot is not always a guarantee that you will find conditions the same when you return. Don't forget that the position of the sun can change in a matter of minutes, and the car you left nicely shaded half an hour before can be getting full sunlight much sooner than you may realize. So if you have a dog in the car, check back frequently to ascertain his safety.

Make obedience training a game with your puppy while he is still extremely young. Try to teach him the meaning of "Come," "Stay," "Sit," "Down," and "Heel," along with the meaning of "*No!*" even while he is still too young for formal obedience training classes. It gives you a head start, and you will be pleased and proud to note how much in the way of good manners even a baby Poodle can pick up through gentle early lessons. These are intelligent dogs, so take advantage of the fact right from the beginning.

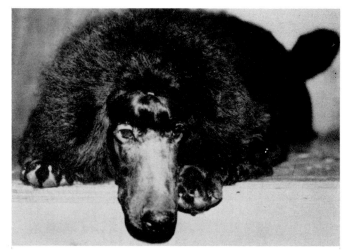

A relaxed pose of Ch. Cabryn's Von Hurrican of Remm, owned by Mr. Dennis and Mrs. Katherine McElligot, Tucson, Arizona.

Miss Sue Forsyth, at age 3½, showing off Kayesett Kennels black Standard dog, Ch. Kaye's Trojan Knight, at the Manhattan Savings Bank Dog Exhibition in New York City.

Overleaf:
Above: The Miniature Poodle bitch, Ch. Lin-Ed's Mystoria, is handled to a good win under judge Ed Dixon by Peggy Hogg for Edward B. Jenner. **Below:** Am. Can. Ch. Dhubne Darth Vader winning the Non-Sporting Group at Chintimini Kennel Club, handled by Marie Langseth for owner, Carroll Ann Irwin.

Highlane Voodoo, a Miniature owned by Marie Zogame, is handled here by Jane Kamp Forsyth to Best of Variety at the Saw Mill River Kennel Club Dog Show, 1969, under judge Lydia Coleman Hutchinson.

Christmas 1969. Freeland's Finesse (by Ch. Freeland's Flashlight from Ch. Hollycourt Vida de Plata) and Freeland's Fille de Joie, eight months old, help celebrate the occasion with true holiday spirit. Monique Devine, owner.

Overleaf:
Above: The look of a future "star". Handsome puppy champion Viscara Vagabond King, is handled by Luc Boileau for Edward B. Jenner. Mrs. Ramona Van Court Jones, judge. **Below:** Poodle Club of Massachusetts, 1976, Ch. Caron Fan Fare by Ch. Capilon Showlad ex Denaire Classic takes Best of Winners under Mrs. Usherson for owner-breeder Mrs. Lewis Lewellyn. Wendell Sammet is handling.

FIRST

GILBERT PHOTO

Winsomore Living Doll, U.D., contemplates the fruits
of her success as she sits surrounded by trophies at
Helsonae Kennels, owned by Helen and Sonja Petlitzki,
Detroit, Michigan.

Overleaf:
Above: Ch. Pinafore Panda Bear, C.D., by Ch. Alekai Ahi ex Puttencove Day Lily, C.D., owned and bred
by Mrs. Philip J. Harney, Woodinville, Washington. **Below:** A future Best in Show winner as a puppy.
The black Miniature, Ch. Helsonae Sunday Special, shown taking the Best Puppy in Show award at the
Washington Poodle Club Specialty under Anne Rogers Clark.
Helsonae Poodles, Detroit, Michigan.

CHAPTER NINETEEN

Poodles In Obedience

Trinket of Rye Top, U.D., is trained, owned, and handled by Mrs. Joseph Longo, Harrison, New York.

I very sincerely doubt that there has ever been any breed of dog more readily adaptable to obedience training and obedience work than the Poodle. Their high degree of intelligence and their willingness to please add up to the principal requisites for distinction in this field, and Poodles have surely proven proudly their talents along these lines.

For its own protection and safety, every dog should, at the very least, recognize and obey the commands "Come," "Heel," "Down," "Sit," and "Stay." Doing so at some time might save the dog's life and in less extreme circumstances will certainly make him a better-behaved, more pleasant member of society. If you are patient and enjoy working with your dog, study some of the excellent books available on the subject and personally teach your Poodle these basic manners. If you need the stimulus of working with a group, find out where obedience training classes are available (usually your veterinarian, your dog's breeder if in or near your area, or a dog-owning friend can tell you), and you and your dog join up. Or you can send the dog to class,

letting someone else do the training, although this is the least rewarding, really, as you lose the opportunity of working with your dog.

If you are going to do it yourself, some basic rules are that you must remain calm and confident in attitude. Never lose your temper and frighten or punish your dog unjustly. Never resort to cruelty. Be quick and lavish with praise each time a command is correctly followed. Make it fun for the dog, and he will respond by eagerness to please you. Repetition is the keynote but should not be continued without recess to the point of tedium. Limit the training sessions to ten- or fifteen-minute periods at a time.

Formal obedience training can be followed, and very frequently is, by entering the dog in obedience competition to work toward an obedience degree or several, depending on the dog's aptitude and your own enjoyment. Obedience trials are held in conjunction with the majority of all-breed conformation dog shows and also frequently as specialty events. For a list of trials, if you are working alone with your dog, inquire

Overleaf:
Above: A study in Poodle elegance! Carroll Ann Irwin's magnificent Standard, Am., Can. Ch. Dhubhne Darth Vader, earned his titles in each Country with four consecutive wins. Sired by Ch. Meyowne Rudolph (white) from Ch. Springtime Bittersweet (black). **Below:** All sired by Ch. Bel Tor Big Picture, here we see Bel Tor Enchanted Eye taking Best of Winners, Ch. Juel Destiny's Showoff taking Best of Opposite Sex to Best of Variety, and Ch. Bel Tor Blissful going Best of Variety under judge, Henry Stoecker, at Bryn Mawr Kennel Club a few years back.

BEST OF
WINNERS

GILBERT PHOTO

WINNERS
DOG

ASHBEY PHOTO

of your veterinarian, your pet supply dealer, the breeder of your Poodle, or contact the American Kennel Club. If you have been working with a training class, you will find information readily available to you regarding dates and locations of trials.

The goals for which one works in the formal A.K.C. Member or Licensed Trials are the following titles: Companion Dog (C.D.), Companion Dog Excellent (C.D.X.), and Utility Dog (U.D.). These degrees are earned by receiving three "legs" or qualifying scores at each level of competition. The degrees must be earned in order, with one completed prior to starting work on the next. For example, a dog must have earned C.D. prior to starting work C.D.X. Then C.D.X. must be completed before U.D. work begins. The ultimate title possible to attain in obedience work is that of Obedience Trial Champion (O.T.C.). To gain this one, dogs must have received the required number of points by placing first or second in Open or Utility after having earned their U.D. There is also a Tracking Dog title available, to be earned at tracking trials, and a new, more difficult to attain degree, Tracking Dog Excellent (T.D.X.).

When you see the letters C.D. following a dog's name, you will know that the dog has satisfactorily completed the following exercises: heel on leash, heel free, stand for examination, recall, long sit, and long stay. C.D.X. means tests have been passed in all of the above plus heel free, drop on recall, retrieve over high jump, broad jump, long sit, and long down. While U.D. indicates that additionally the dog has passed tests in scent discrimination (leather article), scent discrimination (metal article), signal exercises, directed retrieve, directed jumping, and group stand for examination.

The letters T.D. indicate that the dog has been trained and passed the tests to follow the trail of a stranger along a path on which the trail was laid between 30 minutes and two hours previously. Along this track there must be more than two right angle turns, at least two of which are well out in the open where no fences or other boundaries exist for guidance of dog or handler.

Doing her obedience routine, Am., Can. Ch. Carillon Michelle, Am. C.D.X., Can. U.D.T., foundation bitch for the Wycliffe Poodles owned by Mrs. Donald Lyle, Vancouver, British Columbia. Photographed in 1955.

Henry Stoecker with Ch. Pillicoc Reverie and Ch. Pillicoc Prunella.

Overleaf:
Above: Ch. Torbec Roi Soleil, by Torbec Big Cheese ex Torbec Sunflower, handled by Wendell J. Sammet to Best of Winners at Westminster in 1978. Canadian-bred by Mrs. T. G. McIntyre. **Below:** An eight-month-old puppy of exceptional promise, the Miniature dog, future Ch. and Obedience Trial Ch. Andechez Zachery Zee is pictured here taking Winners Dog under judge Lydia Coleman Hutchinson. Owned by Blanche and Rebecca C. Tansil, Andechez Poodles.

Tar of Rye Top, U.D., Mrs. Joseph Longo's first High Score in Trail obedience winner.

Mrs. Milton Erlanger putting her marvelous Ch. Pillicoc Rumpelstiltskin through his Obedience paces. "Curly" was one of the first Poodles to earn a C.D. degree, published in 1935. Photo courtesty of Henry Stoecker.

The dog wears a harness and is connected to the handler by a lead 20 to 40 feet in length. Inconspicuously dropped at the end of the track is an article to be retrieved, usually a glove or wallet, which the dog is expected to locate and the handler pick up. T.D.X. is a more difficult version of the above, with a longer track and more turns to be worked through.

Almost without exception, Poodles are to be found in the list of top-scoring dogs in any obedience training club. They have distinguished themselves admirably in this field. You will note as you turn the pages of this book how tremendously many bench show champions also carry one or more of the Obedience titles following their names, some in just one country, but many in two or more. Beauty and brains certainly are well-combined in all three varieties of this breed, which undoubtedly is one of the reasons Poodles enjoy such great popularity with the dog-loving public.

The first Poodle ever to have won a Non-Sporting Group and his class in Obedience on the same day, according to history, was Champion Carillon Courage, C.D.X., while probably the most famous combined bench show and obedience winner of all time was the renowned Champion Carillon Jester, U.D.T., Blanche Saunders' magnificent Standard that really put Poodles in Obedience on the map.

Over the past decades, many, many others of all three varieties have joined these distinguished Poodles as outstanding obedience performers. In case anyone feels that Toy or Miniature Poodles may be less clever than their larger kin, this is not at all true. Champion Pulaski's Masterpiece, a very well-known Toy Poodle owned by Count Alexis Pulaski of New York some thirty years ago, had a U.D. degree. At present, Mrs. Joseph Longo of Harrison, New York, among others, is making exciting records with her Miniatures, of which we shall tell you more.

Mrs. Longo in earlier days had owned the world-famous Rye Top Boxers, which included the renowned Best in Show bitch Champion El Wendie of Rockland. But Poodles were a new breed to her when one named Toby came as a

Overleaf:
Above: Ch. Wissfire Miss Kitty, a big winning Toy Poodle, going Best under Anna K. Nicholas at James River Kennel Club Show in 1979. Owned by Joan Scott, handled by F. C. "Bud" Dickey.

Below: Ch. Pinafore Barrymore shown finishing his title as he takes Winners Dog at the Columbia Poodle Specialty, July 1980. Owner Mrs. P. J. Harney; handler, Marie Langseth.

GROUP
FIRST

JAMES RIVER
KENNEL CLUB
1979

GILBERT PHOTO

BEST OF
WINNERS

GILBERT PHOTO

Topper of Rye Top, U.D., being obedience trained by his owner, Mrs. Joseph Longo of Harrison, New York. A) learning to "sit".

C) Learning the meaning of "down".

D) Starting lesson in "heel."

B) Learning to "stay".

E) Turning into "heel" position.

Overleaf:
Above: Ch. De Man For Jet Stream winning Best Toy Poodle at the Greenspring Specialty in 1969. A handsome little dog being beautifully presented by Vernelle Hartman, now Mrs. William L. Kendrick.
Below: Ch. Andechez Yolanda taking Best of Winners at Westminster, 1979. Owned by B. and R. Tansil of Parkton, Maryland.

F) Learning the jumps.

H) Hand signals.

I) Hand signals.

G) Learning the jumps.

Overleaf:
Above: A very well known Standard Poodle, Am., Can. Ch. Torbec Hey There Peterson, taking Best in Show at the Sportsmen's Show in 1979 under Glen Sommers. Garrett Lambert handles this dog for breeder-owner T. G. McIntyre, Bolton, Ontario, Canada. Peterson was Winners Dog at the Poodle Club of America en route to his American title. **Below:** Mrs. Edward Solomon of Pittsburgh, Pennsylvania, owns this glamorous Standard Poodle bitch, Ch. Dassin Rita La Rose, handled by F. "Bud" Dickey to first in the Non-Sporting Group at Kennel Club of Northern New Jersey, 1980. The judge is Anna Katherine Nicholas.

POODLE CLUB
OF
SOUTHEAST MICHIGAN
MARCH 8 1974

WINNERS
STANDARD
DOG
JUDGE
MRS GERTRUDE EDGE
PHOTO BY BOOTH

gift from a member of the golf club at which her husband is the golf professional. Mrs. Longo, with the thought in mind of making him a well-mannered pet, started taking Toby to obedience school, which has been the starting point for so many of our obedience fans. Toby amazed his owner by showing such aptitude that she was persuaded to enter him in official obedience trials. He was great in Novice and Open Classes, but really hated the Utility work. Being a novice herself at training, Mrs. Longo felt she had much to learn, but even so, Toby pleased her by gaining a C.D.X.

Having come to thoroughly enjoy this new interest, the Longos purchased their second Poodle, this one a silver Miniature who became Tammy of Rye Top. After completing her U.D., she was bred to Toby, in due time producing a litter of four from which the Longos kept three, selling the other. Two of those they kept, Topper of Rye Top and Trinket of Rye Top, were cream, and the third, Tar of Rye Top, was charcoal. All three completed their U.D. titles. Tar of Rye Top made the *Dog World* Award for his C.D. and C.D.X. degrees, plus he scored a High in Trial (i.e., Comparable to Best in Show, this being the dog making the highest score of any dog entered in the obedience classes that day). Trinket of Rye Top finished her U.D., and Topper of Rye Top gained his U.D., won two High in Trial awards, and was also in the Top Ten Non-Sporting Obedience Dogs in the country.

The Longos bred Toby and Tammy for a second time, and from six puppies they kept three and sold three. Those they kept were Tinsil, Toddy, and Tina, all of Rye Top, who all gained their U.D. titles with ease. Tina of Rye Top became a very famous little figure in the obedience rings, taking no less than six High in Trial Awards, a Canadian C.D. and High in Trial, and then, as frosting on the cake, was three times in the Top Ten Non-Sporting Obedience Dogs in the United States. This must surely have been very gratifying to her breeder, owner, trainer, and handler!

It is particularly interesting, as well, that Topper of Rye Top until his 1981 retirement was

A most intelligent Standard. This is Ch. Colonel Mint Julip of the Nass, U.D., Non-Sporting Group, High Score in Trial and High Combined Score in Trial winner. Beauty plus brains well describes this handsome dog, owned by Francis P. Fretwell, Monfret Poodles, Moore, South Carolina.

Tina of Rye Top, U.D., a five-pound Toy owned, trained and handled by Mrs. Joseph Longo. Pictured here winning the top Obedience award at Elm City Kennel Club, 1978. Gaining her ninth High Score in Trial trophy on the day, with a score of 196½ out of a possible 200 points. "Tina" also won the Utility competition. This double victory gave her the Highest Combined Score trophy as well.

Overleaf:
Above: Ch. Dassin Debussy, Best of Breed, Pittsburgh Poodle Club, with Joseph Vergnetti. Ch. Dassin Busby Berkley, center, Best of Winners with Bud Dickey, and Ch. Dassin Dancing Daffodil. Three handsome Dassin Farm-bred Poodles. **Below:** Ch. Dassin Broadway Joe, black Standard son of Ch. Wisshire's Country Gentleman ex Ch. Jocelyene Marjorie. A noted winning Poodle that is also a great producer with more than 29 champions to his credit. Pictured here, as a youngster en route to the title, taking Winners Dog at the Poodle Club of Southeast Michigan. Bred and owned by Dassin Farm, F. C. Dickey and Joseph Vergnetti, Medina, Ohio.

Showing all the intelligence of expression confirmed by her many Highest Scoring Dog in Trial Awards, her American U.D. and Canadian U.D.T., this lovely headstudy of Am., Can. Ch. Wycliffe Jacqueline portrays as well a Top Producing Dam in the Poodle Breed and a Best in Show winner. She is the first Poodle owned by Mrs. Donald Lyle.

Jean Lyle and Blanche Saunders (America's Miss Obedience), photographed during the summer of 1960, with Lynn Taylor. Shown is Am., Can. Ch. Carillon Michelle, Can. U.D.T., Am. C.D.X., Mrs. Lyle's head foundation bitch purchased from Miss Saunders. The cream is Wycliffe Katrina. In the background Wycliffe Jacqueline is peering over the gate.

one of the leading scent hurdle racing dogs. He has been out in veteran's class and has won on each occasion.

Next comes Tanya of Rye Top, who the Longos purchased in Florida as a seven-week-old puppy. She is not only a U.D., but became the Longos' very first Obedience Trial Champion (O.T.C.) and got the *Dog World* Award for her American and Canadian C.D.X. titles. During the summer of 1980, the Longos went to Bermuda for the first time, and Tanya gained her C.D. and won highest aggregate score for all the trials. She also has to her credit six High in Trial awards.

Tanya was bred to a breed champion, and the Longos have two of her daughters from this litter, Rye Top's Tuesday and Rye Top's Thumbelina, now two and a half years old. Tuesday has won a High in Trial from Novice, and Thumbelina earned her Utility degree, following C.D.X., in her first three shows, so is now working for points on her Obedience Trial Championship. Tuesday needs just one leg more on her C.D.X.

Last but not least, the Longos also have Tobyna of Rye Top, also a U.D.

We tell this story to give our readers an idea of the pleasure one can have personally training and showing their Poodles in this field. Mrs. Longo started out as a complete novice in obedience, never before having attempted anything along these lines. Now, not too many years later, she points with pride to the ten Poodles she has put through to U.D. and hopes that, by the time you are reading this, Tuesday will have become the eleventh.

It was back in 1948 that eight Poodle owners from New York City met for the purpose of training their Poodles for obedience. As a result of this, in 1951 the Poodle Obedience Training Club of Greater New York was formed, its purpose having been to encourage the training and showing of pure-bred Poodles in obedience. The lady so highly respected in her field, Miss Blanche Suanders, was training supervisor for the group, and its success was almost astronomical. Over the years, this Club's li-

Overleaf:
Above: Ch. Valhalla's Kristine owned by Mr. and Mrs. William Tow and Catherine Kish, bred by Catherine Kish. An all-breed Best in Show and consistent Group winner, she was Best Puppy in Show, Poodle Club of America 1978, judged by Ed Jenner. Pictured winning the Group at Staten Island in 1980 under William Bergum. Handled by Wendell J. Sammet. Below: Mrs. Lewis Lewellyn owns Ch. Capillone Showlad pictured here winning Best of Breed at the Poodle Club of Massachusetts under judge, Elaine Usherson. Wendell Sammet handling.

S.I.K.C.
JUNE 22, 1980

NON SPORTING
GROUP 1ST

BEST OF
BREED

GILBERT PHOTO

438

censed Specialty Shows have been exciting, well-attended events. Members have earned an amazing number of titles with their Poodles, and their dogs have appeared with regularity at all sorts of exhibitions, benefits, and other such events. The Poodle Obedience Training Club of Greater New York became affiliated with the Poodle Club of America in 1956.

It was back in August, 1935, that the American Kennel Club awarded its first C.D.X. Poodle degrees. Cadeau de Noel, Carillon Epreuve, and Tango of Piperscroft received them.

Ch. Fayward Claude, C.D., April 1957. Owned by Mrs. Raymond Alexander, Framingham Centre, Massachusetts. Handled by Jane Kamp Forsyth.

Jap. Ch. L'ambria Grand Prix (by Ch. Arundel A Lovin' Spoonful), a Best in Show and Specialty Show winner. One of the many outstanding Toy Poodles owned by Mr. and Mrs. Yukichi Fukazawa, prominent Poodle breeders in Japan.

Toby of Rye Top, C.D.X., the little Poodle that started Mr. and Mrs. Joseph Longo's fabulously successful string of obedience winners. "Toby" is the sire of six U.D. winners.

Obedience Trial Champion Tanya of Rye Top with her daughter, Rye Top's Tuesday, C.D.X. Mrs. Joseph Longo is owner, trainer and handler.

Overleaf:
Above: Ch. Alekai All Together, by Ch. Alekai Argus ex Ch. Alekai Brilliance, finishing a championship at Lehigh Valley Kennel Club 1980 at 18 months of age. Bred and owned by Mrs. Henry J. Kaiser, Alekai Poodles, here handled by Wendell J. Sammet. **Below:** Terri Meyers of Brooklyn Park, Minnesota, congratulates the gorgeous Standard Poodle bitch Ch. Lou Gin's Kiss Me Kate, following an exciting win. "Miss Kate" belongs to Terri and the Jack Phelans of Hammond, Indiana.

Canadian Obedience Trial Ch. Evanz Tantalizing Tina, Am., Bda., Can. U.D. and Mex., Bda. C.D.X., pictured winning one of her High Score in Trial awards, handled by Joyce Klevering of Ann Arbor, Michigan. "Tina" is sired by Ch. Evanz Lord Happiness Is ex Can., Mex. Ch. Pomero's La Sweet Martisse. She has a High in Trial one or more times in the United States, Mexico and Bermuda, plus a High in Trial Series for all four days in the shows on the Bermuda Circuit. Co-owned by Miss Klevering and Marilyn Pauley.

Obedience Trial Champion Tanya of Rye Top winning High Score in Trial at Greater Lowell Kennel Club, 1980, with her owner-trainer-handler, Mrs. Joseph Longo, Harrison, New York.

Overleaf:
Above: Ch. Manorhill's Classic Touch, handled by owner, Mrs. Frances M. Herms, to five times Best of Variety and four times Best of Opposite Sex. **Below:** Am., Can., Mex., Bda., Int. Ch. Evanz Daring Debutante. Top Winning Toy Poodle in Canada and No. Eight in United States for 1979. A multiple Best in Show winner, handled by Allan Chambers for Marilyn Pauley, Evanz Poodles, Saline, Michigan.

BEST OF
VARIETY

GILBERT PHOTO

BARRIE
KENNEL CLUB
BEST in SHOW

1979

BEST OF
BREED
OR VARIETY
BOOTH PHOTO

BARRIE
KENNEL CLUB

Best of Winners

1980

Stonham Photography

The beautiful Standard bitch, Ch. Longleat Hulagan,
with her puppies. Owned by J. Lester and Alisia Duffy.

Overleaf:
Above: The elegant and typey Champion Greylock Ribbon Raider, by Ch. Nilsson of Silcresta ex
Chrisward Naughty Marietta, owned by Judy Goldberg, Greylocks Poodles, Tonawanda, New York, and
handled by William Cunningham. *Below:* Can. Ch. Judel's Jumpin Jack Flash, bred by Judy E. Brown,
owned by William and Beverly Curry,

CHAPTER TWENTY

Breeding Poodles

This is Temar's Attention Please, sire of at least 24 champions. This noteworthy Miniature is owned by A. Monroe McIntyre, Atlanta, Georgia, and by Nancy Hafner of Tennessee.

The Poodle Brood Bitch

In a previous chapter we have discussed selection and purchase of Poodle puppies on through to a bitch you plan to use for breeding. Remember when you start out to make the latter important purchase that the bitch you hope will become the foundation of your kennel must be of the most desirable bloodlines, with good temperament and excellent type, and free of major faults or unsoundness. There is no such thing as a "bargain" brood bitch. If you are offered one, be wary and bear in mind that you need only the *best*, and that the price will be correctly in ratio to the quality.

Conscientious Poodle breeders feel quite strongly that the only possible reason for producing puppies is the desire to improve and uphold quality and temperament within the breed, certainly not because one hopes to make a quick cash profit on a mediocre litter, which never works out that way in the long run and can very well wind up adding to the nation's shocking number of unwanted canine waifs. The only reason for breeding a litter is the ambition to produce gorgeous Poodles of high show poten-

tial and sound temperament. That is the thought to be kept in mind right from the moment you begin to yearn for puppies.

Poodle bitches should not be mated earlier than their second season, by which time they should be from fifteen to eighteen months old. Many breeders prefer to wait and finish their bitches first to championship, then breed them, as pregnancy can be disaster to a show coat and getting it back in shape again takes time. Whenever you have decided will be the proper time, start watching at least several months ahead for what you feel would be the perfect mate to best complement her quality and bloodlines. Subscribe to the Poodle magazines and some of the all-breed ones in order to familiarize yourself with outstanding Poodles in other parts of the country. There is no necessity to limit your choice to a nearby dog unless you feel him to be suitable, as bitches are being shipped all over the country for breeding and suffering no ill results. Bear in mind that you need a stud dog strong in those features where your bitch is weak or lacking. Especially note if

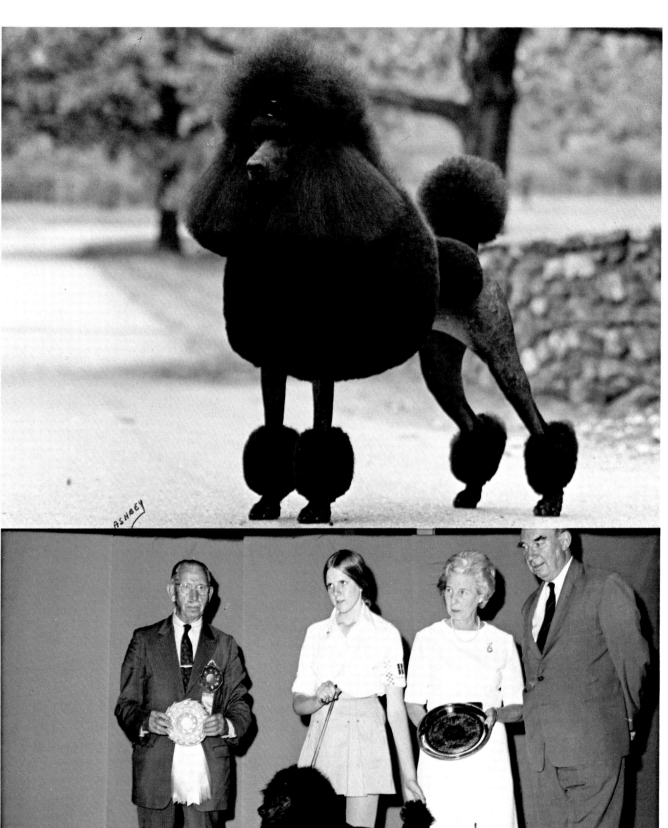

CANADIAN
NATIONAL
SPORTSMEN'S

DOG SHOW

BEST IN SHOW

1969

BEST OF
WINNERS

GILBERT PHOTO

there is a similarity between the background of your bitch and the stud dog, and of your bitch and those who, bred to him, have produced the progeny you admire. If so, he would seem to be a suitable selection for her. Stud fees usually run from $100.00 to $500.00—sometimes under special circumstances for an especially noted sire they can be even more. It is money well spent, though. *Do not* breed to a dog because he is less expensive than the others unless you really honestly think he can sire the kind of puppies for which you are striving.

If you will contact the owners of the stud dogs you find interesting, they will send you pedigrees, which you then can study in relation to your bitch's own or discuss with other breeders who are knowledgeable, including the one from whom your bitch was purchased. You may not always get an entirely unbiased opinion (particularly if the person giving it also has an available stud dog), but discussion is a fine

teacher. Listen to what they say and consider the value of their comments, and as a result you will be better qualified to reach a knowledgeable and intelligent decision of your own.

Once you have decided on the course you wish to follow, immediately contact the owner of the stud that is your first choice to find out if this will be agreeable. You will be asked about your bitch's health, soundness, temperament, and freedom from serious faults. A copy of her pedigree may be requested, or perhaps just a discussion of her background over the phone may suffice. The owner of the stud may require

Winning the Brood Bitch Class at the Poodle Club of America, 1969, is Ch. Kaye's Cocoa Nicole (left), with her daughter, Ch. Kaye's Viva Victoria, center, and her son, Champion Kaye's Ring Master. All belong to Mr. and Mrs. J. Herbert Kaye, Kayesett Kennels.

Overleaf:
Above: The lovely apricot Miniature, Ch. Harmo Gay Prospector, winning Best in Show at the Canadian National Sportsmen's in 1969. William J. Trainor handling for Harmo Kennels, Amherst, New Hampshire. **Below:** Champion Regence's El Picador, by Ch. Peeple's Silver Whistle from Regence's Star Spray. Bred and owned by V. Jean Craft and Margaret M. Klotz, Regence Poodles, Vienna, Virginia.

that the bitch be tested for brucellosis, which should be done not more than a month prior to the breeding.

Find out which airport will be most convenient for the person meeting and returning the bitch if she is to be shipped, and also what airlines use that one.

You will find that airlines also have special requirements on acceptance of animals for shipping. These include weather limitations and types of crates which are acceptable. The weather limits have to do with extreme heat or extreme cold at the point of destination, as some

A fabulous headstudy, made in 1968, of the black Miniature male, Eng., Am., Can. and Mex. Ch. Montmartre Bartat By Jingo owned by Mrs. Marjorie A. Tranchin of Dallas, Texas. This magnificent dog, in addition to his show successes in four Countries, also sired 27 champions.

airlines will not fly dogs into temperatures above or below certain levels, fearing for their safety. The crate problem is a simple one, as if your own is not suitable (which quite possibly it is not) most of the airlines have available crates designed for the purpose which can be purchased at a fair price. It is a good plan to purchase one of these if you intend to be shipping your Poodles even fairly frequently. These crates are made of fiberglass and are the safest type to be used for shipping.

You normally must notify the airline several days in advance to make a reservation, as they are able only to accommodate a certain number of dogs on each flight. Plan on shipping the bitch on about her eighth or ninth day of her season, but be careful to figure *not* to ship her on a weekend. The schedules often vary then, and some freight offices do not open at all on those days, which means that your bitch may be delayed in reaching her destination. Whenever you can, ship on a *direct* flight. Changing planes always carries a certain degree of risk of a dog being overlooked or wrongly routed at the middle stop, so avoid this danger when possible. The bitch must be accompanied by a health certificate which you must obtain from your veterinarian before taking her to the airport. Usually it will be necessary to have the bitch at the airport about two hours prior to flight time. Before finalizing arrangements, find out from the stud's owner at what time of day it will be most convenient to have the bitch picked up promptly upon arrival.

If you plan on bringing your bitch to the stud dog, it is more simple in the long run, particularly if you live even fairly near. Some people feel that the trauma of going by plane may cause the bitch to not conceive. Be sure to leave yourself sufficient leeway to assure your arrival at the proper time for breeding, which is normally the tenth to fourteenth day following the first signs of color. If you want the bitch bred twice, you must allow a day between. Do not expect the stud owner to house you while you are there. Locate a nearby motel that accepts dogs and make that your headquarters.

Overleaf:
Above: Swag Kennels' Standard Poodle, Wentworth George, with Terri Meyers, going Best of Variety at Key City Kennel Club 1977. **Below:** Surrounded by her family, Ch. Lou Gin's Kiss Me Kate seems also to be smiling about her just-won Best in Show, as are Paul Ann Phelan, Bob Walberg, Terri Meyers, and Jean (Mrs. Bob) Walberg.

BEST OF VARIETY
KEY CITY K.C.
APRIL 17, 1977
OLSON PHOTO

LAWTON FORT SILL KNL CLUB
LAWTON OKLAHOMA
OCT 28 1978
BEST IN SHOW
JUDGE
MR FRANK HAZE BURCH

LAWTON·FORT SILL
KENNEL CLUB

BEST IN SHOW

BEST OF
BREED OR VARIETY
WESTMINSTER
KENNEL CLUB
1979
GILBERT PHOTO

Just prior to your bitch coming into season, you should take her for a visit to her veterinarian. She should be checked for worms and should receive all necessary booster shots, plus one for parvo virus. The brucellosis test can be done then and her health certificate obtained for shipping if she will travel by air. If the bitch is slightly overweight, now is the time to get it off. She should be in good condition, neither underweight nor overweight, at the time of breeding.

Finally the day arrives when you notice the swelling of the vulva, and within a day or two color appears. Immediately phone the stud dog's owner and settle on the day of shipping or make the appointment for you and the bitch to be there for the breeding. If you are shipping, the stud fee check should be mailed immediately, leaving ample time for it to have arrived when the bitch does and the mating takes place. Be sure to call the airline for her reservation right then, too.

Do not feed the bitch before shipping her. Be certain that she has had a drink of water and has been well-exercised before closing her in the crate. Several layers of newspapers topped with some shredded newspaper will make a good bed and can be discarded when she arrives at her destination and replaced with clean paper for the return trip. Remember that the bitch should be brought to the airport about two hours before flight time.

If you are taking the bitch by car, be certain that you will arrive at a reasonable time of day. Do not appear late in the evening. If your arrival in town is not until then, get a good night's sleep and contact the stud's owner in the morning. If possible, leave the children and relatives at home, as they will only be in the way and possibly not welcomed by the stud's owner. Most stud dog owners prefer not to have many people on hand during the actual mating.

After the breeding has taken place, if you wish to sit and visit for awhile and the stud's owner has the time, return your bitch to her crate in your car. She should not be permitted to urinate for at least one hour following the breeding.

Eng., Am. and Can. Ch. Braeval Boomerang photographed in 1962 is the sire of 15 champions. Mrs. Marjorie Tranchin, owner.

Am. and Can. Ch. Wycliffe Hadrean, born July 1968, by Wycliffe Uranus ex Wycliffe Ysolt, at 15 months. Hadrean became the sire of 25 champions. Mrs. Donald Lyle bred and owns this handsome dog.

Overleaf:
Above: Kisses for co-owner Paul Ann Phelan and handler Bob Walberg as the aptly named Ch. Lou Gin's Kiss Me Kate closes out her show career, having won her 140th Best in Show award moments before. Sharing the happiness of the occasion were breeder Lou Dunston and co-owners Terri Meyers and Jack Phelan. **Below:** Ch. Mari A Spring Song, by Ch. Syntifny Piece of the Rock, was the Top Winning Toy Poodle for 1978. Mari was also a multiple Best in Show winner, going Best in Show twice at the Poodle Club of America, and being a Variety winner at the Garden. Todd Patterson handles for owner, Patricia Averill.

Am. and Can. Ch. Wycliffe Leroy, a Top Producer, is shown winning at the Poodle Club of America Specialty, 1965. Jane Forsyth handling. Owned and bred by Mrs. Donald Lyle.

Ch. Beritas Benito of Wybun winning the Watchung Mountain Poodle Club Specialty during the late 1970's. An outstanding producer and excellent show dog.

This is the time when you get the business part of the transaction attended to. Pay the stud fee, upon which you should receive your breeding certificate and, if you do not already have it, a copy of the stud dog's pedigree. The owner of the stud dog does not sign or furnish a litter registration application until after the puppies have been born.

Upon your return home, you now settle down to planning for the puppies in happy anticipation of a wonderful litter. A word of caution! Remember that even though she has been bred, your bitch is still an interesting target for all male dogs, so guard her carefully for the next week or until you are absolutely certain that her season has entirely ended. This would be no time to have any unfortunate incidents with another dog!

The Poodle Stud Dog

Choosing the right stud dog to best complement your bitch is often very difficult. Two principal factors to be considered are the stud's conformation and his pedigree. Conformation is fairly obvious. You want a dog that is a good example of the breed according to its Standard of Perfection. Understanding pedigrees is a bit more subtle, since the pedigree lists the ancestry of the dog and will also tell you the various bloodlines involved, plus many times their color.

If you are a novice in the breed, the correct interpretation of a pedigree may be difficult for you. Therefore I suggest that you study the pictures in this book, which include many of the famous Poodles whose names you will find, plus make an effort to discuss the various dogs behind your proposed stud with some of the veteran, more experienced breeders, who should include the breeder of your bitch. Frequently these folks will be personally familiar with at least many of the dogs in question, can offer opinions on them, and may have access to additional pictures you would benefit by seeing.

It is very important that the stud's pedigree should be harmonious with that of the bitches you plan on breeding to him. Do not rush out and breed to the latest winner with no thought of

Overleaf:
Above: Can. Ch. Evanz Slingapore Swing, silver Toy male, owned by Bernice Henderson, British Columbia, Canada. Top Winning Silver Toy in Canada, 1976. The sire of Top Producing bitch, Evanz Puffenz Pooed D'Naer, whose best known daughter is Ch. Evanz Daring Debutante. **Below:** Ch. Ravendune Ken D'Lee Typesetter, by Jeanie's Black Dina-Mite, was Winners Dog at Westminster, 1979. Bred and owned by Todd Patterson and Jeri Kendall, handled by Todd Patterson.

whether or not he can produce true quality. By no means are all great show dogs great producers! Take time to check out the progeny of the dog or dogs you are considering.

Breeding dogs is not a money-making operation. By the time you pay a stud fee, care for the bitch during gestation, whelp the litter, and rear the puppies through shots, worming, etc., you will be fortunate to break even financially once the puppies have been sold. Your chances of doing so are better if you are breeding for a show-quality litter, which will bring high prices as the pups are sold as show prospects. Therefore your best investment is to use the best dog available regardless of the cost, as you should then wind up with more valuable puppies. Remember that it is equally expensive to raise mediocre puppies as top ones, and your chances of financial return are better with the latter. So breed to the most excellent, most suitable stud dog you can find and do not quibble over the amount you are paying in stud fee.

You will have to decide which course you wish to follow when you breed your bitch, as there are three options. These are in-breeding, line-breeding, and out-crossing.

In-breeding is normally considered to be father to daughter, mother to son, or brother to sister. Line-breeding is breeding a bitch to a dog belonging originally to the same family, being descended from the same ancestors, such as half brother to half sister, niece to uncle, or cousin to cousin. Out-cross breeding is, of course, breeding a dog and a bitch with no mutual ancestors.

Each of these methods has its fans and its detractors. I would say that line-breeding is probably the safest course, especially for the novice, who should leave the more sophisticated in-breeding to the very experienced long-time breeders who thoroughly know and understand the line involved, the risks, and the possibilities. Out-crossing normally is done when you are trying to bring in a specific feature, such as shorter backs, better movement, more correct head, coat, etc.

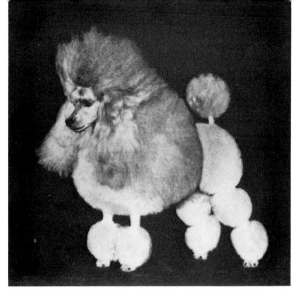

An Anita McMullen portrait of the silver Toy male, Am. and Can. Ch. Evan's Lord Happiness Is, sire of 25 champions at 11 years old. Owned by Marilyn Pauley, Evanz Poodles, Saline, Michigan.

Ch. Aizbel The Aristocrat has won two all-breed Bests in Show, four specialty Bests (including the Poodle Club of America National, 1978) and 20 Non-Sporting Groups, owner-handled on all but two of the latter occasions. He is the sire of 22 champions to date, and belongs to Mr. and Mrs. Luis Aizcorbe, Miami, Florida.

Wycliffe Rowena of Highlane, is pointed, though she has not gained her title yet. She is the dam of ten champions from a total of 18 puppies. Mrs. Donald Lyle, West Vancouver, Canada, owner.

Overleaf:
Above: Greenspring Poodle Club 1977, Best of Winners goes to Ch. Breng-Mar's Brunette, by Legagwan Pen-del Sirius from Breng-Mar's Baby Ruth. Owned by V. Jean Craft and Margaret M. Klotz, Regence Poodles, Vienna, Virginia. Wendell J. Sammet, handler. **Below:** Ch. Cotian Just In Time, Winners Bitch at Greenspring Poodle Club, 1978, still in puppy clip. This lovely brown Toy was sired by Poodletown's Polaris ex Cotian Delicate Delinquent, bred by Cotian Poodles, and owned by Mr. and Mrs. Loring Wentzel. Wendell J. Sammet, handler.

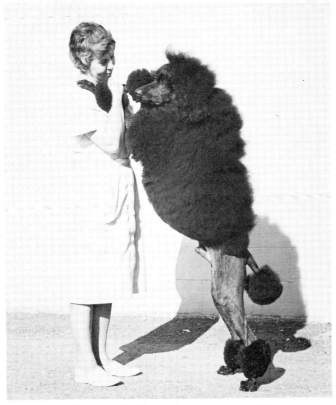

Multiple Best in Show winner and sire of 66 champions, Am. and Can. Ch. Wycliffe Kenneth is pictured with his "Mama", Mrs. Donald Lyle, Vancouver, Canada.

It is every breeder's ambition to develop their own strain or bloodline. However, it must be realized that this will take time and at least several generations before you can claim the achievement. The safest way to embark on this plan is by the selection of one or two bitches, the best that you can buy and from Top Producing lines, from which to breed. In the beginning you really have to own a stud dog. In the long run it is less expensive and sounder judgment to pay a stud fee when you are ready to breed a bitch than to purchase a stud dog and feed him all year, because a stud dog does not win any popularity contests with owners of bitches to be bred until he at least becomes a champion, has been successfully "specialed" for awhile, and has been at least moderately advertised, all of which adds up to a quite healthy expenditure.

The wisest course of an inexperienced breeder toward success in dogs is starting out as I have outlined above. Keep the best bitch puppy from the first several litters. After that you may wish to consider keeping a stud dog, if there has been a particularly handsome male in one of your litters that you feel has great potential, or if you know where there is one available that you are interested in, with the feeling that it would fit in nicely with the breeding program on which you are working. By this time, with several litters already born, your eye should have developed to a point enabling you to make a wise choice, either from one of your own litters or from among dogs you have seen that appear suitable.

When you make the decision to acquire your own stud dog, the greatest care should be taken in his selection. He must be of highest quality as he may be responsible for siring many puppies each year. Ideally he should come from a line of excellent Poodles on both sides of his pedigree, which themselves are, and which are descended from, top producers. This dog should have no glaring faults in conformation, being of quality and type to hold his own in keenest competition of his breed. He should be in good health, virile, and a keen stud dog, a proven sire able to transmit his correct qualities to his puppies. Need I say that such a dog will be enormously expensive unless you have the good fortune to

Overleaf:
Above: Ch. Bentwater Benita's Shiloh, the sire of nine or more champions, with his owner-handler, Joseph Vergnetti, collecting a win en route to the title. **Below:** Ch. Merrimar Marc Anthony, black Miniature dog, is pictured here with Virginia Davis. Owned by Mrs. William H. Ball and handled during an exciting ring career by Patrick F. Norwood.

BEST OF
WINNERS

GILBERT PHOTO

breed it? But to buy and use a lesser dog at stud is downgrading your breeding program unnecessarily since there are so many dogs fitting this description whose services can be used for a fee!

You should *never* breed to an unsound dog or one with serious faults. Not all champions by any means pass along their best features, and occasionally you will find a great stud dog that never gained a championship title due to some unusual circumstances. What you want to know most of all about a stud dog is what type puppies he produces, and with what bloodlines, and whether he himself possesses the physical attributes considered essential to outstanding show Poodles.

If you go out to buy a stud dog, obviously he will not be a puppy but will be a grown, proven male with as many of the above attributes as possible. He will be an expensive investment. But if you choose well and proceed toward his selection with study, care, and forethought, he will prove one of the best you've ever made.

Perhaps you may be so fortunate as to find that a young male, which you finally decided to keep from one of your homebred litters because he showed tremendous potential for the ring, matures into a stud dog such as we have been discussing. In this case he should be managed with care, for he is a valuable property that can contribute inestimably to Poodles in general and your kennel in particular.

Do not permit your young stud dog to be used until he is at least close to a year old, and even then he should be bred to a mature, proven matron accustomed to being bred who will make this first experience pleasant and easy for the stud. A young dog can be turned off breeding forever by a maiden bitch who fights and resists his advances. Never allow this to happen. Always start out a stud dog with a bitch who is mature, has been bred previously, and is of even temperament. The first breeding should be performed in quiet surroundings with only you and one other person to hold the bitch. Do not make a circus out of this first time, as the experience will determine the dog's outlook about being bred in the future. If he does not enjoy this first

A beautiful photo of an outstanding Toy Poodle. Jeanie's Black Dina Mite is a Top Producer, sire of 17 champions, and is a son of Ch. Ardyna's Nicodemus of Molynews ex Aspen Black Diamond. He is owned by Jeanie Mazza of Wayne, New Jersey.

Taken some years ago, this interesting photo is of Ch. Braeval Busker, a Group winning sire of champions and Best in Show winners. Handled here by Pat Norwood for owner, Marcella Gant.

Overleaf:
Above: Ch. Daktari Apogee Capezio, younger brother to Ch. Daktari-Apogee Aja, going Best of Winners from the puppy class to finish at the Poodle Club of America Specialty 1979. One of the many gorgeous Poodles at Daktari-Apogee Kennels. **Below:** Ch. Melrose Corky, handled by William Cunningham, taking Best of Winners at the Western Reserve Kennel Club Dog Show, August, 1980. One of the excellent Toy Poodles belonging to Jean Holley of Olmsted Falls, Ohio.

Am. and Can. Ch. Wycliffe Fitzherbert, Best in Show winner, the sire of 45 champions is by Am. and Can. Ch. Wycliffe Xcellente of Shamlot ex Am. and Can. Ch. Wycliffe Genevieve. Mrs. Donald Lyle, West Vancouver, Canada.

Ch. Bentwater Aztec, the sire of nine champions, is a son of Ch. Bentwater Benita's Shiloh. Handled here by Joseph Vergnetti at the Quinnipiac Poodle Club Specialty, 1974. Owned by Jan Bray.

experience or associates it with any unpleasantness, you may well have a future problem with which to contend.

Your young stud must permit help with the breeding, as later there will be bitches that will not be cooperative. If right at the beginning you are there helping him and praising him, he will accept and expect assistance

Things to have handy before you introduce your dog and the bitch are K-Y jelly, which is the only lubricant that should be used, and either an old stocking (for a Standard) or a length of gauze with which to tie up the bitch's muzzle should it be necessary to keep her from biting you or the dog. Some bitches put up a fight while others do not, and it is safest to be prepared.

At the time of the breeding the stud fee becomes due, and it is expected that it will be paid immediately. Normally a return service is offered if the bitch misses or fails to produce at least one live puppy. Conditions of service are what the stud dog's owner makes them, and there are no standard rules covering this. The stud fee is paid for the act, not the result. If the bitch fails to conceive, it is customary for the owner to offer a free service, but this is a courtesy and not to be considered a right, particularly in the case of a proven stud who is siring consistently and whose fault the failure obviously is *not*. Stud dog owners are always anxious to see their clients get good value and to have winning young stock by their dog in the ring, therefore very few refuse to mate the second time, but it is wise for both parties to have the terms of the transaction clearly understood at the time of the breeding.

If the return service has been provided and the bitch has missed a second time, that is considered to be the end of the matter and the owner would be expected to pay a further fee if it is felt that the bitch should be given a third chance with the stud dog. The management of a stud dog and his visiting bitches is quite hard work, and a stud fee has usually been well-earned when one service has been achieved, let alone by repeated visits with the same bitch.

Overleaf:
Above: Ch. Daktari Apogee Enda by Eng., Am. Ch. Tiopepi Typhoon ex Ch. Daktari Asia, was Best of Winners and Best of Opposite Sex for 5 points over Best in Show winning "specials" at Westminster 1981 under judge Mrs. Betty Dexter. Enda finished her title with three 5-point majors, breeder-owner-handled by A. Monroe McIntyre who co-owns with Nancy Hafner. **Below:** Looking to the future, is the puppy that matured to become Ch. J.L.C. Critique, a Best in Show winner, a Specialty Best of Breed winner, twice a Westminster Non-Sporting Group winner. Owned during the major portion of his exciting show career by Robert Koeppel, "Tiki" is now at home with Mrs. Rita Cloutier. This is how a future top winning Miniature looks at an early age.

BEST OF
WINNERS

WESTMINSTER
KENNEL CLUB
1981
GILBERT PHOTO

The accepted litter is one live puppy. It is wise to have a breeding agreement certificate printed up which the owner of the stud dog and the owner of the bitch both sign. This should list in detail the conditions of the breeding as well as the dates of the mating. At this time the owner of the bitch receives a copy of the stud dog's pedigree if one has not previously been provided. The owner of the stud does not sign the litter registration until the puppies have been born.

Upon occasion, arrangements other than a cash stud fee are made for a breeding, such as the owner of the stud taking the pick-of-litter puppy in lieu of money. This should be clearly specified on the breeding certificate along with the terms of at what age the stud's owner will select the puppy, whether it is to be specifically of a stated sex, or whether it is to be the pick of the entire litter.

The price of a stud fee varies according to circumstances. Usually, to prove a young stud dog his owner will permit the first breeding to be quite inexpensive; then once a bitch has become quite clearly pregnant by him, he becomes a "proven stud" and the fee rises accordingly for bitches that follow. The sire of championship-quality puppies will bring a stud fee of at least the purchase price of one show-type puppy as the accepted "rule of thumb." Until at least one champion has finished by your stud dog, the fee will remain equal to the price of one pet puppy. When his list of champions starts to grow, so does the amount of the stud fee. For a Top Producer sire of consistent champions, litter after litter, the stud fee will rise accordingly.

Almost invariably it is the bitch that comes to the stud dog for the breeding. Immediately upon having selected the stud dog you wish to use, the owner of that dog should be contacted to discuss details. It is the stud dog owner's prerogative to refuse to breed any bitch deemed unsuitable for the stud dog, therefore your bitch's pedigree and, if requested, a picture of her should be submitted. Stud fee and method of payment should be discussed at this time and a decision reached whether it is to be a full cash transaction at the time of mating or a pick-of-litter puppy when

A particularly lovely little Toy Poodle, Ch. Bel Tor Impossible Dream, makes a fine win for his owner, Mrs. J.A. Mason, during 1970.

Troymere Toblerone, one of the splendid producers from Troy Tanner's Troymere Kennels at Sidney, Australia.

Regence's Dare Devil taking Winners Dog at Westminster, 1975. Handled by Wendell J. Sammet, Dare Devil is by Legagwann Pen-Del Sirius from Regence Daughter of Darkness.

they are eight weeks old. The stud dog owner should be given an approximate idea of when the bitch is expected to be coming into heat, which can vary quite widely, as many bitches do not keep to a regular six-month cycle. It should be decided whether the bitch will be brought to the stud dog or shipped in by plane. If the latter, there may be an additional charge depending on the stud owner's proximity to the airport, based on time, gasoline, and tolls required in making the trips to meet and return her. The normal length of time for the stud owner to keep the bitch is five days, these being the day of arrival, the day she will be bred the first time, one day between, the day of the second breeding, and the day shipped home. Board for this is included in the stud fee, but if for some reason the bitch must remain longer, her owner is charged board for the additional time at the normal boarding rate for the breed.

The day you see signs of your bitch being in season, you should call the stud's owner to finalize arrangements. I have known cases where this has been put off until the final moment, only to find that the stud dog and his owner are off at shows and thus unavailable, which could have been avoided had the call been made promptly. Let the stud's owner know the airline, flight number, and scheduled time of arrival, which information he will in turn give to you for the bitch's trip home.

It is essential that the owner of a dog being offered at public stud have proper facilities for the care of visiting bitches. Nothing can be more heartbreaking than to have a bitch either misbred or, worse still, get away and become lost. There must be a safe place for her to be both housed and exercised, and the owner of the stud should be very certain of this before undertaking to have bitches visit his dog.

As already mentioned, breeding dogs is no road to riches. It may seem that the stud fee you are paying or charging is astronomical, when actually it is far from being that, everything taken into consideration. Remember all the time, effort, and expense that have gone into the making of a Poodle to which other people wish to breed!

Overleaf:
Above: This beautiful apricot Miniature is Can. Ch. Murwyn's Bonnie Tinkerbelle, owned by Mrs. Ruth L. Clarkson, North Gower, Ontario. By Ch. Murwyn Golden Guardsman ex Bonfire of Lindenwald.
Below: Ch. Lochranza Rumbaba, a brown Miniature in residence at Daktari Apogee Poodles. This import is pictured taking Best of Winners at the Poodle club of America, October, 1978 from judge, Mrs. Ann Stevenson.

2nd in Group
T.I.K.O.

Poodle Club of America

BEST OF WINNERS
POODLE CL. OF AMER.
OCTOBER 5, 1978
OLSON PHOTO

Credit Valley K.C.

Best of Winners   Best Opp. Sex

1979

Stonham Photography

BEST OF
BREED

POODLE CLUB
OF AMERICA
1986

GILBERT PHOTO

466

There is no dog more valuable than the proven sire of champions, Group Winners, and Best in Show dogs! Once you have such a dog, guard his reputation well and *do not* permit him to be bred to just any bitch that comes along. It takes two to make the puppies; even the most dominant stud can not do it all. Never permit him to be bred to a bitch you consider unworthy. Remember that when the puppies arrive it will be your stud dog who will be blamed for any lack of quality, while the bitch's shortcomings will be quickly and conveniently overlooked.

Going into the actual management of the mating is a bit superfluous here. If you have had experience, you will know. If you have not, you should not attempt to follow a book but should have a veterinarian, breeder friend, or handler there to help you the first few times. You *do not* just turn the dog and bitch loose together and await developments; too many things can go wrong. Someone should hold the dog and the bitch (one person each) until the tie is made and should stay with them during the entire act.

If you get a complete "tie," probably then only the one mating is absolutely necessary. However, especially with a maiden bitch or one that has come a long distance for this breeding, we prefer following up, leaving one day between, with a second breeding. This way there should be no problem.

Once the "tie" has been completed and they release, be certain that the male's penis goes completely back within its sheath. He should be allowed a drink of water, a short walk, and then put into his kennel or somewhere alone where he can settle down. Do not allow him to be with other dogs for awhile, as they will notice the odor of the bitch on him and, particularly with other males, he may become involved in a fight.

The bitch, however, should not be permitted to relieve herself immediately or for at least an hour. In fact, many people feel that she should be "up-ended" for several minutes to assure the sperm traveling further within. She should be crated and kept quiet for an hour or so.

Can. Ch. Syntifny Snapshot, sire of seven champions and a Top Producer. By Ch. Syntifny Piece Of The Rock. Jane A. Winne, owner, Syntifny, Three Rivers, Michigan.

The Miniature Poodle, Marsden Black Vandal, is a proven producer of excellent quality. Bred and owned by John and Phillip Warburton, Glenore, New South Wales, Australia.

Overleaf:
Above: Betty Mahaffy is pictured here with her lovely Toy Poodle, Ch. Ashwood's Little Bit Black, by Ch. Ashwood's Bit O Trouble out of Brown Bonanza of Grayco, taking Best of Winners at the Central New York Kennel Club Dog Show 1979. **Below:** Gaining Best of Breed at the Poodle Club of America Specialty Show, 1980 is the Standard bitch, Ch. Dassin Rita La Rose. With her handler, F. L. Dickey, she earns the supreme honor of the Poodle year for owner, Mrs. Edward Solomon.

Your Poodle's Gestation, Whelping, and Litter

Once the bitch has been bred and is back at home, be reminded to keep an ever-watchful eye that no other male gets to her until at least the twenty-second day of her season. It will still be possible for an unwanted breeding to take place, which at this point would be catastrophic. Remember she actually can have two separate litters by two different dogs, so take care.

In other ways she should be treated quite normally. It is not necessary for her to have any additives until she is at least four to five weeks pregnant. Also it is unnecessary for her to have additional food. It is better not to overfeed the bitch this early, as the puppies do not strain her resources until the last stages of her pregnancy. A fat bitch is not an easy whelper.

Controlled exercise is good and necessary for the bitch. She should not be permitted to just lie around. At about seven weeks along, this should be slowed down to several walks daily, preferably on leash.

At four to five weeks of the pregnancy, calcium may be added to the diet, and at seven weeks the one meal a day may be increased to two meals with some nutritional additives in each. Canned milk may be added to her meal at this time.

A week before she is due to whelp, your Poodle bitch should be introduced to her whelping box so that she will have accustomed herself to it and feel at home there by the time the puppies arrive. She should be encouraged to sleep there but permitted to come and go as she pleases. The box should be roomy enough for her to lie down and stretch out, but not too large or the pups will have too much room in which to roam and may get chilled if too far from the mother. Be sure that there is a "pig rail" for the box, which will prevent the puppies from being crushed against the side of the box. The room where the box is placed, either in the home or the kennel, should be free from drafts and should be kept at about 70 degrees Fahrenheit. In winter it may be necessary to have an infra-red lamp over the

This beautiful Miniature Poodle is Ch. Sangueree Shannon who finished her championship at nine months of age. A producer of champions, Shannon belongs to Michael Hagen and Aileen Tobias, Monrovia, Maryland.

Am. and Can. Ch. Bell Aire's Cara Mia Jewel is owned by Helen and Sonja Petlitzki, Helsonae Poodles, Detroit, Michigan.

Overleaf:
Am. Ch. Pomroth Chanel is pictured here winning under judge Jay Schaeffer. Bud Dickey handling for owner, Mrs. Helen Hamilton.

WINNERS

CARROLL

KENNEL CLUB

MAY 1979

ASHBEY

Mari Carlos
1980

470

whelping box, in which case guard carefully against this being placed too low or close to the puppies.

Keep a big pile of newspapers near the box. You'll find that you never have enough when you have a litter, so start accumulating them ahead of time. Also have a pile of clean towels, scissors, and a bottle of alcohol ready at least a week before the bitch is due to whelp, as you never know when she may start.

The day or night before she is due, the bitch will become restless, going in and out of her box and in and out of the door. She may refuse food, and at this point her temperature will start to drop. She will start to dig at and tear up the newspapers in her box, shiver, and generally look uncomfortable. Only you should be with the bitch at this point. She does not need an audience. This is not a side show, and several people hovering over her may upset the bitch to the point of her hurting the puppies. Stay nearby but do not fuss too much over the bitch. Eventually she will settle down in her box and begin to pant, very shortly thereafter starting to have contractions. Soon a puppy will start to emerge, sliding out with the contractions. The mother immediately should open the sac, cut the cord, and then clean up the puppy. She will also eat the placenta, which you should permit. Once the puppy is cleaned, it should be placed next to the bitch unless she is showing signs of having the next one immediately. The puppy will start looking for a nipple on which to nurse. You should make certain that it is able to latch on successfully.

If a puppy is a breech (i.e., born feet first), then you must watch carefully that it is completely delivered as quickly as possible and the sac removed fast so that the puppy does not drown. Sometimes even a normally positioned birth will seem extremely slow in coming. Should this occur, you might take a clean towel and, as the bitch contracts, pull the puppy out, doing so gently and with care. If once the puppy is delivered it shows little signs of life, take a rough (turkish) towel and rub quite briskly back and forth, massaging the chest. Continue this for

Two of the foundation Poodles of Beaujeau Poodles, Ch. Diablotin Autumn Leaf, brown Miniature bitch (left) and Beaujeau Diablesse. Autumn Leaf was the dam of five champions.

Griggswood Cadenza, dam of four champions, is pictured winning at the Montreal Club Canin, September, 1977. Jennifer Griggs is handling this daughter of Ch. Griggswood Double Entry ex Ch. Griggswood Harmony. Owned by Griggswood Poodles, Quebec.

Overleaf:
American and Canadian Champion Dhubhne Darth Vader with his three-month-old puppy, Dhubhne Dream Waltz, the latter named for a world champion five-gaited mare. Both Poodles belong to Carroll Ann Irwin, North Hollywood, California.

Am. and Can. Ch. Wycliffe Zara, a multiple Best in Show winner and a Top Producer is owned by Mrs. Donald Lyle, Wycliffe Poodles, West Vancouver, B.C.

This is the great Miniature Poodle, Ch. Aizbel The One And Only, sire of 30 champions. Owner-handled he has gained three all-breed Bests in Show, three specialty Bests in Show, and 20 Non-Sporting Group Firsts. Bred and owned by Mr. and Mrs. Luis Aizcorbe, Miami, Florida.

about fifteen minutes and be sure that the mouth is free from liquid. It may be necessary to try mouth to mouth breathing. This is done by pressing the puppy's jaws open and, using a finger, depressing the tongue which may be stuck to the roof of the mouth. Then blow hard down the puppy's throat. Bubbles may pop out of its nose, but keep on blowing. Rub with the towel again across the chest and try artificial respiration, pressing the sides of the chest together, slowing and rhythmically, in and out, in and out. Keep trying one method or the other for at least fifteen minutes before giving up. You may be rewarded with a live puppy that otherwise would not have made it.

This puppy should not be put back with the mother immediately, as it should be kept warm. Put it in a cardboard box near the stove, on an electric pad, or, if it is the time of year for your heat to be running, near the radiator until the rest of the litter has been born. Then it can go in with the others.

The bitch may go for an hour or more between puppies, which is fine as long as she seems comfortable and is not straining or contracting. I would not allow her to remain unassisted for more than an hour if she does continue to contract. Now is the time to call your veterinarian, whom you should have already alerted of the possibility. He may want the bitch brought in so that he can examine her and perhaps give her a shot of Pituitrin. In some cases the veterinarian will find a Caesarian section is necessary due to a puppy being lodged in some manner making normal delivery impossible. Sometimes this occurs due to size, but sometimes it is just that the puppy is turned wrong. If the bitch does require a section, the puppies already born must be kept warm in their cardboard box with a heating pad under the box.

Once the section is done, get the bitch and the puppies home. Do not attempt to put the pups in with the bitch until she is at least fairly conscious, as she may unknowingly hurt them. But do get them back with her as soon as possible for them to start nursing.

Overleaf:
One of the many fine homebred winners belonging to Edward B. Jenner of Knolland Farms, Ch. Knolland Magnolia is pictured here with Gary Wittmeier handling.

If the mother lacks milk at this point, the puppies must be fed by hand, kept very warm, and held onto the mother's teats several times a day in order to stimulate and encourage the secretion of milk which should start shortly.

Assuming that there is no problem and the bitch whelps naturally, you should insist that she go out to exercise, staying just long enough to make herself comfortable. She can be offered a bowl of milk and a biscuit, but then should settle down with her family. Be sure to clean out the whelping box and change the newspapers so that she will have a fresh bed.

Actually, unless some problem occurs, there is little you must do now about the puppies until they become three to four weeks old. Keep the box cleaned and with newpapers. When the pups get to be a couple of days old, towels should be tacked down to the bottom of the box so that the puppies will have traction when they move.

If the bitch has difficulties with her milk supply, or if you should be so unfortunate as to lose the bitch, then you must be prepared to either hand-feed or tube-feed the puppies if they are to survive. I personally prefer tube feeding as it is so much faster and easier. If the bitch is available, it is best that she continue to clean and care for the puppies as normal excepting for the food supplements you will provide. If anything has happened so she is unable to do this, you must learn to gently rub the puppy's abdomen with wet cotton to make the puppy urinate, and the rectum should be gently rubbed to open the bowels. This must be done after each feeding.

Newborn puppies must be fed every three to four hours around the clock. The puppies must be kept warm during this time. Have your veterinarian show you how to tube-feed. Once learned, it is really very simple.

After a normal whelping, the bitch will require additional food to enable her to produce sufficient milk. She should be fed twice daily now, and, in addition, given some canned milk several times during the day.

At two weeks old, you should clip the puppies' nails, as they are needle sharp at this stage and can hurt or damage the mother's teats and stomach as the pups hold on to nurse.

Puget Sound Poodle Club Specialty, June, 1977. Am. and Can. Ch. Wycliffe Fitzherbert, aged three, is pictured with his children winning the Stud Dog Class. Am. and Can. Ch. Denaire Black Dahlia, 12 months; Am. and Can. Ch. Wycliffe Joyous Jacqueline, 18 months; Can. Ch. Rondel Wycliffe Caprice and Am. and Can. Ch. Rondell Critic's Choice, both 19 months.

Overleaf:
Am., Can. Ch. Marney Bonnie Doone, Miniature, bred and owned by Mrs. Margaret Durney and handled by Tim Brazier.

Mr. William M. Schmick, vice-president of the American Kennel Club, and his wife, Cynthia, are former Poodle breeders. Highly successful breeders their Standards have included this beautiful Best in Show winner, Ch. Caledonia Honey Bear, owner-handled to an exciting award in 1954. Honey Bear was a noted producer as well as show bitch.

This brown Miniature dog is the very famous Ch. Campbell's Razz-Ma-Tazz, owned by Nancy Cutler and Peggy Hogg, by whom he was handled. Shown as a special for only a year, he accounted for half a dozen Bests in Show, along with a good number of Group victories. This dog is the all time Top Producing Brown Sire, all three Varieties, with 39 champions to his credit so far including Best in Show winners. He is as well the sire of seven Top Producers.

Between three and four weeks of age, weaning of the puppies should be started. Scraped beef (prepared by scraping it off slices of beef with a spoon, so that none of the fat or gristle is included) may be offered in very small quantities a couple of times daily for the first few days. Then by the third day you can mix up ground puppy chow with warm water as directed on the package, offering it four times daily. By now the mother should be kept away from the puppies and out of the box for several hours at a time until, when they reach five weeks, she is left in with them only overnight. By the time they are six weeks old, the puppies should be entirely weaned and the mother should only check them out with occasional visits.

Most veterinarians recommend a temporary D.H.L. (distemper, hepatitis, leptospirosis) shot when the puppies are six weeks of age. This remains effective for about two weeks. Then at eight weeks the series of permanent shots begins for the D.H.L. protection, and it is also a good idea now since the prevalence of the dreaded parvo virus to discuss the advisability of having these shots, too, for your puppies. Each time the pups go in for shots, you should bring stool samples to be checked for worms, even though the previous one may have proved negative. Worms go through various stages of development and may be present although they do not appear positive in every check. So do not neglect to keep after this.

The puppies should be fed four times daily until they are three months old. Then you can cut back to three feedings daily. By six months of age, two meals daily are sufficient. Some people feed their dogs twice daily throughout their lifetime, while others go to once a day when the puppy reaches a year of age.

The ideal time for puppies to go to new homes is between eight and 12 weeks old, although some do so successfully at six weeks. Be sure that they go to their future owners accompanied by a diet list and schedule of the shots they have received and those they will still need. These should be included with the registration application and a copy of the pedigree.

Overleaf:
Ch. Bel Tor Playing It Cool makes an attractive picture of Poodle type and elegance. Owned by Mrs. J. A. Mason.

BEST OF
WINNERS

NORTHWESTERN
CONNECTICUT
DOG CLUB

SEPTEMBER 1978

ASHBEY

Mrs. Henry J. Kaiser has always thoroughly enjoyed her Poodles for their personality as well as for their beauty. Here she romps with two of her favorites.

Overleaf:
Am., Can. Ch. Pomroth Custom Maid belongs to Mrs. Helen M. Hamilton, Pomroth Poodles, Reg. This handsome puppy is handled here by Tim Brazier.

CHAPTER TWENTY-ONE

Responsibilities of Poodle Breeders And Owners

The brown Toy, Ch. AA Love Tiffany, handled by Wendell J. Sammet to Group First at Carrol County Kennel Club, 1971, under judge Louis Murr. Mrs. Marge McNelis, owner.

The first responsibility of a person breeding Poodles nowadays is to do so with care, forethought, and deliberation. It is inexcusable to breed more litters than you need to carry on your show program or perpetuate your bloodlines. A responsible breeder should not cause a litter to be born unless there are plans for definite disposition of the puppies and unless the breeder has a waiting list to assure that each healthy puppy will be welcomed into a good home and happy future. Overpopulation is the dog world's most heartbreaking tragedy. Those of us who truly love and are involved with dogs should not add to it. Breeding programs should be planned so that a Poodle bitch never whelps a litter without a definite purpose. If you have any reason to feel that placing the puppies may become a problem, wait for a more propitious moment before you bring them into the world. Certainly no Poodle owner wants to find himself running frantically around in search of someone to take some of the puppies off his hands, even if he has to give them away, and the latter frequently is not a good idea. I am a firm believer that people getting a Poodle should *buy* that Poo-

dle, paying a fair price for it. A Poodle is a dog that demands *care*, and I have found that a lot of the people in the world who simply cannot resist "something for nothing" have little intention of putting themselves out in the least over the dog.

A responsible Poodle breeder makes absolutely certain, so far as is humanly possible, that the home to which one of his puppies will go is a *good* home from the dog-ownership point of view. I have tremendous admiration for those who carefully check out the people to whom they are selling a dog, and I think that all should follow suit on this important issue. We do not want Poodles winding up in Humane Society shelters, in experimental laboratories, or as victims of speeding cars. While complete control of such a situation may be almost an impossibility, it should never be forgotten that when we place a puppy in a new home, there is always a chance of such things happening. Family problems arise or people grow bored with a dog, and thus the dog becomes the victim. As a Poodle breeder, the future of these magnificent dogs is in your hands. Guard it well and with conscience.

Overleaf:
Above: The Miniature Poodle with which Bill Cunningham won his first Best in Show, Ch. Villa Cesca Ebony August, brown Miniature bitch owned by Barbara Powers, Tenpenny Poodles. Mr. Cunningham handled to the top award at Progressive Dog Club of Wayne County in 1975. This lovely bitch became the second Top Miniature Poodle Bitch in the United States, and was retired upon winning Best of Opposite Sex at Westminster. Photo courtesy of Mr. Cunningham. **Below:** Winning the 1979 Watchung Mountain Poodle Club Specialty Show, Ch. J.L.C. Critique with his handler, Paul Edwards, takes the honors from judge Ann Seranne on the left. Mrs. Rita Cloutier owns this fine sparkling white Miniature Poodle.

PROGRESSIVE

BEST OF OPP. SEX

BEST OF BREED
WATCHUNG MOUNTAIN
POODLE CLUB

DECEMBER 1979

ASHBEY

481

A superb headstudy of the white Standard dog, Ch. Alekai Argus, owned by the Aldeblou Poodles of Mr. and Mrs. Terrence Levy, Huntington, New York.

Waiting at ringside is Am. and Can. Ch. Kayesett Barbie Doll owned by Kayesett Kennels, Muriel P. and J. Herbert Kaye, Woodbridge, Connecticut.

The unique and beautiful Poodle kennel owned by Mr. and Mrs. Henry J. Kaiser on their Hawaiian estate. The original home of Alekai, the design, beauty and workability of this well-planned layout earned tremendous admiration and acclaim from everyone so fortunate as to have seen it.

The final obligation every dog owner shares, be there one dog or many dogs involved, is that of making detailed, explicit plans for the future of our dearly loved animals in the event of the owner's death. Far too many of us are apt to leave this important matter unattended to, feeling that they will "make out alright" or that "someone" will "see to them." This is not very likely unless you have gone to some trouble to assure that this will be the case.

Life is filled with the unexpected, and even the youngest, healthiest, person most obviously slated to be around for the next several decades, may be the victim of a fatal accident or sudden illness. *One never knows.* The fate of our dogs, so entirely in our hands, should never be left to chance. If you have not already done so, please get together with your lawyer and set up a clause in your will saying exactly what you want done with each of your dogs, to whom they will be entrusted (after first making absolutely certain that the person is willing and able to assume this responsibility), and telling the location of all registration papers, pedigrees, and kennel records. Just think of the possibilities of what might happen otherwise. If there is another family member who shares your love of the dogs, that is good. But if your heirs are not dog oriented, they will hardly know how to proceed, and your dogs may wind up being disposed of in a way that would break your heart were you alive to know about it.

In our family, we have specific directions in each of our wills for each of the dogs. A friend, also a "dog person," has agreed to take over their care until they can be placed accordingly and will make certain that all will work out as we have planned. We have this person's name and telephone number prominently displayed in our van and in our wallets. Our lawyer is aware of this fact; it is all spelled out in the wills. The friend has a signed check to be used in case of an emergency or accident when we are traveling with the dogs to be used for her to come and see

to them should anything happen making it impossible for us to do so. This we feel is the least any dog owner must do, should our dogs suddenly find themselves without us. There have been so many sad cases of dogs unprovided for by their loving owners, left to heirs who couldn't care less and who disposed of them in any way at all that was the least trouble, that it should be a *must* to all of us to prevent any such thing happening to our own dogs.

The registration certificates of all these dogs are enclosed in the envelope with our wills. The person who will be in charge knows each dog so that there will be no problem about identification. These are points to be considered and provided for.

We also owe an obligation to our older dogs that is too often disregarded. It disgusts me that there are people in the world, supposedly dog fanciers, who are only interested in getting an older dog out of the way once its show career has ended, in order to make room for new litters. The people I like and consider to be genuine dog lovers are the ones who permit their dogs to live out their lives in happy comfort as long as they are in reasonably good health and enjoying doing so. How quickly some forget the thrill and happiness that dog has brought with exciting wins or the beautiful puppies produced from him or her, in which we have taken such pride.

Ch. Daktari Apogee Aja, a Group winner from the puppy class and winner of five Non-Sporting Groups. Sired by Eng. and Am. Ch. Tiopepi Typhoon ex Ch. Daktari Asia.

DASSIN FARM, INCORPORATED

Names of Dog: Ch. Dassin Broadway Joe — PA395022

Ch. Dassin Sum Buddy

Owner Truman Dickey   Breeder Dickey

Sire: Ch. Wanshire Country Gentleman

- SIRE Haus Brau Aladdin
  - SIRE Ch. Wycliffe Ian
  - DAM Ch. Haus Sachse Rebecca
- DAM Haus Brau Cheri Biri Bin
  - SIRE Ch. Wycliffe Murdock
  - DAM Ch. Haus Brau Angelique

Dam: Ch. Jodyne Marjorie

- SIRE Ch. Wycliffe Virgil
  - SIRE Ch. Wycliffe Timothy
  - DAM Ch. Wycliffe Jacqueline
- DAM Mogenes Beaugeaut
  - SIRE Footprints Go Gay Go
  - DAM Mogenes Amber

Date Issued _____   Signed Joseph Vergnetti

SEX Male   COLOR White   DATE WHELPED April 28th 1945

REGISTERED WITH AKC   DATE OF PURCHASE Nov 20 '4?   NAME OF PURCHASER Blakeen Kennels

Ch Snow Boy of Fircot

- Harwee of Mannerhead (Black)
  - Eng Ch Eric Brighteyes (Black)
    - Popinjay
      - Eng. Ch. The Monarch
      - Blue Love Bird
    - Bonny Forget Me Not
      - The Aide De Camp
      - Belinda Blue (Grey)
  - Eng. Ch. The Mistress of Mannerhead (Black)
    - Harpendale Gay Lord
      - Ch. The Ghost (Grey)
      - Bettina
    - Harpendale Loretta
      - Ch Chieveley Chopstick (Grey)
      - Harpendale Nippy
- Solitaire of Piperscroft (White)
  - Russet of Piperscroft (Brown)
    - Eng. Ch. Barty of Piperscroft (Grey)
      - Monty of Piperscroft (Black)
      - Manon of Piperscroft
    - Priscilla of Piperscroft
      - Plata of Eathorpe (Grey)
      - Chieveley Chatty
  - Heatherbelle of Piperscroft
    - Swanhill Silver King (Grey)
      - Vendas Blue Masterpiece (Blue)
      - Vendas Zeeta
    - Vendas Gold Dollar (Apricot)
      - Eng. Ch. Petit Morceau of Piperscroft (Black)
      - Vendas Ice Fairy (White)

I HEREBY CERTIFY THAT TO THE BEST OF MY KNOWLEDGE AND BELIEF THE ABOVE PEDIGREE IS TRUE AND THAT ALL ANCESTORS NAMED ABOVE ARE OF THE SAME BREED.

SIGNED THIS _____ DAY OF _____ 19 ___

OWNER, SIGNATURE Mrs Sherman R Hoyt   ADDRESS _____

BRED BY Mrs Thomas

Ch. Tamara of Stonebridge, by Ch. Alekai Ahi ex Ch. Alekai Maunalua, bred and owned by Stonebridge Poodles, Dorothy Baranowsky. Handler, Wendell J. Sammet.

Ch. Monfret Fiorello, C.D.X., a multiple Group winner from the Monfret Kennels of Francis P. Fretwell.

Beresford Alladin, a Miniature, is handled here by Jane Kamp Forsyth for Alice Bradshaw and Irene Donovan to a first in the Non-Sporting Group at Suffolk County Kennel Club, 1970.

These two well-dressed little Poodles are out for a walk with their owner, well bundled up in their overcoats as is Ellington, their cat friend. Small Poodles living as house dogs and in short clip appreciate the warmth of a coat when taken out on cold days. These two are Toughy's Chocolate Fancy and Toughy of Junkin, both owned by Marcia Foy.

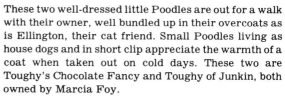

Beverely Merritt's Toy Poodle, Am. and Can. Ch. Wilmar Howlene Stone Broke is being handled by Todd Patterson to Best of Winners at the Greater Cincinnati Poodle Club Specialty show en route to the title.

Ch. Kayesett Zarina taking Best of Variety in 1971 under judge, Iris de la Torre Bueno. Jane Forsyth handling for Mr. and Mrs. J. Herbert Kaye.

Ch. Dassin Blue Lilac, a daughter of Ch. Jocelyene's Marjorie, is bred and owned by F.C. Dickey, Medina, Ohio.

The black Miniature Ch. Beritas Ronlyn Danger Man, an English import, is pictured winning at Middlesex County, June 1968. Owned by Petwill Kennels, handled by Wendell J. Sammet. By Eng. Ch. Beritas Bonaparte ex Eng. Ch. Ronly's Miss Irresistable.

The multiple Best in Show winning Standard, Am., Can. Ch. Monfret Merlin. Francis P. Fretwell, owner. Sired by Ch. Carillon Dilemma, U.D., ex Ch. Kah's Kollector's Item, C.D.

PEDIGREE

OF

BLAKEEN KING DOODLES .... AKC N-146438

BREED	BORN	KENNEL NAME	COLOR	SEX
Poodle _Toy_	Jan.9, 1952	"Doodles"	Black	Male

BREEDER	ADDRESS OF BREEDER	DATE PURCHASED
Blakeen Kennels	Stamford, Conn.	

GRANDPARENTS	GREAT GRANDPARENTS	GREAT GREAT GRANDPARENTS
	Barnell's Tres Joli	Ch. Gremlin
		Ch. Cherin
Voltaire II	Gaite Parisienne	Ch.Galcit's Priority of St. Elmo
		Ch. Von's Jitsie Lou

sire was toy

Baron De Gladville *toy*
SIRE AKC N-104152 /20042
COLOR black

	Andre Boy	Ch. Le Monde Chic de Larson
		Ch. Miss Perfection of Rosbar
Barnes' Mimi	Orsie's Mega-Mega	Kingsland's Bobbie
		Kingsland's Xmas Mary

all dams were mini alius

Ch. Puttencove Antonio	Ch. Anthony of Revemir	Ch.**Cartlane Augustin**
		Revemir Georgette
	Ch. Revemir Bitsie of Puttencove	Ch. Blakeen Bitzie Boy
		Revemir Babette

Puttencove Dot
DAM AKC N-102034
COLOR black

Sirod Doris of Blakeen	Ch. Vendas The Black Imp of Catawba *blk*	*min* Jambo
		Ch. Vendas Maid of Honour *Amelia*
	Ch. Fiddown Floride	Charcot
		Ch. Pailette of Groton

REMARKS

SOLD TO	ADDRESS	DATE	PRICE
Robert D. Levy	Miami Beach, Florida	3/25/53	$2500.00

Certificate of Pedigree

Name _CH. SYNTIFNY'S RIGHT ON THE HOOK_

Breed _____ Color _____

Sex _____

Date of birth _MARCH 31, 1974_

SIRE _AMBERLY'S CHIP OFF OF DELRAH_

- CH. AMBERLY'S DESTINY OF RALEIGH
  - CH. ROMO PATTY FINGA OF CHARIOT
    - CALVINELLE NIGHTWATCH
      - CH. A.O. DASHING BANDITER
      - OU-CHULA VON DER MOORHEIDE
    - GREGOIRE'S HI DOLLY
      - CH. LOCHRANZA ALI BABA
      - GREGOIRE'S DROP IN THE BUCKET
  - AMBERLY ROMO SHEER FANTASY
    - ARUNDEL HEIR APPARENT
      - CH. FRIDIA'S FAVORITE SON
      - CH. U. WILLINI ABBLE
    - ROMO CINDERELLA
      - CH. ROMO LITTLE PRINCE
      - ROMO LADY OF THE NIGHT
- ROMO CINDERELLA
  - CH. ROMO KINKY RULZY
    - CH. J.O. KING POODLES
      - CH. LAMBER KIM POODLES
      - SANSTERRE LIVING DOLL
    - POODTOWN RITZY
      - POODTOWNE PINKY KINKY
      - CANDICE DE PECHE
  - ROMO LADY OF THE NIGHT
    - CH. CASTLEBROOK WEE CAVALIER
      - MILANTO AL KHALIF
      - CASTLEBROOK SPARKLE
    - KUR AJ TWINKLE TOES

DAM _SHANNON VALLEY'S WINTER_

- SHANNON VALLEY'S FROSTY O
  - CH. SNO ENVY OF SASSAFRAS
    - CH. ENVY ME OF SASSAFRAS
      - CH. SASSAFRAS THE SNO BALL
      - PETITE SNOW IMP
    - SNOW MONIQUE OF SASSAFRAS
      - CH. MONIQUE OF SASSAFRAS
      - PETITE MONIQUE EVETTE
  - DIXON'S SASSAFRAS ICE CRICKET
    - LIL CH. SNOW SHEOT OF SASSAFRAS
      - CH. SAPPHIRE OF SASSAFRAS
      - INFANTARINA OF SASSAFRAS
    - DIXON'S PETITE SNOW GINGER
      - CH. SASSAFRAS THE SNO BALL
      - WHITE SWAN'S LITTLE LAMBIE PIE
- LEE'S LIL BIT-O-SNO
  - NOMARS SAUCI PRINZ
    - CH. NOEL SNOW OF SASSAFRAS
      - SARSPARILLA OF SASSAFRAS
      - COLLETTE NOEL
    - NOMAR'S DOLLY
      - BALANCE CANOPE
      - NOMAR'S CHA CHA
  - BON LEE'S LIL BIT O'LICORICE
    - CH. BELLE FLEUR LITTLE MIDGE
      - ARDLUSSA CHINQUAPIN
      - LITTLE SIR ECHO'S MIDGET
    - SKULAN'S LADY TINA
      - RHODA'S MR. PEPPY
      - RHODA'S LADY FELICIA

Reg. No. _____

Bred By _JANE A. WINNE SYNTIFNY_

Whelped _____

This Pedigree is certified to be correct to the best of my knowledge.

Signed _Jane A. Winne_ Date _11/26/80_

Ch. Cutler's Ebony Wysteria. Photo courtesy of Peggy Hogg.

CHAPTER TWENTY-TWO

Veterinarian's Corner

by Joseph P. Sayres, DVM

Eng., Am., Can., Mex. Ch. Montmartre Maria-Lina owned by Beaujeau Poodles.

By way of introduction to this chapter concerning the medical aspects of the care of your Poodle, I think we should devote a few paragraphs to how to choose your veterinarian.

Until recent years, there has been a lot of misunderstanding and even animosity between veterinarians and breeders. Some distrust arose on the breeders' part because most veterinarians were not familiar with or even interested in learning about pure-bred dogs. Some of the problems encountered were peculiar to certain breeds, and some would crop up at inconvenient times. Veterinarians were then beset by breeders who thought that they knew more about the medical problems of their dogs than the vets did. The veterinarians very often were only called for emergencies or when it was too late to save a sick dog who had been treated too long by people in the kennel. Another problem was that many breeders had never included veterinary fees in their budgets and were slow to pay their bills, if indeed they paid them at all.

Fortunately, these problems have been to a large extent solved. Education and better communication between breeders and veterinarians have eliminated most areas of friction.

Today, veterinary education and training have advanced to a point paralleling that of human standards. This resulted from advances in the field of Veterinary Science in the last two decades. Sophisticated diagnostic procedures, new and advanced surgical techniques, and modern well-equipped hospitals all make for improved medical care for our dogs.

Educated breeders now realize that while they may know more about the general husbandry of their dogs and the unique traits of the poodle, they should not attempt to diagnose and treat their ailments.

In choosing your veterinarian, be selective. He or she should be friendly, should be interested in your dogs, and, in the case of breeders, should be interested in your breeding programs. Veterinarians should be willing to talk freely with you. Such things as fees, availability for emergencies, and what services are and are not available should be discussed and understood before a lasting relationship with your veterinarian can be established.

You can expect your veterinarian's office, clinic, or hospital to be clean, free of undesirable odors, well-equipped, and staffed by sincere, friendly personnel who willingly serve you at all times. All employees should be clean, neat in appearance, and conversant with whatever services you require. You may also expect your dog to be treated carefully and kindly at all times by the doctor and his staff.

Your veterinarian should participate in continuing education programs in order to keep up with changes and improvements in his field. He should also be aware of his limitations. If he doesn't feel confident in doing certain procedures, he should say so and refer you to qualified individuals to take care of the problem. Seeking second opinions and consultation with specialists on difficult cases are more the rule than the exception nowadays. That is as it should be.

You will know that if your veterinarian is a member of the American Animal Hospital Association, he and his facility have had to measure up to high standards of quality and are subjected to inspections every two years. Many excellent veterinarians and veterinary hospitals by choice do not belong to the American Animal Hospital Association. You can satisfy your curiosity about these places by taking guided tours of the facilities to learn by word of mouth about the quality of medicine practiced at these hospitals.

So far we have discussed only what you should expect from your veterinarian. Now, let's discuss what the veterinarian expects from his clients.

Most of all, he expects his clients to be open and frank in their relations with him. He doesn't like to be double-checked and second-guessed behind his back. He also wants you to handle your pet so that he, in turn, can examine him. He also expects you to leash your dog to control him and keep him from bothering other pets in the room. He expects to be paid a fair fee and to be paid promptly for services rendered. Fees in a given area tend to be consistent, and variations are due only to complications or unforeseen problems. Medicine is not an exact science, therefore things unpredictable can happen.

If you are dissatisfied with the services or fees, then ask to discuss these things in a friendly manner with the doctor. If his explanations are not satisfactory or he refuses to talk to you about the problem, then you are justified in seeking another doctor.

The veterinarian expects to provide his services for your animals during regular hours whenever possible, but he also realizes that in a kennel or breeding operation emergencies can occur at any time and that his services will be needed at off hours. You should find out how these emergencies will be handled and be satisfied with the procedures.

No veterinarian can be on duty 24 hours of every day. Today cooperative veterinarians group together to take turns covering each other's emergency calls. Some cities have emergency clinics that operate solely to take care of those catastrophes that seem usually to happen in the middle of the night or on weekends.

My conclusion, after 30 years of practice, is that most disagreements and hard feelings between clients and veterinarians are a result of a breakdown in communication. Find a veterinarian that you can talk to and can be comfortable with, and you'll make a valuable friend.

In using veterinary services to their best advantage, I believe that you will find that prevention of diseases and problems is more important than trying to cure these things after they occur. In other words, an ounce of prevention is worth a pound of cure.

Poodle Club of America, 1956. Left to right: Walter Morris with Ch. Nibroe Gary; Jane Forsyth with Ch. Icarus Duke Otto; Bob Forsyth with Ch. Alfonco v.d. Goldenen Kette.

The three varieties of Poodles have their share of congenital defects. From the publication *Congenital Defects in Dogs*, published by Ralston Purina Company, as well as other reliable sources, the following conditions are listed as congenital defects in poodles.

TOY POODLES

A) Generalized progressive retinal atrophy. This is a weakening of retinal vessels affecting young dogs and is first noticed as night blindness.

B) Ectasia Syndrome. This condition is characterized by abnormal retinal vessels, optic discs, retinal detachments, and occasional bleeding within the eye.

C) Patent ductus arteriosis. A heart defect in which the duct between the aorta and pulmonary artery fails to close.

D) Patella luxation. A dislocation of the knee cap usually accompanied by the rotation of the tibia (shin bone) and a shallow groove for the knee cap to insert. Lameness may occur as early as six months of age and is indicated by animals moving by hopping if both rear legs are affected.

E) Fibrosis of the plantaris muscle. This is a hardening of muscles in the back feet so the dogs cannot stand on their hind feet.

F) Collapsed trachea. A softening of the cartilaginous rings in the windpipe.

G) Unilateral or bilateral cryptorchidism. Nondescent of the testicles.

H) Predisposition to dystochia. Abnormal labor when whelping usually due to anatomical peculiarities, fetal deaths, or over-nervousness of the dam.

MINIATURE POODLES

A) Generalized progressive retinal atrophy. See description under Toy Poodles.

B) Ectasia syndrome. Same as described under Toy Poodles.

C) Globoid cell leukodiptrophy. An enzyme deficiency which causes a collection of those cells in the central nervous system. Signs of stiffness in the back legs or trouble walking may start as early as three to six months of age.

D) Cystinuria. Excessive cystine in the urine causing a predisposition to bladder stones.

E) Patent ductus arteriosis. Described above in the Toy Poodle section.

F) Partial alopecia. Hair loss in some areas of the body.

Ch. Arden Applause, winning the Greater Pittsburgh Poodle Club Specialty Show. Carolyn Wolfe, Owner. Sired by Jeanie's Black Dina Mite from Vernlil Arden Free Style.

G) Hypoplasia of the jaw—Odontoid process, dysplasia. Abnormal development of first two neck vertebrae which may produce a dislocation of the joint between the vertebrae.

H) Epiphyseal dysplasia. Impaired calcification of long bone cartilage producing abnormally short legs.

I) Patella luxation. As described in Toy Poodle section.

J) Dislocation of shoulder.

K) Unilateral or bilateral cryptorchidism. Described in Toy Poodle section.

L) Predisposition to dystocia. Similar to description under Toy Poodles.

M) Hemophilia A. Deficiency which prevents or retards blood clotting.

N) Narcolepsy. Abnormal sleep patterns.

STANDARD POODLES

A) Cataracts, bilateral. Opaque lenses; a recessive mode of inheritance.

B) Distichiosis. The presence of two rows of eyelashes, resulting in irritation and excessive tears.

C) Atopic dermatitis. A skin inflammation with severe itching which may be due to a defect in the immune system.

D) Hip dysplasia. Refer to section of this subject at the end of this chapter.

E) Unilateral or bilateral cryptorchidism. Described under Toy Poodles.

F) Hemophilia A. Explained in the Miniature Poodle section.

By proper and vigilant vaccination programs, the following contagious diseases can be eliminated: distemper, hepatitis, leptospirosis, rabies, parainfluenza, and parvovirus enteritis. With proper sanitation and the guided use of insecticides and vermifuges, the following conditions can be made extinct or of only minor importance: roundworm infestation, hookworm infestation, whipworm infestation, coccidiosis, tapeworm infestation, fleas, ticks, and lice. These problems will be dealt with individually as our chapter progresses.

The following vaccination schedule should be set up and strictly followed to prevent infectious diseases:

Disease:	Age to Vaccinate:
Distemper	Six to eight weeks old; second inoculation to be given at 12 to 16 weeks of age; revaccinate annually.
Hepatitis (adenovirus)	Same as distemper.

Parainfluenza
(kennel cough)   Same as distemper.
Leptospirosis   Give first vaccine at nine weeks old; revaccinate with second D.H.L.P. (distemper, hepatitis, leptospirosis, parainfluenza) at 12 to 16 weeks of age; revaccinate annually.
Parvovirus   Give first vaccine at six to eight weeks old; second vaccine two to four weeks later; duration of immunity from two injections established at only four months at the time of this writing; revaccinate annually; revaccinate before going to dog shows or going to boarding kennels if more than six months have elapsed since the last shot.
Rabies   First inoculation at three to four months old, then revaccinate when one year old and at least every three years thereafter; if dog is over four months old at the time of the first vaccination, then revaccinate in one year and then once every three years.

Vaccines used are all modified live-virus vaccines except for leptospirosis, which is a killed bacterium, and parvovirus vaccine, which is a killed strain of feline distemper virus. New and improved vaccines to immunize against parvovirus will appear shortly.

Communicable diseases for which no vaccines have been perfected as yet are: canine brucellosis, canine coronavirus, and canine rotavirus.

Infectious Diseases

Distemper

Distemper is caused by a highly contagious airborne virus. The symptoms are varied and may involve all of the dog's systems. A pneumonic form is common, with heavy eye and nose discharges, coughing, and lung congestion. The digestive system may be involved, as evidenced by vomiting, diarrhea, and weight loss. The skin may show a pustular type of rash on the abdomen. Nervous system involvement is common, with convulsions, chorea (twitches and incoordination), and paralysis as persistent symptoms. This virus may have an affinity for nerve tissue and cause encephalitis and degeneration of the spinal cord. These changes for the most part are irreversible, and death or severe crippling ensues.

We have no specific remedy or cure for distemper, and recoveries when they occur can only be attributed to the natural resistance of the patient, good nursing care, and control of secondary infections with antibiotics.

That's the bad news about distemper in most areas today because the efficiency of the vaccination has been effective in almost eradicating this dreaded disease.

Hepatitis

A contagious viral disease affecting the liver, this is not an airborne virus and can only be spread by contact. Although rarely seen today because of good prevention by vaccination programs, this virus is capable of producing a very acute, fulminating, severe infection and can cause death in a very short time. Symptoms of high temperature, lethargy, anorexia (loss of appetite), and vomiting are the same as for many other diseases. Careful evaluation by a veterinarian is necessary to confirm the diagnosis of this disease.

The old canine infectious hepatitis vaccine has been replaced by a canine adenovirus type-two strain vaccine which is safer and superior. The new vaccine seems to be free of post-vaccination complications such as blue eye, shedding of the virus in the urine, and some kidney problems.

Leptospirosis

This is a disease that seriously affects the kidneys of dogs, most domestic animals, and man. For this reason it can become a public health hazard. In urban and slum areas the disease is carried by rats and mice in their urine. It is caused by a spirochete organism (a type of bacteria) which is very resistant to treatment. Symptoms include fever, depression, dehydration, excessive thirst, persistent vomiting, occasional diarrhea, and jaundice in the latter stages. Again, it is not always easy to diagnose, so your veterinarian will have to do some laboratory work to confirm it.

We see very few cases of leptospirosis in dogs, and then only in the unvaccinated ones. The vaccine is generally given concurrently with the distemper and hepatitis vaccinations. Preventive inoculations have resulted in the almost complete demise of this dreaded disease.

Parainfluenza

This is commonly called kennel cough. It is caused by a throat-inhabiting virus that causes an inflammation of the trachea (wind pipe) and larynx (voice box). Coughing is the main symptom, and fortunately it rarely causes any other systemic problems. The virus is airborne, highly contagious, and is the scourge of boarding kennels. A vaccine is available that will protect against this contagious respiratory disease and should be given as part of your vaccination program along with the distemper, hepatitis, leptospirosis, and parvovirus shots. Pregnant bitches should not be vaccinated against parainfluenza because of the possibility of infecting the unborn puppies. As there may be more than one infectious agent involved in contagious upper respiratory disease of dogs, vaccination against parainfluenza is not a complete guarantee to protect against all of them.

Rabies

This is a well-known virus-caused disease that is almost always fatal and is transmissible to man and other warm-blooded animals. The virus causes very severe brain damage. Sources of the infection include foxes, skunks, and raccoons, as well as domesticated dogs and cats. Transmission is by introduction of the virus by saliva into bite wounds. Incubation in certain animals may be from three to eight weeks. In a dog, clinical signs will appear within five days. Symptoms fall into two categories depending on what stage the disease is in when seen, the *dumb* form and the *furious* form. There is a change of personality in the furious form; individuals become hypersensitive and over react to noise and stimuli, and they will bite any object that moves. In dumb rabies, the typical picture of the loosely hanging jaw and tongue presents itself. Diagnosis is only confirmed by a laboratory finding the virus and characteristic lesions in the brain. All tissues and fluids from rabid animals should be considered infectious, and you should be careful not to come in contact with them. Prevention by vaccination is a must because there is no treatment for rabid dogs.

Contagious Canine Viral Diarrheas

There are three related diseases covered under this heading.

A) *Canine Coronavirus (C.C.V.):* This is a highly contagious virus that spreads rapidly to susceptible dogs. The source of infection is through infectious bowel movements. The incubation period is one to four days, and the virus will be found in feces for as long as two weeks. It is sometimes hard to tell the difference between cases of diarrhea caused by coronavirus and parvovirus. Coronavirus generally is less severe or causes a more chronic or sporadic type of diarrhea. The fecal material may be orange in color

and have a very bad odor. Occasionally it will also contain blood. Vomiting sometimes precedes the diarrhea, but loss of appetite and listlessness are consistent signs of the disease. Fever may or may not be present. Recovery is the rule after eight to ten days, but treatment with fluids, antibiotics, intestinal protectants, and good nursing care are necessary in the more severe watery diarrhea cases. Dogs that survive these infections become immune for an unknown length of time.

To control an outbreak of this virus in a kennel, very stringent hygienic measures must be taken. Proper and quick disposal of feces, isolation of affected animals, and disinfection with a 1:30 dilution of Clorox are all effective means of controlling an outbreak in the kennel.

There is no vaccine yet available for prevention of canine coronavirus. Human infections by this virus have not been reported.

B) *Canine Parvovirus (C.P.V.):* This is the newest and most highly publicized member of the intestinal virus family. Cat distemper virus is a member of the same family but differs from canine parvovirus biologically. It has been impossible to produce this disease in dogs using cat virus as the inducing agent, and conversely canine parvovirus will not produce the disease in a cat. However, vaccines for both species will produce immunity in the dog. The origin of C.P.V. is still unknown.

Canine parvovirus is very contagious and acts rapidly. The main source of infection is contaminated bowel movements. Direct contact between dogs is not necessary, and carriers such as people, fleas, instruments, etc., may carry and transmit the virus.

The incubation period is five to 14 days. The symptoms are fever, severe vomiting and diarrhea, often with blood, depression, and dehydration. Feces may appear yellowish gray streaked with blood. Young animals are more severely affected, and a shock-like death may occur in two days. In animals less than six weeks old, the virus will cause an inflammation of the heart muscle, causing heart failure and death. These pups do not have diarrhea. A reduction in the number of white blood cells is a common finding early in the disease.

The virus is passed in the feces for one to two weeks and may possibly be shed in the saliva and urine also. This virus has also been found in the coats of dogs. The mortality rate is unknown. Dogs that recover from the disease develop an immunity to it, but the duration of this immunity is unknown.

Control measures include disinfection of the kennels, animals, and equipment with a 1:30 dilution of Clorox and isolation of sick individuals. Treatment is very similar to that for coronavirus, namely intravenous fluid therapy, administration of broad-spectrum antibiotics, intestinal protectants, and good nursing care. Transmission to humans has not been proved.

Clinical studies have proved that vaccination with two injections given two to four weeks apart of the approved canine vaccine will provide good immunity for at least four months and possibly longer, as future studies may show. At present puppies should be vaccinated when six to eight weeks old, followed with a second injection two to four weeks later. Full protection does not develop until one week following the second injection. The present recommendations are for annual revaccinations with an additional injection recommended before dog shows or boarding in kennels if a shot has not been given within six months.

C) *Canine Rotavirus (C.R.V.):* This virus has been demonstrated in dogs with a mild diarrhea, but again with more severe cases in very young puppies. Very little is known about this virus. A milder type diarrhea is present for eight to ten days. The puppies do not run a temperature and continue to eat. Dogs usually recover naturally from this infection. There is no vaccine available for this virus.

Canine Brucellosis

This is a disease of dogs that causes both abortions and sterility. It is caused by a small bacterium closely related to the agent that causes undulant fever in man and abortion in cows. It occurs worldwide.

Symptoms of brucellosis sometimes are difficult to determine, and some individuals with the disease may appear healthy. Vague symptoms such as lethargy, swollen glands, poor hair coat, and stiffness in the back legs may be present. This organism does not cause death and may stay in the dog's system for months and even years. The latter animals, of course, have breeding problems and infect other dogs.

Poor results in your breeding program may be the only indication that brucellosis is in your kennel. Apparently normal bitches abort without warning. This usually occurs 45 to 55 days after mating. Successive litters will also be aborted. In males, signs of the disease are inflammation of the skin of the scrotum and shrunken or swollen and tender testicles. Fertility declines, and chronically infected males become sterile.

The disease is transmitted to both sexes at the time of mating. Other sources of infection are aborted puppies, birth membranes and discharge from the womb at the time of abortions.

Humans can be infected, but such infections are rare and mild. Unlike its presence in the dog, the disease in humans responds readily to antibiotics.

Diagnosis is done by blood testing, which should be done carefully. None of the present tests are infallible, and false positives may occur. The only certain way that canine brucellosis can be diagnosed is by isolating the organism from blood or aborted material, and for this special techniques are required.

Treatment of infected individuals has proven ineffective in most cases. Sterility in males is permanent. Spaying or castrating infected pets should be considered, as this will halt the spread of the disease and is an alternative to euthanasia. At present there is no vaccine against this important disease.

Our best hope in dealing with canine brucellosis is prevention. The following suggestions are made in order to prevent the occurrence of this malady in your dogs.

1) Test breed stock annually and by all means breed only uninfected animals.

2)Test bitches several weeks before their heat periods.

The black Standard bitch, Ch. Longleat Hulagan, photographed in 1974. Owned by Longleat Poodles, Mr. and Mrs. James Lester and bred by the owners. Handled by Wendell J. Sammet. By Ch. Prince Philip of Belle Glen ex Ch. Alekai Hula.

3) Do not bring any new dogs into your kennel unless they have two negative tests taken a month apart.

4) If a bitch aborts, isolate her, wear gloves when handling soiled bedding, and disinfect the premises with Roccal.

5) If a male loses interest in breeding or fails to produce after several matings, have him checked.

6) Consult your veterinarian for further information about this disease, alert other breeders, and support the research that is going on at the John A. Baker Institute for Animal Health at Cornell University.

External Parasites

The control and eradication of external parasites depends on the repeated use of good quality insecticide sprays or powders during the warm months. Make a routine practice of using these products at seven-day intervals throughout the season. It is also imperative that sleeping quarters and wherever the animal commonly stays be treated also.

Fleas

These are wingless brown insects with laterally compressed bodies and strong legs; they are blood-suckers. Their life cycle comprises 18 to 21 days from egg to adult flea. They can live without food for one year in high humidity but die in a few days in low humidity. Able to multiply rapidly, they are more prevalent in the warm months. They can cause a severe skin inflammation in those individuals that are allergic or sensitive to the flea bite or saliva of the flea, and they can act as a vector for many diseases and do carry tapeworms. Control measures must include persistent, continual use of flea collars, flea medallions, sprays, or powders. The dog's bedding and premises must also be treated because the eggs are there. Foggers, vacuuming, or the use of professional exterminators may have to be used. All dogs and cats in the same household must be treated at the same time.

Ticks

There are hard and soft species of ticks. Both types are blood-suckers and at times cause severe skin inflammations on their host. They act as vectors for Rocky Mountain spotted fever as well as other diseases. Hibernation through an entire winter is not uncommon. The female tick lays as many as 1,000 to 5,000 eggs in crevices and cracks in walls. These eggs will hatch in about three weeks and then a month later become adult ticks. Ticks generally locate around the host's neck and ears and between the toes. They can cause anemia and serious blood loss if allowed to grow and multiply. It is not a good idea to just pick ticks off the dogs because of the danger of a reaction in the skin. Just apply the tick spray directly on the ticks, which then die and fall off eventually. Affected dogs should be dipped every two weeks. The premises, kennels, and yards should be treated every two weeks during the summer months, being sure to apply the insecticide to walls and in all cracks and crevices. Frequent or daily grooming is effective in finding and removing ticks.

Lice

There are two kinds of lice, namely the sucking lice and the biting lice. They spend their entire life on their host but can be spread by direct contact or through contaminated combs and brushes. Their life cycle is 21 days, and their eggs, known as nits, attach to the hairs of the dog. The neck and shoulder region, as well as the ear flaps, are the most common areas to be inhabited by these pesky parasites. They cause itchiness, some blood loss, and inflammation of the skin. Eradication will result through dipping or dusting with methyl carbonate or Thuron once a week for three to four weeks. It is a good idea to fine-comb the dogs after each dip to remove the dead lice and nits. Ask your veterinarian to provide the insecticides and advice or control measures for all of these external parasites.

Worms

Ascarids

These include such things as roundworms, puppyworms, stomachworms, milkworms, etc. Puppies become infested shortly after birth and occasionally even before birth. They can be difficult to eradicate. When passed in the stool or thrown up, the worms look somewhat like cooked spaghetti when fresh or like rubber bands when they are dried up. Two treatments at least two weeks apart will eliminate ascarids from most puppies. An occasional individual may need more wormings according to where in its life cycle the worm is at the time of worming. Good sanitary conditions must prevail, and immediate picking up of bowel movements is necessary to keep the worm population down.

Hookworms

This is another troublesome internal parasite that we find in dogs. They are blood-suckers and also cause bleeding from the site of their attachment to the lining of the intestine when they move from one site to another. They can cause a blood-loss type of anemia and serious consequences, particularly in young puppies. Their life cycle is direct, and their eggs may be ingested or pass through the skin of the host; yards and runs where the dogs defecate should be treated with 5% sodium borate solution, which is said to kill the eggs in the soil. Two or three worm treatments three to four weeks apart may be necessary to get rid of hookworms. New injectable products (administered by your veterinarian) have proved more effective than remedies used in the past. Repeated fecal examinations may be necessary to detect the eggs in the feces. These eggs pass out of the body only sporadically or in showers, so it is easy to miss finding them unless repeated stool testing is done. As with any parasites, good sanitary conditions in the kennel and outside runs will help eradicate these worms.

Whipworms

These are a prevalent parasite in some kennels and in some individual dogs, where they cause an intermittent mucous diarrhea. As they live only in the dog's appendix, it is extremely difficult to reach them with any worm medicine given by mouth. Injections seem to be the most effective treatment, and these have to be repeated several times over a long period of time to be effective. Here again, repeated fresh stool samples must be examined by your veterinarian to be sure that this pest has been eradicated. Appendectomies are indicated in only the most severe chronic cases. To repeat, cleanliness is next to godliness and most important in getting rid of these parasites.

Tapeworms

These are another common internal parasite of dogs. They differ from the roundworms mentioned above in their mode of transmission, as they have an indirect life cycle. This means that part of their cycle must be spent in an intermediate host. Fleas, fish, rabbits, and field mice all may act as intermediate hosts for various tapeworms. Fleas are the most common source of tapeworms in dogs, although dogs that live near water may eat raw fish and hunting dogs that eat the entrails of rabbits may get them from those sources. Another distinguishing feature of the tapeworms is the suction apparatus, the part of the head that enables the tapeworm to attach itself to the lining of the intestine. If after worm-

ing just the head remains, it has the capability of regenerating into another worm. This is one reason why they are so difficult to get rid of. It will require several treatments to get all the tapeworms out of a dog's system. These worms are easily recognized by the egg-containing body segments which break off and appear on top of a dog's bowel movement or stick to the hair around the rectal area. These segments may appear alive and mobile at times but most often are dead and dried up when found. They look like flat pieces of rice and may be white or brown when detected. Elimination of the intermediate host is an integral part of any plan to rid our dogs of these worms. Repeated wormings may be necessary to kill all the adult tapeworms in the intestine.

Before leaving the topic of worms, it should be stressed that all worming procedures must be done carefully and only with the advice and supervision of your veterinarian. The medicants used to kill the worms are to a certain extent toxic, so they should be used with care.

Heartworm

Although heartworms are a type of roundworm, the disease is so important it requires separate treatment.

Just as the name implies, this disease is caused by an actual worm that goes through its life cycle in the blood stream of its victims. It ultimately makes its home in the right chambers of the heart and in the large vessels that transport the blood to the lungs. They vary in size from 2.3 inches to 16 inches. Adult worms can survive up to five years in the heart.

By its nature this is a very serious disease and can cause irreversible damage to the lungs and heart of its host. In its most advanced state heartworm disease can result in heart failure and lung pathology. The disease is carried by female mosquitoes that have infected themselves after biting an infected dog; they then pass it on to the next dog that they come in contact with.

The disease has been reported wherever mosquitoes are found, and now cases have been reported in man and cats. It is most prevalent in warmer climates where the mosquito population is the greatest, but hotbeds of infection exist in the more temperate parts of the United States and Canada also.

Concerted effort and vigorous measures must be taken to control and prevent this serious threat to our dog population. The most effective means of eradication, I believe, will come through annual blood testing for early detection, by the use of preventative medicine during mosquito exposure times, and also by ridding our dog's environment of mosquitoes.

Annual blood testing is necessary to detect cases that haven't started to show symptoms yet and thus can be treated effectively. It also enables your veterinarian to prescribe safely the preventative medicine to those individuals that test negative. There is a 10 to 15% margin of error in the test, which may lead to some false negative tests. Individuals that test negative but are showing classical symptoms of the disease such as loss of stamina, coughing, loss of weight, and heart failure should be further evaluated with chest X-rays, blood counts, and electrocardiograms.

Serious consequences may result when the preventative medication is given to a dog that has heartworm already in his system; that is why it is so important to have your dog tested annually before starting the preventative medicine.

In order to be most effective, the preventative drug diethylcarbamazine should be given in daily doses of 2.5 mg. per pound of body weight or 5 mg. per kilogram of body weight of your dog. This routine should be started 15 days prior to exposure to mosquitoes and should be continued until 60 days after exposure. Common and trade names for this drug are Caricide, Styrid-Caricide, and D.E.C. It comes in liquid and tablet forms.

This drug has come under criticism by some breeders and individuals that claim that it affects fertility and causes some serious reactions. Controlled studies have shown no evidence that this drug produces sterility or abnormal sperm count or quality. Long-term studies on reproduction when the drug was given at the rate of 4.9 mg. per pound of body weight (three times the preventative dose level) for two years showed no signs of toxic effects on body weight maintenance, growth rate of pups, feed consumption, conception rate, number of healthy pups whelped, ratio of male to female pups, blood counts, and liver function tests. It is reported as a well-tolerated medication, and many thousands of dogs have benefited from its use. From personal experience, I find just an occasional dog who will vomit the medicine or get an upset stomach from it. The new enteric coated pills have eliminated this small problem.

However, if you still don't want to give the preventative, especially to your breeding stock, an alternative procedure would be to test your dogs every six months for early detection of the disease so that it can be treated as soon as possible.

Heartworm infestation can be treated successfully. There is a 1 to 5% mortality rate from the treatment. It can be expected that treatment may be completed without side effects if the disease hasn't already caused irreversible problems in the heart, lungs, liver, kidneys, etc. Careful testing, monitoring, and supervision are essential to success in treatment. Treatment is far from hopeless these days, and if the disease is detected early enough a successful outcome is more the rule than the exception.

In conclusion, remember that one case of heartworm disease in your area is one too many, especially if that one case is your dog. By following the steps mentioned, we can go a long way in ridding ourselves of this serious threat to our dogs.

Other Parasites

Less commonly occurring parasitic diseases such as demodectic and sarcoptic mange should only be diagnosed and treated by your veterinarian. You are wise to consult your doctor whenever any unusual condition occurs and persists in your dog's coat and skin. These conditions are difficult to diagnose and treat at best, so that the earlier a diagnosis is obtained, the better the chances are for successful treatment. Other skin conditions such as ringworm, flea bite allergy, bacterial infections, eczemas, hormonal problems, etc. all have to be considered.

Home Remedies and First Aid

You have repeatedly read here of my instructions to call your veterinarian when your animals are sick. This is the best advice I can give you. There are a few home remedies, however, that may get you over some rough spots while trying to get professional help.

I think it is a good idea to keep some medical supplies on hand, for example a first aid kit. The kit should contain the following items: a roll of cotton; gauze bandages; hydrogen peroxide; tincture of metaphen; cotton applicator swabs; B.F.I. powder; a rectal thermometer; adhesive tape; boric acid crystals; tweezers; and a jar of petroleum jelly.

A word here on how to take a dog's temperature may be in order. Always lubricate the thermometer with petroleum jelly and carefully insert it well into the rectum. Hold it in place for two to three minutes and then read it. The thermometer should be held firmly so that it doesn't get sucked up into the rectum.

Stopping Vomiting

Mix one tablespoon of table salt to one pint of water and dissolve the salt thoroughly. Then give one tablespoonful of the mixture to the patient. After waiting one hour repeat the procedure and skip the next meal. The dog may vomit a little after the first dose, but the second dose works to settle the stomach. This mixture not only provides chlorides but acts as a mild astringent and many times in mild digestive upsets will work to stop the vomiting.

Giving Medicines

To administer liquid medicines to dogs, simply pull the lips away from the side of the mouth, making a pocket for depositing the liquid. Slightly tilt the dog's head upward and he will be able to swallow the liquid properly. Giving liquids by opening the mouth and pouring them directly on the tongue is an invitation to disaster because inhalation pneumonia can result. Putting it in the side of the mouth gives the dog time to hold it in his mouth and then swallow it properly.

Tablets are best administered by forcing the dog's mouth open and pushing the pill down over the middle of the tongue into the back of his mouth. If put in the right place, a reflex tongue reaction will force the pill down the throat to be swallowed. There also is no objection to giving the pills in favorite foods as long as you carefully determine that the medicine is surely swallowed with the food.

Diarrhea

In the case of the Standard Variety, give three or four tablespoons of Kaopectate or milk of bismuth every four hours. Use one fourth of this dosage for Miniature and Toy Poodles. Skip the next meal, and if the bowels persist in being loose, then start a bland diet of boiled ground lean beef and boiled rice in the proportions of half and half. Three or four doses of this medicine should suffice. If the diarrhea persists, and particularly if accompanied by depression, lethargy, and loss of appetite, your veterinarian should be consulted immediately. With all the new virus-caused diarrheas floating around, time is of essence in securing treatment.

A Mild Stimulant

Dilute brandy half and half with water, add a little sugar, and give a tablespoonful of the mixture every four to five hours. For Miniature and Toy Poodles, reduce the dosage to a teaspoonful of the mixture every four to five hours.

A Mild Sedative

Dilute brandy half and half with water, add a little sugar and give a tablespoon of the mixture every 20 to 30 minutes until the desired effect is attained. For Miniature and Toy Poodles, reduce the dosage to a teaspoonful of the mixture every 20 to 30 minutes.

Using brandy for both sedation and stimulation is possible by varying the time interval between doses. Given every four to five hours it's a stimulant, but given every 20 to 30 minutes it acts as a sedative.

Treatment of Minor Cuts and Wounds

Cleanse them first with soap and water, preferably tincture of green soap. Apply a mild antiseptic such as Bactine or tincture of metaphen two or three times daily until healed. If the cut is deep, fairly long, and bleeding, then a bandage should be applied until professional help can be obtained.

Whenever attempting to bandage wounds, apply a layer or two of gauze over the cleaned and treated wound, then a layer of cotton, and then another layer or two of gauze. The bandage must be snug enough to stay on but not so tight as to impair the circulation to the part. Adhesive tape should be applied over the second layer of gauze to keep the bandage as clean and dry as possible until you can get your dog to the doctor.

Tourniquets should be applied only in cases of profusely bleeding wounds. They are applied tightly between the wound and the heart, in addition to the pressure bandage that should be applied directly to the wound. The tourniquets must be released and reapplied at 15-minute intervals.

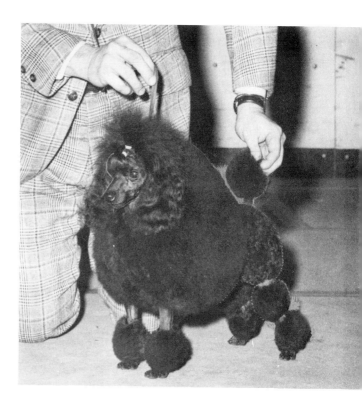

Burns

Application of ice or very cold water and compresses is the way to treat a skin burn. Apply cold packs as soon as possible and take the dog immediately to your vet.

Frost Bite

The secret in treating this uncommon condition is to restore normal body temperature gradually to the affected parts. In other words, use cold water and then tepid water to thaw out the area slowly and restore circulation. In cases of severe freezing or shock due to bitterly cold temperature, take the animal to the veterinarian as soon as possible.

Abscesses and Infected Cysts

Obvious abscesses and infected cysts that occur between the toes may be encouraged to drain by using hot boric acid packs and saturated dressings every few hours until professional aid can be secured. The boric acid solution is made by dissolving one tablespoon of crystals to one pint of hot water. Apply frequently to the swollen area. Further treatment by a veterinarian may involve lancing and thoroughly draining and cleaning out the abscess cavity. As most abscesses are badly infected, systemic antibiotics are generally indicated.

Heat Stroke or Exhaustion

A word about the serious effects of heat on a dog is appropriate. It never ceases to amaze me how many people at dog shows have to be warned and advised not to leave their dogs in cars or vans with the windows closed on a warm day.

A dog's heat regulating mechanism is not nearly as efficient as ours. Consequently, they feel the heat more than we do. Keep them as cool and as well ventilated as possible in hot weather. Another opportunity for shock is taking your dog out of a cool air-conditioned vehicle and exposing him immediately to the hot outdoors. Make that change as gradual as you can because a rapid change can cause a shock-like reaction.

In cases of suspected heat stroke—which manifests itself with very high body temperatures (as high as 106-107-108°F. sometimes), severe panting, weakness, shaking, and collapse—act quickly to get him into a cold bath or shower or put ice cold compresses on his head. Then without delay rush him to the nearest veterinarian for further treatment.

Prevention is the key here, and with a little common sense heat stroke and exhaustion can be avoided.

Poisons

Many dogs are poisoned annually by unscrupulous people who hate dogs. Many others are victims of poisoning due simply to the careless use of rat and ant poisons, insecticides, herbicides, antifreeze solutions, drugs, and so forth. Dogs also frequently insist on eating poisonous plants either in the house or outdoors, which can lead to serious consequences. Common sources of these toxic products are named in the following section.

Plants that can be a source of poison for dogs are listed here. This list contains only the most common ones. Garden flowers: daffodil, oleander, poinsetta, mistletoe, philodendron, delphinium, monkshood, foxglove, iris, and lily of the valley. Vegetables: rhubarb, spinach, tomato plants, and sunburned potatoes can be harmful. Trees and shrubs: rhododendron, cherry, peach, oak, elderberry, and black locust. Wild plants: Jack in the pulpit, Dutchman's breeches, water hemlock, mushrooms, buttercups, poison hemlock, nightshade, jimson weed, marijuana, locoweed, and lupine. Also, grain contaminants can exist in dog food. The most common ones are ergot, corn cockle, and gratolaria.

Poisonous *animals* are such snakes as vipers, rattlesnakes, copperheads, water moccasins, and the coral snakes. The only poisonous lizards are the Gila monster and Mexican beaded lizard, both deadly. Some toads, spiders, insects, and fishes also are potential sources of trouble.

Chemicals comprise perhaps the largest and most common source of poisoning in our environment. These are hazards that our dogs may be exposed to every day. Careful handling and storage of these products are essential. Toxic materials are found in all of the following groups of materials. Arts and crafts supplies, photographic supplies, automotive and machinery products (such as antifreeze and de-icers, rust inhibitors, brake fluids, engine and carburetor cleaners, lubricants, gasoline, kerosene, radiator cleaners, and windshield washers), cleaners, bleaches and polishes, disinfectants, and sanitizers all contain products that potentially are dangerous. Even health and beauty aids may contain toxic materials if ingested in large enough quantities. These include some bath oils, perfumes, corn removers, deodorants, antiperspirants, athlete's foot remedies, eye makeup, hair dyes and preparations, diet pills, headache

Ch. Arden Aggravation, owned by Cornelia Crissey and handled by Richard Bauer, here is making a good win. Aggravation is sired by Jeanie Mazza's, Jeanie's Black Dina-Mite.

remedies, laxatives, liniments, fingernail polish removers, sleeping pills, suntan lotions, amphetamines, shaving lotions, colognes, shampoos, and certain ointments. Paints and related products also can be dangerous. Caulking compounds, driers, thinners, paints, paint brush cleaners, paint and varnish removers, preservatives, and floor and wood cleaners all fit into this category. Pest poisons for birds, fungi, rats and mice, ants, and snails all can be toxic and sometimes fatal to dogs. Miscellaneous items like fire extinguishers and non-skid products for slippery floors can be unsafe. Almost all solvents like carbon tetrachloride, benzene, toluene, acetone, mineral spirits, kerosene, and turpentine are bad.

The previous paragraph only serves to illustrate how many products in our everyday environment exist which can be hazardous or fatal to our dogs.

In cases of suspected poisoning, one should be aware of what to do until professional help can be obtained.

a) Keep the animal protected, quiet, and warm.

b) If contact is through the skin, eye, or body surface, cleanse and flush the area with copious amounts of water. Do this also if the dog gets something in his eye. Protect him from further exposure.

c) Inducing vomiting may be dangerous and should be done only on the advice of a veterinarian. Giving peroxide may induce vomiting in some cases. It is better to allow the animal to drink as much water as he wants. This will dilute the poison. Giving milk or raw egg whites is helpful many times to delay absorption of the toxic products.

d) Do not attempt to give anything by mouth if the patient is convulsing, depressed, or unconscious.

e) Do not waste time. Get veterinary service as quickly as possible. Take any vomited material or suspected poisons and their containers with you to the vet. When the suspected product is known, valuable time can be saved in administering specific treatment. The suspected specimens should be uncontaminated and put in clean containers.

A word to the wise should be sufficient. Keep all products away from your dog that in any way can harm him.

Bloat

One of the most serious and difficult problems and real emergency situations that can occur is that of bloat. Other names for this condition are torsion and acute indigestion. This condition generally occurs in larger breeds after the consumption of a large meal (usually dry feed) and then drinking a lot of water immediately after eating. Follow this with a vigorous exercise period, and the stage is set for bloat. The stomach, being pendulous and overloaded at this point, can become twisted or rotated. This, of course, cuts off the circulation to the stomach and spleen and may also interfere with the large blood vessels coming to and from the liver. A shock-like syndrome follows, and death may ensue shortly if heroic measures are not undertaken to save the stricken animal. If ever there was an emergency, this is truly one. Dry heaves, painful loud crying, and abdominal enlargement take place in a very short time. Relief of the torsion requires immediate surgery to right the stomach to its normal position and to keep it there. Circulation may then return to normal.

In cases of acute indigestion without torsion, the distress and bloat may be relieved by passing a stomach tube to allow the gas to escape. At the risk of being redundant, it must be said that this condition is very acute and requires immediate and heroic action to save the victim.

Preventative measures for bloat include dividing the dog's normal diet into three or four meals a day. Water should not be given for one hour before and one hour after each meal, and no exercise is advisable for an hour or two after eating.

With breeders and veterinarians becoming more aware of the bloat syndrome, I feel that more of these cases will be saved than in the past.

Whelping

We cannot leave the subject of emergencies without considering the subject of whelping. Most bitches whelp without any problems. It is wise, however, to watch them closely during this time. I feel that no bitch should go more than two hours in actual labor without producing a puppy. This includes the time before the first one as well as between puppies; if more than two hours elapse, then the dam should be examined by a veterinarian. It will then be determined if she is indeed in trouble or is just a slow whelper. This rule of thumb gives us time to find out if there is a problem, what it may be, and have time to save both dam and puppies in most cases.

It is good practice to have your bitches examined for pregnancy three and a half to four weeks after mating as well as at term around the 58th or 59th day. These procedures will enable the veterinarian to discover any troubles that may occur during pregnancy, as well as alerting him as to when the whelping is going to take place. Knowing this, he can plan to provide service if needed during off hours.

Bitches that are difficult to breed, miss pregnancies, or have irregular reproductive cycles should have physical exams including laboratory tests to determine the cause of the trouble. These tests may be expensive, but a lot of breeding and sterility problems due to sub-par physical condition, hormonal imbalances, or hypothyroidism can be corrected. If a valuable bitch is restored to her normal reproductive capacity, the reward more than offsets the medical costs.

Another important thing to remember about whelping and raising puppies is to keep them warm enough. This means a room temperature of 75° to 80° F. for the first ten days to two weeks until the puppies are able to generate their own body heat. Be sure the dam keeps them close. Leave a light burning at night for the first week so she won't lose track of any of them or accidentally lie on one of them. Chilling remains the biggest cause of death of newborn puppies. Other causes are malnutrition, toxic milk, hemorrhage, and viral and bacterial infections. Blood type incompatibilities have been discovered lately to be causes of trouble.

Consultation with your veterinarian concerning these and any other breeding problems you've had in the past may result in the solution of these problems. This may result in larger litters with a higher survival rate.

Approaching Old Age

Providing medical services from cradle to grave is the slogan of many veterinarians, and rightly so. The average life expectancy for our dogs these days is about 13 years. Sad to say, this is a short time compared to our life span. Larger breeds historically do not live as long as the medium sized or smaller breeds. However, I think that with proper care all Poodles should be expected to reach this expectancy. This, then, is a good time to speak about approaching old age and some of the problems we can expect during that time. Arthritis, kidney disease, heart failure, and cataracts are probably the most common ailments in older dogs; when our pet has trouble getting up in the morning, jumping up, or going upstairs, you can bet that some form of a joint problem is starting. Giving two enteric coated aspirin tablets three times a day for five days very often will help these individuals. This dosage is for a Standard Poodle, but adjusted dosages for Miniature and Toy Poodles are also helpful. This is relatively free of side effects and as long as nothing else is wrong, your dog will get a bit of relief.

The Veteran's Class, Poodle Club of America, 1964.

502

Signs of kidney weakness are excessive drinking, inability to hold urine through the night, loss of weight, lack of appetite, and more than occasional bouts of vomiting and diarrhea. If any of these signs present themselves, it would be worthwhile to have a checkup. Very often corrective measures in diet and administering some medicine will prolong your dog's life.

Some form and degree of heart failure exists in a lot of older animals. Symptoms of chronic congestive heart failure consist of a chronic cough, especially after exercise, lack of stamina, lethargy, abdominal enlargement, and labored breathing at times. If diagnosed and treated early in the disease, many heart patients live to a ripe old age.

Cataracts form in the lenses of most, if not all, old dogs. They are a part of the normal aging process. Total blindness from cataracts generally does not result for a long time, and distant and peripheral vision remain satisfactory for the expected life span of the dog. Rarely is total blindness produced by these aging cataracts before the dog's life expectancy is reached. There is no effective treatment for cataracts other than their surgical removal, which is not recommended in the older patient that has any vision at all left.

Hip Dysplasia

It is becoming more evident that most of the arthritis in older dogs of large breeds is the result of problems in bone growth and development when the individual was very young. Problems such as panosteitis, hip dysplasia, elbow dysplasia, and osteochondrosis dessicans all are often precursors of arthritis. In Standard Poodles, according to information from the Orthopedic Foundation for Animals, hip dysplasia is found in 24% of the cases presented to them. The smaller varieties of the Poodle are seldom if ever afflicted with hip dysplasia.

At any rate, hip dysplasia seems to be a developmental condition and not a congenital anomaly. It is thought to be an inherited defect, with many genes being responsible for its development. Environmental factors also enter into the severity of the pathology in the hip joints. Nutrition during the growth period has been an important factor. Over-feeding and over-supplementation of diets have caused an abnormal growth rate with overweight puppies. These individuals, if they were susceptible to hip dysplasia in the first place, show more severe lesions of hip dysplasia. Restricted feeding of growing dogs is necessary for normal bone growth and development.

Signs of hip dysplasia vary from one dog to another, but some of the more common ones are: difficulty in getting up after lying for awhile, rabbit-like gait with both rear legs moving forward at the same time when running, lethargy, and walking with a swaying gait in the rear legs. In many cases, a period of pain and discomfort at nine months to one year old will resolve itself and, even though the dysplasia is still there, most of the symptoms may disappear.

It is recommended that dysplastic individuals not be bred, that they not be allowed to become overweight, and that they have moderate exercise. The selection of dysplastic-free individuals for breeding stock eventually will result in the production of sounder hip joints in affected breeds. This factor, of course, is only one consideration in the breeding and production of an overall better Standard Poodle.

This beautiful Standard head belongs to Ch. Puttencove Perdita (by Ch. Alekai Luau ex Puttencove Primrose), a Top Producing foundation bitch at Valhalla Kennels. Owned by Catherine Kish.

Pictured is Ch. Dassin Busby Berkley, litter brother to
Ch. Dassin Rita La Rose, both of which are owned by
Mrs. Edward Solomon, Pittsburgh, Pennsylvania.
Both handled by F.C. Dickey, Medina, Ohio.

504

Harmo

AMHERST · NEW HAMPSHIRE
ZIP CODE 03031

AREA CODE 603 673-2200

Pedigree
OF

Harmo Gay Prospector
REGISTERED NAME

Male
SEX

Nov. 23, 1964
WHELPED

Poodle MINIATURE
BREED

A. K. C. NO.

Buster
CALL NAME

Harmo Kennels & Dorothy L. Ekstrom
BREEDER

Apricot
COLOR

PARENTS	GRAND PARENTS	GREAT GRAND PARENTS	GREAT GR. GRAND PARENTS
		Victor of Fircot	Eng.Ch.Cremola of Swanhill
			Cream Puff of Fircot
	Spotlight of Summercourt GRAND SIRE		
		Venda's Falaise	Venda's Zante
			Venda's Madam Bovary
Int.Ch.Summercourt Square Dancer of Fircot SIRE REG. NO. N-388678			
		Pippo of Montfleuri	Eng.Ch.Toomai of Montfleuri
			Eng.Ch.Philippa of Montfleuri
	Mistress of Pipers Lane GRAND DAM		
		Mangeur of Bushhill	Mandarin of Mannerhead
			Fifi of Swale
		Millbrook Rouge D'Or	Sherwood Golden Trumpet
			Sherwood Angela
	Applewood's French Toast GRAND SIRE		
		Applewood's Tiny Sunbeam	Broughton Golden Prince
			Drakeway La Marquise D'Apr
Harmo Golden Gaiety DAM REG. NO. N-978581			
		Broughton Bright Penny	Broughton Another Eric
			Canito's Tina Too
	Harmo Contessa GRAND DAM		
		Broughton Golden Treasure	Broughton King Midas
			Broughton Golden Trinket

● This Certifies That, the above Pedigree
is true and correct to the best of
my knowledge and belief.

DATE OF PURCHASE

SIGNED

NAME OF PURCHASER

BLAKEEN KENNELS

PEDIGREE

OF

CH. BLAKEEN DING DING

AKC   N-207369

BREED	BORN	KENNEL NAME	COLOR	SEX
Poodle, Toy	Oct. 30, 1953		White	Female

BREEDER: Arda L. Schriber and Ethel S. Keeler

ADDRESS OF BREEDER: Livingston Manor, New York.

DATE PURCHASED: April 9, 1954

	GRANDPARENTS	GREAT GRANDPARENTS	GREAT GREAT GRANDPARENTS

SIRE
Ch. Wilber White Swan
AKC COLOR N-133530

- Ch. Leicester's Bonbon's Swan Song
  - Ch. Leicester's Bonbon
    - Ch. Pruden's Little Skipper
    - Ch. Leicester's Fidele de Lafferty
  - Leicester's Alouette
    - Ch. Robin Goodfellow
    - Minette
- Wilber Victoire
  - Wilber Valentine
    - Barrack Hill Bomber
    - Barrack Hill Truffle
  - Gamin Greenleaf
    - Dorem Geminette

DAM
Blakeen Solitaire
AKC COLOR N-90124

- Ch. Snow Boy of Fircot
  - Solitaire of Piperscroft
    - Eng.Ch.Russet of Piperscroft
    - Heatherbelle of Piperscroft
  - Harwee of Manner-head
    - Harwee of Mannerhead
    - Eng.Ch.The Mistress of Mannerhead
- Ch. Blakeen Snow Flurry
  - Ch. Snow Boy of Fircot
    - Solitaire of Piperscroft
    - Harwee of Mannerhead
  - Ch. Blakeen Minikin
    - Ch. Barrack Hill Bomber
    - Eng.Ch.Eric Brighteyes
    - Fifi of Swanhill
    - Mince Ruissaune

REMARKS

SOLD TO   ADDRESS   DATE   PRICE

Ch. Lou-Gin's Kiss-Me-Kate

Call Name of Dog: Katie

	Breed	Sex	Color
	Poodle	Female	White

Date Whelped: May 23, 1976

Litter Reg. Number

Individual Reg. Number

Registered with: AKC

Name of Breeder: Louis Dunson

Address of Breeder

SIRE Am. Can. Ch. Iley Barclay C.D.

GRAND SIRE
Ch. Haus Brau Executive of Acadia

- Ch. Haus Brau Clarion
  - Am.Can.Ch. Wycliffe Murdock
  - Ch. Haus Brau Angelique
- Am.Can.Ch. Haus Brau Adorable Regina
  - Am.Can.Ch. Wycliffe Ian
  - Am.Can.Ch. Haus Brau Sachse Rebe

GRAND DAM
Am.Can.Ch. Chantilly Felice CD.

- Am.Can.Ch. Wycliffe Ian
  - Ch. Wycliffe Thomas
  - C.D.
- Ch. Wycliffe Ian

DAM Am. Can. Ch. Lou-Gin's Chateau Chalon

GRAND SIRE
Ch. Acadia Command Performance

- Ch. Haus Brau Executive of Acadia
  - Ch. Haus Brau Clarion
  - Haus Brau Adorable Regina
- Am.Can.Ch. Chantilly Felice
  - Am.Can.Ch. Wycliffe Ian
  - C.D.

GRAND DAM

- Ch. Lou-Gin's Chateau Chalon
  - Ch. Haus Brau Executive of Acadia
    - Ch. Haus Brau Clarion
    - Haus Brau Adorable Regina
  - Am.Can.Ch. Wycliffe Simon
  - Ch. Acadia Conversation Piece

Eng., Am., Mex., C.A.C.I.B. Ch. Montmartre Super
Lad, at Westminster, 1976. Handled by Barbara
Humphries for Marjorie Tranchin, Dallas, Texas.

Glossary

To the uninitiated, it must seem that fanciers of pure-bred dogs speak a special language all their own, which in a way we do. To help make this book more comprehensive to our readers, the following is a list of terms, abbreviations, and titles which you will run across which may be unfamiliar to you. We hope that they will lead to fuller understanding, and that they will also assist you as you meet and converse with others of similar interests in the world of pure-bred dogs.

A.K.C. – See American Kennel Club.

ALMOND EYE – The shape of the tissue surrounding the eye creating an almond-shaped appearance.

AMERICAN KENNEL CLUB – The official registry for pure-bred dogs in the United States. Publishes and maintains the Stud Book, handles all litter and individual registrations, transfers of ownership, etc. Keeps all United States dog show award records, issues championships and other titles as earned, approves and licenses dog show and obedience judges, licenses or issues approval to all point shows or recognized match shows. Creates and enforces the rules and regulations by which the breeding, raising, exhibiting, handling, and judging of pure-bred dogs in this country are governed. Clubs, not individuals, are members of the American Kennel Club, represented by a delegate chosen from their own membership for the purpose of attending the quarterly American Kennel Club Delegates' Meetings. A.K.C. is the commonly used abbreviation of American Kennel Club. The address of A.K.C. is 51 Madison Avenue, New York, N.Y. 10010.

ANGULATION – The angles formed by the meeting of the bones, generally referring to the shoulder and upper arm in the forequarters and the stifle and hock in the hindquarters.

BAD BITE – One in which the teeth do not meet correctly according to the specifications of the breed Standard.

BAD MOUTH – Can refer to a wryness or malformation of the jaw or to incorrect dentition.

BALANCE – Symmetry and proportion. A well-balanced dog is one in which all the parts appear in correct ratio to one another: height to length, head to body, neck to head and body, and skull to foreface.

BEEFY – Refers to over-musculation or over-development of the shoulders, hindquarters, or both.

BEST IN SHOW – The dog or bitch chosen as the most representative of any dog in any breed from among the six Group winners at an all-breed dog show.

BEST OF BREED – The dog or bitch that has been adjudged the best of its breed in competition at a dog show. In Poodles, this award is made only to the dog or bitch taking the award of Best over the two other Best of Variety winners at that event.

BEST OF OPPOSITE SEX – The dog or bitch adjudged Best of Opposite Sex to the one adjudged Best of Variety. If the Best of Variety is a dog, then the Best of Opposite Sex is a bitch adjudged best of her sex over the Winners Bitch and any other bitches entered for "Best of Variety Competition," or vice versa. At an independent separately held specialty where Best of

Breed is selected from the three Best of Variety winners, then Best of Opposite Sex to Best of Breed is selected from the winners of Best of Opposite Sex in each of the three varieties.

BEST OF VARIETY—Since Poodles are divided into three varieties which do not compete together except in the case of an independent separately held specialty show (not held in conjunction with an all-breed show), there is a Best of Variety selected in each of the three varieties, Miniature, Standard, and Toy, denoting that the winner has been chosen best of all the entries in his variety of Poodle at that show. The Miniature and Standard Poodle Best of Variety winners then both compete in the Non-Sporting Group; the Toy Best of Variety in the Toy Group.

BEST OF WINNERS—The dog or bitch selected as the better of the two between Winners Dog and Winners Bitch.

BITCH—The correct term for a female dog.

BITE—The manner in which the dog's upper and lower teeth meet.

BLOOM—A word used to describe coat in good condition.

BLUE RIBBON WINNER—A Poodle who has won first prize at an A.K.C. point show.

BRACE—Two dogs, or a dog and a bitch, closely similar in appearance and moving together in unison.

BREED—Pure-bred dogs descended from mutual ancestors refined and developed by man.

BREEDER—A person who breeds dogs.

BREEDING PARTICULARS—Name of the sire and dam, date of breeding, date of birth, number of puppies in the litter, sex, name of the breeder, and name of the owner of the sire.

BRISKET—The forepart of the body between the forelegs and beneath the chest.

BROOD BITCH—A bitch used primarily for breeding.

CACIB—A Challenge Certificate offered by the Federation Cynologique Internationale toward a dog's championship.

CANINES—Dogs, jackals, wolves, and foxes as a group.

CANINE TEETH—The four sharp pointed teeth at the front of the jaws, two upper and two lower, flanking the incisors; often referred to as fangs.

CARPALS—Pastern joint bones.

CASTRATE—Neuter a dog by removal of the testicles.

CAT-FOOT—A short-toed, round, tight foot similar to that of a cat.

CHAMPION—A dog or bitch who has won a total of 15 points including two "majors," the total under not less than three judges, two of whom must have awarded the "majors" at A.K.C. point dog shows. Ch. is the abbreviation of the word Champion.

CHARACTER—Appearance, behavior, and temperament considered correct in an individual breed of dog.

CHEEKY—Cheeks which bulge or are rounded in appearance.

CHEST—The part of the body enclosed by the ribs.

CHISELED—Clean-cut below the eyes.

CHOKE COLLAR—A chain or leather collar that gives maximum control over the dog. It is tightened or relaxed by the pressure on the lead caused by either pulling of the dog or tautness with which it is held by the handler.

CHOPS—Pendulous, loose skin creating jowls.

CLODDY Thickset or overly heavy or low in build.

CLOSE-COUPLED—Compact in appearance. Short in the loin.

COAT—The hair which covers the dog.

CONDITION—A dog said to be in good condition is one carrying exactly the right amount of weight, whose coat looks alive and glossy, and who exhibits a general appearance and demeanor of well-being.

CONFORMATION—The framework of the dog, its form and structure.

COUPLING—The section of the body known as the loin. A short-coupled dog is one in which the loin is short.

COARSE—Lacking in refinement and elegance.

COW-HOCKED—When the hocks turn inward at the joint, causing the hock joints to approach one another with the result that the feet toe outward instead of straight ahead.

CRABBING—A dog moving with its body at an angle rather than coming straight on to you. Otherwise referred to as sidewheeling or sidewinding.

CREST—The arched portion of the back of the neck.

CROPPING—The cutting of the ear leather, usually performed to cause the ear to stand erect.

CROSSING ACTION—A fault in the forequarters caused by loose or poorly knit shoulders.

CROUP—The portion of the back directly above the hind legs.

CRYPTORCHID—An adult dog with testicles not normally descended. A disqualification; a dog with this condition cannot be shown.

CYNOLOGY—Study of canines.

DAM–Female parent of a dog or bitch.

DENTITION–Arrangement of the teeth.

DEW CLAWS–Extra claws on the inside of the legs. Should generally be removed several days following the puppy's birth. Required in some breeds, unimportant in others and sometimes a disqualification, all according to the individual breed Standard.

DEWLAP–Excess loose and pendulous skin at the throat.

DIAGONALS–The right front and left rear leg make up the right diagonal. The left front and right rear the left diagonal. These diagonals move in unison as the dog trots.

DISH-FACED–The condition existing when the tip of the nose is placed higher than the stop.

DISQUALIFICATION–A fault or condition so designated by the breed Standard or by the American Kennel Club. Judges must withhold awards at dog shows from dogs having disqualifying faults, noting the reason in the Judges' Book for having done so. The owner may appeal this decision, but a disqualified dog cannot again be shown until it has been officially examined and reinstated by the American Kennel Club.

DISTEMPER TEETH–A condition so-called due to its early association with dogs having suffered from this disease. It refers to discolored, badly stained, or pitted teeth.

DIVERGENT HOCKS–Frequently referred to as bandy legs or barrel hocks as well. The condition in which the hock joints turn outward, thus the exact opposite of cow-hocks.

DOCK–Shortening a tail by cutting it.

DOG–A male of the species. Also used to collectively describe male and female canines.

DOG SHOW–A competition in which dogs have been entered for the purpose of receiving the opinion of a judge.

DOG SHOW, ALL-BREEDS–A dog show in which classification may be provided, and usually is, for every breed of dog recognized by the American Kennel Club.

DOG SHOW, SPECIALTY–A dog show featuring one breed only. Specialty shows are generally considered to be the showcases of a breed, and to win at one is an especially coveted honor and achievement, competition at them being particularly keen.

DOMED–A condition of the top-skull by which it is rounded rather than flat.

DOUBLE COAT–A coat that consists of a harsh, weather resistant protective outer coat, with a short, soft undercoat providing warmth.

DOWNFACED–Describes downward inclination of the muzzle towards the tip of the nose.

DOWN IN PASTERN–A softness or weakness of the pastern causing a pronounced variation from the verticle.

DRAG–A trail having been prepared by dragging a bag, generally bearing the strong scent of an animal along the ground.

DRAWING–The selection by lot of dogs that decides in which pairs they will be run in a specific field trial.

DRIVE–The powerful action of the hindquarters which should equal the degree of reach of the forequarters.

DROP EAR–Ears carried drooping or folded forward.

DRY HEAD–One exhibiting no excess wrinkle.

DRY NECK–A clean, firm neckline free of throatiness or excess skin.

DUDLEY NOSE–Flesh colored nose.

ELBOW–The joint of the forearm and upper arm.

ELBOW, OUT AT–The condition by which the elbow points out from the body rather than being held close.

EVEN BITE–Exact meeting of the front teeth, tip to tip with no overlap of the uppers or lowers. Generally considered to be less serviceable than the SCISSORS BITE, although equally permissible or preferred in some breeds.

EWE NECK–An unattractive concave curvature of the top area of the neckline.

EXPRESSION–The typical expression of the breed as one studies the head. Determined largely by the shape and placement of the eye. Should be alert and keenly interested in Poodles.

EYETEETH–The upper canines.

FAKING–The artificial altering of the natural appearance of a dog. A highly frowned upon and unethical practice which must lead, upon discovery by the judge, to instant dismissal from competition in the show ring, with a notation stating the reason in the Judges' Book.

FANCIER–A person actively involved in the sport of pure-bred dogs.

FANCY–Dog breeders, exhibitors, judges, and others actively involved with pure-bred dogs comprise the Dog Fancy.

FANGS–The canine teeth.

F.C.I.–See Federation Cynologique Internationale.

FEDERATION CYNOLOGIQUE INTERNATIONALE–A canine authority representing numerous countries, principally European, all of which consent to and agree on certain practices and breed identification. F.C.I. is the abbreviation.

FEET EAST AND WEST—An expression describing toes on the forefeet turning outward rather than pointing straight ahead.

FIDDLE FRONT—Caused by elbows protruding from the desired closeness to the body, resulting in pasterns which approach one another too closely and feet turning outward, the whole resembling the shape of a violin.

FINISHING A DOG—Refers to completing a dog's championship or its obedience title.

FLANK—The side of the body through the loin area.

FLAT BONE—Bones of the leg which are not round.

FLAT SIDED—Ribs that are flat down the sides rather than slightly rounded.

FLEWS—A pendulous condition of the inner corners of the upper lips.

FLYER—An especially promising or exciting young dog.

FLYING EARS—Ears correctly carried dropped or folded that stand up or tend to "fly" upon occasion.

FLYING TROT—The speed at which you should never move your show dog in the ring. All four feet actually leave the ground briefly during each half stride, making correct evaluation of the dog's normal gait virtually impossible.

FOREARM—The front leg from elbow to pastern.

FOREFACE—The muzzle of the dog.

FRONT—The forepart of the body viewed head-on, including the head, forelegs, shoulders, chest, and feet.

FUTURITY—A competition for dogs less than 12 months of age for which puppies are nominated at or prior to birth. Usually highly competitive among breeders, with a fairly good purse for the winners.

GAIT—The manner in which a dog walks and trots.

GALLOP—The fastest gait. Never to be used in the show ring.

GAY TAIL—Tail carried high.

GOOSE RUMP—Too sloping (steep) in croup.

GROOM—To bathe, brush, comb, and trim your dog.

GUN SHY—Fear of the sight or sound of a gun.

HACKNEY ACTION—High lifting of the forefeet, in the manner of a hackney pony.

HAM—Muscular development of the upper hind leg. Also used to describe a dog that loves applause while being shown, really going all-out when it occurs.

HANDLER—A person who shows dogs in competition, either as an amateur (without pay) or as a professional (receiving payment for the service).

HARE FOOT—An elongated paw, like the foot of a hare.

HAW—A third eyelid or excess membrane.

HEAT—The period during which a bitch can be bred. Also referred to as season.

HEEL—A command ordering the dog to follow close to the handler.

HINDQUARTERS—Rear assemblage of the leg.

HOCK—The joint between the second thigh and the metatarsus.

HOCKS WELL LET DOWN—Expression denoting that the hock joint should be placed low toward the ground.

HONORABLE SCARS—Those incurred as a result of working injuries.

INCISORS—The front teeth between the canines.

INTERNATIONAL CHAMPION—A dog awarded four CACIB cards at F.C.I. dog shows.

JOWLS—Flesh of lips and jaws.

JUDGE—Person making the decisions at a dog show, obedience trial, or field trial. Must be approved and licensed by A.K.C. in order to officiate at events where points toward championship titles are awarded.

KENNEL—The building in which dogs are housed. Also used when referring to a person's collective dogs.

KNEE JOINT—Stifle joint.

KNITTING AND PURLING—Crossing and throwing of forefeet as a dog moves.

KNUCKLING OVER—A double-jointed wrist, sometimes accompanied by enlarged bone development in the area, causing the joint to double over under the dog's weight.

LAYBACK—Used in two different ways. A) As description of correctly angulated shoulders. B) As description of a short-faced dog where pushed-in nose placement is accompanied by undershot jaw.

LEATHER—The ear flap. Also the skin of the actual nose.

LEVEL BITE—Another way of describing an even bite, as teeth of both jaws meet exactly.

LEVEL GAIT—A dog moving smoothly, topline carried level as he does so.

LIPPY—Lips that are pendulous or do not fit tightly.

LOADED SHOULDERS—Those overburdened with excessive muscular development.

LOIN—Area of the sides between the lower ribs and hindquarters.

LUMBER—Superfluous flesh.

LUMBERING—A clumsy, awkward gait.

MAJOR—A dog show at which there are three or more points awarded the Winners Dog and/or Winners Bitch.

MATCH SHOW—An informal dog show where no championship points are awarded and entries can usually be made upon arrival, although some demand pre-entry. Excellent practice area for future show dogs and for novice exhibitors, as the entire atmosphere is relaxed and congenial.

MATE—To breed a dog and a bitch to one another. Litter mates are dogs which were born in the same litter.

MILK TEETH—The first baby teeth.

MISCELLANEOUS CLASS—A class provided at A.K.C. Point Shows in which specified breeds may compete in the absence of their own breed classification. Dogs not yet recognized by A.K.C. are permitted to compete in this class prior to becoming recognized and with their own classification.

MOLARS—Four premolars are located at either side of the upper and lower jaws. Two molars exist on either side of the upper jaw, three on either side below. The lower molars have two roots, the upper molars have three roots.

MONORCHID—A dog with only one properly descended testicle. This condition disqualifies from competition at American Kennel Club dog shows.

NICK—A successful breeding that results in puppies of excellent quality is said to "nick."

NOSE—Describes the dog's organ of smell, but also refers to his talent at scenting. A dog with "a good nose" is one adept at picking up and following a scent trail.

OBEDIENCE TRIAL—A licensed obedience trial is one held under A.K.C. rules at which it is possible to gain a "leg" toward a dog's obedience title.

OBEDIENCE TRIAL CHAMPION—Denotes that a dog has attained Obedience Trial Championship under A.K.C. regulations, having gained a specified number of points and first place awards. O.T.Ch. is an abbreviation of this title.

OBLIQUE SHOULDERS—Shoulders angulated so as to be well laid back.

OCCIPUT—Upper back point of skull.

O.F.A.—Orthopedic Foundation for Animals.

ORTHOPEDIC FOUNDATION FOR ANIMALS—This organization is ready to read the hip radiographs of dogs and certify the existence of or freedom from hip dysplasia. Board Certified radiologists read vast numbers of these films each year. O.F.A. is a commonly used abbreviation.

OUT AT ELBOW—When the elbows point away from the body.

OUT AT SHOULDER—A loose assemblage of the shoulder blades.

OVAL CHEST—Deep with only moderate width.

OVERSHOT—Upper incisors overlap the lower incisors.

PACING—A gait in which both right legs and both left legs move concurrently, causing a rolling action.

PADDLING—Faulty gait in which the front legs swing forward in a stiff upward motion.

PADS—Thick protective covering of the bottom of the foot. Serves as shock absorber.

PAPER FOOT—Thin pads accompanying a flat foot.

PASTERN—The area of the foreleg between the wrist and the foot.

PIGEON-CHEST—A protruding, short breastbone.

PIGEON-TOED—Toes which point inward, as those of a pigeon.

POLICE DOG—Any dog that has been trained to do police work.

PUT DOWN—To prepare a dog for the show ring.

QUALITY—Excellence of type and conformation.

RACY—Lightly built, appearing overly long in leg and lacking substance.

RANGY—Excessive length of body combined with lack of depth through the ribs and chest.

REACH—The distance to which the forelegs reach out in gaiting, which should correspond with the strength and drive of the hindquarters.

REGISTER—To record your dog with the American Kennel Club.

REGISTRATION CERTIFICATE—The paper you receive denoting your dog's registration has been recorded with A.K.C., giving the breed, assigned name, names of sire and dam, date of birth, breeder and owner, along with the assigned Stud Book number of the dog.

RESERVE WINNERS DOG OR RESERVE WINNERS BITCH—After the judging of Winners Dog and Winners Bitch, the remaining first prize dogs or bitches remain in the ring where they are joined by the dog or bitch that placed second in the class to the one awarded Winners Dog or Winners Bitch, provided he or she was defeated by that one dog or bitch only on the day. From these a Reserve Winner is selected. Should the winners Dog or Winners Bitch subsequently be disallowed due to any error or technicality, the Reserve Winner is then moved

up automatically to Winners in the A.K.C. records and the points awarded to the Winners Dog or Winners Bitch then transfer to the one which placed Reserve. This is a safeguard award, for although it seldom happens, should the winner of the championship points be found to have been ineligible to receive them, the Reserve dog keeps the Winner's points.

ROACH BACK—A convex curvature of the topline of the dog.

ROCKING HORSE—An expression used to describe a dog that has been overly extended in forequarters and hindquarters by the handler, the forefeet placed too far forward and the hind feet pulled overly far behind, making the dog resemble a child's rocking horse. To be avoided in presenting your dog for judging.

ROLLING GAIT—An aimless, ambling type of action correct in some breeds but a fault in others.

SADDLE BACK—Of excessive length with a dip behind the withers.

SCISSORS BITE—In which the outer sides of the lower incisors touch the inner side of the upper incisors. Generally considered to be the most serviceable type of jaw formation.

SECOND THIGH—The area of the hindquarters between the hock and the stifle.

SEPTUM—The vertical line between the nostrils.

SET UP—To pose your dog in position for examination by the judge. Sometimes referred to as stacking.

SHELLY—A body lacking in substance.

SHOULDER HEIGHT—The dog's height from the ground to the withers.

SIRE—The male parent.

SKULLY—An expression referring to a coarse or overly massive skull.

SLAB SIDES—Flat sides with little spring of rib.

SOUNDNESS—Mental and physical stability.

SPAY—To neuter a bitch by surgery.

SPECIAL—A dog or bitch entered only for best of breed competition at a dog show.

SPECIALTY CLUB—An organization devoted to sponsoring an individual breed.

STANCE—The natural position a dog assumes in standing.

STANDARD—The official description of the ideal specimen of a breed. The Standard of Perfection is drawn up by the Parent Specialty Club, approved by its membership and by the American Kennel Club, and serves as a guide to breeders and to judges in decisions regarding the merit or lack of it in individual dogs.

STIFLE—The joint of the hind leg corresponding to a person's knee.

STILTED—Refers to the somewhat choppy gait of a dog lacking rear angulation.

STOP—The step-up from nose to skull. An indentation at the juncture of the skull and foreface.

STRAIGHT BEHIND—Lacking angulation of the hindquarters.

STRAIGHT SHOULDERED—Lacking angulation of the shoulder blades.

STUD—A male dog that is a proven sire.

SUBSTANCE—Degree of bone size.

SWAYBACK—Weakness in the topline between the withers and the hipbones.

TAIL SET—Placement of the tail at its base.

T.D., T.D.X.—See Tracking Dog, Tracking Dog Excellent.

TEAM—Generally four dogs.

THIGH—Hindquarters from the stifle to the hip.

THROATINESS—Excessive loose skin at the throat.

TOPLINE—The dog's back from withers to tail set.

TOPKNOT—The hair on top of the Poodle's skull.

TRACKING DOG—A title awarded dogs that have fulfilled the A.K.C. requirements at licensed or member club tracking tests. T.D. is an abbreviation.

TRACKING DOG EXCELLENT—An advanced tracking degree. T.D.X. is an abbreviation.

TRAIL—Hunting by following a ground scent.

TROT—The gait in which the dog moves in a rhythmic two-beat action, right front and left hind foot and left front and right hind foot each striking the ground together.

TUCK-UP—A noticeable shallowness of the body at the loin, creating a small-waisted appearance.

TYPE—The combination of features which makes a breed unique, distinguishing it from all others.

U.D., U.D.T.—See Utility Dog, Utility Dog Tracking.

UNDERSHOT—The front teeth of the lower jaw overlap or reach beyond the front teeth of the upper jaw.

UPPER ARM—The foreleg between the forearm and the shoulder blade.

UTILITY DOG—Another level of obedience degree. U.D. is an abbreviation.

UTILITY DOG TRACKING—Indicates that the dog has gained both Utility Dog and Track-

ing Dog degrees.

WALK – The gait in which three feet support the body, each lifting in regular sequence one at a time off the ground.

WALLEYE – A blue eye, fish eye, or pearl eye caused by a whitish appearance of the iris.

WEEDY – Lacking in sufficient bone and substance.

WELL LET DOWN – Short hocks, hock joint placed low to the ground.

WET NECK – Dewlap or superfluous skin.

WHEEL BACK – Roached back with topline considerably arched over the loin.

WINNERS DOG OR WINNERS BITCH- – The awards which are accompanied by championship points, based on the number of dogs defeated, at A.K.C. member or licensed dog shows.

WITHERS – The highest point of the shoulders, right behind the neck.

WRY MOUTH – When the lower jaw is twisted and does not correctly align with the upper jaw.

Ch. Tedwin's Top Billing, Best of Variety winner at Westminster when he was ten years old.

Overleaf:
Kayesett Poodles do well Coast to Coast. Here is Ch. Kayesett Kensington winning a Non-Sporting Group in California. Mr. and Mrs. J. Herbert Kaye, owners.

Kenn

Ludwig

BEST OF
WINNERS

QUINNIPIAC
POODLE CLUB

1980

ASHBEY

INDEX

This index is composed of three separate parts: a general index, an index of kennels and an index of names of persons mentioned in the text.

Overleaf:
This is the latest champion from Griggswood Poodles owned by Mrs. D. E. Griggs, Ormston, Canada. Ch. Griggswood Prelude is by Ch. Putencove Presentation ex Ch. Griggswood Harmony, and is handled here by Wendell Sammet to take Best of Winners under judge Iris de la Torre Bueno at the Quinnipiac Poodle Club Specialty, 1980.

The Index continues on pages 520 and 521

Overleaf: Am., Can. Ch. Wilmar Howlene Stone Broke, a noted Toy Poodle winner owned by Beverly Merritt and handled by Todd Patterson. Mrs. Rebecca Mason makes the award.

Index of People

Overleaf:
A lovely picture of an exquisite Poodle. The famed white Standard bitch, Ch. Rimskittle Bartered Bride, is winning under Edward B. Jenner. Handled by Tim Brazier, this elegant Poodle racked up an impressive record in keenest competition. Owned by Margo Durney.

The Index continues
on pages 524 and 525.

Overleaf:
Ch. Kayesett Douglas taking Best of Winners at eight months of age. Mr. and Mrs. J. Herbert Kaye,
owners; Wendell J. Sammet, handler.

BEST OF
WINNERS

EASTERN
DOG CLUB

DECEMBER 1977

DOUGLAS

WINNERS

SOUTHERN MARYLAND
KENNEL CLUB

1980

ASHBEY

Overleaf:

This is Ch. Cabryn's Von Hurrican of Remm, Standard Poodle owned by Mr. Dennis and Mrs. Katherine McElligott of Tucson, Arizona. Pictured taking Winners at the Southern Maryland Kennel Club, 1980, under judge, Frank Oberstar. Handled by Paul Edwards, bred by Carolyn J. O'Rourke.

Endpapers: Ch. Harmo Rapport (Annie), and Ch. Harmo Rhapsody (Janie) winning Best Brace in Show at Beverly Hills. Mrs. Anna Boardman owns these attractive brown Miniatures, William J. Trainor handling.

Mr. and Mrs. Royal E. Peterson are breeder-owners of this handsome white Standard, Ch. Popcorn of Deryabar, handled by Wendell J. Sammet. Popcorn is by Ch. Alekai Rumble of Stoneridge ex Ch. Hexton Jonquil.

BEST
IN TH

Cammar